The
SUPERMARKET
Epicure

The Cookbook for Gourmet Food at Supermarket Prices

BY

Joanna Pruess

ILLUSTRATIONS BY RAY SKIBINSKI

QUILL
WILLIAM MORROW
New York

Library of Congress Cataloging-in-Publication Data

Pruess, Joanna.
  The supermarket epicure.
  Includes index.
  1. Cookery. 2. Marketing (Home economics)
I. Title.
TX652.P78 1988   641.5   88-5213
ISBN 0-688-08569-5

Printed in the United States of America

First Quill Edition

1 2 3 4 5 6 7 8 9 10

BOOK DESIGN BY MINA GREENSTEIN

This book is dedicated to:

My wonderful children, Nicole, Ben, and Justin. They are my constant source of joy, inspiration, and support.

My mother, Harriet Rubens, who nourished and nurtured an amazing brood; and whose love of travel allowed me to experience the pleasures of different cuisines.

In loving memory of my father, Gerald Rubens, who taught me that if I asked enough questions, nothing was beyond my reach; and whose "crazy concoctions" inspired my own sense of invention.

ACKNOWLEDGMENTS

In writing this book, I have learned what almost every cookbook author before me has written: A book is the collective efforts of many people giving generously of their time, talents, and commitment to the cause. These thank-yous cannot begin to express my gratitude.

To my dear friend Sandy Talcott, who motivated me to write this book by asking for it again, and again, and again over the years.

To Barbara Soyster, Barbara Somers, Cheryl Kleinman, and Kathleen Kenny Sanderson: my four pillars of strength. Without their knowledge, humor, and loving support, as well as untold hours spent in reading and evaluating the recipes and text, this book would not have come into being.

To Karen Berk and Carole Walter, dear friends and extremely competent food professionals, who listened tirelessly to my ideas, helped me to get through the rough spots, and always offered encouragement.

To Donna Brady and Ivan Schneider, for their typing and computer skills.

To many friends who willingly tested and retested the recipes, and especially to Maureen Connolly and Terry Taffer.

To Allen Bildner, and all his associates at King Supermarkets, for sharing their knowledge. And special thanks to all the Cooking Studio staff.

To my agent, Bill Adler, for his guidance and assistance from the beginning.

Finally, to my editor, Maria Guarnaschelli, for helping me to find my own voice, offering a myriad of helpful suggestions, and enthusiastically believing in this book.

CONTENTS

INTRODUCTION

Supermarkets have been a part of my life for as long as I can remember. In my childhood, family outings were often coupled with a stop for weekly grocery specials. Five children—my brother, three sisters, and I—each checking out with two bottles of ketchup was not unusual. Through the years, I watched as modern convenience foods like TV dinners, cheese that made funny, squiggly designs when squirted from the can, and frozen vegetables made their debut. Canned spaghetti bore little resemblance to the Italian prototype or my Mom's slowly simmered version. But, it was easy and fast to prepare. Julia Child had yet to show us the joys of French cooking, and "good food" was simple, basic fare.

At twenty, I moved to France, where my ideas about what was good to eat were radically redefined. There I saw and tasted a broad range of foods I had never known. Shopping at the local butcher, cheese, fruit, and vegetable merchants became an ever-changing ritual for almost eight years. Choices fluctuated daily, and each season brought new reasons to celebrate gastronomically. Even the smells and sounds varied. With time, my meals were inspired by what looked best in the market each day, and I became more demanding of each product as I chose it.

A switch had flipped in my head, and I fell madly, passionately in love with food. Tender, thin green beans made me euphoric. A perfectly roasted chicken was a masterpiece. And ripe melons from Cavaillon were celestial gifts. Thanks to Le Cordon Bleu and friends, I learned to touch, feel, and smell what I was buying. Big wasn't necessarily best, and taste was more important than appearances. But appearances were part of the seduction, too.

Along the way, I also learned that shopkeepers had rigidly set hours. When I missed them (which was often), I found myself exploring the local supermarkets, which stayed open when all other stores were closed. Although the food never seemed quite as fresh, my gnawing hunger pains and fascination with new products were more than nourished. The clerks were willing to let me sample or buy the tiniest portion of a pâté or salad. I watched as other shoppers carefully considered their choices. Under these conditions, I learned a valuable shopping lesson: No matter where you are, celebrate the best of what is available. By choosing carefully, asking questions, and experimenting, you can prepare great meals from ordinary sources.

When I returned to the United States, my first trips to the supermarket left me feeling that I was shopping in an impersonal, plastic-wrapped world. Apples were tightly sheathed in cellophane, meats were half concealed in cardboard, and salads were sealed in plastic tubs. There was no one to talk to about food, no one to ask questions of, no smells, no tastes. I resolved to do all my shopping in the many specialty shops that were springing up not far from our home. A job and three infants soon made this a forgotten dream. Happily, times were changing in the supermarket world.

In the 1930's, the pioneers of the industry had revolutionized shopping by creating one-stop food centers complete with everything from canned vegetables and fresh meat to laundry supplies. The idea was successful and spread. But, by the fifties and sixties, modern technology had streamlined food handling to where it had all but replaced human hands. Meat was packaged on an automated line. It was a rare market that had a butcher to ask for specialty cuts or how to cook something. Produce was wrapped, scaled, or weighed and protected from the view of knowing eyes. As big chains gobbled up small entrepreneurs, personal attention and individuality were sacrificed to the "bottom line." Eventually, customers felt alienated and began looking to smaller, more intimate food stores.

In the mid-seventies, supermarkets began taking a hard look at themselves, their lost customers, and how to win them back. What they found was a change in their customers' needs. Women with or without husbands are out the door and winning the bread. Fathers are raising children alone. Seniors and singles have their own demands. Interest in nutrition is making mediocre, chemical-ladened foods less desirable, while improved take-out and quick-heat items have sky rocketed in popularity because of their ease of preparation.

Since I went to work in this industry, I have seen the general population "turn on" to high-quality foods. With a little assistance, shoppers are willing to experiment and invest in newer, less familiar foods. While the general trend may be away from cooking all the time, there is a strong renewed interest and pride in preparing at least part of the meal oneself. Couples cook and entertain together. Children, too, have taken to the kitchen—and, not simply to make chocolate chip cookies.

Even the smallest store now offers what was once considered exotic foods from around the world. Progressive supermarkets recognize that beyond high-quality ingredients, only personalized service and convenience can distance them from the competition. Catering managers, chefs, and cooking teachers are being added to their staffs, while the "super" part of their name is being expanded to include more nonfood products like fresh flowers, general merchandise, and party supplies. To keep customers informed, a wealth of printed and spoken information is available. Longer hours of operation, telephone ordering, and even entertainment are part of today's planning. The tide has definitely turned for many supermarkets.

With so much available in one place, a new problem has evolved: how to navigate these giant markets, deal with take-out and prepared foods, and buy, store, and present food to its best advantage? Having spoken with thousands of shoppers, I know that to be a smart shopper, a strategy is necessary. To assist you, the chapters of this book are divided like the sections of your supermarket: Vegetables, Meat, Frozen Foods, even Take-out. There is general information in the introduction to each chapter and specific information about buying the main ingredients in the recipe headnotes. At the end of many recipes, there are Did You Know? tips on smart buying, storing, or using your food. Look for this symbol:

Finally, between chapters, there are Strategy Pages dealing with larger supermarket issues, such as: "Label Literacy," "Surviving the Supermarket," "Seasonality," and "Let Your Supermarket Work for You."

With some practice and thought, these skills will help you to translate your purchases into meals worthy of a three-star restaurant. Your table may or may not be graced with the latest exotica from far-off lands. But you will dine very, very well. Remember that food is an intensely personal experience. Discover what pleases *you* and carefully choose what is really best that day in the market. That's the beginning. Most recipes are only meant to be a guideline. Baking is the exception. If basil is called for and oregano is more to your liking, make the substitution. If the broccoli looks great and the asparagus are old, the choice should be obvious, even if the recipe suggests asparagus. Great cooks in Paris or Chicago don't dwell on what isn't; they celebrate the positive.

Finally, it takes more than correctly prepared recipes to make a great meal. Success comes from proper selection and storage. Presentation and table decor also play an important role in creating the total experience. A meal should be a temptation for all the senses. Eyes see and noses smell before a morsel of food reaches the mouth. Many of the tools for creative entertaining and wonderful everyday eating are found in today's markets. Through this book I've added suggestions and tips on how best to master today's supermarket in the hopes that you, too, will feel as I do: that you can create wonderful dining celebrations from your local supermarket.

The
SUPERMARKET
Epicure

Let Your Supermarket Work for You

Supermarkets are making monumental strides in updating their images from one-stop utilitarian food markets to one-stop "super" stores, offering an abundance of food—both fresh and prepared—and nonfood products and many services formerly available only in food boutiques or specialty stores. In order to survive today's dramatically larger—45,000 to 50,000 square feet is not unusual—and more complicated markets, customers need to choose the supermarket(s) that best meets their needs. Confronted with this task, I have developed certain criteria to help me make the decision after visiting the quality markets in an area.

For me, the two most important considerations are *Cleanliness* and *Consistency*.

Cleanliness is vital to how good I feel about a market; it tells me a lot about the food sold there. First impressions lead me to certain conclusions about quality and the degree of management's concern for food safety. Even before entering the store, I make judgments; if garbage is strewn carelessly around, I think the same might be true in the meat-packing room or elsewhere. If the containers in the Take-Out or Deli sections are dirty, the food looks old, or clerks are sampling while serving customers, I fear that bacteria is lurking nearby and I may end up sick. If spills are not quickly wiped up, leaving treacherous puddles, or there are unpleasant odors, I know that this is not where I want to do my shopping on a regular basis.

Consistency is more important to me than finding the newest variety of herb or most exotic fish. Why? Because initially I always spend a lot of mental energy sizing up where I shop and getting used to cooking with certain kinds of ingredients. There is comfort in a more or less predictable quality. Sure, foods vary from day to day. But if, on a regular basis, you can do your general shopping or dash in at the last moment and still find respectable ingredients, it is a great time saver. I also look for consistent store policies and clerks or department managers who are usually willing to be helpful. It is a great luxury to know that specially ordered products will be delivered as promised.

Along with consistency, I look for markets that are *ordered*, bright, and easily navigated. Especially in smaller markets with narrower aisles, if the store is well lit and well signed, shopping is easier and less claustrophobic.

Service and *Cooperation* make shopping easier, too. They are part of the market's desire to meet customer needs. More than any other product, today's stores offer a variety of services to distinguish themselves from their competition. How successful they are seems to be as much a result of their attitude as the actual assistance they give. I think about how helpful the staff is and whether I feel that they sincerely care about my requests. On more critical issues, such as food recalls, complaints, or even simple returns, the staff's reaction affirms or denies a commitment to the store's customers.

Finally, *Flexibility* and *Change* show me that a supermarket is trying to keep abreast of current food trends and improved technology.

To make shopping easier and more efficient, I suggest preparing a market list in the order of the store's layout. Use it as a guide, but don't overlook the choicest item or best buy in the store because you are so intent on finding the next item on your list. Shopping once a week and planning ahead helps avoid wasteful impulse buying. However, only buy the amount of fresh food you can use to best advantage.

Whether you choose your produce, meat, fish, or poultry first is not significant. Rather, keep in mind that if the food you want is too highly priced, not of top quality or unavailable, you should make a substitution on the spot. Often these spontaneous changes have become some of my greatest successes.

Investigate the newer special services now available in many markets before you actually need them. For catering I ask for references from past catering jobs. I also taste this department's food and watch how platters and take-out foods are prepared.

And take it from one who knows: If possible, don't go to the market when you are hungry!

·1·
VEGETABLES

INTRODUCTION

The vegetable section of the Produce department is one of the largest and most changeable areas of a supermarket, often fluctuating daily because of seasonality and availability. An appreciation for ethnic cuisines and an awareness of the important role vegetables play in good health have prompted merchandisers to offer us less familiar produce along with staples like carrots, onions, and celery. Although many markets are selling vegetables unwrapped, careful selection and storage are vital if you want the best quality. Be sure to glance at the tips included with each recipe.

GENERAL BUYING SUGGESTIONS

Look carefully at every vegetable you buy. Turn it over, look at the roots or leaves, check it for bruises and drying.

Bulk-packed vegetables can save you money—but only when used within a reasonable period of time. Be sure to evaluate the over-all quality. Money spent on discarded foods is also thrown away.

Where uniform size is important to even cooking or appearance, take the time to *handpick* vegetables, if possible. If they are plastic wrapped, examine the packages carefully for broken or damaged product. Some Produce clerks will actually open containers for you if asked.

Some vegetables, like celery and carrots, are frequently sold cello-packed. Look to see that the bright orange color is on the carrots, not a grid pattern on the bag. With sealed bags, like packages of spinach, check for broken, wet leaves. They decay quickly.

Make a point of becoming friends with the Produce manager. He or a clerk can sometimes find fresher produce from the storage room if asked, or he can order an item specially. When in doubt on how much to buy or how to cook a new vegetable, ask advice.

Newer produce, such as miniature vegetables, nopales (cactus leaves), and exotic mushrooms, often come with recipe folders to give you additional storage and cooking tips. Unless your market has a good turnover on these items, examine them carefully. In some markets they tend to get old before they are bought. When faced with unfamiliar vegetables, I read about them, then I cook them for myself to become familiar with their taste and texture, before I use them for entertaining.

SALAD GREENS

Not long ago, iceberg, romaine, and Boston lettuce were usually the entire "salad greens" department of a market. Today, that trio has exploded into a seemingly endless array of leaf and head lettuces, sprouts, and even edible flowers. No matter how many choices there are, each item should be carefully stacked in a cool bin and frequently misted to remain fresh-looking.

A quick word about hydroponically grown greens, such as Boston lettuce, spinach, and some herbs: while they are usually picture perfect and clean, their flavor is often diminished.

Knowing that greens are delicate, choose them carefully, slip each choice into a plastic bag, and place them in your shopping cart where they will not be damaged. At the checkout register, I ask to have my produce packed separately from the rest of my order—potatoes, onions, and other heavy items at the bottom of the bag, more crushable items on top.

Just about everyone loves a good salad, from crisp mixed greens to those composed of more exotic ingredients. With attention to the selection, storage, and preparation of your ingredients, an unlimited variety can be yours.

Selection

Look each head of lettuce over carefully for damaged outer leaves and brown spots. Colors should be bright. Some stores trim lettuce for better value and to make it more saleable.

Whether soft-leafed (Boston) or crisp-leafed (romaine), lettuce should not be limp. If it is, it may have been soaked in water or otherwise mistreated. Don't buy it. Lettuces should be misted periodically and kept cool.

Choose heads that feel firm and heavy.

Storage

Whole Heads

Keep lettuces whole until needed. They will last longer—two to four days at most.

Do not wash them (it causes rust), but remove excess dirt and damaged leaves that may hasten decay.

Place each head in a plastic bag, squeeze out excess air, fasten, and refrigerate in the vegetable bin.

Washed Leaves

Place washed leaves on paper towels in layers and put them into sealed plastic bags. Punch a few holes in the bags to allow air to circulate. Leaves will stay fresh up to two days.

Do not store lettuces near any fruit, such as cantaloupes or apples, that gives off ethylene gas. It will cause rust spots.

Preparation of Lettuce for Salads

Lettuce is a delicate green, so it needs to be treated carefully. It bruises when forced into a small space, and it wilts when left unchilled.

Fill the sink with lukewarm to cool water. Break off the leaves and discard the core. Swirl the lettuce gently in the water. Then rinse each leaf separately (except iceberg), and remove any rust spots and thickened ribs.

Spin dry in a salad spinner or swing in a lettuce basket. Pat the leaves dry with paper towels, if necessary.

Store whole leaves, wrapped in paper or cloth towels, in the refrigerator to chill and crisp before being dressed. Or, tear the leaves, place them in a salad bowl, cover with a slightly dampened towel, and refrigerate, for up to two hours.

Combining Ingredients

Combine crisp, sharper-flavored lettuces like chicory, watercress, or radicchio with subtler leaves like Boston or green and red leaf.

Vary textures and colors, but be selective. Three or four different lettuces are plenty.

Dressing a Salad

Do not overdress a salad. Eight cups of lightly packed leaves only need ¼ to ⅓ cup of dressing.

Vary the oils, vinegars, and herbs. Walnut oil goes well with delicate greens, such as Bibb lettuce or arugula. Crunchy romaine likes a fruity olive oil. This is where your own taste and creativity are important.

Dress the salad just before serving. The acid of vin-

egar or lemon juice will cause lettuce leaves to go
limp.

**SOME OF MY
FAVORITE SALADS**

Blanched green beans, minced shallots, boiled and
sliced new potatoes, and cubed beets, tossed with
MUSTARD VINAIGRETTE (page 363) and served on
red lettuce leaves.

Arugula, radicchio, crumbled goat cheese, walnuts,
and torn Boston lettuce leaves, tossed with MUS-
TARD VINAIGRETTE (page 363), substituting raspberry vinegar and walnut oil for the lemon juice
and olive oil.

Torn romaine lettuce, julienned turkey breast, red
onion rings, broken walnut pieces, and pear slices
arranged on plates with ROQUEFORT VINAIGRETTE
(page 364) spooned on top.

Blanched pea pods, yellow pepper slices, cherry tomato halves, shredded carrots, and blanched cauliflower florets tossed with SWEET AND TANGY
ORIENTAL VINAIGRETTE (page 366) and served on
Bibb lettuce leaves.

Avocado and papaya slices arranged with chopped
eggs and watercress sprigs on a bed of Boston
lettuce leaves with CURRIED MAYONNAISE (page 370).

Boiled shrimp, blanched pea pods, cubed jicama, and
diced red pepper tossed with SPICY OLD BAY TO-
MATO DRESSING (page 365) and served in a steamed
artichoke with the choke removed. Or serve on
toasted sourdough bread.

Sliced zucchini, red or yellow pepper slices, quartered
small mushrooms, toasted pine nuts, sprouts, and
thinly sliced scallions tossed with PURÉED CHICK-
PEA VINAIGRETTE (page 365) served on a bed of
chicory and salad bowl lettuce leaves.

Cucumber slices, cubed beets, sliced boiled potatotes,
and tomato slices, tossed with TUNA NIOISE SAUCE
(page 379) served on a bed of romaine and endive
leaves with garlic croutons.

HERBS

Happily, the explosion of greens in supermarkets now
includes fresh herbs, as well. Contemporary, lighter
cooking stresses that herbs are an excellent way to add
lots of flavor, but no calories, to our foods. Here,

freshness counts a lot. And since we often use a small amount of most herbs, markets and growers have taken a cue from their customers' needs in their merchandising, selling herbs in a variety of ways.

Selection

With all herbs, look for brightly colored, fresh-looking leaves, free of bruised spots, excess moisture, or wilting.

Herbs growing in small plastic pots afford the potential advantage of continual growth on your windowsill or of being transplanted. Since they need to be watered, if the soil seems very dry and the leaves are wilted in the market, pass them up. Remember to attend to this at home, too. I've had the greatest success with chives, which seem to thrive in the steamy atmosphere near the kitchen sink. If the plant flowers, great! Add the blossoms along with other edible flowers, such as nasturtium, to your salad. Freeze-dried chives, by the way, are usually limp and tasteless. Substitute fresh scallions.

Hydroponically grown herbs sealed in plastic bags are available for immediate use, since they are quite clean. However, they are often more expensive, and the flavor is usually milder. Be sure to check the bag for condensation and moisture-wilt.

Larger bunches of familiar herbs, such as flat-leaf and curly parsley, dill, and basil, are usually available to use immediately or to store. As you choose each bunch, put it into a plastic bag to keep it moist. The smaller tied bunches of thyme, rosemary, oregano, marjoram, and the like are appearing year around from local growers. Look at their condition carefully. If they are withered and limp, you may be better off with a new bottle of the dried herb.

Even tiny plastic see-through boxes with a tablespoon or two of chopped herbs are found in many markets today. Here, all the work has been done for you, there is information concerning the herb's use on printed cards alongside, and the boxes are dated. But, be aware that the leaves are often moldy or wilted and thus unusable, making the already high price exorbitant.

Care of Fresh Herbs

Once home, use herbs quickly or prepare them for storage. Do *not* wash herbs before refrigerating. Properly wrapped and sealed in a plastic bag, most herbs make their own mini-environment and will stay fresh in the refrigerator for up to a week.

If there are no roots, wrap a damp paper towel around the stem ends, pull off any wilted leaves, and place the herb in an airtight plastic bag. If the leaves are very moist, a dry paper towel in the bag will help absorb excess moisture.

Herbs with roots should be placed in a glass with a couple of inches of water. Use a plastic bag to tent the top.

When herbs begin to wilt, they may be frozen for four to six months in small, airtight bags with the air removed. Or, they may be puréed first, frozen in a small amount of water in an ice cube tray, and then stored in bags. Although they will not retain their appearance, their flavor will remain quite fresh, and they can be used in cooking or in herb butters and vinegars.

Another solution is to dry herbs. While some dried herbs have more flavor than commercially jarred ones, they are, after all, still dried. Generally, when substituting dried herbs for fresh in a recipe, use one-third the amount: 1 teaspoon dried thyme leaves in place of 1 tablespoon fresh.

Using Herbs

Because herbs are so delicate, they need to be handled with care when washed and chopped.

Rinse herbs under cool water and gently pat them dry with paper towels, or dry them in a salad spinner.

Where appearances are important, a sharp knife bruises delicate leaves less than a food processor. If using a food processor, it is important to *pulse* a minimum of times.

Add fresh herbs toward the end of cooking, but crumble dried herbs and add them early to release their flavor.

Just a hint: An easy way to remove the tiny leaves of herbs with inedible, coarse stems is to grasp a stem between your thumbnail and index fingernail, and with light pressure, strip the leaves opposite from their growing direction, i.e., from tip to root end.

A sprig of fresh rosemary is wonderful in a soup or stew, but also see how herbs are used in my HERBED CREAM CHEESE DIP (page 270) or in MUSTARD VINAIGRETTE (page 363). Herb butters are a combination of finely minced herbs and softened butter (about 1 tablespoon herb to a stick of butter, depending on how pungent the herb is and personal taste). Use unsalted butter. Salt may be added afterward. Pipe the herbed butter into rosettes, or form it into a cylinder, chill, and slice as a garnish for grilled fish, meats, poultry, or soups and stews. Frozen, these butters last for up to three months.

Basic Kitchen Herbs from the Supermarket

Basil

Basil is very fragrant with a mildly spicy flavor. It is a staple of Italian cooking, since it goes so well with tomatoes, vegetables, and pasta. Try it, too, in salads, soups, and stews. It does not withstand long cooking, so add it at the end. The taste of opal basil is the same as that of green leaf. Lemon basil has a subtle hint of citrus.

Bay Leaf is a pungent leaf of the laurel tree. Use it sparingly in soups and stews; it should be removed before serving, since the leaf does not soften during cooking.

Bay leaf

Chervil is not easily found fresh. It is a delicate cousin of parsley and complements vegetable and egg dishes. It is used in *fines herbes*.

Chives are a mild-flavored relative of the onion family. They do not withstand cooking, so they are often stirred into soups or other dishes at the end of cooking, chopped and sprinkled on salads, or used whole as a garnish.

Chives

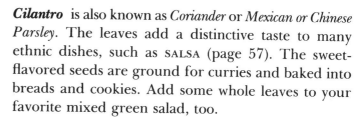

Cilantro

Cilantro is also known as *Coriander* or *Mexican or Chinese Parsley*. The leaves add a distinctive taste to many ethnic dishes, such as SALSA (page 57). The sweet-flavored seeds are ground for curries and baked into breads and cookies. Add some whole leaves to your favorite mixed green salad, too.

Dill leaves have a subtle licorice taste and are used in soups and vinaigrettes, and with potatoes, cucumbers, and fish. The seeds are used for breads, pickles, and soups.

Dill

Fennel has a strong licorice flavor in its feathery leaves or edible bulb, which is made milder by cooking. The seeds are commonly used to season sausages and richly flavored meat dishes. Eat the raw or braised bulb as you would celery.

Marjoram is a mild cousin of oregano, frequently used in Italian cooking or with creamed vegetable soups, poultry, and stuffings.

Mint has a cool, refreshing flavor. Spearmint and peppermint are the most common varieties found in markets. It is used in jellies, sauces, and desserts, and with peas, and new potatoes.

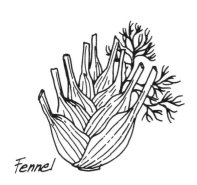
Fennel

Oregano is similar to its relative, marjoram, but has a more pronounced flavor. It is used for foods like pizza, stews, and other full-flavored dishes where its robust flavor will not overpower.

Marjoram

Mint

Oregano

Parsley

Parsley is the most widely used of the culinary herbs. Curly parsley is mild and most often used as a garnish. Flat-leaf parsley, also called Italian parsley, has a more distinct flavor and is used to enhance the flavor of other herbs and many foods. When chopping parsley, note that the stems have the most flavor.

Rosemary has a pinelike scent that can be overpowering if the herb is used to excess. Use it in small amounts to season lamb, beef, veal, and game, as well as some sauces. It is especially nice with garlic.

Sage has a strong flavor which can easily dominate others. It is best used with game, poultry, and cheese and is found in many sausages. Fresh leaves don't taste as musty as the dried or powdered herb.

Sage

Tarragon is a sweet herb with an aniselike taste, often used in French cooking to enhance delicately flavored chicken, fish, veal, and egg dishes, as well as sauces such as béarnaise and beurre blanc.

Thyme has a pungent distinctive scent. It is a popular herb used in strongly flavored stuffings, pâtés, and soups, as well as poultry and fish dishes.

With herbs more readily available, it is becoming easier for supermarket cooks to experiment with these culinary treasures.

Tarragon

Thyme

Rosemary

SALAD BARS: CONVENIENCE BEYOND LETTUCE

In a hurry? Try the Salad Bar. Cooking for a small family? The Salad Bar's got just the right amount. Need a handful instead of a bunch? The Salad Bar is an answer that is finding more and more popularity with on-the-go-shoppers.

More than bite-size lettuce leaves, tomato wedges, and onion rings—although they are there, too—the Salad Bar in most supermarkets now offers an array of vegetables, legumes and nuts, seasonal fruits, toppings, and salad greens. At first glance, it may seem to be the answer to the consumer's dream. But let's discuss it first.

First impressions count

What you see often indicates the quality of the Salad Bar. Look for one that is appetizing.

It should be well tended, with appropriate utensils in place for each item.

The should be no spillage.

Food trays should be set in ice, and a protective "sneeze" guard should extend upward or down from above to prevent shoppers from leaning over the food.

Containers and lids, as well as a selection of dressings, should be neat and easily accessible.

Empty trays should be refilled promptly. A high turnover is a good indication of freshness.

Think of the cost

If all you are buying is lettuce, radishes, and shredded carrots, then $2.99 or so a pound is extravagant.

If you want olives, marinated artichoke hearts, a few nuts, or berries for garnish, then what you are paying for is the convenience of prepreparation and the savings realized from the availability of small portions.

Beyond walking around and creating your own mixed green salad, there are endless possibilities that the Salad Bar offers. Here are just a few ideas:

Crudités

This is a traditional French first course of cooked and uncooked vegetables.

Pick up a head of lettuce, rinse and dry it, and place several leaves on each salad plate. Mix shredded or julienned carrots from the Salad Bar with lemon juice, olive oil, salt, and pepper, and mound them to one side. Cubed or sliced beets are next. Then add a mound of shredded cabbage with vinaigrette spooned over. Next, add sliced mushrooms or hard-cooked eggs, and finally a scoop of three-bean salad. Serve with a knife and fork, and voilà.

A Vegetarian Oriental Stir-Fry

Quickly sauté 1 or 2 split garlic cloves in a small amount of oil, and discard the garlic. Starting with the large, denser vegetables, add approximately 1 cup each of broccoli and cauliflower florets, ½ cup each sliced celery, diced red pepper, sprouts, onion rings, or scallions, and even some baby corn if it is available. Sauté the vegetables for a minute or two until crisp-tender. Stir in some soy sauce, sesame oil to taste, and hoisin sauce, if you have it. Freshly grated ginger is another plus. Serve with rice and/or crisp noodles.

AS A VARIATION: Add leftover chicken, tofu, or steak for a heartier dish.

Italian Rice or Orzo Salad

This is a variation on the DOMED COLD ORZO SALAD WITH SHRIMP on page 385.

Improvise a delicious salad by boiling and draining 1 cup of rice or pasta. Slice some pitted black olives, add chopped red onion rings and scallion slices, a handful of peas, and chopped watercress. If there are sun-dried tomatoes on the Salad Bar, mince and add them, too. Mix with vinaigrette and serve.

Mixed Fruit Salad

Look at MARGARITA'S FRUIT SALAD IN A HONEYDEW MELON (page 89).

Melons, mangoes, and bananas are perfect go-togethers, or make your own combination. Add some cassis, Grand Marnier, or tequila. Serve on a pretty platter with a sprinkle of coconut and a squirt of lemon or lime.

Spinach, Mushroom, and Red Onion Salad

Add canned mandarins, fresh orange segments, or chopped hard-cooked eggs to the basic ingredients. If there are real bacon bits, sprinkle them on, too. Use the store's vinaigrette or make your own. Two soups are a natural from the Salad Bar:

Quick Vegetable Soup

Choose an assortment of basic vegetables, such as tomatoes, zucchini slices, carrot sticks, celery and onion slices, chick-peas, and kidney beans. At home, place them in a medium-size saucepan with beef or chicken broth to cover, season with salt and pepper to taste and with dried herbs you have on hand (perhaps thyme and basil). Simmer, partially covered, for an hour or so. Ten minutes before serving time you might want to stir in 2 to 3 tablespoons of orzo (rice-shaped pasta). Finish cooking, taste for seasonings, and serve with crisp bread.

Gazpacho

This cold vegetable soup from Spain calls for the simplest of fresh ingredients, finely chopped by hand or in a food processor or blender.

Choose green peppers, scallions and onions, tomatoes, cucumbers, and celery. Add salt, pepper, Tabasco sauce, and a bit of minced garlic. Chop, chill well, and serve in pretty balloon glasses topped with black olive slices.

Presto Primavera

Buy small quantities of broccoli florets, carrot slices, onion rings, mushrooms, and peas. Steam or sauté them just until the vegetables are crisp-tender. Meanwhile, boil pasta to the al dente stage and drain well. Toss the pasta with the steamed vegetables, some crushed garlic, cream and/or olive oil, a good sprinkling of grated Parmesan cheese (about ½ cup for ½ pound of pasta), and freshly ground black pepper.

Granita

This is a soft and refreshing Italian ice.

Freeze cubes of fruit or berries on a cookie sheet for a couple of hours or until frozen solid. Once frozen, transfer them to a food processor, add a simple sugar syrup (see MANDARIN CRANBERRY SORBET, page 339), and pulse with an on-off motion until almost smooth. I like my granita with some texture, so I work quickly. Then scoop into bowls and serve.

FOR A FRUIT SORBET: Add an egg white, refreeze the purée in a brownie pan, and reprocess before serving.

VEGETABLE VERSATILITY

Vegetables are a special passion of mine, not only because of their variety, but because I can use them for everything from hors d'oeuvres to dessert (look at SPICY PUMPKIN MOUSSE on page 340). I also use them to make glamorous centerpieces and serving containers (see the last chapter).

Your choices change hourly in a supermarket. With a little flexibility on your part—choosing what is best rather than what you had written on a list—the possibilities are tremendous. In this era of health consciousness, vegetables deserve resounding kudos. They are filling, fibrous, and often nonfattening. For me, they are also my favorite foods.

Artichokes Stuffed with Russian Potato Salad

Serves 4

Although artichokes are available most of the year, they are most plentiful and reasonable in April and May—just in time to serve them stuffed with this caviar-and-dill potato salad.

Artichokes should feel solid with smooth leaves. They should be bright green, but don't be concerned about bronze-colored tips on the leaves. That happens normally during winter and won't affect the taste. Artichokes may be served hot, cold, or at room temperature with many sauces. I adore them every way.

4 large artichokes
1 tablespoon white or red wine vinegar

FOR THE POTATO SALAD
1½ pounds boiling potatoes
2 medium stalks celery, finely chopped
3 scallions, thinly sliced, including most of the green parts
2 tablespoons finely chopped fresh dill
½ cup sour cream
⅓ cup mayonnaise
1 tablespoon white or red wine vinegar
2 ounces red salmon caviar
Salt and freshly ground black pepper to taste

FOR THE SAUCE
1 cup mayonnaise
2 tablespoons finely chopped fresh dill
1 large shallot, peeled and minced
2 teaspoons white or red wine vinegar

1. PREPARE THE ARTICHOKES Pull off the small lower leaves around the stem. Cut the stems to about ¾ inch. Using a serrated stainless steel knife, cut off the top ¼ of the artichoke and, with kitchen shears, cut off the prickly tip of each remaining leaf. Rinse the artichokes under cool water. Rub lemon juice over the cut stems or drop them into a bowl of acidulated water to prevent discoloration if they will not be cooked right away. Fill a nonaluminum pot just large enough to hold the artichokes with about 2 inches of water. Add 1 tablespoon of vinegar, and the artichokes, stem sides down. Cover the pot, and bring to a boil. Boil gently until the leaves pull off easily and the heart is tender when pricked with a fork, about 20 to 40 minutes, depending on the size. (Or place them in a steamer and cook them for approximately the same time.) Check from time to time to be sure that the water has not evaporated.

2. When the artichokes are tender, remove them to a collander and let them drain until cool enough to handle. Gently pull the leaves apart to reveal the choke. Lift it off and, with a spoon, carefully scrape off the fuzzy part which remains on the heart. Put them in a bowl, cover, and set them aside to cool.

3. MAKE THE POTATO SALAD In a large saucepan, boil the potatoes just until tender when pierced with a sharp knife, about 14 to 17 minutes. Drain, peel, and cut them into ¾-inch cubes.

4. Transfer the potatoes to a bowl, add the celery, scallions, and dill. Combine the sour cream, mayonnaise, and vinegar in a small bowl, then add it to the potatoes, and turn gently to mix. Add the caviar, salt, and plenty of black pepper. Toss gently. Spoon the potato salad into the artichokes.

5. PREPARE THE SAUCE In a small bowl, combine the cup of mayonnaise with the dill, shallot, and vinegar. Spoon some mayonnaise onto each plate for dipping the artichoke leaves and pass the extra sauce at the table.

DID YOU KNOW? When selecting potatoes, choose new (less starchy) potatoes for boiling and salads. They have thinner skins and are firmer. As potatoes get older, they become starchier. Baking potatoes, because they stay in the ground a longer time, have a mealy texture and thicker skins. Choose potatoes that are solid and without sprouts. Store them unwrapped in a cool pantry or drawer.

Fettuccine with Asparagus and Lemon Cream

Serves 4 to 6 as a main course or 8 as a first course

This colorful pasta dish, with lemon-scented cream, red peppers, and asparagus, is perfect for spring—just when asparagus comes into season. It's worth waiting for these graceful stalks since the out-of-season variety is frequently quite expensive and less flavorful.

Asparagus only lasts a couple of days, even when carefully stored, so I buy it as close to eating time as possible. Try to select spears that are of uniform size (I prefer the narrow ones, about ½ inch in diameter), with closed buds, and stiff stalks. That's the surest way to guarantee even cooking. If the only choice you have is rubberbanded bunches, select carefully for size and quality. Once the bright green begins to get slightly mottled or the stalks droop, the magic is gone.

1 pound imported dried or QUICK HOMEMADE FETTUCCINE pasta (page 383)
Kosher or coarse salt
4 tablespoons (½ stick) unsalted butter
1½ cups heavy cream
Grated zest of 1 large lemon
Salt and white pepper to taste
Pinch of freshly grated nutmeg
1½ pound tender, young asparagus, cleaned, trimmed, and cut into 1½-inch pieces (see Did You Know?)
1 small red bell pepper, peeled, seeds and membranes removed, cut into fine dice
1 cup freshly grated imported Parmesan cheese
¼ cup fresh flat-leaf parsley leaves, coarsely torn for garnish

1. Bring a large pot of salted water to boil. Add the dried pasta, stirring to separate the strands. Follow the package directions and cook until al dente, 10 to 15 minutes. If using fresh pasta, cook it for 1 to 2 minutes after the sauce is ready.

2. Meanwhile, melt the butter in a large, heavy skillet over low heat. When it is melted, stir in the cream, lemon zest, salt, pepper, nutmeg, and asparagus and simmer gently, shaking the pan occasionally, until the asparagus is crisp-tender, about 7 to 8 minutes. Stir in the red pepper and continue cooking for another

DID YOU KNOW? Wait to clean asparagus until you are ready to use them. Otherwise, they will dry out. Then, *break* off the fibrous bottom where each spear snaps naturally. With a sharp knife, pare off the thin outer layer almost up to the bud. The spears will cook faster and be uniformly tender this way. If you must keep asparagus for a day or two, stand the spears upright in a container with about an inch of water or wrap the bottoms with wet paper towels. Cover with plastic to maintain the moisture.

2 to 3 minutes. Taste to adjust the seasonings, if necessary.

3. When the pasta is cooked, drain it, and stir it into the sauce. Sprinkle half the Parmesan cheese over the pasta, and toss to blend well. Transfer to a heated serving platter, garnish the top with parsley leaves and serve immediately. Pass the remaining cheese at the table.

Chilly Beet Soup

Serves 8 as a first course

When the days are hot and hunger strikes, this cool, beautiful, dark pink soup with a wispy garnish of chives is a perfect refreshment. For a light summer meal, serve a larger bowl of the soup accompanied by a sandwich. The flavor is a surprising combination of beets, green apples, cucumbers, leeks, and yogurt. It is creamy and slightly sweet, with a little tangy bite.

Fresh beets have a truly wonderful taste and texture. (For soups and purées, the canned variety is fine.) Select bunches with uniformly medium-size beets so they will cook evenly. The leaves should not be wilted. Beets will last in your refrigerator for at least a couple of weeks. I especially like to steam washed and quartered beets until just tender. Then I toss them with a little melted butter, a little orange juice, salt, pepper, and a sprinkling of chopped parsley.

3 medium leeks, white parts only, washed and thinly sliced
½ cup chicken or vegetable stock
3 8½-ounce cans sliced beets, undrained
2 large Granny Smith or other tart green apples, washed and seeded but *unpeeled*
1 medium cucumber, peeled, quartered, and seeds removed
1 cup chicken or vegetable stock
2 cups plain low-fat yogurt
Chives or ¼ cup thinly sliced scallion tops for garnish

1. In a small saucepan, combine the leeks and ½ cup stock. Bring just to a simmer and cook for 1 to 2 minutes, until the leeks have begun to soften. Transfer the leeks and stock to a small bowl and set aside to cool.

2. In the bowl of a food processor fitted with a steel chopping blade, or in a blender, purée the beets until almost smooth. Add the cucumber and apples and process until a slightly chunky texture is obtained, scraping down the sides of the bowl as needed.

3. Combine the remaining stock with the yogurt in a small bowl, stirring until very smooth. Scrape this mixture into the beet purée, and process just until well blended. Transfer the soup to a large bowl, stir in the leeks, cover, and chill until cold. To serve, ladle the soup into bowls, and place 2 or 3 chives or several slices of scallions in the center of each bowl.

Oriental Broccoli Salad

Serves 8 for lunch

In this flavorful salad, bright green broccoli and sweet red peppers are combined with firm-style tofu, or bean cake, found in your Dairy case. Tofu's creamy color, slightly soft texture, and delicate taste are marvelous against the broccoli and the tangy ginger-soy dressing. However, you can use diced cooked chicken breasts or shrimp instead.

Thank goodness for broccoli. It's one of the most consistently good buys in supermarkets all year long, providing it has been kept cool. And it's so versatile. Take an extra moment to select a bunch that is dark green with tightly closed florets. The stalks should be firm, without leggy branches. As broccoli ages, the color lightens and the stalks become fibrous and hollow. Turn the bunch over and look. Also, the stronger broccoli smells, the older it is.

1 large bunch (1¾ pounds) broccoli, rinsed, leaves removed, stalks separated and cut into thirds *or* 10 cups broccoli florets
1 large onion, peeled and thinly sliced
2 large red bell peppers, peeled, seeded, and sliced
8 ounces firm-style tofu, cut into small cubes
1 recipe SWEET AND TANGY ORIENTAL VINAIGRETTE (page 366)
3 tablespoons sesame seeds, toasted until light brown

1. With a sharp paring knife, remove the tough outer layer of the broccoli stalks, then steam them in a large pot until just tender, about 4 to 5 minutes once the water under the steamer boils. Drain the broccoli in a colander, rinse with cold water to stop the cooking, blot dry, then cut it into bite-size portions.

2. Place the onion in a medium-size bowl. Pour boiling water over it and let it wilt, about 1 minute. Drain and blot dry.

3. In a large bowl, combine the broccoli, onion, red pepper, and tofu, and toss with approximately half the Oriental vinaigrette. Chill for about 2 hours.

4. Add the sesame seeds and approximately half of the remaining dressing (see Note below). Toss and serve.

NOTE: Salads composed of steamed vegetables and other porous ingredients like pasta tend to absorb the flavor of their dressings. Therefore, if chilling the salad before serving, add about half of the vinaigrette to the salad before refrigerating to moisten and allow the flavors to blend. Then, add some more dressing just before serving to refresh the flavor.

Broccoli Almond Soup

Serves 8

This elegant, creamy soup is a great autumn favorite of mine. The only cream used is for garnishing at the end. It is actually thickened with toasted ground almonds and puréed broccoli—an ambrosial combination. The coriander adds a delicate sweetness. This is an ideal recipe in which to use broccoli stalks when you have used the florets elsewhere. I would, however, save 8 tiny florets for the final garnish.

1 large bunch (1¾ to 2 pounds) broccoli, rinsed, leaves removed, stalks separated and cut into thirds *or* 10 cups broccoli stalks
8 tablespoons (1 stick) unsalted butter
1 large onion, peeled and thinly sliced
3½ ounces blanched almonds, toasted
4–5 cups chicken stock, preferably homemade
2 teaspoons ground coriander seed
1 teaspoon salt, or to taste
⅛ teaspoon white pepper
2 tablespoons sour cream (optional)
2 tablespoons light cream (optional)

1. Remove the tough outer layer of the broccoli and then steam it in a large pot until just tender, about 4 to 5 minutes once the water under the steamer has boiled. Remove from the steamer and set aside. Reserve 8 small florets for garnish.

2. In a large saucepan, melt the butter over medium heat just until it foams. Add the onion and sauté it until translucent, about 5 minutes. Add the broccoli, cover, and cook over medium-low heat until the broccoli is very tender—about 20 minutes.

3. Transfer the broccoli-onion mixture along with the almonds to the bowl of a food processor fitted with a steel chopping blade. Process until smooth, scraping down the sides of the bowl as needed.

4. Return the purée to the saucepan and stir in the chicken stock, coriander, salt, and pepper. Cook over medium heat until hot. Taste for seasonings.

5. Combine the sour and light creams in a small bowl, if desired. To serve, ladle the soup into heated bowls and garnish with a dollop of cream with a small broccoli floret on top.

NOTE: This soup may be made several days ahead of time, refrigerated, and reheated when needed; or freeze it for 2 to 3 months.

Broccoli and Cheese in Golden Phyllo Dome

Serves 8 as a first course or vegetable side dish

The simple garnish of two broccoli florets visually identifies this green-centered golden dome for my guests. Once they take a bite, they'll detect the cheese, but this way they don't even think of peas or green beans as the other important flavor.

If stored with wet paper towels around the stalks, broccoli will remain in good condition in a cold refrigerator for up to a week. I almost never buy frozen broccoli. The texture seems to become soft and mushy. However, since the vegetable is puréed in this recipe, frozen stalks or pieces would be a reasonable substitute. Cook broccoli uncovered in a nonaluminum pan to retain the bright green color.

1 large bunch (1¾ pounds) broccoli, rinsed, leaves removed, and stalks separated, peeled, and cut into thirds
1 tablespoon unsalted butter
1 medium onion, peeled and finely chopped
1 cup shredded Gruyère or Swiss cheese
2 eggs, beaten
2 tablespoons finely chopped fresh dill *or* 2 teaspoons dried
¼ teaspoon freshly grated nutmeg
¼ teaspoon dry mustard
Pinch of ground red pepper
Salt and freshly ground black pepper to taste
4 tablespoons (½ stick) unsalted butter, melted
8 phyllo leaves (see page 344)

1. Butter a 7-cup oven-safe bowl and preheat your oven to 375°F.

2. Steam the broccoli just until tender, about 5 to 6 minutes after the water under the steamer comes to a boil. Reserve 2 florets for garnish and transfer the remaining broccoli to the bowl of a food processor fitted with a steel chopping blade.

3. Melt 1 tablespoon of butter in a small skillet just until it foams. Add the onion and sauté it over medium-high heat until wilted and lightly colored, about 5 to 6 minutes. Add it to broccoli and process with on/off pulses until fairly smooth, stopping to scrape down the sides of the bowl. Add the cheeses, eggs, dill, nutmeg, dry mustard, red pepper, salt, and black pepper. Process just until well blended.

4. Place 1 phyllo leaf, long end near you, on a clean work surface and brush it lightly with butter. Fold the phyllo lengthwise in half, then in half lengthwise again, forming a long strip of four layers. Drape it in the buttered bowl, crossing the center of the bowl and leaving the ends extending over the edge. Repeat with a second leaf, placing it at right angles to the first. Use the remaining 6 leaves in the same fashion, covering the entire inside of the bowl.

5. Scrape the broccoli mixture into the bowl, smoothing it down with the back of a spoon or a spatula. Turn the ends of the phyllo strips over the filling, starting with the last strip and ending with the first. Brush with the remaining melted butter. Bake

DID YOU KNOW? Not only does paring the tough, fibrous outer layer off the broccoli help it to cook faster, it makes it easier to digest and more attractive when served as a crudité. Even on a raw vegetable platter, I prefer to blanch the florets for a couple of minutes to brighten the color and remove the slightly dusty look of the raw buds. Dip broccoli into TAPENADE (page 370) or CURRIED MAYONNAISE (page 370) as an hors d'oeuvre.

it on the middle rack of the preheated oven until the top is golden brown, about 40 minutes.

6. Remove the bowl from the oven and invert it onto an oven-safe platter. Remove the bowl and return the phyllo dome to the oven until the top is golden brown, about 8 minutes. Remove and let it stand for 10 minutes. Then place the 2 remaining florets in the middle of the timbale and present it at the table. Cut the timbale into wedges with a serrated knife and serve. This vegetable dish is an elegant accompaniment to roast chicken or grilled fish. It also makes an unusual first course.

Mexican Cole Slaw

Serves 6 to 8

This cole slaw is hardly mild-mannered. Tossed with a sunny Mexican mole-flavored sauce, the vibrant colors and crunchy textures of sliced radishes and finely chopped green peppers add a festive touch.

When buying radishes, you will find that the freshest ones are those in a bunch with the leaves still attached. The greens should be crisp, and the radishes should look firm and smooth. Smaller, round radishes are usually milder with a better texture. Once home, remove the greens before storing the radishes to prevent moisture loss. They will only last a few days.

1 tablespoon apple cider or red wine vinegar
2 tablespoons mole sauce
3 tablespoons vegetable oil
1 8-ounce can crushed pineapple packed in juice, drained, juice reserved
1 teaspoon tomato paste
⅛ teaspoon celery seeds
½ cup commercial sour cream
1½ pounds white or green cabbage, cored and finely shredded
1 large green pepper, seeds and membranes removed, minced
1 cup thinly sliced radishes
Salt and freshly ground black pepper to taste

1. In a small bowl, combine the vinegar and mole sauce, stirring to blend well. Whisk in the vegetable oil, reserved pineapple juice (approximately 2 tablespoons), tomato paste, celery seeds, and sour cream, cover, and refrigerate while preparing the vegetables.

2. Combine the cabbage, pepper, radishes, and pineapple in a large bowl. Spoon the sauce on top, season with salt and pepper, and toss to blend. Serve at once. This salad tends to get watery when it sits around.

Caramelized Cabbage in Strudel

Serves 6 to 8

When I first tasted the caramelized sweetness of slowly browned onions and cabbage wrapped in flaky pastry as prepared by my Hungarian great-grandmother, I understood why my grandmother loved this dish so much. It quickly became a favorite of mine. With the convenience of purchased strudel leaves (phyllo) available fresh in the Dairy department or in the Frozen Foods aisle, you can easily prepare this vegetable dish for game and roasts. Like cabbage, this strudel seems to go with the cold weather.

When buying cabbage in the market, I look for the familiar white, green, and purple heads to feel solid with no signs of damage to the outer leaves. These cabbages last in my vegetable crisper for at least 10 or 12 days. Elegant curly-leafed Savoy, Napa, and Chinese cabbage used mainly in stir-frying last only a week before the leaves look limp. Cabbage is not only reasonably priced, low in calories, and quite healthy, but the purple heads make a most dramatic centerpiece! See for yourself on page 442.

4 tablespoons (½ stick) unsalted butter
2 large onions, peeled and chopped
1 large green or white cabbage, approximately 2
    pounds, cored and shredded
Salt and plenty of freshly ground black pepper to
    taste
4 tablespoons unsalted butter, melted
7 phyllo leaves
3 tablespoons toasted fresh bread crumbs

1. Heat 4 tablespoons of butter in a heavy, deep, nonaluminum pan large enough to hold all of the cabbage. When it foams, add the onions and sauté them over medium-high heat until lightly colored, about 7 to 8 minutes. Add the cabbage and stir over medium heat until softened and golden brown in color, 40 to 45 minutes. If the cabbage cooks too quickly and begins to brown before it is completely softened, stir it well, adjust the heat down, and cover the pot for a few minutes to allow moisture to form. Then remove the lid, stir, turn the heat back to medium, and continue. Or, add ½ cup water, stir up the browned cabbage, and continue cooking. The water should evaporate. (You may have to do this a couple of times, stirring each time so that the cabbage at the bottom of the pot does not burn.) Stir in the salt and plenty of pepper. Set aside uncovered.

2. Preheat your oven to 375°F and butter a cookie sheet or jelly roll pan.

3. Spread out a clean towel on a flat surface. Lay 1 leaf of phyllo with the long side close to you on the towel, and brush lightly with melted butter. Keep the remaining phyllo covered with a towel. Sprinkle about 1 tablespoon of bread crumbs over the phyllo. Add a second leaf of phyllo, brush with butter, but *do not* add bread crumbs. Continue with the remaining leaves of phyllo, using bread crumbs only on the fourth and sixth leaves. *Do not* brush the last (seventh) leaf of phyllo with butter.

4. Spoon the cabbage mixture in a strip along the long edge of the layered phyllo, forming it into a compact cylinder, and leaving about a 1½-inch border at each short end. Using both hands, flip the sides of the towel toward the back, causing the front edge of

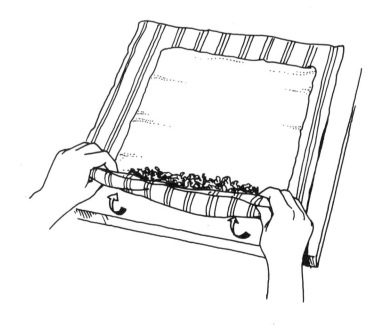

the strudel to roll back over the cabbage. (See illustration.) Turn the sides of the phyllo in and continue rolling in the same manner. With the last roll, flip the strudel onto the jelly roll pan with the seam on the bottom. Brush the top and sides of the strudel with the remaining butter, and with a sharp, pointed instrument (like a trussing needle or awl) make 6 to 8 small holes through the strudel dough to the filling for excess moisture to escape.

5. Transfer the pan to the middle of the preheated oven and bake until the top is crisp and golden brown, about 25 to 30 minutes. This strudel may be kept in a 250°F oven for at least 1 hour. To serve, cut with a serrated knife into 1½-inch slices.

NOTE: Cabbage strudels may be made 1 or even 2 days ahead of time, covered with a buttered piece of aluminum foil, and refrigerated until ready for baking. If the foil is stuck to the phyllo, begin baking the strudel with the foil. Once the butter melts, it will lift off easily.

Holiday Cranberry Carrots

Serves 8

I love carrots not only for their versatility and sweet flavor, but also for the color contrast they add to any plate. In this festive recipe, their orange tone is intensified as the cranberries pop during cooking and blend with the marsala wine to form a dazzling glaze. The orange zest and cardamom (a surprise here) add a subtle warmth and richness to the taste.

You can tell if carrots are old. They are often cracked, pale colored, and large. They may even be sprouting roots. You can be pretty sure that they will be tasteless and tough. Select, instead, the thinnest, brightest carrots you can find. Since carrots are available all year, this should not be a problem. I prefer to buy mine with the tops still on as a guarantee of freshness. This way, carrots keep for a couple of weeks in a refrigerator. With a few exceptions (such as purées), I prefer not to use frozen carrots, since their texture is poor.

2 pounds young carrots, peeled and sliced into ¼-inch rounds
4 tablespoons (½ stick) unsalted butter
1½ tablespoons grated orange zest
8 cardamom pods, hulled and seeds pounded in a mortar *or* ¼ teaspoon ground cardamom
¼ cup dry marsala wine
¾ cup fresh cranberries
Salt to taste

1. Steam the carrot slices just until tender, about 5 to 6 minutes. *Do not overcook.*

2. Melt the butter in a large, heavy skillet over medium-high heat just until it foams. Add the carrots, orange zest, and cardamom. Cook, stirring occasionally, for 2 to 3 minutes. Add the marsala and cranberries, turn up the heat to high, and cook, stirring frequently until the liquid has evaporated, about 3 to 5 minutes. The cranberries will pop during this time. Season to taste with salt.

NOTE: This dish may be prepared several hours or even a day ahead of time and reheated over low heat.

🛒 DID YOU KNOW? Another method of peeling carrots, parsnips, or salsify for cooking is to boil or steam them whole for a few minutes, then run them under cold water. Their skins will slide off. Then slice, julienne, or cook them longer, as needed. This works well when there are lots of carrots to be cleaned.

Cauliflower and Potato Purée with Parmesan

Serves 8

When combined with potatoes and Parmesan cheese, the flavor of cauliflower is subtle and a good balance to more highly seasoned meats or vegetables. I like to pipe this purée through a pastry bag to add brightness and texture to a plate.

Cauliflower is another winter vegetable whose aroma gets stronger as it gets older. And if the smell is pungent, the taste will be less than sweet. I use cauliflower within a couple of days of buying it. Look for heads that are firmly bunched and uniformly pale-colored without any brown spots.

1 head of cauliflower, approximately 1¼ pounds, broken into florets
1 large red potato, peeled and cubed
3 tablespoons light cream or milk
2 tablespoons unsalted butter
¼ teaspoon freshly grated nutmeg
Salt and white pepper to taste
½ cup freshly grated Parmesan cheese

Vegetable purées add variety to a meal. They are a cinch to make in the processor. If you are piping the purée through a pastry tube, add a potato for substance to vegetables that do not contain starch. Always make sure that the nonstarchy vegetable is very smooth before adding the cooked potato, since overbeating the potatoes will release too much of their starch and produce a gummy texture. Since people today are so "roughage" conscious, a food mill is another way of making a more textured purée.

1. Steam the cauliflower over boiling water until tender, drain well, and transfer to the bowl of a food processor fitted with a steel chopping blade. In a separate pot, boil the potato until tender, drain, and keep covered until needed.

2. Add the cream or milk and butter to the cauliflower bowl and process until smooth. Add the potato, nutmeg, salt, and pepper; process just until smooth. Over-processing will make the potato gummy. Mashing can be done with a potato ricer or food mill.

3. Add the Parmesan cheese and pulse a few times to combine. Taste and adjust seasonings, if necessary.

4. Pipe the purée through a pastry bag fitted with a large star tip into a circular mound on each plate or spoon some onto each plate and decorate with fork tines. I serve this purée with NOISETTES OF LAMB FLORENTINE (page 191).

Roasted Eggplant with Tahini on Endive Leaves

Serves 6 as a first course

This attractive do-ahead first course can easily double as an hors d'oeuvre or vegetable accompaniment for roast lamb. The tangy sweet Middle Eastern flavors of roasted eggplant and tahini (check in the International Foods section for this ground sesame-seed purée) seem to improve with time.

We are fortunate to have excellent eggplants available almost all year in supermarkets. Recently, the large purple ones have been joined by smaller Japanese (look at the end of this recipe for an idea on how to use them) and white varieties. Your fingers can really be the best guide to good selection. All eggplants should have shiny, tight skin without any brown spots, and the crown should be green. But, don't judge by appearances alone. *Gently* push with your thumb or forefinger. If the flesh gives slightly but then bounces back, it is ripe. If the indentation remains, it is over ripe, and the insides will be mushy. If there is no give, the eggplant was picked too early. Unfortunately, these aubergine treasures don't last well, at all. I try to use mine within a day. If you must refrigerate them, do so only for a day or two and without any wrappings. Since they don't like extreme cold, place them in the top part of the refrigerator; a cool pantry is even better.

1 tablespoon olive oil
2 medium eggplants
3 large cloves garlic, peeled and cut into slivers
2 plum tomatoes, peeled
½ cup tahini
Salt and freshly ground black pepper to taste
2 tablespoons minced flat-leaf parsley
⅓ cup olive oil
7–8 tablespoons fresh lemon juice
⅓ cup pignoli (pine nuts), toasted until light brown
30 Belgian endive leaves, approximately the same size
6 cherry tomatoes, for garnish

1. Preheat your oven to 375°F. Lightly oil a cookie sheet.

2. Wipe the eggplants with a cloth or paper towels. Cut them in half lengthwise and make several deep gashes in the flesh but do not pierce the skin. Insert the garlic slivers into the eggplants and place the halves cut side down on the cookie sheet. Transfer to the preheated oven and let them steam for about 40 minutes until the flesh is very soft.

3. Remove the eggplants from the oven and let them cool slightly. Scoop out the pulp and put it into a food processor fitted with a steel chopping blade or mash with a fork. Be sure to include the garlic. Add the tomatoes, tahini, salt, pepper, parsley, olive oil, and most of the lemon juice and process until smooth. If doing this by hand, mash the tomatoes, then mix all the ingredients together. Scrape into a bowl, cover, and refrigerate for several hours or overnight.

4. Before serving, stir in the pignoli and taste to adjust seasonings, adding additional lemon juice, if necessary. Place 5 endive leaves in a petal design on each plate, the tapered end pointing out. Spoon a large tablespoon of the eggplant mixture onto each leaf and place a cherry tomato in the center. Little slices of toasted French bread, brushed with olive oil and lightly dusted with crumbled tarragon leaves, would be a nice addition.

DID YOU KNOW? Tahini is made from ground raw, hulled sesame seeds. You will find it with Baking Supplies or Health Foods in the market. It is frequently used in Middle Eastern cooking. Once opened, this fragile condiment should be refrigerated, as it goes rancid easily. Use it within 1 to 2 months.

To make GRILLED JAPANESE EGGPLANT: Buy 1 per person, using the same selection guide as above. Split the eggplant in half lengthwise, brush all over with a little sesame oil, and place on a hot grill or barbecue, cut-side down. Turn once after 2 to 3 minutes, brush lightly with some hoisin sauce (from the Oriental section), and cook for another 2 minutes or until the eggplants are tender when pierced with a fork. Sprinkle a few sliced scallions over the eggplant halves and serve.

Velouté of Fennel

Serves 8 to 10

Veloutés are among the most elegant and richest of creamed soups. With the addition of cream and egg yolks to the flour and butter roux, they live up to their name which means "velvety." Like the fabric of the same name, this is party fare. In this delicate version, the star is the beautiful anise-flavored pale-green bulb found in markets from October to March.

As you reach in the grocer's shelf, feel that the fennel bulbs are solid and without soft spots. Freshness counts a lot here, since fennel does not last well even under refrigeration (1 to 3 days is optimum). As this vegetable ages, some markets trim the lacy green stalks off when they go limp. I prefer mine crisp and uncut. If fennel is unavailable or the outsides are cracked and brown, substitute 1 pound of celery and 1 tablespoon of fennel seeds.

4 tablespoons (½ stick) unsalted butter
6 large heads fennel, trimmed and thinly sliced
6 tablespoons (¾ stick) unsalted butter
6 tablespoons unbleached all-purpose flour
8 cups chicken stock, preferably homemade
4 egg yolks
¾ cup heavy cream
Salt and white pepper to taste
Chopped fresh chives for garnish

1. Melt 4 tablespoons of butter in a large, heavy skillet over medium heat. Add the fennel, cover, and slowly braise, stirring occasionally, until the fennel is completely softened and lightly browned, about 30 to 35 minutes. Transfer the fennel to a food processor fitted with a steel chopping blade and purée. Set aside.

2. Melt the remaining butter in a large, heavy saucepan over medium-low heat. When the butter foams, add the flour and stir with a wooden spoon until the flour is cooked but still light in color, about 3 to 4 minutes. Slowly add the stock to the flour mixture, stirring constantly. Bring it to a boil, then reduce the heat to low and simmer gently for 30 minutes. Stir in the prepared fennel. Pass the soup through a fine strainer, if desired. The soup may be prepared ahead to this point.

3. Just before serving, bring the soup to a simmer. Combine the egg yolks and cream in a small bowl and

HAVE YOU TRIED? Fennel (*finocchio* in Italy) in Pinzimonio: Trim the fennel stalks at the point where they meet the bulb, and shave a narrow slice off the base. Rinse under cold water, then cut the bulbs into quarters or eighths. Arrange attractively on a small serving dish that also holds a small bowl of extra-virgin olive oil and one of coarse salt. Pick up a piece of fennel with your fingers (in pinzimonio) and dip it first into the oil and then the salt. This also makes an interesting variation for your favorite crudité.

beat well. Gradually add about 1 cup of soup into the yolk mixture, beating constantly. Slowly blend the yolk mixture back into the remaining soup. (Be careful not to let the soup boil or the eggs will curdle.) Season to taste with salt and pepper. Ladle into warm bowls and garnish with chives.

Green Bean and New Potato Salad from Vernon

Serves 8

So many French towns are renowned for producing the finest quality of a certain product: Cavaillon for small, perfumed melons; Bresse for white chickens. Vernon, northwest of Paris on the way to Rouen, justly prides itself on its wonderful, tender green beans. Some friends from the region first introduced me to this simple salad with its garlicky vinaigrette, an addicting combination for bean and potato lovers like me. In an effort to duplicate their dish, I have been known to pick out each thin, crisp, deep green bean individually from the produce bin at the market. Uniformity shows in the appearance and taste.

At home, refrigerate beans in a partially opened plastic or brown paper bag. Or punch a couple of holes in a sealed bag. Moisture will cause the beans to become moldy. If they won't be used within 2 days, I would boil or steam the beans until bright green but still crisp, then rinse them under cold water to stop the cooking, blot dry, wrap, and refrigerate. They will stay in top condition for 3 or 4 days this way. Or you could freeze them, partially cooked and well dried, in airtight wrapping for up to 6 months.

1¼ pounds tender, young beans, rinsed, tips
   removed
1 pound red potatoes, of equal size, scrubbed
1 recipe MUSTARD VINAIGRETTE (page 363)
2 large cloves garlic, peeled and mashed
2 tablespoons finely chopped flat-leaf parsley
Freshly ground black pepper to taste

1. Bring a large pot of salted water to a boil. Add the green beans and cook until just tender, about 3 to 4 minutes after the water returns to a boil. Drain the beans in a colander or strainer, rinse with cold water, then blot dry on paper towels. (The beans may also be steamed.)

2. Add more water to the pot and boil the potatoes until just tender, about 12 to 14 minutes. They should be easily pierced with a knife, but not crumbly. Drain and let them air cool until slightly warm. Do not rinse them. With a sharp knife, cut them into ¼-inch slices without peeling.

3. Mound the beans in the center of a large bowl and place the potato slices overlapping one another around the outside edge. If you are not serving this right away, drizzle a little olive oil over the potatoes to keep them from drying out. Just before serving, pour the Mustard Vinaigrette with the extra garlic and parsley over the beans and potatoes. Add plenty of black pepper. Toss carefully and serve.

NOTE: Occasionally I add pieces of leftover roasted chicken or turkey breast to this salad for a more substantial picnic dish.

Gnocchi with Peas and Tomato Sauce

Serves 8 to 10 as a first course

A Tuscan farmer woman first taught me to make these heavenly potato dumplings (or *gnocchi*). Her sauce included the giblets from the fresh chicken that was served at the next course, roasted to crunchy perfection (see CRUNCHY OVEN-ROASTED CHICKEN, page 133). This recipe is rustic and very satisfying.

FOR THE SAUCE
2 tablespoons olive oil
1 small clove garlic, peeled and minced
1 small onion, peeled and finely chopped
1 small carrot (or ½ medium), scraped and finely chopped
1 small stalk celery, finely chopped
4 ounces thickly sliced prosciutto or similar-type cured ham (not smoked), chopped
Giblets from 1 chicken (neck, liver, heart, and gizzard), cleaned and chopped
¼ cup freshly chopped flat-leaf parsley
1 tablespoon freshly chopped basil *or* 1 teaspoon dried
1 28-ounce can Italian tomatoes, drained and puréed
Salt and freshly ground black pepper to taste
½ cup shelled peas or small frozen peas, defrosted
4 ounces freshly grated Parmesan cheese

FOR THE GNOCCHI
1½ pounds boiling potatoes, quartered
2–3 cups all-purpose flour
½ tablespoon salt

DID YOU KNOW? I think the best mashed potatoes are still made the old-fashioned way—with a potato ricer or masher rather than a processor, which makes them gummy. (I only use the processor when I make vegetable purées and add the potato at the last minute.) Peel and quarter the potatoes. Then boil them in salted water until tender. Drain and let them dry out slightly, either in the pan over low heat for a minute, or in a bowl partially covered with a clean towel. Then mash them by hand. Beat in some milk or a little of the boiling liquid, some butter, a pinch of nutmeg (if you like), and salt and pepper to taste. Don't keep stirring! Thin-skinned, boiling potatoes make creamier mashed potatoes than the baking variety (russets). Be sure to cut off any green spots on the potatoes before cooking them.

1. PREPARE THE SAUCE Pour the olive oil into a large, heavy, nonaluminum pot and heat it until fragrant. Add the garlic, onion, carrots, and celery, and sauté over medium-high heat until wilted, 7 or 8 minutes. Add the prosciutto, giblets, parsley, and basil, and cook until the giblets are browned and separated. Stir in the tomatoes, salt, and pepper, and simmer for 20 minutes or longer, while preparing the gnocchi. Toward the end of the cooking time, add the peas and cook until tender, about 5 to 7 minutes, if using fresh peas.

2. PREPARE THE GNOCCHI Place the potatoes in a large pot of water and bring to a boil. Cook until the potatoes are tender when pierced with a knife (about 12 to 14 minutes), drain, and peel them while still hot. Set them aside until they are just cool enough to work with.

3. Lightly sprinkle a large workboard with some flour. Press the potatoes through a potato ricer or food mill (*not a processor*), and spread them out to cool. Begin incorporating flour by ½ cupfuls into the po-

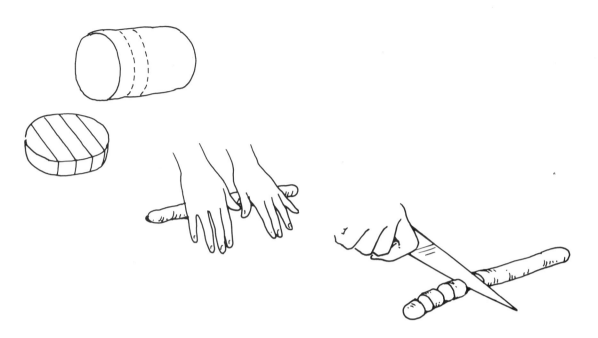

tatoes, dusting your hands, the board, and the potatoes with flour repeatedly as you work until the dough is smooth, uniform, and slightly sticky. (Some potatoes take more flour than others, so the amounts may vary by up to 1 cup.) Knead gently for 3 to 4 minutes more, then form the dough into a large cylinder about 4 to 5 inches in diameter.

4. Cut off slices about 1 inch thick, then cut these slices into 1-inch strips. (See illustration.) Roll each strip into a cylinder about the thickness of your thumb. Cut it into 1-inch lengths. Place the gnocchi on a floured board and do not handle them.

5. Bring a large pot of salted water to a boil. Add about 2 dozen gnocchi at a time. After the water has returned to a boil and the gnocchi rise to the surface, boil them for another 30 to 40 seconds. Remove them with a skimmer or wide-slotted spoon to a large, warmed serving bowl. Repeat with the remaining gnocchi. You will have about 4 or 5 batches of gnocchi.

6. TO SERVE Alternate layers of the gnocchi with large spoonfuls of the Peas and Tomato Sauce. (You will need only about half the amount of sauce prepared above. Pass extra sauce at the table and/or freeze what is left.) Sprinkle with the Parmesan cheese, toss gently, and serve about 8 to 10 gnocchi per person.

Sautéed Julienne of Leeks and Cucumbers

Serves 4 to 6

This pale green vegetable dish is quite delicate yet flavorful. The cucumbers, cut into crescent shapes, are blanched and then sautéed with matchstick-thin strips of leeks. The result is a refreshing accompaniment for fish, poultry, or pork.

Texture is important here, so choose the vegetables with care. Unfortunately, cucumbers in supermarkets are often shipped with a waxy coating, which I abhor, even though it's meant to retard moisture loss. I generally leave mine in a plastic bag from the Produce department, and peel them just before using. Feel each cuke to be sure it is solid and without any soft spots. I prefer to buy medium-size cucumbers, as the large ones often have big seeds, as well.

Size is also important with leeks. Once the root end has become enlarged, the leek is likely to be tough and not as sweet. Leeks are best when they are firm and young with bright green leaves. They should measure under an inch and a half in diameter at the base. Wrapped in plastic bags in a refrigerator, they will keep for at least 10 days before turning brown.

4 young leeks, about 1¼ inch in diameter, outside
    leaves removed
2 tablespoons unsalted butter
2 medium-size cucumbers, peeled
Salt and freshly ground black pepper to taste
1 tablespoon light cream (optional)
2 teaspoons fresh lemon juice
1 generous teaspoon minced flat-leaf parsley

1. Trim off the root end of the leeks and the greens 1 inch above the white part. Insert the tip of a sharp paring knife about ¼ inch from the trimmed root and make a deep incision up the length of the leek. Spread the leaves apart with your fingers and rinse under cold running water to remove any sand. Cut them in half lengthwise, then in thirds crosswise, and finally into thin lengthwise strips.
2. Melt the butter in a large, heavy skillet over medium heat. Add the leeks and slowly sauté them until softened, but not browned. Set aside.
3. Cut the cucumbers into half lengthwise, and scoop out the seeded center parts with a pointed spoon or a melon baller. Cut each half crosswise into thin cres-

cent-shaped slices. Bring some water to a boil in a medium-size saucepan. Add about a teaspoon of salt, then drop in the cucumber slices and cook for about 30 seconds until they are just transparent. Remove with a skimmer or slotted spoon and blot dry on paper towels. Add the cucumber to the skillet with the leeks, toss to combine, and raise heat to medium.

4. Add the salt, pepper, and cream, shaking the pan until the cream evaporates. Add the lemon juice and parsley. Toss again and taste to adjust the seasonings, if necessary.

Chunky Mushroom and Barley Soup

Serves 8

DID YOU KNOW? If you have saved the soaking liquid from dried porcini mushrooms (page 53), you can strain it through several layers of cheesecloth or paper towels and use it in place of part of the beef stock (about 1 to 1½ cups). It will add an earthy flavor to this soup. A couple of chopped porcini added to the sliced cultivated mushrooms would be superb, as well.

Here is my variation on a traditional Eastern European favorite soup. The rich flavor of the sautéed vegetables is complemented by the subtle tanginess of the sour cream and lemon juice. This is a good place to use up the mushroom stems from the PESTO MUSHROOMS on page 43. But, do buy that extra quarter pound of mushrooms to slice at the end of the recipe. They not only add texture, they are a visual clue to the taste, as well.

When buying cultivated white mushrooms, make sure to buy the freshest, whitest ones you can find. If they are loose, turn them over to inspect the undersides. As they lose moisture, the ridged part of the cap separates from the stems. When appearances are less important, the prepacked baskets are sometimes a better buy. But be careful. Some larger mushrooms are labeled "stuffers" and cost more, an unnecessary expense when size is not important. When storing mushrooms in the refrigerator, keep them in a brown bag, or plastic bag with holes cut into it, to let them breathe. These cultivated mushrooms are usually so clean that a wipe with a damp towel is all they need.

½ cup medium barley
2 cups water
½ pound parsnips, scraped and finely chopped
½ pound carrots, scraped and finely chopped
½ pound onions, peeled and finely chopped
5 tablespoons unsalted butter
2 tablespoons vegetable oil
1 pound mushrooms, wiped, stems trimmed, finely chopped
3 tablespoons finely chopped flat-leaf parsley *or* 1 tablespoon dried
1 large clove garlic, peeled and crushed
3 cups beef stock, preferably homemade
1 cup light cream
1 tablespoon lemon juice
Salt and freshly ground black pepper to taste
2 tablespoons unsalted butter
¼ pound mushrooms, wiped, stems trimmed, thinly sliced
½ cup sour cream

1. Bring medium-size saucepan of water to a boil. Add the barley, adjust the heat down, and simmer, covered, until tender, about 25 minutes. Drain and reserve.

2. Melt 5 tablespoons of butter and oil in a large, heavy saucepan just until the butter foams. Add the chopped parsnips, carrots, and onions; stir to coat with butter; and cover. Cook over low heat, stirring occasionally, until the vegetables are tender, about 10 minutes.

3. Add the mushrooms and parsley to the vegetables and continue cooking until the mushrooms are separated, about 5 minutes. Add the garlic, then stir in 1 cup of broth and mix well.

4. Ladle the mixture by batches into the bowl of a food processor fitted with a steel chopping blade, and purée it until almost smooth. Return the purée to the saucepan, stir in the remaining stock, light cream, lemon juice, and cooked barley, and season with salt and pepper. Simmer for 10 minutes or until heated through.

5. Meanwhile, sauté the remaining ¼ pound of mushrooms in 2 tablespoons butter until just wilted, about 30 seconds to 1 minute. When the soup is hot, remove the saucepan from the heat, whisk in the sour cream, and stir in the mushrooms. Ladle the soup into bowls and serve.

Pesto Mushrooms

Makes 16

Fresh basil is a sure sign of summer and a passion of many cooks. In season, a walk in the Produce department of most supermarkets will reveal bunches of this tender aromatic herb—hopefully misted and not left to become limp or bruised. There may even be purple or other varieties to experiment with (their taste is similar). But, what about the bags of hydroponic basil that we now find in winter? They certainly are clean and easy to use. Pick off a leaf and rub it between your fingers. Sometimes all this clean living diminishes the intensity of flavor.

For years, I have been saucing pasta with pesto (this heavenly basil, pine nut, and cheese purée). I found that when there were extras in the refrigerator, I'd spread it on thin crackers (or my fingers!). Finally, I added a little cream cheese to soften the flavors and stuffed mushrooms with it. The just-warmed crunchy caps and the soft filling are a decadent hors d'oeuvre. Or, serve one large pesto mushroom with other vegetable accompaniments for a main course.

🛒 DID YOU KNOW? To flute mushrooms, a citrus stripper is an easier way to create the design than trying to master turning and cutting out the decorative ridges with a small paring knife.

To prepare fluted mushroom caps ahead of time, Roger Vergé's Le Moulin de Mougins, a great restaurant in southern France, cooks them for a few seconds in a little boiling water with a few drops of lemon juice and a small amount of butter. They are then removed, patted dry, and stored tightly covered in the refrigerator. When needed, run them quickly under the broiler fluted side up, to color them.

2 cups loosely packed fresh basil leaves, rinsed
  and gently blotted dry
¼ cup olive oil
2 tablespoons pine nuts (pignoli)
2 tablespoons walnuts—*or* all walnuts, if desired
2 large cloves garlic, peeled and split
1 teaspoon salt
Freshly ground black pepper to taste
2 ounces cream cheese
⅓ cup grated imported Parmesan cheese
⅓ cup grated Romano cheese—*or* all Parmesan
  cheese
16 medium-large mushrooms
2 tablespoons unsalted butter
1 large clove garlic, peeled and minced
Salt and freshly ground black pepper

1. Place the basil, olive oil, pine nuts, walnuts, garlic cloves, salt, and pepper in the bowl of a food processor fitted with a steel chopping blade and process until smooth. Scrape down the sides of the bowl, add the cream cheese, and process until smooth.

2. Scrape the basil mixture into a bowl and stir in the cheeses. Adjust the seasonings, if necessary.

3. Remove the stems from the mushrooms and wipe the caps. (Reserve the stems for stock or CHUNKY MUSHROOM AND BARLEY SOUP on page 41.) In a small skillet, melt the butter and stir in the minced garlic; cook over low heat for 30 seconds, then turn off the heat. Brush the inside and outside of the mushroom caps lightly and season with salt and pepper.

4. Place the mushrooms in a shallow baking dish. Fill each cap with some of the pesto mixture, mounding it slightly in the center. Cover them loosely and refrigerate for 1 to 2 hours. (This recipe may be prepared up to this point at least a day ahead of time.)

5. Preheat your oven to 400°F. Bake the mushrooms uncovered for 5 to 6 minutes or until the filling is softened and the mushrooms are warm but still firm. Serve at once. I usually put each cap in a small decorative fluted paper cup, like the mini muffin liners often found in the Baking section of the market.

Incredibly Light Onion Rings

Serves 4

Onions in every shape and size are a personal passion of mine. The wire egg basket that hangs in my kitchen overflows with white, red, and yellow onions, as well as garlic, all year long. I adore onions thinly sliced and raw on sandwiches, but also baked, braised, or fried to a crisp. These crunchy, *ungreasy* onion rings are really fun to make. This is the easiest (and best) version I've tried. What's more, they can be made at least an hour ahead of time and left in a warm oven. Be warned, they disappear quickly!

Choose onions individually, feeling them to be sure they are solid, without any soft spots and that the skins are dry and papery. Smell them, too; they should be sweet. Only a deteriorating onion will smell pungent before it is cut.

Mild shallots, too, go in the basket. Scallions and tiny pearl onions (when I can find them) I leave in a plastic bag in the vegetable drawer of my refrigerator.

DID YOU KNOW? This flour-and-water batter is excellent for deep frying zucchini blossoms, too. Hold each blossom by the stem and dip it completely into the batter. Lift the blossom out and let any excess batter drip back into the bowl. Carefully place each squash blossom into hot oil and fry it until it is golden brown on the first side, then turn and continue cooking until the second side is well colored. Only fry as many blossoms as will fit comfortably in the skillet at a time. Drain on paper towels and sprinkle with salt. I usually squeeze on a few drops of lemon juice for flavor. Serve at once. This is an hors d'oeuvre to make for your friends in the kitchen. Or leave the fried blossoms in a warm oven and serve them along with sautéed zucchini as a vegetable accompaniment to CRUNCHY OVEN-ROASTED CHICKEN (page 133).

FOR THE BATTER
1 cup unbleached all-purpose flour
1 cup cold water

FOR THE ONIONS
2 very large yellow onions, peeled and thinly sliced
Olive oil *or* a combination of olive and vegetable oils for deep-frying
Salt to taste

1. **PREPARE THE BATTER**   Place the cold water in a bowl large and deep enough to hold the onions separated into rings. (They may be coated in batches.) With a strainer or a sifter, sift the flour into the bowl in small amounts, stirring with a wooden spoon or whisk to incorporate it evenly into the batter. The batter should be smooth and the consistency of light cream. Set aside.

2. Separate the onion slices into rings and place them in the batter, turning to cover.

3. Turn your oven on to 275°F. Line a cookie sheet with paper towels.

4. Pour the oil into a large, heavy skillet to a depth of ½ inch and heat it until very hot but not smoking,

300°F on a deep-fat thermometer. (If the oil becomes too hot during cooking, take the skillet off the heat for a minute to let it cool down slightly.) Remove some of the onion rings from the batter with a fork or slotted spoon, allowing excess batter to drip back into the bowl. Fry only a few rings at a time, keeping the oil very hot. Do not crowd the pan. If the top side does not brown, turn to fry both sides, about 3 to 4 minutes. When golden brown, remove with tongs or a fork to the paper towel-lined pan to drain. Place the pan in the warm oven and continue with the remaining onion rings. Sprinkle with salt to taste before serving. They will remain crisp for at least an hour.

Marinated Three Onion Salad

Serves 6 to 8

This simple creamy dill-flavored salad is a colorful side dish for an informal dinner or buffet. Don't worry about all those onions. Blanching subdues their pungent bite. Serve with MADE-TO-BE-LEFTOVER MEAT LOAF (page 171), pâtés, and roast chicken.

Both large Spanish and red Bermuda onions seem milder to me when bought in the late spring. They are my first choice for eating raw if I cannot find some of the newer sweet onions sold seasonally like Vidalias (from Georgia), Walla Wallas (from Washington), or Mauis (from Hawaii). All three make wonderful eating, but watch the price ticket—these "gourmet" varieties are apt to be a couple of dollars more than yellow onions. If you are putting them into a stew, remember their special flavor will be lost.

2 large yellow or Spanish onions, peeled and thinly sliced
2 large red Bermuda onions, peeled and thinly sliced
1 large bunch scallions, trimmed and thinly sliced (including most of the green parts)
2 tablespoons salt
2 teaspoons Dijon mustard
3 tablespoons fresh lemon juice
2 tablespoons olive oil
1 cup plain low-fat yogurt
1 tablespoon sugar
⅓ cup finely chopped fresh dill
Freshly ground black pepper to taste

1. Separate the red and yellow onion slices into rings and place them in a large bowl. Cover with boiling water and 2 tablespoons of salt. Allow them to stand for about 10 minutes, or until wilted. Drain and blot them well on paper towels.

2. Rinse and dry the bowl. In the bowl, combine the mustard and lemon juice, then whisk in the olive oil and yogurt. Add the sugar, dill, and pepper. Stir in the onions and scallions. Mix well and refrigerate for at least an hour. The flavor improves as the salad sits.

Hearty Onion Soup

Serves 4 to 6

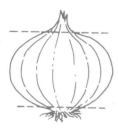

This thick, puréed onion soup is quite unlike the classic clear French version. Here, slowly caramelized onions and Riesling wine are combined with chicken stock and a splash of sherry. Sautéed strands of golden onion are added before serving for another flavor dimension. The Gruyère cheese croutons are a splendid complement to the creaminess of the soup. I find them far more appealing than a thick lid of cheese on soggy bread which often camouflages the taste of the soup.

Supermarkets often sell 3-pound bags of onions. It's a quick way to buy the right amount for this recipe.

FOR THE SOUP
5 tablespoons unsalted butter
2½ pounds yellow onions, peeled and thinly sliced
2 tablespoons unsalted butter
½ pound yellow onions, peeled and thinly sliced
½ cup Riesling wine
4–5 cups chicken stock
1 teaspoon salt, or to taste
⅛ teaspoon white pepper
¼ cup medium sherry

FOR THE CROUTONS
8–12 thin slices of a narrow French bread
1 clove garlic, split
2 tablespoons olive oil
3–4 ounces Gruyère cheese, finely shredded

1. In a large, heavy pot, melt 5 tablespoons of butter just until it foams. Add the 2½ pounds of onions

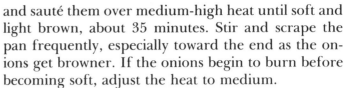

Place the flat, cut part on the board and make even slices almost through the onion, working from the right (or left) to the center. Once at the center, turn the onion 180 degrees and then slice the other half, holding the first slices together against the middle so that all the slices are equally thick or thin.

To chop, trim off the top and only the smallest amount from the root end of the onion. It should stand steady. You do not need to slice off anything from the side (as above). Cutting from the top down, make narrow or wide slices almost to the root. Turn the onion 45 degrees and slice the onion, again almost to the root. Cut the onion through the root in the center, and with the flat center on the workboard, slice the onion into pieces working from the top to the root end.

and sauté them over medium-high heat until soft and light brown, about 35 minutes. Stir and scrape the pan frequently, especially toward the end as the onions get browner. If the onions begin to burn before becoming soft, adjust the heat to medium.

2. Meanwhile, in a medium-size skillet, melt the 2 tablespoons of butter over medium heat, and slowly sauté the remaining onion slices until golden brown, about 6 to 7 minutes. Set these onions aside to add at the end.

3. Add the wine to the large pot, stir, and bring the mixture to a boil, then reduce the heat and simmer for 5 minutes.

4. Stir about ½ cup of the chicken stock into the onion mixture, transfer the onions in batches to a food processor fitted with a steel chopping blade, and purée. Or use a blender: Fill it ⅓ of the way and purée the onions in batches. Return the puréed onions to the pot, add another 2½ cups of stock, the salt, pepper, and sherry, and stir well. Add more stock as needed. Stir in the sautéed onions and keep the soup warm over medium-low heat.

5. Prepare the croutons by toasting the bread slices until lightly browned, rubbing them with garlic and then brushing with olive oil. Place them on a cookie sheet, sprinkle with Gruyère cheese, and place under the broiler until the cheese is melted and light brown. Ladle the soup into heated bowls and place 2 croutons on top.

Parsnips and Pomegranates

Serves 8

Parsnips and pomegranates have been used in cooking for centuries. I have never seen them combined before, but cooking is creative, and there are very few rules in the kitchen. Parsnips have a lot of natural sugar which caramelizes during sautéing or frying. With a hint of orange and the jewellike pomegranate seeds, this vegetable dish is a regal addition to any fall meal—just the season to find these items in your market.

Try to buy parsnips loose; they'll keep better (at least a couple of weeks) when not wrapped airtight. Even though their size varies dramatically, unless a parsnip is wrinkled and dehydrated-looking, it should still be delicious. When cooking them, if some are very thin and others thick, cut the parsnips into pieces, and split the wide end in half.

½ teaspoon salt
8 medium parsnips, tops and tips trimmed, cut into 2-inch lengths, wider tops split in half lengthwise
2 tablespoons unsalted butter
1½ cups orange juice
½ teaspoon salt, or to taste
¾ cup fresh pomegranate seeds, white membranes removed, about 1 large pomegranate
2 tablespoons finely chopped chives

1. Bring a large pot of water to a boil. Add the salt and the parsnips. Cover the pot and return the water to a boil. Remove the lid and cook until the parsnips are just tender when pierced with a knife. Drain and rinse them under cold running water. The skins should slip off. Thinner ends will be done within about 4 to 5 minutes. Thicker pieces will take longer. Do not let them get too soft. Cut the pieces into approximately ½-inch strips and blot dry on paper towels.

2. In a large, heavy skillet, melt the butter over medium-high heat just until it foams. Add the parsnips, shaking to coat them evenly and continue cooking, turning occasionally, until they start to color, about 7 to 8 minutes.

3. Pour in the orange juice, turn up the heat, and boil until the orange juice evaporates, about 3 to 4 minutes. Stir in the salt. Add the pomegranate seeds

DID YOU KNOW? There are lots of things you can do with parsnips aside from boiling and puréeing them. They are wonderful sliced and sautéed with tangy apple slices. Or, blanched, they add texture and taste to salads of mixed greens or chicken.

and chives and gently turn to mix and warm the seeds. To serve, spoon the parsnips onto a dish in a ring shape with another green vegetable, such as baby peas, in the center.

Pasta Primavera

Serves 6 generously as a first course

This vibrant pasta dish blossoms like spring (*primavera* in Italian) with intensely green asparagus, broccoli, and peas. Tiny flecks of carrots and leeks in the creamy sauce elevate the flavor and add a little crunch of texture. If your time is short the vegetables may be cleaned and blanched in advance, even the night before. Then, the dish is quick and easy to finish.

3 tablespoons olive oil
2 large carrots, scraped and minced
2 leeks, white part only, rinsed and minced
1½ cups chicken stock
2 tablespoons finely chopped flat-leaf parlsey
1 cup light cream
⅓ pound prosciutto, finely chopped
½ pound mushrooms wiped, stems trimmed, sliced
½ pound asparagus, trimmed, blanched, and cut into fourths
3 cups broccoli florets, trimmed and blanched
1 10-ounce package frozen tiny peas, defrosted
½ cup light cream
1 pound fresh or homemade fettuccine noodles
1 cup freshly grated imported Parmesan cheese
Salt and freshly grated black pepper to taste

1. Heat the oil in a medium-large skillet until hot but not smoking. Add the carrots and leeks and sauté them over medium-high heat until wilted. Add the chicken stock, parsley, and 1 cup of cream. Stir to blend and gently boil to reduce by half.

2. While the cream is reducing, bring a large quantity (at least 5 quarts) of water to a boil in a pot. Add salt.

3. Add the prosciutto, mushrooms, asparagus, broccoli, and peas and the remaining cream to the skillet. Heat until the vegetables are warmed and just cooked through.

4. While the vegetables are heating, add the pasta

to the boiling water, stirring to separate the strands, and cook until al dente. Drain the pasta well, add the sauce, pepper, salt, and Parmesan cheese. Toss and serve at once.

Sautéed Snow Peas, Radishes, and Cherry Tomatoes

Serves 3 to 4

This colorful medley of vegetables literally takes only a minute to cook. Much more, and the brilliance begins to fade. Blanched pea pods are tossed with split cherry tomatoes and icicle or regular radishes, splashed with a little balsamic vinegar, and the magic is done. Plenty of crunch and a subtle touch of sweetness make this a terrific side dish for roasted chicken or INDIAN GAME HENS MARINATED IN YOGURT AND SPICES (page 148).

Unlike garden peas, snow peas are found almost the year around in the market. I prefer to buy them small and of a similar size. They should be bright green and look very crisp. Buying trays of wrapped snow peas can be risky if there are many broken or oversized ones. In that case, buy a bit more than you need. As soon as you return home, punch holes in the wrapping and refrigerate. Eat snow peas within a day or two.

Icicle radishes are narrow elongated white radishes. They are quite similar to other summer red, round radishes.

6 ounces snow peas, tips and strings removed
2 tablespoons unsalted butter
1½ cups sliced icicle or red radishes
1¼ cups split cherry tomatoes
1 tablespoon sugar
1 tablespoon balsamic vinegar
Salt and freshly ground black pepper to taste

1. Bring a medium-size saucepan of salted water to a boil. Add the snow peas and blanch them for 25 to 30 seconds to set the color. Drain and rinse with cold water. Blot them dry on paper towels.

2. In the same saucepan, melt the butter over medium-high heat until it foams. Add the radishes, cherry tomatoes, sugar, and balsamic vinegar and shake the pan to coat the vegetables, cooking for about 30 seconds. Add the pea pods, season with salt and pepper, and toss. Serve at once.

DID YOU KNOW? The French call Chinese snow peas *mange-tout*, which means "eat it all."

Red Pepper Butter

Makes 1 cup; about 16 to 18 rosettes

This colorful composed butter is easily made ahead of time, piped into decorative swirls, and refrigerated until serving time. It is a festive addition to grilled swordfish or tuna steaks. Try it on broiled chicken breasts or steamed broccoli and asparagus.

Bright, firm, sweet red bell peppers always capture my eye in the market. I buy only those that have no bruises and feel the heaviest. As these peppers (which are ripe green bell peppers) get older, they become dehydrated and their skin wrinkles. Store them unwrapped in a vegetable crisper. Unlike their green cousins, these beauties are already ripe, and their good looks fade after only a couple of days.

2 large red bell peppers, peeled, seeds and membranes removed, *or* 2 red peppers from a jar, packed in water (not oil and vinegar) and blotted very dry
1 large clove garlic, peeled
12 tablespoons (1½ sticks) unsalted butter, at room temperature
½ teaspoon Worcestershire sauce
¾ teaspoon salt
1 tablespoon freshly snipped chives *or* finely chopped scallions

1. To peel the peppers, char them over a gas flame or under a broiler, turning to blacken all sides of the flesh. Transfer them to a small brown bag, close tightly, and allow them to steam and to cool enough to handle. The charred skin will peel easily with the help of a small paring knife. If needed, run under cold water to remove any blackened bits. Blot dry, and remove the seeds and membranes before using.

2. Place the peppers and garlic in the bowl of a food processor fitted with a steel chopping blade and process until smooth, scraping down the bowl as needed. Add the softened butter, Worcestershire sauce, and salt and process, starting with an on-off motion, into a smooth mixture.

3. If desired, fill a pastry bag fitted with a star tip with the butter and pipe it into swirls about the size of a half dollar onto sheets of wax paper. (Or roll into a cylinder about 1¼ inches in diameter, wrap in plastic, chill, and then slice it into ½-inch slices.) Drizzle chives on top of each swirl or slice and refrigerate

🛒 **DID YOU KNOW?** A Quick Fresh Red Pepper Sauce to serve with grilled scallops or roasted chicken breast that has been sliced and fanned:

Combine 2 large peppers (peeled and seeded), 2 tablespoons of olive oil, salt, and pepper together in a food processor fitted with a steel chopping blade. Purée them until smooth. Transfer to a bowl and stir in ¼ cup finely chopped flat-leaf parsley. Makes 1 cup. I like the combination of grilled foods with a room-temperature sauce.

until needed. If butter is not to be used for several hours, place wax paper with swirls into a flat dish and cover it with foil or plastic wrap. Add the chives shortly before the butter is to be served.

Pumpkin and Porcini

Serves 6

Porcini are Italian wild mushrooms, called *cepes* in French, with a woody, pungent flavor. They are available dried and packed in small cellophane bags in many markets, often in the Produce department. Or check in the aisle with canned mushrooms. Sometimes they are hanging on "J" hooks there. As porcini are quite expensive, look at each package and select the one with the largest number of whole pieces. Dried porcini keep for months in a cool pantry. Combined with the sweetness of fresh pumpkin and the other aromatic ingredients, they make this a colorful and unusual side dish for autumn game dinners.

Pumpkins will keep in perfect condition for at least a month if stored in a cool, dry spot. Once they are bruised or cut, they need to be covered, refrigerated, and used within a week. Be sure to look at the recipe for PUMPKIN BLACK BEAN SOUP on page 373 if you want to toast the seeds.

1½ ounces dried porcini mushrooms
Flour and salt for dredging
4 cups pumpkin, peeled, seeded, cut into cubes
    about 1 x 1 x ½ inches (see Note)
6 tablespoons olive or vegetable oil
3 ounces thick sliced bacon, cut into ½-inch pieces
1 cup finely chopped onion
½ cup dry marsala
5 juniper berries, crushed
1 teaspoon salt, or to taste
Freshly ground black pepper to taste
2 tablespoons balsamic vinegar

1. Place the porcini mushrooms in warm water to cover and let them soak for about 25 to 30 minutes until soft. Transfer the mushrooms to a clean bowl, removing all grit and fibrous pieces. Pour the mushroom liquid through several layers of cheesecloth and reserve for use at another time. It's wonderful added to CHUNKY MUSHROOM AND BARLEY SOUP (page 41) or to SAUTÉED VEAL CUTLETS WITH MUSTARD, CAPERS, AND PEPPERS (page 204). Rinse the mushrooms again and squeeze gently to remove excess water.

2. Combine the flour and salt together in a flat dish. Dredge enough pumpkin cubes to cover the bottom of a large, heavy skillet without crowding and shake off excess flour. Heat 4 tablespoons of the oil in the skillet over medium-high heat until it is hot and almost smoking. Add the floured cubes and sauté them until lightly colored, turning to color all sides. With a slotted spoon, remove them to a bowl and continue dredging and sautéing until all the cubes are cooked.

3. Clean the skillet. Pour in the remaining 2 tablespoons of oil, heat until it is hot and fragrant, add the bacon, adjust the heat to medium, and sauté until the bacon pieces are separated and translucent, about 2 to 3 minutes. Add the onion and continue to cook slowly another 10 minutes, stirring occasionally, until the onion is light brown.

4. Stir in the marsala, then the juniper berries, porcini mushrooms, salt, and pepper. Raise the heat and bring the mixture to a boil, cooking until the liquid is reduced by half.

5. Add the vinegar and pumpkin and cook for a few minutes longer to warm the pumpkin through. Adjust seasonings, if necessary.

NOTE: Other squashes or sweet potatoes may be substituted for pumpkin, if desired.

Those Potatoes!

Serves 6 to 8

This potato dish is so popular that I usually double the recipe for my friends. The serpentined pepper strips make a beautiful design. And the aroma from the garlicky potatoes will fill your room. Gratins will be crunchier if baked in a porous dish so moisture can escape. The terracotta ovals or rectangles made in France and Italy are perfect.

If you eat a lot of potatoes, then buying in bulk is fine. However, often large quantities of foods left to go bad end up costing more money because of what is thrown away. I prefer to select each potato separately. That way I can buy them all the same size and look for cracks and blemishes. At home, I leave my potatoes loose in a drawer.

1 tablespoon unsalted butter
2 pounds medium-size red or other waxy potatoes, peeled and cut into ⅛-inch slices
2 large red bell peppers, peeled, seeds and membranes removed, cut into thin strips
½ cup milk
¼ cup cream *or* all milk
2–3 large cloves garlic, peeled and minced
1 teaspoon salt, or to taste
⅛ teaspoon white pepper
2 tablespoons cream
2 tablespoons freshly chopped flat-leaf parsley for garnish

1. Preheat your oven to 350°F. Butter a large (10 × 14-inch) earthenware or porcelain baking dish.

2. Place the potato slices in an overlapping pattern, reversing directions from one row to the next. Drape strips of peppers around the edges of the potato slices, forming an undulating design. Use any extra pieces of pepper around the edge of the dish.

3. In a small saucepan, bring the milk and cream, garlic, salt, and pepper to a simmer and cook for about 30 seconds over low heat, then pour it over the potatoes, including all the garlic, and transfer the baking dish to the lower third of the preheated oven. After 1 hour, spoon the remaining cream over the potatoes. Bake until the top of the gratin is crusty and well colored, about 1 hour and 20 minutes. If the potatoes become too dry during cooking, spoon over a couple more tablespoons of cream.

4. Remove the dish from the oven and sprinkle parsley over the top. Cut into portions along the edges of the potato slices and serve.

AS A VARIATION: Sauté 2 to 3 thinly sliced large onions in some butter or olive oil until lightly browned. Spread them evenly in the gratin dish and layer the potatoes over them. Continue as above, omitting the red pepper and stirring a teaspoon of Dijon mustard into the cream. Ten minutes before removing the potatoes from the oven, sprinkle ½ cup of Parmesan cheese on top and return the dish to the oven until the top is brown.

NOTE: This dish may be cooked ahead of time and reheated for 10 to 15 minutes in a 350°F oven. Add a little more cream, if needed, to make the top shiny.

Tomato Coulis

Makes 1½ cups

Something has happened to tomatoes, and it is not very good. For the most part those solid light-red rocks, perfectly shaped and uniform in size, marketed under the misnomer t-o-m-a-t-o-e-s taste like cellulose to me. Frankly, I almost *never* buy fresh tomatoes except in the late summer. There are exceptions: First, for extravagance and reasonably good flavor, there are imported Israeli tomatoes. Second, plum tomatoes are often quite good. The secret is to smell them. Do they smell tomatoey? If they feel very hard, leave them. Finally, please do not put your tomatoes in a refrigerator. They will taste much better at room temperature. Barring any decent alternatives, I prefer canned imported Italian tomatoes: Look at CHUNKY HOMEMADE TOMATO SAUCE (page 377). This simple uncooked tomato sauce below is a celebration of how wonderful real tomatoes can be.

Use this sauce on ZUCCHINI GRATIN (page 63).

3 firm, ripe tomatoes, peeled and seeded
½ teaspoon salt, *or* to taste
Freshly ground black pepper to taste
½ teaspoon sugar
1 tablespoon freshly chopped mint *or* basil

1. To peel and seed the tomatoes, drop them in a saucepan of boiling water for about 20 to 30 seconds. Remove with a slotted spoon and use a sharp paring knife to peel away the skin. Then, cut the peeled tomatos in half horizontally. Place the rounded side in the palm of your hand and squeeze gently so the seeds fall out.

2. Process the tomatoes in a processor fitted with a steel chopping blade. The purée can be very smooth or chunky, depending on the texture you want. Add the salt, pepper, sugar, and mint or basil and taste to adjust seasonings, if necessary.

DID YOU KNOW: The word *coulis* originally referred to all sauces that were derived naturally from cooking meat. Later it came to mean a thick purée of meat, poultry, fish, game, or vegetables that was also used for sauces and soups. Today, we usually use the word to refer to a cold, puréed sauce made from uncooked or only slightly cooked ingredients, such as this TOMATO COULIS. Both the strawberry sauce for the FLOATING ISLANDS (page 291) and the raspberry sauce for the FRESH PEAR TART WITH GINGER CREAM (page 97) are coulis.

Salsa

Makes 2½ cups

Salsa is an addicting uncooked chunky tomato sauce that most Tex-Mex restaurants put on their tables in bowls along with baskets of tortilla chips. It may vary from semi-fiery to three-alarm blazing hot. I've developed a real passion for salsa, since it is low in calories and very flavorful. Use it, mixed with yogurt, for dipping raw vegetables, or stir it into the sour cream for MEXICAN SHRIMP BASKETS (page 242) to make a piquant dressing. Ladled over an omelet, it's colorful and zesty. You need flavorful tomatoes for this sauce.

Cilantro, also called "Chinese parsley" and "fresh coriander," looks like flat-leaf parsley, but it has a unique and somewhat stronger flavor. Supermarkets have recently begun to stock this staple of Oriental and Mexican cooking. The best way to maintain cilantro is to place it in Ziploc bags with a damp paper towel around the roots and seal it tightly. It should last 4 or 5 days. If it is very wet, blot it first with dry paper towels. This also works well for parsley and mint.

1 cup minced onion
1½ cups finely chopped firm, ripe tomatoes
1–2 large jalapeño peppers (about 2 inches long), membranes and seeds removed, minced (see Note)
2 cups washed and loosely packed cilantro leaves, chopped
2 tablespoons red wine vinegar
Freshly ground black pepper to taste

1. Combine all ingredients in a small bowl. Store salsa in glass screw-top jars in the refrigerator. It will last for a couple of weeks.

NOTE: Working with hot chile peppers can be risky. The oil in the peppers can get on your hands, under your nails, or just about anywhere. *Do not touch your eyes* after you have been working with peppers, even if you have washed your hands. The hottest parts of the peppers are the seeds and membranes. Remove as much of these as your taste allows. Peppers vary widely in heat. One jalapeño might be enough today. But, a second may be needed another time.

DID YOU KNOW? The smaller the top of a chile pepper, the hotter it is likely to be!

Summer Tomato Soup with Basil Cream

Serves 6

This delicate tomato soup is a perfect celebration for August and September, when tomatoes are at their best. Served lukewarm or cool, it is a refreshing and colorful beginning to a meal or a marvelous partner for sandwiches at a light meal. Served with lightly salted basil-scented whipped cream, it is elegant.

Chopping basil is best done by hand with a sharp knife, unless you want the leaves puréed. A food processor bruises the leaves.

2 tablespoons unsalted butter
4 large shallots *or* 1 medium onion, peeled and thinly sliced
2 teaspoons salt, or to taste
3 pounds juicy, ripe tomatoes, peeled, seeded, and coarsely chopped
1 pint rich chicken stock (see Note)
1 pint milk
White pepper to taste
½ cup heavy cream, chilled (optional)
½ teaspoon salt, or to taste
½ cup loosely packed fresh basil leaves, finely chopped
Small basil leaves for garnish (optional)

1. In a heavy, medium-size saucepan, melt the butter just until it foams. Add the shallots or onion, and sauté them over medium heat just until wilted and very lightly colored, about 7 to 8 minutes.

2. Stir in the 2 teaspoons of salt and the tomatoes, cover tightly, and simmer until the tomatoes are soft, about 12 minutes.

3. Transfer the mixture to the bowl of a food processor fitted with a steel chopping blade and purée until smooth. Or, for more texture, pass the mixture through a food mill. Return the purée to the saucepan, stir in the chicken stock and milk, season with white pepper, and heat gently for a few minutes. Set aside to cool.

4. If desired, beat the heavy cream in a chilled bowl just until it forms soft peaks. Stir in the salt and basil. Otherwise, stir the chopped basil into the soup. Ladle the soup into bowls, add a good-size dollop of the basil cream in the middle of each bowl, and place a couple of basil leaves in the center. To make a decorative design, swirl the cream outward in a circular or sunburst pattern from the center, using the tip of a knife or a spoon handle.

NOTE: To enrich a canned or weak chicken stock, add 1 medium celery stalk, chopped; ½ small onion, chopped; 1 small carrot, scraped and chopped; a couple of sprigs of parsley; and a couple of black peppercorns to 3½ cups (2 cans) of stock. Bring the liquid to a boil, then lower the heat and boil gently until the liquid has reduced to 2 cups, approximately 15 to 20 minutes. Strain.

Fried Turnip Crisps

Serves 8

I always laugh when I serve these crunchy, almost sweet chips to my friends. They never expect that turnips are the base for these delicious morsels. Turnips, parsnips, celery root (celeriac), and sweet potatoes, when thinly sliced, become crisp like potato chips. They are a delightful predinner snack or can be served in place of a starch.

Turnips are always the best in spring, when the tender, smaller ones are in the market. Alas, so many people turn up their nose at this vegetable and its bigger cousin, the rutabaga, that they have no idea how wonderfully sweet they can be. Store turnips without their greens in the refrigerator for up to a week. And, try the ROASTED SQUABS STUFFED WITH TURNIPS, OLIVES, AND FIGS (page 158) for a special meal.

Vegetable oil for deep frying
6–8 medium-size turnips, peeled and cut into
⅛-inch slices
Salt
Fresh lemon juice (optional)

1. In a deep skillet, pour oil to a depth of about 1 inch and heat until hot but not smoking.
2. Pat the turnip slices dry on paper towels and add them in small bunches, so that the oil remains hot. Continue cooking, stirring frequently, so that all the crisps cook evenly, about 7 to 8 minutes. Once they are golden brown, remove them to paper towels and serve while still hot. Or place in a warm oven until ready. Continue with the remaining turnips. Sprinkle

lightly with salt and, if desired, drizzle a little fresh lemon juice over them.

Meatball-Vegetable-Alphabet Soup for Kids of All Ages

This recipe makes a lot of soup—approximately 16 to 18 generous servings. But it keeps in the refrigerator for several days and freezes well. As with all country or rustic soups, ingredients and proportions may be changed with personal preferences. I created this for my children originally but found my friends like it, as well. It is particularly satisfying on a blustery winter day when the rich blend of vegetables will warm you through. Serve it with thick slices of homemade bread.

FOR THE SOUP
⅓ cup olive oil or vegetable oil
3 ounces salt pork, blanched and cut into ½-inch cubes
3 large onions, peeled and cut into ¼-inch slices
2 medium parsnips, scraped and cut into ¼-inch slices
3 medium zucchini, trimmed and cut into ¼-inch slices
1 pound carrots, scraped and cut into ¼-inch slices
3 medium stalks celery, trimmed and chopped
5 small turnips, peeled and diced
1 large potato, peeled and cut into ½-inch dice
½ head green cabbage, cored and shredded
2 large cloves garlic, peeled and slivered
2 cups cooked Great Northern beans (*or* substitute the canned variety)
1 28-ounce can crushed Italian tomatoes
1 bay leaf
¼ cup finely chopped flat-leaf parsley *or* 1½ tablespoons dried
Salt and freshly ground black pepper to taste
1½ teaspoons dried thyme
6 cups beef stock
6 cups water
¾ cup dried alphabet macaroni

FOR THE MEATBALLS
1 pound lean ground beef
1½ tablespoons chopped flat-leaf parsley
½ teaspoon salt, or to taste
Freshly ground black pepper
2 tablespoons vegetable oil

1. In a very large, heavy stockpot, heat the oil, stir in the salt pork and cook over medium heat for about 3 minutes. Add the onions and cook until lightly colored, 5 to 7 minutes.

2. Add the parsnips, zucchini, carrots, and celery and continue cooking until they begin to wilt, another 4 minutes. Add the turnips, potatoes, and cabbage and cook 4 minutes longer.

3. Stir in the garlic and beans and cook for an additional 2 minutes. Cover and let the vegetables stew for 10 to 12 minutes, stirring occasionally. Add the tomatoes, seasonings, and liquid; bring the mixture to a boil; reduce the heat; and let the soup simmer, partially covered, for 1 hour.

4. Meanwhile, prepare the meatballs by combining the beef, parsley, salt, and pepper. Mix well and form into small meatballs no larger than 1 inch in diameter. Fry them in the oil over medium-high heat for about 2 minutes, turning to brown evenly. Drain and add them to the soup.

5. Cook the alphabets in boiling water until just tender. Drain and add to the soup. Simmer until all the ingredients are hot, about 5 minutes.

Winter Vegetable Stew Dijon Style

Serves 6 to 8

Dijon, France, is justly famous for its spicy mustard. In this hearty dish, it adds a rich flavor to the sauce and practically no calories—a boon to dieters. Notice, as well, that the only cream is half-and-half; the sauce is thickened, instead, with a little cornstarch. I don't think you will feel cheated. When it is served over brown rice or barley, the varied textures and colors of this medley are especially satisfying. While vegetables at the peak of freshness are my preference, this is a good spot to use up those that may have been slightly neglected.

4 tablespoons (½ stick) unsalted butter
1 tablespoon vegetable oil
¾ pound tender carrots, scraped and sliced about
   ¼ inch thick (approximately 3 cups)
1 head cauliflower, broken into small florets
¾ pound yellow onions, peeled and sliced ¼ inch
   thick (approximately 3 cups)
3 medium yellow squash, sliced about ¼ inch
   thick (approximately 3 cups)
¾ pound small white mushrooms or quartered
   larger mushrooms, wiped and stems trimmed
⅓ cup white wine
2 cups chicken or vegetable stock
2 teaspoons salt, or to taste
Freshly ground black pepper to taste
2 tablespoons freshly chopped dill *or* 1 tablespoon
   dried
½ cup half-and-half
4 tablespoons Dijon mustard
1½ teaspoons cornstarch
1 10-ounce package frozen petite peas, defrosted
Chopped toasted pecans for garnish, optional

1. Melt the butter and oil in a large, heavy casserole over medium heat just until the butter foams. Add the carrots and sauté them for 2 to 3 minutes; add the remaining vegetables except the peas and continue cooking until they start to wilt, 5 to 6 minutes longer. Pour in the wine and bring the liquid to a boil. After 1 minute, add the stock, cover, adjust the heat down, and simmer until the vegetables are almost tender, 8 to 10 minutes.

2. Add the salt, pepper, dill, and half-and-half into which you have stirred the mustard. Stir to blend and continue to cook slowly over medium-low heat for another 8 to 10 minutes.

3. Remove about ½ cup liquid and stir the cornstarch into it. Return the liquid to the casserole and blend well, cooking gently for a few minutes more until the stew has thickened. Adjust the seasonings, adding more mustard if needed. Stir in the peas. Serve over noodles, cooked barley and brown rice, or other grains. Top with chopped nuts, if desired.

FOR VARIETY: Stews are ideal for adding or changing ingredients to suit your own taste. This vegetarian version would be sensational with cubes of leftover chicken or turkey added at the end to warm them through. Or fresh shrimp, again added at the end and allowed to turn pink, would be a flavorful and colorful addition. Or, how about broccoli florets or roasted red peppers? I have used all of them at various times.

Cool and Tangy Watercress Sauce

Makes 3 cups

This is a refreshing and light sauce for fish in pastry or grilled trout. Crisp dark green bunches of watercress—essential here for color and taste—need to be stored wrapped in damp towels and a light protective wrapping if they are to last more than a day. Once again, don't make the mistake of airtight wrapping. Vegetables need air circulation.

2 large bunches watercress, washed
½ cup mayonnaise
½ cup plain low-fat yogurt
½ cup heavy cream, whipped to soft peaks
Salt and freshly ground black pepper to taste

1. Remove any yellow leaves and trim the coarse stems from the watercress. Place it in a food processor fitted with a steel chopping blade and purée. Add the mayonnaise and yogurt and pulse just until blended.
2. Transfer the sauce to a bowl and fold in the cream, salt, and pepper.

Zucchini Gratin with Tomato Coulis

Serves 8

This is a versatile late-summer dish to serve warm or at room temperature. I first tasted it near Grasse, in the south of France, where the vegetables had come fresh from the garden. If you do not grow zucchini, summer squash is one of the easiest vegetables to find in a supermarket.

I prefer zucchini small—no longer than 6 inches, solid, and with no signs of dehydration. Since zucchini has such a high percentage of water, they will last only a few days in the refrigerator. Make sure to take them out of the plastic bag. If you are lucky enough to grow zucchini, check on page 45 for deep frying their beautiful golden blossoms. What a treat!

3 tablespoons unsalted butter
1 tablespoon vegetable oil
3 medium zucchini, washed and cut into ¼-inch
    slices
2 large shallots, peeled and finely chopped
2 eggs
½ cup milk
½ cup freshly grated imported Parmesan cheese
⅓ cup cooked white rice
¼ teaspoon freshly grated nutmeg
Salt and freshly ground black pepper to taste
1 recipe TOMATO COULIS (page 56)

1. Preheat your oven to 350°F. Butter an 8-inch-square baking dish with 1 tablespoon of butter. Set aside.

2. In a large, heavy skillet, heat the remaining 2 tablespoons of butter and the oil just until the butter foams. Add the zucchini slices and sauté them over medium-high heat, shaking the pan often, until they are wilted and lightly colored, about 5 minutes. Reduce the heat to medium, stir in the shallots, and cook for 2 minutes longer, until the shallots are wilted.

3. In a bowl, beat the eggs and milk together. Add the zucchini mixture, half the grated cheese, and the rice, nutmeg, salt, and pepper. Stir and adjust the seasonings, if necessary. Pour the mixture into the prepared baking dish, smooth the top, and sprinkle on the remaining cheese.

4. Bake in the center of the preheated oven until a knife inserted in the center comes out clean, about 20 minutes. Remove the gratin from the oven and let it cool on a wire rack for at least 10 minutes. Cut into squares and serve with TOMATO COULIS spooned on top.

Buying by the Seasons

So much has been written recently about foods that are flown in from growers around the world and how we no longer need to wait for peaches in the summer, pears in the fall, or tomatoes in August. While it is true that sophisticated farming and shipping technology affords us many more varieties of fruits, vegetables, fish, and meat than ever before throughout the year, an intelligent shopper must still consider seasonality as an important issue when buying in a supermarket for several reasons.

PRODUCE

Many fruits and vegetables stop ripening once they are picked. Since tree- or vine-ripened fruits, such as peaches or tomatoes, are extremely perishable, they are often picked underripe for easy transport. This is especially true for long-distance shipping where a longer shelf life translates into less spoilage and higher revenues. While the color may brighten and the fruit may soften, no more sugar is being produced, so the produce cannot develop optimum flavor and texture, even when left to ripen at room temperature.

When fruit is picked ripe—as with berries shipped from South America—by the time it arrives in the supermarket, it is usually at the tail end of its shelf life. If not used that day, it is wasted. Where possible, ask for fruit from the closest grower.

Price is another consideration. Out-of-season items usually cost at least twice as much as seasonal ones. For my money, taking the risk of having to discard spoiled or tasteless produce isn't worth it. In season, even the least expensive supermarket should have a good selection to choose from. Just be sure to pick carefully and read the selection tips with each recipe.

Respecting seasonality also means recognizing that some foods, while available all year, go through different stages. Garlic, for example, is usually milder in the spring and summer. Split a clove open during the winter months and you are likely to find a green shoot growing inside; this is often bitter and should be discarded before use.

Other foods in the Produce department are often a better buy in another form during most of the year:

The wonderful sweet peas of summer come and go quickly, leaving behind only large, waxy green marbles. On the other hand, boxes of frozen petite peas are delicious. Fresh unblemished spinach, even hydroponically grown, is often hard to find and takes a lot of time and effort to prepare. Boxes of frozen are more than acceptable.

Tomatoes for sauces and soups are another disappointment. Experience has taught me that showy hothouse and imported varieties are usually inferior to the canned imported Italian (San Marzano region) ones.

Modern technology allows growers to flash-freeze berries individually in the fields at the height of the season. During winter months, these packages are a more reliable choice than imported fresh berries when appearance is less important. While fresh-squeezed orange or grapefruit juice is wonderful, it is no more nutritious than frozen juice, which is usually substantially less expensive.

MEAT, POULTRY, AND FISH

While supermarkets sell meat, poultry, and fish all year, they do gear up for holiday and seasonal merchandising. You might consider buying during peak availability, when prices are lower, especially if you have a freezer in which to store multiple purchases.

Notice that lamb is often featured in Easter newspaper ads, while during the rest of the year it is hardly mentioned. It is available twelve months of the year, but traditionally the price is lower in the spring.

A more diversified selection of fish is featured during the Lenten season, and markets run plenty of specials. This is a good time to sample an unfamiliar fish or to discuss a new recipe with the clerk.

Although turkeys are the traditional mainstay of Thanksgiving, with more cuts and sizes available, this bird's popularity is spreading, especially as a substitute for pricier veal.

More adventurous markets are selling game birds, usually in the fall and winter months, when more substantial foods are appropriate.

Certain cuts of meat are seasonal favorites. Steaks are a barbecue special, so the price is often lower in winter when there is less demand, and pork chops are less costly in summer.

DAIRY

Seasonal differences here are not as noticeable.

But, as June is Dairy Month, look for butter to be substantially lower in price. It freezes well for a long time, so it's a good buy.

The variety of cheeses is highest during the cool months and during Lent.

For holiday baking, heavy cream is sold in quart cartons. The rest of the year, half pints are the norm. If your market sells "pasteurized" cream in addition to "ultra pasteurized," it is more often available during winter months when it is less likely to spoil.

STAPLES

While the shelves in the center of the market appear to be about the same all year around, there are subtle changes that you might notice. It is very difficult to convince a supermarket to change its familiar ordering patterns. But, with enough requests, they often listen.

Specialty flours, candied fruits, chocolates, and some nuts are associated with autumn and holiday baking. For the rest of the year, they may be missing or in short supply, since shelf space is always at a premium. If you use these items regularly, be sure to check with the department manager about special orders, or, if your space at home permits, buy extra.

Other baking supplies, such as parchment paper and decorative foil cups, are also easier to find in the fall.

Chestnuts, currants, and dried fruits are more often used in winter cooking.

During the warmer months, barbecue sauces, decorative paper plates and napkins, charcoal, and other paraphernalia for outdoor cooking are more in demand, and there will be more variety.

The more delicate a food, the more important the question of seasonality becomes. For food in optimum condition, with the longest shelf life, at the best price, supermarket shoppers are best served by selecting foods in their prime growing and shipping times. This does not mean that there are no exceptions. I have bought plums and nectarines in February that were sensational. But I've gambled and lost, as well. If the market offers samples, then your decision is made easier. Otherwise, the facts are overwhelmingly in favor of seasonal buying.

INTRODUCTION

Recently, supermarket produce buyers have gone back to school and to the fields to familiarize themselves with many varieties of fruit that were, up until a few years ago, unavailable. With technological advances and global marketing, an ever-widening supply and variety of products now comes into the market place. The spread of smaller ethnic markets has afforded interested cooks the chance to sample unfamiliar fruits like starfruit, mangoes, and fresh lichees. These customers, in turn, then look for these products in their supermarkets. A bit of healthy competition has certainly helped the consumer.

Such plentitude has made fruit even more popular in every dimension of cooking from breakfast through dessert; from juicy berries on cereal to INDIVIDUAL APPLE STRUDELS (page 73). Fruit in combination with other foods adds a sweet acidity to balance flavors. PINEAPPLE BOATS WITH PORK, BLACK BEANS, AND MOLE SAUCE (page 100) or SAUTÉED TURBOT FILLETS WITH SLICED STARFRUIT (page 105) are but two examples. And, it is beautiful enough to make the most exquisite centerpiece.

In order for high expectations to be met, customers need to spend a minute analyzing how good the fruit they reach for actually is. Fortunately, fruit is wrapped far less than it used to be, as looks can be very deceiving. Aside from a visual examination for bruises and texture, the aroma and feel of the fruit can give you some important clues to the taste and texture. A peach, for example, may look beautiful. But, if it is hard as a rock and there is no fragrance, chances are pretty poor that it will get any better even sitting out on your kitchen counter. Tempting though it may be, you will be better off passing it by.

Soft fruit can also be misleading. Remember that each time someone gently pushes the bottom of a melon, it is bruised a little more. Eventually, it may become soft, but it is a long way from ripe. In a bag of apples or oranges, the adage about one bad piece of fruit spoiling the barrel is true. Make sure to inspect these bags carefully. Once home, discard rotten fruit immediately.

Another source of concern in the fruit section is preservatives. Markets and growers need to make a profit, and this may lead to undesirable practices, such as applying a waxy protective coating of *alar* to make apples look shiny and cushion them against bruises. If you have read or heard about these problems, be sure to ask at the market. Here, as elsewhere throughout the market, it sure pays to have a friendly clerk. Not only will he answer questions, but he will help with special orders and assist you in selecting the best of what is available that day.

Seasonal buying, for me, is still the safest and most economical way to buy fruit. Look at the Strategy Pages on Seasonality just preceding this chapter. Another good way to verify quality is to taste fruit from the same crop. Markets know that this often boosts sales and frequently have cut up samples ready and waiting. It's also an appealing way to discover unfamiliar items, provided that the display is clean.

We are fortunate to have the variety of fruits available in supermarkets today. We no longer suffer with ugly cold-storage apples in the spring. Strawberries have become almost seasonless. With a little care in selection, each piece of fruit will be delicious eating, too.

Individual Apple Strudels

Makes 8

Apple strudel has long been one of my favorite desserts. Just thinking about crisp, flaky pastry wrapped around tangy apples laced with walnuts and raisins, cinnamon and a dash of rum, makes my mouth water. Thanks to phyllo, these miniature strudels are easy to make and ideal for serving. No more flakes and broken slices, and everyone gets plenty of crunchy "ends."

It should come as no surprise that Americans eat more apples than any other fruit. However, of the several hundred varieties grown, most are eaten locally and aren't seen in the market. Up until a few years ago, even in fall—the peak season—grocers stocked only few choices like Rome Beauty, red and yellow Delicious, McIntosh, and Greening. Recently, I have found other varieties: Macouns, Empires, Granny Smiths, Cortlands, along with Jonathans and Winesaps in markets around the country.

When choosing apples, buy only firm, brightly colored (appropriate to the variety) fruits. If the skin looks shriveled or there are bruises, make another choice. Most apples will last at least 2 weeks in the refrigerator. They keep nicely in a dark cellar, as well.

½ cup golden raisins
⅓ cup amber or dark rum
3 tablespoons unsalted butter
5 large Granny Smith or other tart apples, peeled, cored, and coarsely chopped (approximately 6½ to 7 cups)
6 tablespoons sugar
2 tablespoons lemon juice
1 teaspoon cinnamon
Zest of 1 large lemon, minced
Pinch of salt
½ cup finely chopped walnuts
¼ cup toasted bread crumbs
¼ cup finely chopped walnuts
5 tablespoons unsalted butter
12 sheets phyllo
Confectioners' sugar for dusting (optional)
½ pint lightly whipped heavy cream, sweetened with sugar (optional)

1. Combine the raisins with the rum in a small bowl and set aside.

2. In a large, heavy skillet, melt 3 tablespoons of butter over medium-high heat. When it has foamed, add the apples and let them cook over medium heat for about 5 minutes until slightly softened, turning to coat with the butter. Add the sugar, lemon juice, rum, raisins, cinnamon, lemon zest, and salt. Adjust the heat to medium high and allow the mixture to boil until almost all the liquid has evaporated, about 3 to 4 minutes. Stir in ½ cup of walnuts and set aside.

3. Butter a cookie sheet or jelly roll pan and preheat your oven to 425°F.

4. Combine the bread crumbs with ¼ cup chopped walnuts in a small bowl.

5. Melt the 5 tablespoons of butter in a small saucepan or skillet.

6. On a clean workspace, place 1 sheet of phyllo horizontally on a towel and brush lightly with butter. Sprinkle a scant tablespoon of the bread crumb mixture over the phyllo. Place a second sheet on top of the first, and again brush lightly with butter, and spread another scant tablespoon of crumbs. Place a third sheet on top of these and cut the stack in half vertically. Spoon about ⅛th of the filling along the lower edge of each stack of phyllo, leaving about a 1¼-inch border on each side.

7. Holding the lower edges of the towel, flip the towel, causing the phyllo to roll over on itself. Fold in the sides of the phyllo and continue to roll. Carefully transfer each strudel to the cookie sheet with the seam side down. Brush the tops with butter. Continue with the remaining phyllo and filling until all 8 strudels have been rolled.

8. Place the pan in the middle of the preheated oven for 12 minutes or until the strudels are crisp and golden brown. Remove the pan and let it stand for at least 10 minutes before serving the strudels. Strudels will keep well in a turned-off oven for at least 1 to 2 hours. Sprinkle with confectioners' sugar. Serve with lightly whipped cream, if desired.

Lemon-Glazed Apricots

Serves 4

This is a simple, refreshing dessert to make for summer meals. Tangy Lemon Curd, combined with a dash of ginger, is spread on fresh apricot halves, which are then baked for a couple of minutes.

Apricots are an almost forgotten luxury in most supermarkets—and specialty stores. Modern technology has so concentrated on shipping fruit that will not bruise, that the ripe, exotically sweet flavor never develops. This is my complaint with the imported varieties found in mid-winter. While they get soft, they are also mushy. If you are on the lookout for apricots, buy large, round, golden-yellow ones that are still firm (not hard), and let them ripen in a bag on your kitchen counter for a couple of days. Don't waste your money on small apricots; they will be mostly pits.

6 ripe apricots, washed and split
¼ cup LEMON CURD (page 90)
½ teaspoon ground ginger
2–3 tablespoons sugar

1. Preheat your oven to 375°F.
2. Place the apricot halves in an oven-safe flat dish. Combine the lemon curd and ginger in a small bowl

AS A VARIATION: Use ripe nectarines or freestone peaches.

and spoon it over the apricots. Sprinkle the sugar on top, and place the apricots in the oven for about 2 minutes, until just warm.

3. Transfer the dish to the broiler section, about 2 to 3 inches from the heat and broil, just until the tops are glazed. Watch carefully to prevent burning. Remove the dish from the broiler and serve 3 apricot halves per person. Sometimes I serve the apricots with a scoop of vanilla ice cream in the center. They also provide a nice accent when served with roasted meats or fowl.

If you have a *baked* tart shell (see pages 310 or 311), double this recipe, spread another ¾ cup of lemon curd over the tart shell, and arrange the baked apricots on top.

Banana-Filled Crêpes Flambées

Serves 6

Bananas in caramelized rum syrup, wrapped in crêpes, and set aflame, are a favorite temptation of mine. To gild the lily, I add softly whipped cream or vanilla ice cream. This is an easy and impressive dessert to make when time is limited. Since the crêpes are made ahead of time, with a short interlude you can ignite the bananas and make a grand entrance.

Happily, bananas are one of the easiest and best fruits to buy anywhere. They are available year round. Rather than looking for perfectly ripe fruit, I prefer to buy mine slightly green, and let them reach perfection on my counter—without bruises and marks. In my house, some of us like bananas with the tiny brown sugar spots, while others like pure yellow. Only after they are as ripe as I want them do I think of refrigerating them. Even though refrigeration turns the skin brown, the bananas are fine.

FOR THE CRÊPES (SEE NOTE)
1 scant cup unbleached all-purpose flour
1¼ cups low-fat milk *or* 1 cup milk + ¼ cup water
1 tablespoon sugar
1 teaspoon salt
1 teaspoon vanilla extract
2 eggs
3 tablespoons unsalted butter, melted
½ teaspoon unsalted butter

FOR THE BANANAS

6 firm, ripe, medium-size bananas without spots
Flour for dusting on the bananas
5 tablespoons unsalted butter
¼ cup sugar
2 tablespoons water
¼ cup sugar
¼ cup water
⅓ cup dark or light rum
1 cup heavy cream softly whipped with the grated
  zest of 1 lemon and a little sugar (optional) *or*
  vanilla ice cream (optional)

1. PREPARE THE CRÊPES In a large bowl, whisk together the flour, milk, sugar, salt, vanilla, and eggs until smooth. Add the melted butter and mix again quickly. The batter should be the consistency of light cream. Cover, and refrigerate for at least ½ hour.

2. Heat the ½ teaspoon of butter in an 8-inch skillet over medium-high heat until hot. Rotate the pan to cover the bottom completely with butter. Stir the batter, then pour about 2 tablespoons into the pan toward 1 side. Lift the pan and rotate it quickly to cover the bottom evenly. Replace the pan on the heat and let the crêpe cook until the edges are light brown, about 1 minute. Adjust the heat to medium if the crêpes seem to be burning before they are cooked through.

3. Slip the edge of a spatula or rounded knife under the edge of the crêpe, grab it with your fingers, and flip it to the other side. Cook the second side about 20 seconds, or until lightly browned in spots. Flip the crêpe onto a plate and continue with the remaining batter. Cover the plate with a second plate inverted on top of the crêpes. If not using the crêpes immediately, let them cool slightly, then cover with plastic wrap. Or separate them into piles of 4 with wax paper between each group. Place them in a Ziploc bag, push out the air, and freeze them for up to 3 months. Be sure to defrost completely before trying to separate them.

4. COOKING THE BANANAS Peel the bananas and remove the strings from the sides. Lightly dust them with flour.

5. In a large, heavy skillet, melt the butter over medium-high heat. When it has foamed, add the bananas and brown them lightly on all sides, rolling them with a wooden spatula. Sprinkle with ¼ cup of

🛒 **DID YOU KNOW?** Three categories of rum are usually sold in U.S. liquor stores. Light-colored, light-bodied rum is from Spanish-speaking areas. The best is from Puerto Rico. Amber rum, made from sugarcane juice, has medium body and comes from Haiti and Martinique. Rich and pungent dark rum is made from fermented molasses and other by-products of sugar production. It comes from English-speaking countries. Jamaican is the best. Which one to use in a recipe is often determined by personal taste.

sugar as you do this. Add 2 tablespoons of water to the pan and continue cooking over medium-low heat for another 5 to 6 minutes, until the bananas are warmed through.

6. Have 6 crêpes ready. Using 2 spatulas, carefully lay a banana on one side of each crêpe, then roll them up and leave them on a plate while finishing the sauce.

7. Add ¼ cup sugar and ¼ cup water to the skillet, and stir well. Over high heat, boil until the syrup turns light brown. Then quickly add the rolled crêpes, spooning the syrup over them. Heat the rum in a small saucepan, and pour it over the crêpes. Carefully ignite the rum, shaking to loosen any caramelized sugar on the bottom of the pan. Serve 1 crêpe to each guest, spooning the syrup over the crêpe. Spoon on whipped cream or vanilla ice cream that has been allowed to soften slightly.

NOTE: This recipe makes 12 to 14 crêpes. Either make all the crêpes and freeze the extras or refrigerate the extra batter in a covered container for up to a week.

Blackberry Tart

Serves 8

🛒 DID YOU KNOW? Like blueberries, blackberries can be frozen by placing them directly on a cookie sheet in the freezer (see page 87). They will last for up to 9 months or a year if correctly stored. While they will not be as firm as fresh fruit, the taste will be perfect. Use them for a shortcake (see page 84), or a MOSAIC OF PEACHES AND BERRIES IN WINE (page 95). They look better if you do not defrost them before using.

Finding beautiful half-pint containers of blackberries neatly lined up in the market of a late-June morning, I quickly celebrated the discovery by making a luscious almond-flavored crust with berries just peeking out from a sweet glaze. While the best berries may be those picked from the bush, I've found this miracle often enough—even in some dumpy looking markets—dark, succulent blackberries *in season* (late May through September) that are superbly flavorful.

Be alert when berry buying. The containers should be covered without any signs of leakage. Each long, plump berry should be dark in color, since even a little redness will mean the fruit is sour. Try asking the clerk if there are fresh containers in back if those on display look picked over. Once home, sort the berries as soon as possible. Bruised and moldy berries can ruin the rest within hours. Store berries covered and refrigerated for up to 2 or 3 days. Then rinse or mist them with cool water just before serving.

1 tart shell (page 311), substituting almonds for
   walnuts, baked
1½ pints blackberries
2 tablespoons kirsch
1 tablespoon cornstarch
½ cup red currant jelly
3 tablespoons sugar
Grated zest of 1 lemon
4–5 slivered almonds, for garnish
1 cup heavy cream, whipped and flavored with a
   little crème de cassis, *or* vanilla ice cream
   (optional)

1. Prepare the tart shell according to directions. Fill
it with the blackberries.

2. Dissolve the cornstarch in the kirsch in a small
bowl. In a small saucepan, combine the jelly, sugar,
lemon zest, and kirsch-cornstarch and bring to a boil.
Boil the mixture until the sugar is dissolved, the jelly
is melted, and the mixture coats the back of a spoon,
about 3 minutes. Remove the pan from the heat, stirring to cool the glaze slightly, then pour it evenly over
the berries. It should just about cover them. Let the
glaze set, then add the almonds in a circle in the center. Serve it with whipped cream flavored with a little
crème de cassis, if desired, or ice cream.

Old-Fashioned Blueberry Pie with Lemon Crust

Lemon and blueberries seem made for each other,
especially in this delectably homey pie, first served
to me by my friend Anne Semmes. The lemony lattice crust holds juicy, fat blueberries laced with lemon
and a touch of crème de cassis. Since blueberries
give off so much liquid, I like to cook some of the
berries partially and then combine them with uncooked berries. The results are a spectacular pie!

Luckily for blueberry lovers, these versatile berries are simple to buy from late May through September, and quite resilient in the refrigerator. They
will keep for at least 10 days. Look for baskets that
have plump, dark fruit, with a minimum of tiny green
berries. If the skins look wrinkled or soft, pass on
that basket. Be sure to check the berries for mold or
bruises, and wash them just before eating.

FOR THE LEMON PASTRY

2 cups unbleached all-purpose flour

¾ teaspoon salt

2 teaspoons sugar

1 teaspoon grated lemon peel

8 tablespoons (1 stick) unsalted butter, chilled and cut into small pieces

¼ cup solid vegetable shortening

1 tablespoon fresh lemon juice

2–4 tablespoons ice water

1 egg white

FOR THE FILLING

3 cups fresh blueberries

2 tablespoons water

¾ cup sugar

2 teaspoons fresh lemon juice

2 tablespoons crème de cassis

3 tablespoons cornstarch

2 cups fresh blueberries

1. PREPARE THE PASTRY In the bowl of a food processor fitted with a steel chopping blade, combine the flour, salt, sugar, and lemon peel, and process for about 15 seconds. Add the butter and shortening, and pulse until the mixture resembles coarse meal.

2. Combine the lemon juice with 2 tablespoons of water. With the machine running, add the lemon water through the feed tube, and process just until the pastry begins to pull into a ball, adding extra water by the teaspoon, if necessary. Remove the dough, divide it into 2 uneven balls, pat each one into a flat disk, lightly dust with flour, wrap, and refrigerate for at least 2 hours.

3. Preheat your oven to 425°F.

4. Lightly dust a workspace with flour. Roll out the larger disk into a circle measuring about 12 inches across, and ⅛ inch thick. Line a 9-inch pie plate with the pastry, leaving the overhanging edge untrimmed. Brush with the egg white.

5. Place 3 cups of the blueberries in a medium-size saucepan with the water, cover, and bring to a boil. Adjust the heat to medium and continue cooking uncovered for about 4 or 5 minutes, until the berries have begun to pop. Drain off approximately ½ cup of the liquid, add the sugar, lemon juice, and crème

DID YOU KNOW? Because blueberries give off so much juice, many people make their pies from canned berries. It is easy to drain off the liquid from them. (It's almost as easy to cook your own.) If using a canned product, note that canned berries are far superior to canned "pie filling," which has loads of sugar and starch in relationship to the fruit.

For another blueberry and lemon idea, bake and let cool a PÂTE BRISÉE or WALNUT PASTRY CRUST (page 310 or 311), spread ½ cup LEMON CURD (page 90) over the bottom, and fill it with blueberries dusted with confectioners' sugar. Extra dough may be cut in lemon shapes, baked with the tart shell, and glazed with the lemon curd. Find some bright green, nonpoisonous leaves and place them next to each lemon cut out on top of the berries.

de cassis mixed with the cornstarch, and the remaining blueberries. Cook for 2 minutes longer over high heat. The fruit mixture should be quite thick. Let it cool for about 15 minutes. Scrape the fruit into the pie shell.

6. Roll out the smaller disk of pie dough into a 9-inch circle and cut it into ½-inch strips. Arrange them over the pie in a lattice pattern, and trim. Bring the edge of the bottom crust over the rim and crimp the edge. If desired, decorate the lattice with leaves and berries cut from the extra pastry scraps.

7. Place the pie on a cookie sheet and transfer it to the middle of your preheated oven for 8 minutes, or until the crust is light brown. Adjust the heat to 350°F and continue baking for 25 to 30 minutes more or until the crust is golden brown and the juices begin to bubble. Put foil around the crust if it becomes too brown before the end of the cooking time. Remove the pie from the oven and let it cool for at least 30 minutes before serving.

Nutmeg-Scented Cantaloupe Sherbet

Makes 1½ quarts

Who's to say that cantaloupes may only be seasoned with a squeeze of lemon juice or a sprinkle of salt? The celebrated American food writer M.F.K. Fisher once told me that her father used ground nutmeg on his melon. That combination, creamy sweet melon with a delicate hint of warm spiciness, proves ethereal in the following sherbet. For parties I cut petals from a circle of melon, fill the center with a scoop of sherbet sprinkled with a pinch of nutmeg, and add a large green leaf (see step 5 below). It always brings raves.

When buying cantaloupes, don't waste money on small melons in April and early May. They are usually disappointing. Instead, wait until late May through early September for firm (not rock hard) round or oval melons with no green showing under the webbed skin. Check the stem end. It should be smooth and slightly indented. While it may give slightly to pressure, a better test of ripeness is the fragrant aroma at the stem end. Any cantaloupe with bruises and sagging-looking skin has seen better days. If the melon is still quite firm, it will taste better if left at room temperature for a couple of days to soften. Refrigerate cut melons and wrap them tightly. They will last for several days.

1 large ripe cantaloupe, peeled and seeded
2 tablespoons strained fresh lemon juice
½ cup superfine sugar
1 teaspoon freshly grated nutmeg
½ teaspoon salt
3 cups cold milk
Freshly grated nutmeg, for garnish
1 large ripe cantaloupe for garnish (optional)
6 large nonpoisonous green leaves, such as lemon, for garnish (optional)

1. Purée the cantaloupe in the bowl of a food processor fitted with a steel chopping blade. There should be about 2½ to 3 cups purée. Add the lemon juice, sugar, salt, and nutmeg and process to blend until smooth, about 30 seconds.

2. Scrape the purée into a large bowl and stir in the milk.

3. Transfer the mixture to an ice cream maker and follow the manufacturer's directions. Once processed, serve within 2 hours. Otherwise, scrape the mixture into a metal container, such as a cake pan, cover and place in the freezer until solid—at least 3 hours.

4. About an hour before serving, cut the frozen sherbet into cubes, and place them in the processor. Begin by pulsing and then process until the sherbet is very smooth and light in color. Serve at once for a softer consistency or return to the freezer for about 1 hour. The sherbet may be reprocessed if serving it on a second or third occasion. Serve in small scoops with a light dusting of freshly grated nutmeg on top.

5. For a decorative presentation, cut the second melon into circular slices about ½ to ¾ inch thick, and remove the seeds. With a small sharp knife, cut 6 of the nicest circles into a petal design (see illustration). Place on individual plates, fill the center with 1 large or 3 tiny scoops of sherbet, dust with nutmeg, and place a large, clean, nonpoisonous green leaf next to the melon. Serve with gingersnaps or MOLASSES SPICE COOKIES (page 328).

NOTE: If you do not have an ice cream maker, the following method may be used. While the texture will not be as smooth, the taste will still be delicious:

1. Combine the cantaloupe purée, sugar, and lemon juice in a bowl and let it stand for at least ½ hour. Stir in the nutmeg, salt, and milk, then scrape the mixture into a flat metal container, such as an 8 × 8-inch square brownie pan, cover and freeze until almost solid—at least 4 to 6 hours.

2. Cut the frozen mixture into cubes and transfer them to the bowl of a food processor fitted with a steel chopping blade and process until smooth. Scrape the sherbet back into the metal pan, cover, and return it to the freezer until firm. Then continue with step 4, above.

DID YOU KNOW? The melon we call cantaloupe in the United States is actually a muskmelon, as is its larger cousin, the Persian. True cantaloupes, like the famous Cavaillon melons of France, have smooth skins and are not grown in the United States.

Cherry-Almond Shortcake

Serves 8

This old-fashioned shortcake is ideal as a base for any seasonal fruits, and it illustrates how wonderful handmade biscuits can be. If you love sweet dark cherries, this is a dessert to make for your Fourth of July celebration or any other summer meal when cherries are abundant. Although it takes about 10 or 15 minutes to remove the pits, you won't remember it by the time you bring this down-home treasure, topped with whipped cream, toasted almonds, and cherries, to the table.

Unless it is cherry season—summer—don't try this confection. Giant bins of fruit mounded high with dark-red cherries are so tempting. They are perfect eaten out of hand. But take a moment to gently feel the fruit (even if that means through cellophane packaging). Are the cherries firm and shiny? A few sun-cracked cherries are OK, but if the lot looks that way, wait for the next shipment. I try to reach toward the back of the display for less picked-over fruit. Wash cherries when you are ready to eat them. They should be stored loosely wrapped or open in a bowl and eaten within a couple of days.

FOR THE FRUIT TOPPING
1¼ pounds sweet dark cherries, pitted
2 tablespoons kirsch
2 tablespoons sugar
¼ cup fresh orange juice

FOR THE SHORTCAKE
1¾ cups sifted unbleached all-purpose flour
¼ cup sugar
4 teaspoons baking powder
1 teaspoon salt
8 tablespoons (1 stick) unsalted butter, chilled and cut into small pieces
½ cup milk
1 tablespoon unsalted butter, melted
1 cup heavy cream
2 tablespoons sugar
¼ teaspoon almond extract
½ cup slivered almonds, lightly toasted

1. MAKE THE TOPPING Combine the cherries, kirsch, sugar, and orange juice in a medium-size saucepan. Bring the mixture to a boil, then reduce the heat to simmer for 4 to 5 minutes. Set aside to cool.

2. FOR THE SHORTCAKE Preheat your oven to 425°F.

3. In a large bowl, sift together the flour, sugar, baking powder, and salt. Add the butter and with your fingers or two knives, cut it into the dry ingredients until it is the size of small peas.

4. Pour in the milk and quickly mix just until blended.

5. Turn the dough out onto a lightly floured board and knead it for about 30 seconds until smooth. Transfer the dough to a 9-inch round unbuttered cake pan, patting it smooth with your fingertips. Brush the top with 1 tablespoon of melted butter and transfer the pan to the preheated oven for 25 minutes, until it is risen and the top is golden brown. Remove the shortcake from the oven and let it cool for about 30 minutes in the pan.

6. While the cake is baking, whip the cream with the sugar and almond extract until soft peaks form.

7. ASSEMBLE THE SHORTCAKE Transfer the shortcake to a cake plate. Ladle the cherries and the juice over it. Sprinkle on the slivered almonds. Once the cake is cut, ladle a generous spoonful of whipped cream over each slice.

Cranberry, Pepper, and Onion Conserve

Makes about 3 cups

While we often think of cranberries in sweets, this tangy relish is a terrific condiment for pâtés, game meats, and that holiday favorite, turkey. The vibrant rosy tones and spicy flavors last for months. It's an easy holiday gift to make.

Cranberries are usually plentiful from early autumn right through mid-winter. For the remaining months, cranberry fanciers can keep them in their plastic bags for at least a month in the refrigerator or freeze them for almost a year. The CRANBERRY HOLIDAY BRAID (page 323) would be lovely on a chilly morning. Be sure the berries are bright and firm.

2 large red peppers
2 tablespoons unsalted butter
1 tablespoon vegetable oil
3 large onions, peeled and sliced very thin
6 tablespoons apple cider vinegar
½ cup sugar
3 cups (1 package) fresh cranberries, washed and picked over
4 cardamom pods, hulled and crushed *or* ¼ teaspoon ground cardamom
2 tablespoons tiny capers

1. Peel the peppers by placing them over a flame and charring the flesh until it is blacked on all sides, approximately 7 to 9 minutes. Place them in a brown paper bag, turn down the top, and let them cool for approximately 20 minutes. Once they have cooled, rub off the blackened skin, split the peppers, remove the seeds and thick membranes, and cut into ¼ inch strips. Set aside.

2. In a large, heavy skillet, melt the butter and oil. When it has foamed, add the onions and stir. Let them sauté over medium-high heat for about 12 to 14 minutes, or until lightly colored. Shake the pan occasionally to cook evenly.

3. Add the vinegar and sugar to the skillet and stir until the sugar is dissolved, about 2 to 3 minutes. Stir in the cranberries and peppers, cover, and cook gently for about 12 to 15 minutes. Remove the lid, crush most of the berries with the back of a wooden spoon.

4. Stir in the cardamom and capers and let the mixture cool. Transfer the conserve to clean jars, cover, and refrigerate for at least 2 days. This conserve will last for many months in the refrigerator.

Chocolate-Dipped Fruit Kabobs

Makes about 12

These amusing little pillars of fruit wrapped in chocolate with a light sprinkle of toasted nuts always elicit squeals of delight from children and nods of pleasure from everyone else. They are easy and fun to make. Often I make them with strawberries, grapes, banana slices, and a marshmallow. Use whatever fruit appeals to you. But, the fruit must be dry (and frozen) for the chocolate to adhere.

The prime season for domestic grapes is from late

summer through November. However, with imports and modern growing techniques, you are apt to find grapes in your market almost the year around. All varieties—from the darkest black Concord to the yellow-green Thompson seedless—should feel firm. Stems should be pliable so the grapes are not falling off. Pick bunches with a minimum of bruises. I prefer to sample a grape or two to find the bunch that tastes best. And I prefer not to wash grapes until I am ready to serve them, as they disintegrate quickly (see note below). Store them in a bowl in the refrigerator for up to 4 days.

12 5-inch bamboo skewers
12 seedless green or red grapes, washed and
　　patted dry
12 marshmallows
12 small strawberries, rinsed under cold water and
　　hulled (if large, split in half)
1½ firm, ripe bananas, peeled and cut into ½-inch
　　slices
1 pound milk or bittersweet chocolate, according
　　to taste
1 cup salted chopped nuts

1. Run each skewer through a grape, marshmallow, strawberry, and banana slice. Put the filled skewers on a cookie sheet covered with wax paper. Place the pan in the freezer for at least 4 hours, or until the fruit is frozen.

2. In the top of a double boiler, slowly melt the chocolate over simmering water, stirring frequently. Once it is melted, let it cool slightly.

3. Remove the fruit from the freezer. With the aid of a metal spatula or knife, apply the chocolate evenly to the kabobs, turning the skewer against the face of the spatula to smooth the chocolate against the marshmallow. Let any excess chocolate run off the fruit and back into the pan.

4. As each skewer is dipped, sprinkle chopped nuts over it and place it back on the wax paper. Work quickly to coat all the skewers. Once they have all been dipped, place the cookie sheet in the refrigerator to let the chocolate harden, 10 to 20 minutes. These kabobs may be made several hours ahead of time.

NOTE: Realizing that the optimum way to store grapes is unwashed, I must say that because my children like grapes so much and because they are always reaching in the refrigerator and pulling them off, I do wash my grapes when I bring them into the house. I then let them drain in a colander and pat them very dry with paper towels. They are then placed in an open bowl near the bottom of the refrigerator. Because they are consumed so quickly, we rarely see them turn bad.

Minted Pink Grapefruit Sorbet

Serves 8

Tangy, citrus-flavored grapefruit and cool crème de menthe are a wonderfully refreshing combination. This delicate sorbet is like an icy breath of fresh air between courses or at the end of a meal. Fresh mint leaves and a segment of the fruit make an elegant presentation.

Although grapefruits are found all year around in the market, the very best ones appear in the late winter to early spring months. If you can find the beautiful ruby reds from Texas, your sorbet will be a vivid pink. But the flavor will be quite similar to both pink and white varieties. The skin should look smooth without any soft, brown, or spongy spots. Don't worry about tiny lines or defects; they won't affect the taste. As you pick up each grapefruit, it should feel heavy and firm. Grapefruits will keep in your refrigerator for at least 7 days.

⅔ cup sugar
2–3 very large pink grapefruit, peeled and
    sectioned, membranes removed (see Note).
    Reserve 8 segments, membranes removed, for
    garnish
5 tablespoons white crème de menthe (see Note)
¼ cup water
Mint leaves, for garnish

1. Combine the sugar, grapefruit, crème de menthe, and water in the bowl of a food processor fitted with a steel chopping blade and purée until smooth. You should have about 3 cups. Let the mixture stand for 30 minutes.

2. Pour the purée into a shallow glass dish or brownie pan and place it in a freezer for 12 to 24 hours, until frozen solid.

3. Transfer the frozen fruit mixture to the processor and process with an on-off motion until it is smooth. Return the mixture to the shallow dish and refreeze for 1 to 1½ hours.

4. Remove the dish from the freezer and let it stand at room temperature for about 10 minutes before serving so it can soften slightly. Scoop into small balls. Serve in bowls with a grapefruit segment and a couple of mint leaves.

NOTE: If pink or red grapefruit are unavailable, white grapefruit are fine. In that case, you can use 2 tablespoons of *green* crème de menthe, if you desire.

Margarita's Fruit Salad in a Honeydew Melon

Makes 7 to 8 cups

Here is another south-of-the-border inspiration to liven up a buffet table or to present as a colorful summer dessert. Carve a handsome honeydew melon into a bowl and fill it with fruit and coconut laced with the Margarita-like flavors of tequila, triple sec, and lime juice to make this a memorable salad.

Choosing a good honeydew melon in the market can be a bit problematical. First, unlike melons such as cantaloupes, honeydews frequently do not give off a sweet smell to let you know when they are ripe. Second, although the flat stem end may give to slight pressure, this area may have been pushed by several shoppers ahead of you. Select a solid, heavy honeydew which has a creamy almost white rind without any traces of green. Soft spots indicate deterioration. At home, I leave honeydews on the counter to soften for a couple of days, unless I am certain they are ripe. Then I refrigerate them for up to 3 days longer. Best time to find a great melon in a supermarket: late May to the end of September.

1 large ripe honeydew
2 tablespoons fresh lime juice
3 large bananas, peeled and cut into slices
1 large mango (about 1¼ pounds), peeled and cut
    into cubes about ¾ inch square
1 cup dark sweet cherries, split and pitted
2 tablespoons tequila (see Note)
3 tablespoons triple sec or curaçao
1 cup shredded sweetened coconut

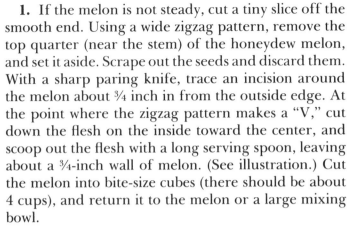

DID YOU KNOW? Mangoes can also be difficult to buy. You need to find a piece of fruit that is firm but gives to slight pressure. When the fruit is ripe, the skin will be shot with yellow and deep-orange streaks through the green, and the smell will be slightly floral. Let mangoes ripen outside the refrigerator, then use them within a day. Although mangoes are shipped from South and Central America during the winter months, they are a better buy during the summer.

1. If the melon is not steady, cut a tiny slice off the smooth end. Using a wide zigzag pattern, remove the top quarter (near the stem) of the honeydew melon, and set it aside. Scrape out the seeds and discard them. With a sharp paring knife, trace an incision around the melon about ¾ inch in from the outside edge. At the point where the zigzag pattern makes a "V," cut down the flesh on the inside toward the center, and scoop out the flesh with a long serving spoon, leaving about a ¾-inch wall of melon. (See illustration.) Cut the melon into bite-size cubes (there should be about 4 cups), and return it to the melon or a large mixing bowl.

2. Add the lime juice, bananas, mango, cherries, tequila, and triple sec to the melon or bowl and toss gently. Before serving, add the coconut and toss again.

NOTE: Unless you make Margaritas, you may not find many uses for tequila, the liquor distilled in Mexico. I'd buy a miniature bottle so you don't clutter your shelf.

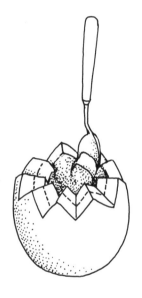

Lemon Curd

Makes 2½ cups

Lemon curd is one of those magical ingredients that can suddenly turn simple ingredients into stars. Keep some on hand in the refrigerator, and use it instead of custard in fresh fruit pies (see 79), as a glaze for LEMON-GLAZED APRICOTS (page 75), or spread on simple cookies, like POGACHEL (page 329).

Happily, lemons are available the year around to spark up the flavor of all kinds of foods from savories to sweets. Look for thin-skinned lemons that feel heavy. Avoid any with brown or moldy spots. Sometimes, the smaller lemons that are sold in plastic bags are actually a better buy than larger lemons. The reason: Some giant lemons have a thick skin that is virtually impossible to squeeze the juice from. In other cases, bagged lemons are old and mushy. Separate bagged lemons at home. They will last for at least 10 days to 2 weeks in the refrigerator.

3 eggs
1 cup sugar
8 tablespoons (1 stick) unsalted butter, melted
¾ cup fresh lemon juice (3 to 4 lemons)
Zest of 3 lemons, minced or finely julienned

1. In a heavy saucepan, stir the eggs and sugar with a wooden spoon until they are smooth and light in color. Add the melted butter and lemon juice, stir to mix well, and set the pan over medium-low heat.
2. Stir the mixture continuously until it is thick and coats the back of the spoon, about 6 to 8 minutes. It is important not to cook this mixture too quickly or the eggs will scramble. Stir in the lemon zest, and scrape the mixture into a clean glass jar. It will keep for at least 1 month in the refrigerator. (If you prefer, you may strain the lemon curd to remove the zest.)

Lime Sorbet in Lime Cups

*Makes 8 small servings or
4 dessert servings*

When the weather is sultry and a small, chilly dessert is in order or a meal is heavy and a palate refresher is called for, these delightful lime cups fill the bill. Make them ahead of time.

Limes are readily available most of the year, but especially in the summer when they add a crisp tangy touch to cool drinks and fresh fruit. Select limes that feel heavy and have firm skins.

⅔ cup sugar
⅔ cup water
5–6 medium-large limes
1 egg white
2 tablespoons gin (optional)
Zest of 1 lime, finely shredded, for garnish
    (optional)

1. In a small saucepan, combine the sugar and water and stir over medium-high heat until the sugar is dissolved. Remove the pan from the heat just before the mixture comes to a boil. Transfer to a covered jar, and chill in the refrigerator until cold.

2. Carefully divide 4 limes in half using a zigzag pattern if you wish to serve the sorbet in lime cups. Remove the zest from another lime, if using it for garnish, and extract the juice from all the limes. You should have 1 cup of juice.

3. Combine the lime juice and sugar syrup, pour it into a flat metal container, cover, and freeze for several hours. When it is solid, cut the mixture into cubes and transfer it to the bowl of a food processor fitted with a steel chopping blade and process until smooth and frothy. Add the egg white and gin and process until blended. Scrape the mixture back into the metal pan, cover, and refreeze for at least 3 hours.

4. To serve between courses of a meal, scrape out the membranes from the 8 lime halves with a grapefruit spoon or other sharp implement. Cut a thin slice off the bottom so that the cups are steady. Using a small (1½-inch) ice cream scoop, fill each cup with a ball of sorbet and place a few strands of the zest on top. Or, serve the sorbet in large scoops with a plate of cookies for dessert.

Orange, Jicama, Watercress, and Olive Salad

Serves 6

Get set for an explosion of flavors with this colorful salad. Tangy sweet orange slices are combined with salty Greek olives, peppery watercress, and delicate jicama—also known as Mexican potato—and tossed with fruity extra-virgin olive oil. It's a fresh, delicious first course for any time of the year.

While some varieties of oranges are found all year, the best ones arrive just when we need them most: in the winter, when most fruits are a fond summer memory. I like navel oranges for salads, especially since they have no seeds. Jicama, on the other hand, is available all year around. It is relatively new to markets, especially on the East Coast where Mexican staples are less familiar. Look for this large circular vegetable with its dark-brown skin. The flesh is crunchy and has a slightly sweet taste. It is almost noncaloric and lasts for at least a week in the refrigerator. Once cut, it should be covered with plastic wrap.

4 navel oranges, peeled
8 ounces jicama, peeled and cut into fine julienne strips (about 2 cups)
⅓ cup Greek olives, pitted and coarsely chopped
2 large bunches watercress, thick stems removed
½ cup extra-virgin olive oil
Salt and freshly ground black pepper to taste
1–2 large heads of Bibb lettuce, washed and dried well

1. Cut the oranges crosswise into ¼-inch slices. Add the jicama, chopped olives, and watercress. Pour on the olive oil, season with salt and pepper, and toss gently.

2. Line 6 salad plates with lettuce leaves. Divide the salad among the plates and serve.

Orange Segments in Orange Sauce with Orange Sherbet

Serves 4

This refreshing triple orange combination is reminiscent of the desserts one enjoys in refined Italian restaurants. With minimal practice, you can cut the oranges so that only the juicy fruit remains. The thin strips of zest are candied and combined with orange liqueur for the sauce. A chilly dollop of home-made or purchased sherbet goes on top.

While navel oranges are only available during the winter months, we have Valencia and other varieties to give us sweet tangy juice and Vitamin C all year. Choose oranges that are firm, without soft, mushy spots. While some varieties have thinner skins, try to avoid oranges that feel light in comparison to their size.

3 navel oranges
Zest of 2 oranges, finely julienned
¼ cup boiling water
1½ tablespoons sugar
¼ cup Grand Marnier, triple sec, or other orange liqueur
1 recipe EASY ORANGE SHERBET (page 415)

1. Wash the oranges to remove any wax or dirt. Remove the zest from 2 of the oranges with a zester or sharp paring knife, avoiding the white pith. If using a knife, cut the zest into thin strips.

2. In a small saucepan, pour the boiling water over the orange zest, add the sugar, and boil, stirring occasionally, over high heat until the liquid has almost evaporated, 5 to 6 minutes. Do not let it brown. Add the Grand Marnier to the pan, stir to mix, and then scrape the orange zest to a bowl, and let it cool while cutting the oranges.

3. Slice off the remaining pith from the oranges with a sharp knife.

4. To remove the segments, cut off a narrow slice at the top and bottom of each orange. Make an incision just next to the membrane of 1 segment, and another cut on the other side of the segment. Continue working around the orange, placing the segments into a bowl. Once all the segments have been removed, squeeze the remaining core and membranes of the oranges with your hand over the orange zest to extract the juice. Mix and pour this sauce over the oranges. Chill for at least 1 hour.

5. To serve, divide the orange segments among 4 plates, spooning the zest and sauce over them. Place a small ball of orange sherbet in the center and put a few strands of the zest on top. Serve at once.

Papaya, Avocado, and Chicken Salad

Serves 4

What beautiful colors nature affords us. In this cool salad, slices of pale orange papaya, yellow-green avocado, and white chicken breast are ribboned with a tangy deep pink dressing. Simple to make; sensational taste.

Papayas are available all year long in some markets. Unfortunately, they are often shipped quite green, which means that they must be allowed to ripen before you can experience their ambrosial taste. They are ready to eat when the skin is almost totally yellow and gives to slight pressure. Leave papayas outside of your refrigerator until they are ripe. Then refrigerate them for up to a week.

Romaine lettuce leaves to line 4 salad plates, coarse stems removed, washed and dried
1 pound boneless, skinless chicken breasts, cooked and cut into thin slices lengthwise
2 ripe medium-size papayas (about 14 ounces each), peeled, seeded, and cut into thin slices lengthwise
2 small or 1 large avocado, peeled, pit removed, cut into thin slices lengthwise (see Note)
1 cup SPICY OLD BAY TOMATO DRESSING (page 365)
4 cherry tomatoes, for garnish

1. Place the lettuce leaves on each plate with the stem ends all together. Divide the chicken, papaya, and avocado slices among the plates in an alternating fanlike design, with the narrow ends toward the stems of the lettuce (see illustration).

2. Spoon a couple of tablespoons of the tomato dressing in a ribbon across each plate, and garnish with a cherry tomato. Pass extra dressing at the table.

NOTE: To loosen the flesh of avocados for easy peeling, run the back of a knife over the skin.

chicken
avocado
papaya

Mosaic of Peaches and Berries in Wine

Serves 10 to 12

The beautiful patterns of summer fruits, chilled in spiced jelled wine, remind me of the tile mosaics one sees in Italy. Each slice is different, and you can choose the variety of wine and fruit to suit your own taste. This hot-weather dessert is low in calories and splendidly refreshing. For a richer variation, add the ZABAGLIONE SAUCE on page 102.

I have not had extraordinary luck with supermarket peaches except in the height of summer, and even then, it is often a hit-or-miss affair. South American imports at other times of the year are never very satisfying, because peaches must ripen on the tree in order to be sweet and juicy. Once mature, peaches are extremely perishable. The best way to select peaches is to make sure the ground color—not the blush—is either entirely cream or golden orange, with no green showing at all. They should feel firm, not stone hard, and smell peachy. At home, leave them on the counter in a brown bag with a couple of holes punched in it for a couple of days, and then eat them. They will only last a day or two more in the refrigerator.

1 liter red or rosé wine (cabernet sauvignon, white zinfandel, etc.)
1 stick cinnamon
6 whole cloves
½ cup sugar
1 2-inch strip orange zest
3 envelopes unflavored gelatin
¾ cup cold water
4 large ripe peaches, peeled and cut into thin slices, about 3 cups (see Note)
½ pint blackberries
½ pint blueberries

1. Lightly oil a $9 \times 5 \times 3$-inch glass or porcelain loaf pan.

2. In a nonaluminum saucepan, combine the wine, cinnamon, cloves, sugar, and orange zest and bring the mixture to a boil over medium-high heat. Reduce the heat to medium, partially cover the pan, and let the mixture simmer for 20 minutes. Meanwhile, sprinkle the gelatin over the water and let it soften.

3. Remove the cinnamon, cloves, and orange zest from the wine mixture with a slotted spoon, and stir in the gelatin. Pour this mixture into a large bowl, let it cool for 1 or 2 minutes, and stir in the fruit gently.

4. Carefully ladle the fruit-wine mixture into the prepared loaf pan. If any liquid remains, reserve it until after the mold begins to solidify—about 1 to 2 hours—then pour it over the mold. Cover and refrigerate the mold until it is solid, at least 8 hours or overnight.

5. To unmold the mosaic, carefully run a sharp knife around the edges, and shake the pan gently. Place a serving platter over the pan, then invert both the platter and pan. The mold should slide free after a few seconds. Cut into ¾-inch slices with a sharp

AS A VARIATION IN COLD WEATHER: Use pears, apples, and bananas. Small pieces of fresh pineapple may be used, too. But, simmer the pineapple first for about 1 minute so it does not prevent the gelatin from jelling.

serrated knife, using a sawing motion so as not to dislodge the berries and peaches. A wide spatula will help you to transfer the slices to individual plates.

NOTE: If the peaches are not ripe, they may be poached with the wine and spices until tender.

Fresh Pear Tart with Ginger Cream

Serves 8

In the dead of winter, when sweet juicy pears rescue us from cold-weather doldrums, this gloriously rich tart with ginger cream can warm our spirits. The tangy raspberry sauce (made from frozen berries) balances the tastes and adds a pretty splash of color.

Good quality pears are easy to find in all markets from early autumn through the winter. Bartlett and Anjou are the most popular selections. Although it is difficult to find perfectly ripe pears—the flesh is delicate and the pears bruise easily at this stage— well-chosen ones will ripen within a few days. Even though they are frequently chilled, most ripening pears will give off a lovely fragrance. The flesh should feel firm, with a slight give, but never hard. Avoid bruises and irregular shapes.

1 baked 11-inch PÂTE BRISÉE tart shell (page 310)

FOR THE GLAZE
½ cup red currant jelly
3 tablespoons sugar

FOR THE PEAR FILLING
5 large Anjou, Bartlett, or Bosc pears, almost ripe
2 tablespoons unsalted butter
⅓ cup sugar
Grated zest of 1 lemon
2 tablespoons freshly grated ginger
¼ cup calvados or applejack
2 cups (1 pint) heavy cream
2 tablespoons sugar

FOR THE RASPBERRY COULIS
1 12-ounce package frozen raspberries, defrosted
½ cup confectioners' sugar, sifted
¼ cup fresh lemon juice

1. FOR THE TART SHELL Bake the tart according to the directions on page 311. Roll out the excess dough and cut out a pear and 2 leaves. Place these cutouts on a lightly buttered cookie sheet and bake them along with the tart, pricking them when they puff up.

2. PREPARE THE GLAZE While the tart is cooking, combine the jelly and sugar in a small saucepan and bring it to a boil over high heat. Boil until the sugar is dissolved and the liquid coats the back of a metal spoon, about 3 minutes. Brush the inside of the tart and the cutouts with the glaze.

3. FOR THE PEAR FILLING Peel, core, and cut each pear into 16 slices. In a large, heavy skillet, melt the butter over medium heat. When it has foamed, add the pears and, depending on ripeness, cook, shaking and gently turning the slices of fruit with a wooden spatula about 3 to 5 minutes, until they start to soften.

4. Sprinkle the sugar over the pears, and continue cooking over medium heat until the sugar melts into a syrup, about 7 to 10 minutes. The pears should be tender without any hard spots. Remove with a slotted spoon to a bowl.

5. Stir the lemon zest, ginger, calvados, and cream into the poaching syrup, raise the heat to medium high, and boil the mixture, stirring continuously with a wooden spoon, until it is thickened and reduced by half, about 15 minutes. As the cream thickens, adjust the heat down so that it slowly bubbles.

6. Drain any liquid from the pears into the cream mixture and boil for 1 minute longer. Arrange the pears in an overlapping decorative pattern in the shell. Pour the cream over the pears, spreading it with the spoon. Sprinkle 2 tablespoons of sugar over the cream.

7. Run the tart quickly under the broiler for a few minutes to color the top or use a salamander. To avoid burning the crust, cover it with aluminum foil. Remove the tart from the broiler, place the pear and leaves in the center, and let it cool to lukewarm or room temperature.

8. PREPARE THE RASPBERRY COULIS While the tart is cooling, or ahead of time, combine the raspberries, sugar, and lemon juice in the bowl of a food processor fitted with a steel chopping blade and purée until the berries are smooth. Pass the mixture through a strainer into a serving bowl. Ladle some of the coulis around each slice as it is served.

DID YOU KNOW? Of all the varieties of pears, the Comice is usually the most expensive and the finest for eating out of hand. The skin should be smooth, firm, and either green-yellow or yellow with a red blush. Unlike other pears, Bosc pears have a rusty brown skin without any gloss to it. The neck is longer than that of other pears. Boscs are very juicy and sweet when ripe. Small Seckel pears, ranging from green to almost ocher, are slightly spicy and sweet and are often used in preserves. Newest in American markets is the Chinese pear. It is far larger than other pears, has a mottled skin, and the flesh is crunchy —almost like an apple.

Pears Poached in Port with Stilton Cream

Serves 4

The English frequently serve pears and Stilton or other blue-veined cheeses along with a glass of port for dessert. Here I have combined these luxurious ingredients into an elegant winter's dessert, made ahead and ready when you are for a smashing final course. A plate of crisp cookies would be most welcomed, too. If you do not find Stilton in your Dairy department, Gorgonzola or a good quality Roquefort are fine substitutions.

Buying pears for cooking is tricky. It is important that they not be completely ripe, lest they fall apart. On the other hand, if they are rock solid, they will have no taste. So I try to buy large, firm, regular-shaped fruit and leave it in a brown bag for at least a day (or up to 3). Once the pears are almost ripe, with the green skin just turning golden (or red with some varieties of Bartlett) I am ready to poach them. If they start to ripen too quickly, refrigerate them. Chilled pears will keep for up to 5 days.

FOR THE PEARS
2 large Anjou or Bartlett pears, almost ripe
1½ cups port
½ cup water
Zest of 1 lemon, minced
1 stick cinnamon
¼ cup sugar

FOR THE CHEESE TOPPING
2 ounces Stilton or other blue-veined cheese, such as Gorgonzola, softened
¼ cup heavy cream, chilled
4 pecan halves, for garnish

1. POACH THE PEARS With a sharp paring knife, peel the pears, cut them in half, and carefully remove the core. A melon baller works well to remove the center part. Cut off a small slice from the back of each pear half so they do not rock.

2. In a large nonaluminum skillet, combine the port, water, lemon, cinnamon stick, and sugar. Place the pears flat side down and slowly bring the liquid to a boil over medium-high heat. Reduce the heat so that the liquid is barely simmering, cover the pan, and let the pears poach for about 15 minutes, or until just tender. Turn them with a wooden spoon after about

8 minutes. Once they are tender, turn off the heat and let the pears cool in the liquid for 5 to 10 minutes. Remove the pears to a wide bowl with a slotted spoon and set aside.

3. Bring the poaching liquid to a slow boil and let it reduce for about 10 to 15 minutes, or until it thickly coats the back of a spoon. Strain the poaching liquid over the pears, cover, and refrigerate for at least an hour until chilled. These pears may be poached 1 to 2 days ahead of time. They become darker the longer they are left in the port.

4. PREPARE THE CHEESE TOPPING Once the pears are cool, mash the cheese until quite smooth. Add the heavy cream and whisk until smooth and thick. Do not overbeat. Transfer the cheese mixture to a pastry bag fitted with a wide star tip, and pipe a swirl onto each pear half. Place a pecan half on top, if desired. Serve at once, or refrigerate for up to several hours. If the pears are refrigerated, remove them from the refrigerator about an hour ahead of time. Serve on individual plates or in a fruit compotier.

Pineapple Boats with Pork, Black Beans, and Mole Sauce

Serves 4 as a main course

Pork and pineapple seem to have a natural affinity. Throw in some black beans and mole sauce—the spicy chocolate-based sauce from Mexico found in jars on the same shelf with other south-of-the-border ingredients—and you have a heady fiesta of taste. Make this concoction ahead of time to allow the flavors to mellow. Then spoon it over quartered pineapple rinds for an unusual serving idea.

Pineapples should be picked and purchased when ripe, not green. Once cut, they will not get any riper. The leaves of the crown should be fresh and bright green, not brown and limp. Some markets stack them up in a great pyramid, making it hard to really examine them. Do ask for a clerk's assistance. I look for the pineapple with the largest body, since there is a fair amount of waste in the skin and core, and a small pineapple will produce little edible fruit. If the pineapple is bruised or leaking liquid, make another choice.

1 pound boneless pork cutlets
1 large ripe pineapple
1 tablespoon unsalted butter
1 teaspoon vegetable oil
1 cup finely chopped onions
1 large clove garlic, peeled and crushed
8 ounces black beans, cooked just until tender and processed or mashed until almost smooth (see Note)
1 cup beef stock
1 teaspoon ground cumin
2 tablespoons tomato paste
3 tablespoons mole sauce
Salt and freshly ground black pepper to taste
¼ cup chopped cilantro leaves
Cilantro leaves for garnish

1. Place the pork cutlets in the freezer for about an hour or just until fairly solid.

2. Split the pineapple into 4 sections, leaving the crown intact, if possible. Carefully remove the pineapple from the rind, leaving a ½-inch shell. Remove the core, then finely chop enough pineapple to make 1 cup. Cut 12 small triangles to be used as a garnish. Set the pineapple aside, reserving the rind.

3. Once the pork is quite chilled, trim all the fat, and cut it into slices about ⅛ inch thick.

4. Melt the butter and oil in a large, heavy skillet over medium-high heat. When the butter has foamed, stir in the onions and sauté them for about 5 minutes, or until softened. Add the pork and cook it for about 3 minutes until just opaque; then add the garlic and cook for 30 seconds. Stir in the beans, stock, cumin, tomato paste, mole sauce, and the cup of chopped pineapple. Season with salt and pepper, adjust the heat to medium, and simmer the mixture for about 20 minutes. Add the chopped cilantro, and cook for 5 minutes longer.

5. Meanwhile, preheat your oven to 325°F.

6. Place the 4 pineapple rinds in a flat pan and heat them in the oven for 15 minutes. Remove the pan from the oven, place a pineapple rind on each plate, and spoon some mole-pork mixture onto each one. Place 3 small triangles of pineapple standing up in the meat mixture, and sprinkle on some cilantro leaves. Serve with boiled rice.

DID YOU KNOW? Although tougher than the rest of the slice, the core of ripe Hawaiian pineapples is edible. Once removed, it makes a nice "swizzle stick" in a tall drink.

NOTE: Black beans, also called "turtle beans," are found with other dried legumes. Most packages are printed with slow and rapid cooking instructions. What works the best for me is to pick over the beans (the amount in this recipe is half the bag), place them in a large saucepan, then cover them with at least 4 times again as much water. Bring this to a boil, cook for 2 minutes, turn off the heat and leave the pan tightly covered for about 2 hours. After this, the beans may need a little longer cooking time to be just tender. I do not like mushy beans. However, if you prefer them very soft, cook the beans longer. To save time, you can substitute drained canned black beans. Use about 1½ 16-ounce cans. This will be about 3 cups of beans.

Broiled Pineapple Slices with Zabaglione Sauce

Serves 6

When pineapples are ripe and juicy, they are wonderful just as they are, cut into either slices or spears. For a little extra pizzazz, I broil the slices briefly and serve them on a decadent pool of cool zabaglione sauce. Wait till you try the combination of marsala, rum, and cream with the tangy sweetness of pineapple. It's addicting.

Puerto Rico, Mexico, and other tropical countries now ship their fruit to our markets. For my money, the biggest and best pineapples still come from Hawaii. Rather than trying to pull a leaf easily from the crown to gauge ripeness, look for a firm pineapple whose skin has a minimum amount of green. Put your nose close to the stem end. It should smell fruity and not at all fermented. To distribute the sugar throughout the pineapple, store it upside down until ready to eat. (Otherwise, all the sweetness settles in the bottom.) I don't refrigerate mine if I plan on eating it within a couple of days. For longer periods, up to a week or more, refrigeration is best.

FOR THE SAUCE

4 egg yolks
5 tablespoons sugar
½ cup marsala
¼ cup light rum
1 cup heavy cream

FOR THE PINEAPPLE

6 slices fresh pineapple about ¾ inch thick, rind removed
3 tablespoons brown sugar
¼ cup chopped pecans

1. PREPARE THE SAUCE In the top of a double boiler and off the heat, combine the egg yolks and sugar and beat them with a wooden spoon until pale yellow, about 1 to 2 minutes. Stir in the marsala and rum.

2. Bring the water in the bottom of the double boiler to a boil. Replace the top of the pot, adjust the heat down so that the water is just simmering, and continue stirring the mixture until it thickly coats the back of the spoon, about 5 minutes. Remove the top part of the pot from the heat and continue stirring for at least 2 minutes longer to cool the sauce slightly. Stir in the heavy cream, transfer the sauce to a bowl, cover and refrigerate it until cold.

3. BROIL THE PINEAPPLE Turn on the broiler, and adjust the rack to about 4 inches from the heat.

4. Place the pineapple slices on a cookie sheet or jelly roll pan. Sprinkle on the brown sugar, and place the pan under the broiler for about 3 minutes, just until the sugar is hot and bubbling and the pineapple is warmed through. Remove the pan and let the slices cool slightly.

5. Pour a generous circle of sauce on each plate. Add a slice of pineapple, a sprinkle of chopped pecans, and serve. This dessert may be made ahead of time. Leave the sauce in the refrigerator and the pineapple at room temperature, once it has been broiled. Serve with MOLASSES SPICE COOKIES (page 328).

DID YOU KNOW? Many supermarkets now have pineapple coring machines in their Produce departments. Not only are they amusing to watch, they afford you the opportunity of selecting a better pineapple at the same price as the uncored ones. Make sure the pineapple is tightly wrapped. Be sure to refrigerate and use it within a couple of days.

Plum-Pear Ketchup

Makes about 2 pints

So you thought that "ketchup" was only a bright-red tomato sauce? Wrong! The word has a long and colorful past dating back to Marco Polo's adventures in China, where he found the natives using a pickled fish brine called "ket-siap" to liven up the taste of bland food. In this intensely flavorful combination, fruit, spices, and vinegar are simmered into a wonderful sauce for spreading on toast or plain cookies like POGACHEL (page 329) or ladling over ice cream. It's also wonderful with PHEASANT PÂTÉ (page 151).

Plums are one of summer's nicest gifts. In season, from May through September, market shelves are brimming with several colorful varieties in all sizes and shapes—from the yellow greengage to blue-black Italian prunes, along with bright-red and purple fruit. The best plums are firm but not too hard and have smooth skins. When picked too early, plums may ripen, but they never seem to develop the wonderful sweetness that makes them ideal for eating out of hand. For that reason, I tend to shy away from expensive air-shipped Chilean plums often sold during the winter. If plums are not quite ripe (and many market specimens aren't), leave them out for a day or two, and then refrigerate. Eat them within a couple of days. This ketchup is a good way to use up less-than-perfect plums or pears.

2 pounds plums, split
5 ripe Anjou or Bartlett pears, peeled, cored, and
   coarsely chopped
¾ cup golden raisins
1¼ cups sugar
20 cloves
3 sticks cinnamon
¾ teaspoon ground coriander seed
½ teaspoon salt
¼ teaspoon white pepper
¼ cup raspberry vinegar
¼ cup water

1. In a large, heavy, nonaluminum pot, combine the plums, pears, and raisins, cover, and bring to a boil over medium-high heat. Adjust the heat to medium and let the fruit simmer for about 20 minutes until it is soft.

2. Remove the lid, mash the fruit with the back of a wooden spoon, stir in the sugar, cloves, cinnamon, coriander, salt, and white pepper and continue cooking slowly, stirring frequently, for another 40 to 50 minutes until the mixture is quite thick. Remove the cinnamon sticks and reserve.

3. Stir in the vinegar and water. Pass the mixture through a food mill or strainer into a large bowl. Fill sterilized jars and place 1 cinnamon stick in each jar. Cap tightly and store the jars in the refrigerator. They will keep for at least 4 to 6 months.

Sautéed Turbot Fillets with Sliced Starfruit

Serves 2

These moist fish fillets with a crunchy almond coating, served with sliced carambola, are dramatic to look at and delightfully pleasing to the taste. Thanks to the carambola's sweet citrusy flavor played against the fish and toasted almonds, this easily prepared dish is a winner.

Carambola or "starfruit" are relatively new to most supermarkets. Fortunately, they are reasonably hearty, as well, since I have seen them sitting on shelves for days. Do take one that is not bruised home and try it. It needn't be peeled, and when cut across the fruit, the slices are a very pretty star. Select firm, shiny-skinned fruit and allow it to ripen to a yellow-orange color with brown edges for maximum sweetness. Once ripe, they can be stored in a bag in your refrigerator for up to 5 days.

2 turbot fillets, approximately 5 to 6 ounces each
⅓ cup ground almonds
2 tablespoons unsalted butter
Salt and freshly ground black pepper to taste
1 medium-large carambola, approximately 5 ounces, thinly sliced
2 ounces pea pods, strings removed, blanched, for garnish (optional)
½ lemon, cut into wedges (optional)

1. Dry the turbot fillets and place them in a dish. Cover one side with half the ground almonds, pressing them gently into the flesh.

2. Melt the butter over medium-high heat in a skillet or pan just large enough to hold both fillets. When it has foamed, add the fish with the coated side down. Season the fish with salt and pepper and sprinkle on the remaining nuts. Spoon some of the melted butter over the nuts. Sauté the fish for about 2 to 3 minutes until lightly colored. Meanwhile, turn on the broiler and adjust the rack to about 4 inches from the heat.

3. Transfer the pan to the broiler and cook for about 1 to 2 minutes longer, watching that the nuts do not burn.

4. Remove the pan from the broiler, put the sliced fruit and pea pods around the outside, and return to the broiler for 30 seconds to 1 minute just to warm the fruit. Serve at once with lemon wedges, if desired.

Individual Strawberry Crème Brûlée Tarts

Makes 4 individual tarts

This stunning dessert is a beautiful celebration of fresh strawberries. A sprinkle of brown sugar on the vanilla custard topping makes this cream "brûlée" or burned-looking. Each crust is simply a folded square of phyllo dough lightly brushed with butter and baked. No mixing or rolling needed. Most of the work can be done ahead of time.

With modern transportation, you are likely to find strawberries in the market almost the year around, often at reasonable prices. To avoid disappointment at home, pick up a basket and check for bruised berries or leakage on the bottom. Strawberries should be firm and bright red. Sort them as soon as you can. The giant Driscoll berries sold with a long stem in some markets are fine for dipping in chocolate or sour cream and brown sugar. It's a shame to pay extra for them if they are not being used for display.

FOR THE PASTRY
4 sheets of phyllo
2 tablespoons unsalted butter, melted

FOR THE CUSTARD AND TOPPING
3 egg yolks
3 tablespoons sugar
1½ cups heavy cream
1 vanilla bean, split, *or* **½ teaspoon vanilla extract**
1½ pints strawberries, washed, hulled, and split
1 teaspoon fresh lemon juice
**1½ tablespoons dark brown sugar, strained to
    remove lumps**

1. PREPARE THE PASTRY Preheat your oven to 400°F.

2. Spread 1 sheet of phyllo on a clean work space and lightly brush it with butter. Fold it in quarters and trim off the folded edge to make a square (see illustration). Place the phyllo square on a cookie sheet, and brush it lightly with butter. Open up the trimmed portion of phyllo (there should now be 2 sheets the same size as the square), place it on top, and brush the top with butter. Continue with the remaining sheets of phyllo in the same fashion.

3. Place the pan in the middle of the preheated oven and bake for 6 to 8 minutes, until light golden in color. Remove the pan and let the pastry cool.

4. FOR THE CUSTARD Off the heat, combine the egg yolks and sugar in the top of a double boiler and stir until it is light yellow in color. Add the cream and the vanilla bean. (If using extract, add this after the custard has thickened.)

5. Bring the water in the bottom of the double boiler just to the simmer and set the top over it. Stir the custard mixture frequently with a wooden spoon until it thickens, about 25 to 30 minutes. Try to avoid forming bubbles on the surface. Once the custard thickly coats the back of the spoon, strain it into a small bowl and chill it until cool, about 25 minutes. This custard may be made ahead of time.

6. Turn on the broiler and adjust the rack close to heat.

7. Cut the berries into halves, and arrange them on the phyllo squares. Brush them lightly with the lemon juice, and spoon on the custard topping. Sprinkle about 1 teaspoon of brown sugar over the custard, and run the tarts under the broiler until the sugar is just melted, watching carefully that they do not burn, about 30 to 45 seconds. *Or* use a salamander if you have one. Remove and serve at once. As a low-calorie alternative, use 1 cup of ORANGE-HONEY YOGURT SAUCE FOR FRUIT, page 277, instead of the crème brûlée.

Minted Watermelon Soup

Serves 4 to 6

This refreshingly cool summer soup is sweet with a pleasant tang and is the epitome of simplicity: ripe, luscious watermelon; tangy buttermilk; and mint. To make a decorative serving tureen, hollow out the rounded end of the melon—about 8 inches in length —and fill it with the delicate pink liquid flecked with green.

This is a good chance to check in with a Produce clerk. If a whole melon is too much and the market sells wedges, ask for a solid, heavy melon to be cut crosswise. Most markets will be accommodating during the summer peak season. This is also a good way to check that the flesh is firm, not mealy, and deep rose or red colored. The rind should be somewhat shiny, and the underside of the melon, where it lay on the ground, should be creamy or slightly yellow, not white. Don't waste your time thumping a watermelon. It will reveal nothing about what is inside. When buying by the piece, find out when the melon was cut. It will only be at its best for a day or two after that and needs to be tightly wrapped. A whole melon may be chilled for up to 4 or 5 days.

5½–6 pounds watermelon (to make 5 cups of
   purée)
1½ cups buttermilk
3 tablespoons chopped fresh mint leaves
Small pieces of watermelon and fresh mint leaves
   for garnish

1. Purée the watermelon in a food processor fitted
with a steel chopping blade or pass it through a food
mill. This should be done in batches. Transfer the
purée to a large bowl and stir in the buttermilk and
chopped mint. Refrigerate the soup for at least 2 hours.
2. Pour the soup into the melon tureen, if desired.
Or serve in chilled bowls with a couple of tiny pieces
of melon in the center and a mint leaf alongside.

Equipping Your Kitchen from the Supermarket

Beyond food, you may find cooking equipment in your market. Some is pretty basic, like can openers and custard cups, and the supermarket is a good place to buy these items. Other markets recognize that they have a captive audience willing to make more substantial purchases when they see a product they want, and price seems to be less important than the convenience of buying in one place. In some cases, a full Cookware Boutique, complete with heavy-gauge pots, chefs' knives, and professional-grade baking supplies, has been installed. While it is impossible to generalize about the quality and variety of cookware in all markets, two important considerations should enter into your decision-making process.

First, whatever you buy should reflect your degree of interest in cooking. If you cook just to get food on the table, bang your knives and pans around and wash them in the dishwasher, even the best quality tools will be ruined in no time. On the other hand, if cooking is something you do for recreation and the results are important, high-quality implements will make your tasks easier and improve the results. With care, equipment will last a very long time. Smart supermarket merchants have put special tools like oyster shuckers or citrus zesters on display near specific foods if they do not have a Kitchen Tools section.

Second, price is not always synonymous with quality. Some inexpensive supermarket gadgets, like vegetable scrapers, steamers, and rubber pot scrapers work as well as more costly models sold at boutiques. Some markets mix the quality of items such as spoons made from hard and soft woods and price them the same. As harder woods don't splinter and crack as readily, it is worth looking closely at purchases. Since cookware merchandising is relatively new to markets, the pricing may be out of line with the competition. If the prices are close, saving a trip (gas and time) is worth considering.

The following equipment is usually a good buy in supermarkets:

MEASURES

- spoons—metal or plastic
- dry measuring cups—metal or plastic
- liquid measuring cups—plastic or glass
- oven, freezer, and instant-read thermometers
- timers

TOOLS

Tools may be carded and hung on "J" hooks or displayed loose. Try to pick up each item and make sure that it is in good condition by testing moveable parts, running a finger along edges to see if they are smooth, and checking the points of connection.

- vegetable scrapers—stainless steel with a swivel blade
- metal spreaders with wood or plastic handles
- rubber pot scrapers
- can and bottle openers
- nutmeg graters
- hand graters with changeable drums
- square graters
- zigzag and plain pastry cutters
- pancake turners and spatulas (often Teflon coated)
- pastry brushes—natural bristles
- vegetable and pot brushes
- ice cream scoops
- strainers—with the basket firmly attached to the rim
- colanders—two-handled with fairly large holes for good drainage
- trivets—to turn almost any pan into a double boiler
- rolling pins—with ball bearings, or a french rolling pin
- citrus zesters—the metal edges of the holes must be very sharp
- nutcrackers and picks
- funnels—plastic or metal
- tweezers (found in Health and Beauty Aids) for removing bones from fish
- 12-inch rulers (from School Supplies) for measuring pastry, etc.
- bulb basters
- whisks—with wires permanently attached to the base

KNIVES

It is difficult to buy knives in the market, since displaying them is a problem, and there is usually little choice or chance for comparison. Manufacturers of some medium-priced lines have attempted selling their cutlery carded on "J" hooks with some success. Inexpensive paring knives are fine for the short term. But for maximum performance, a chef's best friend is a good knife. High-carbon and stainless-steel combinations are the best. They cost money, and few markets are willing to stock these slow turnover items.

PAPER, WOOD, AND CLOTH

These items are generally a good buy. Generic brands of paper goods may be of a thinner gauge and not work as well, especially paper towels. Be sure that towels, mits, and pot holders are more than just pretty.

- wax paper
- plastic wrap
- parchment paper
- aluminum foil—regular and heavy-duty wide
- paper towels—2 ply work better
- Ziploc bags
- freezer paper and tape
- muffin tin liners
- cheesecloth
- string—tightly twisted without any coating
- bamboo skewers
- toothpicks
- oven mits—at least above-wrist length and lined or quilted
- pot holders
- towels—should be of a firm weave, linen or cotton are better than blends

DISHES AND BOWLS

These items are reasonable and readily available.

- Pyrex or porcelain custard cups and soufflé dishes
- stainless steel or Pyrex mixing bowls in graduated sizes
- glass and metal cake pans, pie plates, tart pans with removable bottoms

- cookie sheets, jelly roll pans—heavier weight is preferable
- muffin and mini-muffin tins
- metal ring molds

POTS AND PANS

These are usually not a good buy in the market unless they are promotionally priced for a demonstration. Teflon skillets are reasonable but wear out quickly. Cast-iron skillets and graniteware roasters may be of interest. The copper pans sometimes sold in markets are usually too lightweight and are still expensive. They are best used for display.

When purchasing kitchen equipment from your market, remember to examine it carefully.

·3·
POULTRY AND GAME BIRDS

INTRODUCTION

For a low-fat, inexpensive source of protein, chicken is the number-one choice of supermarket customers. And with good reason. Chicken is incredibly versatile. You can cook it in every conceivable way, from barbecueing to stewing, from whole to minced, and it will be delicious. Ethnic cuisines from around the world combine chicken with local spices and ingredients into an endless array of original dishes. In this chapter you'll find STIR-FRIED CHINESE CHICKEN WITH CASHEWS (page 123), INDIVIDUAL MEXICAN CHICKEN AND CORN-BREAD CASSEROLES (page 121), and EGGPLANT ROASTED WITH MEDITERRANEAN CHICKEN (page 124).

Supermarket cases are filled with chickens, from whole roasters to quartered broilers and fryers and packages of all legs or breasts. In this day when saving time and labor is so important to many of us, cut-up chickens are an appealing convenience, even though they cost slightly more per pound.

Recently, chicken has had to share a little of the limelight with turkey, thanks to a smart market campaign by the turkey people. Why? Because this once-seasonal bird is now available all year long, not only whole in several sizes including very small, but in cutlets and parts, too. Like its smaller cousin, turkey is very economical, comparing quite favorably in taste with veal at a fraction of the cost. Look at SAUTÉED TURKEY CUTLETS IN LEMON BUTTER (page 140). The ratio of turkey meat to bones is higher than in chicken, particularly with larger birds. Smart merchants have picked up on these facts to bring more options to the customer.

Other poultry choices have expanded, too. Along with fresh Cornish game hens, we find fresh and frozen ducks or even the breast alone. Markets with a trendy clientele sell goose, quail, and pheasant. Current interest in chickens "like they used to taste" have led to "corn-fed" and "free-range" birds being stocked or available on special order in markets with service meat counters. Prepared items, like breaded chicken nuggets, turkey cutlets, and duck in orange sauce reflect the spiraling interest in poultry.

With the popularity of poultry comes a heightened awareness of the importance of careful selection and storage. Be sure to take a look at The ABC's of Working with Poultry in this chapter. For their part, markets sell only USDA inspected poultry, an indication that the farm was sanitary. There should be a small seal on the package or a wing tag. Birds are also graded by the Department of Agriculture. The best grade, "A," indicates that the bird is meaty, with a minimum of skin tears, broken bones, bruises, or other defects.

When purchasing poultry, you may notice that the package has some ice crystals on it. This is because supermarkets store their poultry at between 28° and 32°F to retard bacterial growth. To distinguish "fresh chilled" poultry from frozen, push in the flesh. It should not feel solid. Most home refrigerators are substantially warmer than this "chilled" temperature, and it is recommended that poultry be used within 2 days *even if the "sell by" date is later*. If the package is not broken, supermarket wrapping is satisfactory for home storage for 12 to 18 hours. Cooked poultry should be used within 2 days.

Supermarkets are trying to offer us more choices for varied and healthful eating. This task is surely made easier with fresh poultry.

THE ABC'S OF WORKING WITH POULTRY

As Americans have become more health conscious, poultry consumption has risen significantly. To meet the demand, supermarkets offer a huge variety of poultry selections. While poultry is nutritious, economical, and versatile, recent news stories emphasize that poultry is also a good source of bacterial food poisoning.

Both *salmonella* and the lesser known *campylobacter* (which, according to some medical sources, is the second leading cause of food poisoning in the United States today) grow easily in poultry. People infected after eating contaminated foods experience mild to severe cramps, vomiting, fever, and diarrhea, and often attribute these symptoms to "flu." Unless one is very old, very young, or seriously ill, the effects are usually minor and pass quickly. Few people report the experience to the market or a doctor, but they should. If symptoms persist, seek medical assistance.

Rather than experiencing these symptoms or becoming neurotic about the bacteria, become smart and follow these simple tips:

A
Alertness Counts

Always be an alert shopper when selecting poultry products. Don't just reach without looking at what is wrapped inside. Since most supermarket poultry products are already under plastic wrap, it is imperative to know your market. Does it have a high turnover of product? Can you trust the dating policies (with no switching of dated labels in the back room)?

Always check the package date to be certain it is current. The plastic wrap should be intact, the tray should be free of excess juices, and the poultry should look moist and fresh with no blemishes.

Ask the department manager if you have questions or concerns about what you see. At the very least, make another selection.

Ask the checker to place your poultry in freezer bags to keep the temperature cooler and to prevent any juices from leaking onto other foods.

As soon as possible, return home with poultry and place it in the coldest part of your refrigerator. If the ride home has been long or warm, chill poultry in the freezer for about 20 to 30 minutes before refrigerating it to lower the temperature rapidly.

And, if not using poultry within 12 to 18 hours, take it out of the store tray, place it on a clean dish with a lip to prevent spilled juices, and cover loosely with foil to let the air circulate around it.

After 48 hours from time of purchase, poultry should be frozen, rewrapped in tightly sealed freezer paper or Ziploc bags. Be sure it is labeled and dated. Defrost in the refrigerator with a plate underneath to prevent juices from contaminating other foods.

B
Be Scrupulously Clean

Before using any poultry, be sure to wash it under lukewarm water for about a minute while you remove and discard excess fat, unwanted skin, or internal parts. Do not immerse it in water. Drain, and pat dry with paper towels.

Bowls and dishes used for defrosting or marinating must be washed before being used for cooking or serving poultry.

Blot up any liquid on the counter as soon as possible. After working with poultry, it is *imperative* that all work surfaces, sinks, colanders, knives, and your *hands* be washed with hot sudsy water. Wooden boards easily absorb juices; white opaque plastic ones are safer. These surfaces should be sanitized with a solution of 1 tablespoon of bleach mixed with a quart of hot water.

C
Cook Thoroughly

Cook all poultry thoroughly to assure the elimination of any bacteria. Bacteria are killed when the internal temperature reaches 165°F.

Charred flesh on the outside from a barbecue does not mean that the chicken is cooked inside. Pink meat near the bone or in the joints is not only unfashionable, it is dangerous. When poultry is pricked with a fork, the juices should run clear.

Check poultry by making a deep cut before serving.

D
Don't Give Bacteria a Chance to Grow

Don't stuff poultry ahead of time. Many professionals now bake stuffing mixtures in a separate casserole. If birds are to be stuffed, have the ingredients chopped, diced, or sautéed and waiting in the refrigerator. Just before cooking time, mix them together with the dry ingredients and fill the cavity.

Don't leave raw or cooked poultry out in a warm environment for more than 1 hour.

E
Enjoy

With a little care you can *enjoy* poultry often.

Tarragon Chicken Salad in Cream Puff Shells

Fills 28 to 32 cream puffs

Small savory puffs filled with warm tarragon-flavored chicken salad and capped with melted Gruyère cheese add an innovative touch to any cocktail party or buffet. Serve this salad, too, at room temperature, without the cheese, inside a cooked artichoke or on avocado halves. It will serve 6 generously.

If you eat a lot of chicken — and who doesn't — look for family packs, especially when they are on sale. The savings may be up to $.50 per pound. Divide the larger package into serving-size portions and wrap and freeze them for up to 9 months. I find that 2 whole breasts fit nicely into a sandwich-size Ziploc freezer bag.

1 recipe WHOLE WHEAT CREAM PUFF SHELLS (page 313), baked, cooked, and split
2 medium whole chicken breasts, split and skinned
2 cups chicken broth plus enough water to cover the breasts
⅓ cup Pommery mustard (see Note)
3 tablespoons red wine vinegar
3 tablespoons walnut oil
3 tablespoons vegetable oil *or* 6 tablespoons vegetable oil, if not using walnut oil
1 tablespoon dried tarragon, crumbled
½ teaspoon salt, or to taste
Freshly ground black pepper
½ cup light cream
1 cup coarsely chopped walnut pieces, lightly toasted
1 cup thinly sliced scallions, including most of the green parts
1 cup finely shredded Gruyère or Swiss cheese

1. Place the chicken breasts in a large, deep skillet, and cover with the chicken broth and water. Bring the liquid to a simmer. Cover the pan and cook covered until the chicken is just cooked, about 15 to 20 minutes.

2. While the chicken is cooking, combine the mustard and vinegar in a large bowl. Add the oils in a slow steady stream, whisking constantly to form an emulsion. Stir in the tarragon, salt, pepper, and cream. Add the walnuts and scallions and set aside.

3. Preheat your oven to 400°F.

4. With a slotted spoon, transfer the breasts to a

work surface. Remove the meat from the bones, cut the chicken into ¼-inch cubes, and add it to the bowl with the sauce. Stir to coat the chicken with the sauce.

5. Place the bottoms of the cream puffs on a cookie sheet and fill them with the chicken salad. Replace the tops and distribute the grated cheese over them. Transfer the pan to the preheated oven and bake until the cheese is melted and the puffs are warm, about 3 to 4 minutes. Remove from the oven and serve at once.

NOTE: If your market does not carry Pommery mustard, substitute smooth Dijon mustard.

Individual Mexican Chicken and Cornbread Casseroles

Serves 4

These mini-casseroles are a favorite of children and grown-ups alike. They are festive and easy to make ahead for dinner or a casual party. Make the zesty chicken filling and ladle it into the soup bowls (I use the crockery kind usually used for onion soup), then bake them with their cornbread topping when you need them. The tomatoes, corn, olives, and spicy jalapeño peppers, seasoned with chili and other Mexican spices, make this chicken dish vibrant in color and taste. You can also prepare a single, larger casserole.

FOR THE FILLING
1 pound boneless, skinless chicken meat from any part (see Note below if using leftovers)
2 tablespoons olive oil
1 cup finely chopped onions
2 large garlic cloves, peeled and minced
1 tablespoon minced pickled jalapeño peppers (2 medium-size peppers, seeds and membranes removed)
1 28-ounce can whole, peeled Italian tomatoes, drained and chopped not too fine
1½ tablespoons chili powder
1 teaspoon ground cumin
1 teaspoon oregano, crushed
1 cup corn kernels, fresh, frozen or canned
½ cup thinly sliced pitted black olives
2 teaspoons red wine vinegar
3 tablespoons chopped cilantro *or* flat-leaf parsley
Salt and freshly ground black pepper to taste

FOR THE TOPPING
1 cup cornmeal
1½ tablespoons sugar
1½ teaspoons baking powder
½ teaspoon salt
1 egg
½ cup milk

1. PREPARE THE FILLING Fill a large skillet or casserole with water, add the chicken, bring to a boil, then turn off the heat, cover the pan, and let it sit for about 15 to 20 minutes, depending on the thickness of the meat until the chicken is just opaque. Remove the chicken, blot on paper towels, and cut it into bite-size pieces.

2. Meanwhile, in a large, heavy skillet, heat the oil until fragrant. Stir in the onions and sauté them over medium heat for about 6 minutes until limp. Add the garlic and cook for 30 seconds longer.

3. Add the jalapeño peppers, tomatoes, chili powder, cumin, oregano, corn, olives, vinegar, cilantro, and salt and pepper and mix well. Cook over medium heat for 10 to 15 minutes, stir in the chicken, and taste the sauce to adjust the seasonings.

4. Ladle about 1 cup of the chicken mixture into each of 4 oven-safe soup bowls. If not cooking the casseroles at this time, cover the bowls and refrigerate them. Remove them from the refrigerator about 1 hour before baking them.

5. PREPARE THE TOPPING Preheat your oven to 425°F.

6. Sift the cornmeal, sugar, baking powder, and salt into a medium-size bowl. Combine the egg and milk, and whisk them into the dry ingredients until smooth. Ladle the batter on top of the 4 bowls, smoothing it with a knife or small spatula to cover the chicken. Do not worry if the topping sinks, it will rise during baking. Place the bowls on a cookie sheet, transfer them to the lower third of the preheated oven, and bake for about 20 to 30 minutes, until the tops are puffed and golden brown. The time will vary with the width of the bowl. Remove the bowls from the oven and serve. These casseroles are also delicious at room temperature. You may bake them several hours in advance and let them cool.

AS A VARIATION: Use leftover turkey or duck meat.

NOTE: Leftovers are fine for this recipe so long as the chicken is not overcooked and dry. Remove the skin and all fat, and cut it into bite-size pieces.

Stir-Fried Chinese Chicken with Cashews

Serves 6 to 8

This is my children's all-time favorite chicken dish. The combination of crunchy pea pods, water chestnuts, and cashews, along with mushrooms and chicken, in the gingery hoisin-soy sauce appeals to all of us. The cook will love it because it is easy and quick to make in a wok or skillet. Serve with steamed or boiled rice to complete the meal.

The Oriental section of the market should contain the sesame oil, hoisin sauce, rice vinegar, and soy sauce.

⅓ cup sesame oil
⅓ cup rice vinegar
¼ cup dry sherry
2 large cloves garlic, peeled and minced
2 pounds boneless skinless chicken breast, cut into 1-inch cubes
2 tablespoons peanut or vegetable oil
1½ teaspoons cornstarch
⅓ cup soy sauce
⅓ cup hoisin sauce
1 tablespoon sugar
2 tablespoons grated fresh ginger
½ pound pea pods, tips and strings removed, blanched for 30 seconds in boiling water
1 7-ounce-can water chestnuts, thinly sliced
2 cups (8 ounces) cashew nuts, lightly toasted
½ pound white mushrooms, trimmed, wiped, and sliced
1 cup thinly sliced scallions, including the green parts

1. In a large bowl, combine the sesame oil, vinegar, sherry, and garlic. Add the chicken cubes and let them marinate for 1 hour.
2. In a wok or large, heavy skillet, heat the peanut oil over high heat until very hot. Transfer the chicken from the marinade to the wok with a slotted spoon, reserving the marinade. Stir the chicken with a large spatula or spoon until it is opaque on all sides, about 3 to 4 minutes.

AS A VARIATION: Substitute sea scallops or large shrimp for the chicken. In place of the pea pods, look for broccoli florets or mini-ears of corn in the Salad Bar.

3. Combine the cornstarch and soy sauce in a small bowl. Add it along with the marinade, hoisin sauce, sugar, and ginger to the wok and reduce the heat to medium-low.

4. Add the pea pods, water chestnuts, cashews, and mushrooms and continue cooking until the vegetables are warmed through, about 5 to 6 minutes. Sprinkle the scallions over the chicken, toss to blend, cook 1 minute longer, then serve over cooked rice.

Eggplant Roasted with Mediterranean Chicken

Serves 2

In this recipe, hollowed-out eggplants split in two become the serving container for a hauntingly fragrant mixture of sautéed eggplant, chicken, pignoli nuts, tomatoes, ground coriander, and fennel. The unusual flavors are subtly spicy and mellow when served warm or at room temperature. For a crowd, you can quadruple the recipe. Prepare the stuffing several hours ahead of time (even the day before) and refrigerate it. Fill the eggplant shells and bake them on a large cookie sheet when needed.

2 medium-size eggplants, approximately ¾ pound each
1 tablespoon olive oil
Salt and freshly ground black pepper
6 ounces boneless and skinless chicken meat (1 large breast or 3 medium thighs)
2 tablespoons olive oil
1 small onion, peeled and finely chopped
1 large clove garlic, peeled and minced
1 cup canned Italian tomatoes, drained and chopped
⅓ cup chopped flat-leaf parsley
¾ cup cooked rice
¼ cup orange juice
1 teaspoon ground coriander seed
⅛ teaspoon ground fennel
¼ cup pignoli nuts, lightly toasted
¼ cup currants
Salt and freshly ground black pepper to taste
¼ cup freshly toasted bread crumbs
½ small clove garlic, peeled and minced
¼ teaspoon salt
1 tablespoon olive oil

1. Wash the eggplants, remove the leaves of the crown without piercing the skin, and split them in half lengthwise. With a sharp knife, trace around the inside edges leaving about a ¼-inch border. Score the flesh diagonally in both directions, forming about ¾-inch squares (see illustration). Remove the flesh, cutting it into cubes. Scrape out any remaining pieces with a sharp-edged spoon or grapefruit knife, taking care not to pierce the skin. Place the shells in an oven-safe pan, brush them inside and outside with 1 tablespoon of olive oil, and season them with salt and pepper. Set aside.

2. Place the chicken in a large skillet, add water to cover, and bring it to a full boil. Turn off the heat, cover the pan, and let the chicken stand for about 10 to 12 minutes, or until almost cooked through. Remove it from the water and cut it into ¾-inch cubes.

3. Preheat your oven to 350°F.

4. While the chicken is cooking, heat the 2 tablespoons of olive oil until fragrant in a large, heavy skillet. Add the eggplant cubes and onion, and sauté them for 3 to 4 minutes over medium-high heat, turning often. Cover the pan and continue cooking the mixture for another 2 minutes, or until the eggplant cubes are softened but still hold their shape. Stir in the garlic.

5. Add the tomatoes, parsley, rice, orange juice, coriander, and fennel and bring the mixture to a boil. Adjust the heat to medium, stir in the pignoli, currants, salt and pepper, and chicken, and taste the sauce to adjust the seasonings. Cook gently for 1 to 2 minutes longer.

6. Spoon the eggplant mixture into the shell, mounding it in the center. Combine the bread crumbs with the ½ clove of garlic and ¼ teaspoon of salt, and sprinkle over the filled eggplant halves. Drizzle the remaining tablespoon of olive oil over the crumbs and place the pan in the preheated oven for 50 minutes to bake. The dish is ready when the crumbs on top are dark brown, the filling is hot, and a little liquid starts to run out from the eggplant shells. Remove and serve at once or let the dish cool to room temperature. This is a one-dish meal, and I would serve only crusty bread, if anything, with it. Place the eggplants on a bed of chicory leaves with a couple of cherry tomatoes for garnish, if desired.

DID YOU KNOW: By slicing and liberally sprinkling eggplants with salt (preferably kosher), then placing them between layers of paper towels in a colander, with a weight on top, you remove any bitterness and the eggplant will absorb less oil in cooking. Rinse and blot dry before cooking.

Stuffed Chicken Breasts Italiana

Serves 8

These rolled chicken breasts, filled with mushrooms, watercress, and ricotta cheese, are substantial enough to satisfy even the heartiest of appetites. Once the rolls have been quickly sautéed, the light, crunchy coating seals in the moisture and flavors before they are baked in the oven. When entertaining, you can roll and stuff the breasts a couple of hours ahead and refrigerate them. Cooked, they will even wait in a warming oven while you and your guests eat a first course. As a variation, mix a little cornmeal with the flour for coating the chicken.

Many butchers will flatten the chicken breasts needed for this recipe if you order them in advance.

8 half chicken breasts, skinned and boned (about 4 to 5 ounces each after boning)
2 tablespoons unsalted butter
1 tablespoon vegetable oil
1 medium onion, peeled and chopped
¼ pound white mushrooms, wiped, trimmed, and thinly sliced
1 cup whole-milk ricotta cheese
½ cup freshly grated Parmesan cheese
3 tablespoons finely chopped flat-leaf parsley
¼ teaspoon freshly grated nutmeg
⅛ teaspoon ground red pepper
Salt and freshly ground black pepper to taste
2 large bunches watercress, large stems removed
Flour seasoned with salt and pepper for dredging
2 eggs
4 tablespoons light or heavy cream
1 cup freshly toasted bread crumbs
Olive or vegetable oil for sautéeing the chicken
2 cups CHUNKY HOMEMADE TOMATO SAUCE (page 377), warmed
Finely chopped flat-leaf parsley, for garnish

1. If the butcher has not flattened the breasts, place them between 2 sheets of wax paper and pound them to an even thickness of about ¼ inch, using a meat pounder, side of a cleaver or chef's knife, or the heel of your hand. Working with the smooth side of the breast down, pound the flesh from the center of the breast toward the outside, taking care not to break through the meat. The small cutlets may be removed

and used for another dish. If used here, be sure to remove the tendon. Cover the breasts and set aside.

2. In a medium-size, heavy skillet, heat the butter and oil over medium-high heat. When the butter has foamed, stir in the onion and sauté it for 5 to 7 minutes until lightly colored. Add the mushrooms, and continue cooking for 2 to 3 minutes until they are wilted, stirring occasionally.

3. Combine the ricotta and Parmesan cheeses, parsley, nutmeg, red pepper, salt, and pepper in a large bowl. In a saucepan or bowl, blanch the watercress for 15 to 20 seconds in boiling water until just wilted. Drain it well, then transfer it to the bowl of a food processor fitted with a steel chopping blade, and process until somewhat smooth. Scrape the watercress into the bowl with the cheeses, sautéed mushrooms, and onions and mix well.

4. Place the chicken breasts vertically on a clean work space with the narrower end closest to you. Divide the stuffing equally, placing about 2 tablespoons onto the lower edge of each breast. Roll them up, turning in the sides to form a neat cylinder (see illustration).

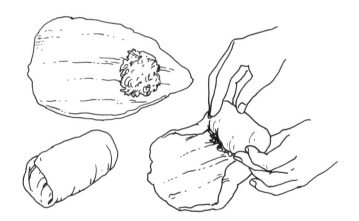

5. Fill a flat dish or pie plate with the flour. In another dish beat the eggs and cream. Fill the third dish with the bread crumbs. Roll each breast first in the flour, making sure to pat some on the ends, then dusting off any excess flour. Next dip it into the egg-cream mixture, and finally, roll the cylinder in the bread crumbs. Place the coated breast on a jelly roll pan or large flat plate and continue with the remaining breasts. Cover and refrigerate for 1 to 2 hours to seal the cylinders.

6. Preheat your oven to 350°F.

7. Add enough oil to a large, heavy skillet to measure ¼ inch in depth and heat it until very hot over medium-high heat. The surface will ripple. Place the rolls 1 at a time in the hot oil, taking care not to crowd them. If necessary, do this in batches. Using 2 wooden spatulas or spoons to help turn, brown the rolls evenly on all sides, approximately 5 to 6 minutes.

8. Once the rolls are golden brown, transfer them to a jelly roll pan with the aid of a wide spatula, and place them in the preheated oven for approximately 15 minutes to finish cooking. Test 1 breast for doneness by cutting partially into it to see that the meat is just cooked through. Remove the pan from the oven and place the breasts on a heated platter or individual plates. Ladle a large spoonful of sauce over the middle of each cylinder, and add a little parsley. Pass remaining sauce at the table. Serve with CREAMED SPINACH (page 411) and a timbale of rice.

NOTE: When preparing the chicken breasts ahead of time, reduce the cooking time to about 12 minutes, turn the oven down to the low setting, and leave the breasts for up to 30 minutes.

DID YOU KNOW? Remember that "a whole chicken breast" refers to both sides of the bird's breast. Chicken breasts are available whole, split (cut in half), and skinless and boneless in the market. If time is short, let the market do the work. Otherwise, save up to $.90 per pound and remove the skin and bones yourself. Follow the directions for boning the turkey breast (page 142), working the knife against the rib bones. In chickens, the flexible white part of the breastbone is cartilage. You can bend the whole breast in half widthwise, and it should separate from the bony part. Then, grab the top of the cartilage and pull it away from the flesh.

Sautéed Chicken Breasts in Dijon Mustard Cream Sauce

Serves 8

This lovely chicken dish is always well received because the breasts are so moist and flavorful. The generous layer of mustard shields the meat and becomes part of the delicious sauce. Originally, a French friend prepared this dish, and when told that my husband loved the chicken, she revealed that the "chicken had very floppy ears!" Her dish contained rabbit (which is equally delicious).

In a dish such as this one, I prefer chicken breasts on the bone. I think they are juicier.

2 tablespoons unsalted butter
2 medium onions, peeled and chopped fairly fine
4 whole medium-size chicken breasts, split, skinned, but *not* boned
Flour for dredging
Salt and freshly ground black pepper
8–10 tablespoons Dijon mustard
2 tablespoons unsalted butter
½–¾ cup heavy cream
Finely chopped flat-leaf parsley for garnish

1. Preheat your oven to 325°F.

2. In a large, heavy skillet, melt 2 tablespoons butter just until it foams. Add the onions and slowly sauté them over medium heat for 6 to 8 minutes until golden brown, stirring occasionally. Once the onions are colored, remove them with a slotted spoon, leaving as much butter in the pan as possible. Reserve the onions until later.

3. In the meantime, pat each breast dry with paper towels and sprinkle lightly with flour. Season with salt and pepper, and generously brush the mustard over the entire breast.

4. Add the remaining butter to the pan, keeping the heat at medium. When it is melted, add the chicken breasts flesh side down and cook until browned, about 8 to 9 minutes; then turn and continue cooking on the second side for another 7 to 8 minutes. Transfer the chicken to a heatproof platter and place it in the preheated oven for 15 to 17 minutes.

5. Turn the heat under the skillet up to high, return the sautéed onions to the pan, and stir in ½ cup of cream, scraping up all the browned cooking bits in the bottom of the skillet. Once the cream starts to

AS A VARIATION: If using rabbit for this dish, cut the skinned rabbit into large serving-size pieces and follow the directions for the chicken above. Cooking time will be about 2 minutes less on each side.

thicken, reduce the heat to medium and taste for seasonings, adding additional mustard, cream, or salt and pepper, to taste. Return the chicken to the pan; turn once or twice to cover with the sauce. Serve with a generous spoonful of sauce ladled over each breast and a little parsley sprinkled on top.

Basque Chicken in Red Wine with Olives and Peppers

Serves 6

I first tasted a rustic *coq au vin* simmered slowly in red wine years ago in the Basque region of southern France. Up to then, I thought of white wine for cooking chicken. In today's cooking, we are more inclined to use red wine with poultry and even fish where the other ingredients in the dish have strong flavors. In this version, colorful peppers and olives give this simple dish a robust taste.

When looking for cut-up chickens in your market, notice that packages labeled "quartered" or "cut up" fryers are usually the same price. For a stew, the advantage of the cut-up bird is that the almost meatless backbone and tail sections are generally cut away from the thigh and breast. Once the chicken is quartered, this is harder to do. Use these bones and the wing tips for stock.

½ pound thick-sliced bacon, cut into ¾-inch strips
1 3½-pound chicken, wing tips removed, cut into serving-size pieces and patted dry *or* 3 pounds thighs
2 large onions, peeled and coarsely chopped
1 large green bell pepper, seeds and membranes removed, coarsely chopped
1 large red bell pepper, seeds and membranes removed, coarsely chopped
1 tablespoon dried sage leaf, crumbled
1 teaspoon dry thyme leaves
1 cup oil-cured black olives
Salt and freshly ground black pepper to taste
1¼ cups hearty red wine

1. In a large, heavy casserole, cook the bacon over medium-high heat for about 2 to 3 minutes, until the pieces begin to separate and the fat has covered the bottom of the pan.
2. Add the chicken, skin side down, and cook for

10 minutes over medium-high heat to lightly color the skin. If the chicken sticks, use a spatula to loosen it. Turn the pieces, add the onions and peppers, and continue cooking for another 5 to 6 minutes. Drain the fat from the casserole.

3. Add the sage, thyme, olives, salt, and a liberal amount of pepper. Pour in the red wine, adjust the heat to high, and boil the liquid for 5 to 6 minutes to reduce it slightly, stirring and scraping up any browned cooking bits. Reduce the heat so the liquid is just simmering and cook for another 15 minutes, stirring occasionally. The chicken may be made a day or two ahead of time and slowly reheated.

Roasted Chicken with Apples, Cider, and Calvados

Serves 4 to 6

The Auge Valley in Normandy is justly famous for its apples and apple products: cider; cider vinegar; and calvados, or apple brandy. In the sauce for this crunchy roasted chicken, they are all combined with that other celebrated Norman product, cream, for a concert of subtle flavor variations. This would be a wonderful main course for an autumnal dinner party when apples and fresh cider are generally available in any market.

With fresh herbs found more frequently in markets, you might find fresh chervil. If you can add this subtle cousin of parsley to the dish, I think you will enjoy its delicate taste.

1 3-pound chicken
1 tablespoon unsalted butter, at room temperature
Salt and freshly ground black pepper
3 tablespoons finely chopped fresh chervil *or* flat-
leaf parsley
1 tablespoon unsalted butter, at room temperature
Salt and freshly ground black pepper
⅓ cup calvados or applejack
¾ cup heavy cream
2 tablespoons unsalted butter
1 tablespoon vegetable oil
½ cup finely chopped shallots
4 large Granny Smith or other tart apples, peeled,
cored, and cut into ⅛ths
½ cup cider, fresh if possible
1½ tablespoons apple cider vinegar
2 tablespoons unbleached, all-purpose flour
2 tablespoons unsalted butter, at room temperature
Salt and finely ground fresh black pepper to taste
Chopped chervil *or* flat-leaf parsley for garnish

1. Preheat your oven to 500°F.

2. Dry the chicken inside and out. Smear 1 table-spoon of butter inside the chicken cavity, season with salt and pepper, and add the chopped chervil. Massage 1 tablespoon of butter into the skin, and season with salt and pepper. Place the chicken, breast side up, on a rack in a shallow roasting pan just large enough to hold it comfortably. Place the pan in the middle of the preheated oven and lower the temperature to 425°F. Roast for 50 minutes.

3. Remove the pan from the oven and transfer the chicken temporarily to a platter. Take out the roasting rack. Drain the excess fat from the pan, add the calvados, and quickly scrape up the browned cooking bits from the bottom. Stir in the cream, return the chicken to the pan, and place it in the oven, leaving the oven on but the door slightly ajar. Cook for 20 minutes, basting twice.

4. While the chicken is roasting, melt 2 tablespoons of butter and the oil in a large, heavy skillet. When it has foamed, add the shallots and cook for 3 minutes over medium heat, until they are limp and translucent. Add the apples, turn once, cover, and let them cook for 8 to 10 minutes over medium heat, or until just softened.

5. When the chicken is done (the leg moves easily in the socket and the juices run clear when the thigh is pricked), drain the juices inside the cavity into the pan. Transfer the chicken to a heated platter and leave it in the turned-off oven while finishing the sauce.

6. On top of the stove, add the cider and vinegar to the roasting pan and bring the liquid to a boil. In a small dish, combine the flour with the remaining 2 tablespoons of butter to make a *beurre manié*. Stir small bits into the sauce until the sauce is thickened. Immediately stop the cooking and taste for seasonings. Stir the apples into the sauce. Cut the chicken into serving pieces or serve whole. Spoon the sauce around the chicken on the platter and garnish with a little chopped chervil or parsley.

Crunchy Oven-Roasted Chicken

Serves 2 to 4

In the hills of Tuscany, fresh chickens stuffed with garlic and herbs are roasted to crunchy perfection in wood-burning ovens. After watching an old farmer woman roast her chickens in high heat, I noticed that she left the oven door open for the last 20 minutes. This, she said, crisps the skin by allowing the moisture which might fall back onto the skin to escape. From that day I have propped my oven door open at the end of the cooking, and the chicken is both succulent and crisp.

In some markets "free-range" and "corn-fed" chickens are sold at the Service Meat Counter. Reputedly, birds fed on natural grains and allowed to roam free taste more like the chickens of years gone by. Corn-fed chickens also eat naturally, and so we benefit when eating them. It is worth investing once to see if you taste a difference in these birds. But be aware that the more hand-care the birds get, the costlier they are. Free-range chickens may be $4.00 per pound. Corn-fed birds are only about $.50 more a pound than commercially raised chickens, I buy these when I can.

DID YOU KNOW? If poultry has a "refrigerator smell," squeeze the juice of half a lemon inside the cavity to refresh it.

1 corn-fed chicken, if available, about 2½ to 3
   pounds (see Note below)
2 tablespoons olive oil
Salt and freshly ground black pepper
4 large fresh sage leaves
2 6-inch sprigs fresh rosemary, stems removed
2–3 large cloves garlic, peeled
Salt and freshly ground black pepper
3 tablespoons dry white wine
3 tablespoons water

1 Preheat your oven to 500°F.

2. Wash the chicken under cold water and dry it inside and out. Smear the inside of the chicken cavity with 1 tablespoon oil and season with salt and pepper. Chop the sage, rosemary leaves, and garlic until they are finely cut and mixed together. Add the herbs to the cavity.

3. Rub the remaining tablespoon of olive oil over the skin of the chicken. Place it breast side up on a rack in a shallow roasting pan just large enough to hold the chicken comfortably. Season with salt and pepper. Pour the wine and water around the chicken and place the pan in the middle of the preheated oven.

4. Adjust the heat to 425°F and roast for 50 minutes. If all the liquid in the pan evaporates during this time, add a little more water. Baste the chicken 2 to 3 times and prick the thigh joint with a fork to release any fat.

5. After 45 to 50 minutes, prop the oven door slightly open and continue cooking for another 20 minutes. Remove the pan from the oven, allow the chicken to rest for about 5 to 7 minutes, then cut it into serving pieces. Serve with ZUCCHINI GRATIN (page 263).

NOTE: For a larger chicken weighing 3½ to 4 pounds, roast the chicken about 20 to 25 minutes longer.

Devilish Crunchy Chicken

Serves 2 to 4

In Italy, this crunchy, piquant chicken is supposedly fare for the devil because of its charred flesh and peppery taste. The chicken is flattened and cooked in a cast-iron (or other heavy) skillet. Once you bite through the darkened exterior, there is succulent, heavenly meat.

1 2½ to 3-pound frying chicken, split in half
½ cup fruity olive oil
¼ cup fresh lemon juice
½ teaspoon Tabasco sauce
Salt and freshly ground black pepper to taste
1–2 large lemons, cut into wedges

1. Wash the chicken under cold water and pat dry. Remove the wing tips and discard them or save them for stock. Trim off excess skin and fat. With a sharp knife, make an incision between the leg and thigh, partially separating the two sections. Repeat with the breast and wing sections (see illustration). With the skin side up, flatten the chicken with a meat pounder, cracking the bones in several places. Remove broken pieces of bones.

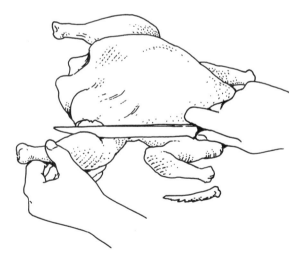

2. In a large bowl, combine the olive oil, lemon juice, and Tabasco sauce and stir to blend. Add the chicken, turning to cover with the liquid, cover the bowl, and let it marinate for about 2 to 3 hours in the refrigerator.

3. Heat a very large, cast-iron skillet over high heat until hot, about 3 minutes. Lift the chicken from the marinade and place it, skin side down, in the pan. Reserve the marinade. Place a flat oven-safe plate or large cake pan over the chicken. It should not be a tight-fitting lid that causes the chicken to steam. Weight it down heavily. I use a large saucepan or tea kettle filled with water.

4. After about 2 minutes, remove the weight, gently loosen the chicken with a spatula if it is sticking to the pan, and baste with some of the reserved marinade. Return the plate and weight and cook for 3 to 5 minutes longer, or until the skin is quite crisp and dark colored. Season the top side with salt and pepper. Turn the chicken, baste with more of the marinade, season with salt and pepper, and continue cooking the second side for 5 to 7 minutes, uncovered.

5. Transfer the chicken to a platter or individual plates, squeeze the juice of 1 lemon over it. Serve either a half or quarter chicken to each guest. Pass additional lemon wedges. Serve with a tossed green salad and rice, if desired.

DID YOU KNOW? While Tabasco sauce may change color from bright orange to rust over a period of time, it does not lose its peppery bite.

Warm Chicken Liver Salad with Red Peppers and Green Beans

Serves 3 for lunch

In an intriguing warm-cool combination of ingredients, sautéed livers are tossed with vibrant red pepper slices and green beans. The pan in which the chicken livers were cooked is deglazed with sherry vinegar, which blends with the olive oil to compose the warm vinaigrette.

Chicken livers freeze beautifully for up to 3 months if carefully wrapped in an airtight container. The plastic tubs from the market are fine if there are no cracks and the lid is tight fitting. Store fresh chicken livers in the coldest part of your refrigerator and use them within 2 days.

1 medium head romaine lettuce
½ medium bunch chicory
1 red or yellow bell pepper, seeds and membranes removed, cut into thin slices
6 ounces tender small green beans, ends removed
½ teaspoon salt
¼ cup fruity olive oil
2 tablespoons finely chopped flat-leaf parsley
1½ tablespoons fruity olive oil
8 ounces chicken livers, split and all membranes and fat removed, patted dry
3 tablespoons sherry or malt vinegar
2 large cloves garlic, peeled and minced
Salt and freshly ground black pepper to taste
¾ cup homemade croutons (optional)

1. Wash and dry the lettuce and chicory and break them into bite-size pieces, discarding the tough lower stems. Place them in a large salad bowl. Add the pepper slices to the bowl. In a small saucepan, bring water for the beans to a boil. Add the salt and beans and boil them for 3 to 4 minutes until wilted but still crisp. Drain and add them to the bowl.

2. Pour the olive oil over the vegetables, add the parsley, and toss.

3. In a medium-size skillet, heat 1½ tablespoons of olive oil until hot over medium-high heat. Add the chicken livers, shaking and turning them for about 3½ minutes, until they are cooked through. Add the sherry vinegar, raise the heat to high, and boil for about 30 seconds, stirring and scraping up any browned cooking bits.

4. Remove the pan from the heat, stir in the garlic, and then turn the hot vinegar and chicken livers over the salad. Season with salt and pepper, add the croutons, and toss very well. Serve at once. The lettuces wilt fairly quickly.

HAVE YOU TRIED? Look at the recipe for SAUTÉED CALVES LIVER LEBANESE STYLE on page 185. It would be just as wonderful prepared with chicken livers which have been sliced and sautéed like the calves liver.

Grilled Marinated Turkey Bites

Makes about 18 cubes

These slightly sweet and spicy morsels are an easy hors d'oeuvre to make, using the convenience of turkey breast meat and a glaze made from currant jelly, sherry, and soy sauce. If you are a dark-meat lover, the thigh meat may be substituted. Think of these nibbles when your barbecue is already fired up for a steak or chicken. Remember to soak your bamboo skewers for a couple of hours so they don't go up in smoke.

As with all meat and poultry marinades, this one should be discarded after use to prevent bacterial infections.

¼ cup currant jelly
¼ cup dry sherry
¼ cup soy sauce
1 large clove garlic, peeled and crushed
½ teaspoon ground ginger
10–12 ounces boneless skinless turkey breast, cut into 1-inch cubes
18 small (about 4 to 5-inch) bamboo skewers, soaked in water

1. In a small saucepan combine the jelly, sherry, soy sauce, garlic, and ginger and bring the mixture to a boil over high heat. Reduce the heat and cook just until the jelly is melted, about 2 minutes. Set aside to cool for 10 minutes.

2. Place the turkey cubes in a flat dish. Pour the marinade over them and toss. Cover and refrigerate the dish for at least 4 hours, turning once or twice. The turkey can be left in the marinade for a day or two.

3. Lift the cubes from the marinade, blot dry on paper towels, and place each cube on a skewer.

4. Adjust the grate of your barbecue to about 4 inches from the heat. When the charcoal is hot, place the cubes on the grill, and cook them for about 4 to 5 minutes on one side, turn them, and cook them for about 4 minutes longer on the second side. They should be nicely browned and cooked through. Place the skewers on a tray and serve them at once. They are delicious alone, or make a bowl of GINGERY PEANUT DIPPING SAUCE (page 368) to pass along with them.

Maria's Chicken and Sausage in Saffron Rice

Serves 4

During the years I lived in Paris, I remember eating this simple paellalike chicken dish often at the home of some friends who had a Portuguese cook named Maria. The wonderful aroma that wafted through the house while it was cooking drew me to the kitchen as soon as I entered the door. When I lifted off the lid, there were the familiar brilliant yellow rice, bright green peas, chunks of garlicky sausage and chicken to feast on.

Because I love the wonderful floral scent of basmati rice, I use it here instead of American long-grain rice (either will work). I also like turkey kielbasa (Polish sausage) for its spicy flavor and lower fat content.

2 tablespoons unsalted butter
1 tablespoon vegetable oil
1 3- to 3½-pound chicken, quartered and patted dry
3 cups coarsely chopped onions, about 2 large onions
Salt and freshly ground black pepper to taste
¼ teaspoon crushed saffron threads
2½–3 cups chicken stock, heated
1 cup basmati or long-grain white rice
8 ounces turkey kielbasa, cut into ½-inch slices
¼ cup coarsely chopped flat-leaf parsley
1 cup frozen petite peas, defrosted

1. In a large, heavy casserole, heat the butter and oil over medium-high heat until hot but not smoking. Add the chicken, skin side down, and cook for 3 to 4 minutes until the skin is lightly browned. Turn and cook for another 3 minutes on the second side. Add the onions, and let them sauté for about 7 minutes, stirring occasionally, or until they are just starting to brown. Season with salt and pepper.

2. While the onions are cooking, add the saffron to the heated chicken stock to let it soften. Stir the rice into the casserole and let it cook for about a minute. Pour 2½ cups of chicken stock over the rice, add the kielbasa slices, raise the heat, and bring the liquid to a boil. Cover the pan, adjust the heat to medium-low so the liquid is just simmering, and cook for about 25 to 30 minutes, until the liquid is absorbed and the rice is tender. After about 20 minutes of cooking,

🛒 **DID YOU KNOW?** In the Deli and the refrigerated Packaged Meat departments, there is a whole range of products using turkey in place of other meats. Bologna, ham, and hot dogs made from turkey rather than pork or beef are usually dramatically lower in calories. But be sure to read the labels. Most of these products still contain almost as much sodium as their pork or beef counterparts.

check to see if there is enough liquid, adding the remaining stock as needed if the rice is not tender. At this time, stir in the parsley and peas, replace the cover, and finish cooking. The chicken should be cooked through and very tender.

Sautéed Turkey Cutlets in Lemon Butter

Serves 4

Turkey cutlets, thinly sliced and pounded until flat, are a splendid and economical alternative to veal. In fact, since turkey breasts are now sold whole, split, boneless, or cut into slices, it's even easier to try your favorite recipes using turkey. Look at the recipe for SAUTÉED VEAL CUTLETS WITH MUSTARD, CAPERS, AND PEPPERS on page 204. An added bonus is that turkey slices stay whole, whereas with veal, if the meat has been cut across muscle groups, you may find the sautéed cutlets breaking into pieces.

This classic version of quickly sautéed cutlets with lemon and butter added to the pan is a breeze for busy night meals, especially if the turkey is pounded in the morning and refrigerated until needed. When you are cooking, be sure to keep the butter and oil sizzling hot to quickly brown each cutlet as it is added to the pan. Otherwise, you will have gray, soggy meat.

2 tablespoons unsalted butter
2 tablespoons vegetable oil
1–1⅓ pound turkey breast, sliced and pounded to about ¼ inch thick (see Did You Know below)
Flour for dredging
Salt and freshly ground black pepper to taste
3 tablespoons fresh lemon juice
2 tablespoons unsalted butter, at room temperature
Finely chopped flat-leaf parsley for garnish
1 small lemon, thinly sliced, for garnish

1. Heat 2 tablespoons each of butter and oil in a large, heavy skillet over medium-high heat. As it is heating, lightly flour 1 cutlet, shaking off the excess flour. Once the butter has foamed and the fat is very hot, slide in the cutlet. If a second cutlet will fit without crowding, flour it quickly, and add it to the pan. The fat should sizzle with each addition.

2. After about 45 seconds or a minute, the cutlet

DID YOU KNOW? Once the raw turkey breast is sliced, there appears to be a thin tendon down the center of it. Do not try to remove it, as it disappears during cooking. However, the smaller cutlet(s) that is often connected to the whole or split turkey breast actually has a stringy tendon that you will want to pull out before cooking.

should be golden brown on the first side. Turn and cook the second side for 30 to 45 seconds. Once it is browned, transfer each cutlet to a warm platter and season with salt and plenty of pepper.

3. Once all the cutlets have been cooked, turn off the heat and add the lemon juice, stirring up all the browned cooking bits. Stir in the 2 tablespoons of softened butter.

4. Return the cutlets to the pan, turning them to cover with the lemon butter, then place them on heated plates. Pour any remaining sauce over the cutlets. Add a couple of thin slices of lemon overlapping on each cutlet and a little chopped parsley. Serve at once.

Lean and Moist Turkey Breast

Serves 6

This boneless turkey roast is so juicy, you might think you are eating a very pricey veal roast. Not only are turkey breasts low in cost, the calories are minimal, particularly when the skin is removed. Dijon mustard, paprika, and lots of parsley on the inside and pan juices deglazed with dry vermouth and orange juice for the sauce make this bird elegant and satisfying— even for Thanksgiving or Christmas. This turkey is also delicious sliced when cold. Serve it with CRANBERRY, PEPPER, AND ONION CONSERVE (page 85).

Thanks to contemporary marketing, turkey parts are now available across the country. They are a boon to small families, and all-white-meat or dark-meat lovers. Look for smaller whole birds, as well, available almost year around. Fresh turkey meat is best used within 2 days of purchase. Cooked turkey lasts for a week in your refrigerator if tightly wrapped in plastic.

1 4½-pound whole turkey breast, boned and
   skinned (2½ pounds boned and skinned weight)
3 tablespoons Dijon mustard
1 tablespoon paprika
¼ cup finely chopped flat-leaf parsley
Salt and freshly ground black pepper
1 tablespoon unsalted butter
1 teaspoon vegetable oil
1 teaspoon paprika
¾ cup dry vermouth
¾ cup orange juice

1. SKIN AND BONE THE TURKEY BREAST Carefully slide your fingers between the meat and the skin on one side of the breast close to the ribs. Grab hold of the skin and pull toward the breastbone. Repeat with the second side, pulling toward the center then up toward the wishbone. The skin should pull off. Use a sharp pointed knife to detach any skin and fat that remain.

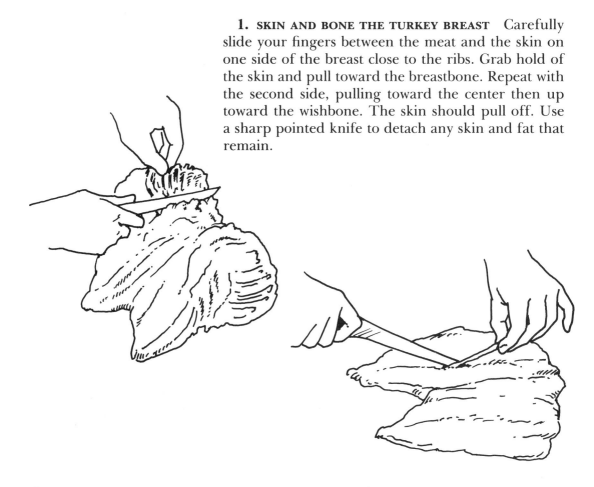

DID YOU KNOW? Although many turkeys come with pop-up timers, they are unreliable or broken far too often to be trusted. Instead, remove this timer and buy an instant-read thermometer, sold in the Meat department or on a "J" hook with other cooking tools, for a quick, accurate temperature check. You will be far more secure about the results.

Frozen turkeys are usually available in any market. Defrost them slowly on a plate in the refrigerator for minimal moisture and flavor loss. When slowly cooked and basted occasionally, they are fine eating. As for the frozen rolled turkey breast roasts, I much prefer to prepare my own. Mine are less expensive and the texture and taste are better.

2. With a sharp boning knife, carefully remove the flesh from the bones by scraping the knife against the rib bones working toward the breastbone. Once at the center bone, carefully work up the breastbone and cartilage, trying to avoid tearing the breast into two parts. (If it does tear, it is not critical, since the roast is tied together.) Repeat with the other side. Remove the tendons from the small cutlets by grabbing the tendon, and scraping the flesh away while pulling the tendon out (see illustrations).

3. Preheat your oven to 350°F.

4. PREPARE THE ROAST Place the breast outside down, with the tip and wishbone horizontal. Brush the inside and under the small cutlets with mustard. Sprinkle on the paprika and then the parsley, salt, and pepper. Roll the turkey from bottom to top, forming a cylinder. Tie it well with string in several places, including a couple of times lengthwise. The roll will measure about 3 to 4 inches in diameter.

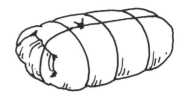

5. In a heavy, shallow, nonaluminum roasting pan or skillet, melt the butter and oil over medium-high heat just until it foams. Add the turkey and brown it on all sides, approximately 5 to 8 minutes. Sprinkle 1 teaspoon of paprika over the turkey, tent it with aluminum foil, and place the pan in the middle of the preheated oven.

6. Roast the turkey for approximately 25 minutes per pound, basting once or twice, or until a meat thermometer registers 145° to 150°F. Remove the foil for the last 20 minutes of cooking. Transfer the turkey to a platter and place it in the turned-off oven while finishing the sauce.

7. FOR THE SAUCE Deglaze the pan with the vermouth and orange juice, scraping up all the browned cooking bits. Turn up the heat to high, and boil the liquid until it is reduced and slightly thickened, about 1 to 2 minutes.

8. Remove the strings and let the turkey stand for a couple of minutes before slicing it into ¾-inch thick slices. Spoon the sauce over the slices before serving. Serve with HEARTY BULGUR PILAF (page 388). Fill the center of the ring with sautéed asparagus.

Two-Days-After Turkey Hash

Serves 2 to 3

If you think that you can't face another turkey sandwich after demolishing a large bird, try this old-fashioned hash for a weekend breakfast or lunch. What a great way to use up those small snippets of meat that are too small to slice. And, it's got just enough seasoning to lift the sautéed turkey, potato, onion, and corn mixture from the mundane to eye-opening satisfaction.

Many people love hash. Because supermarkets now sell turkey parts all year, this morning favorite can be made even when there are no leftovers.

1 medium all-purpose potato, scrubbed and cut into ¼-inch cubes (about 1 cup)
1½ cups cooked turkey, cut into ¼-inch cubes
¾ cup corn kernels, frozen or canned
1½ tablespoons grated onion
2 tablespoons finely chopped flat-leaf parsley
1 teaspoon Worcestershire sauce
¼ teaspoon dry mustard
¼ teaspoon dried thyme leaves
Salt and freshly ground black pepper to taste
2 tablespoons unsalted butter
1–2 tablespoons vegetable oil
¼ cup dry vermouth
2–3 poached eggs (optional)

1. Bring some water to a boil in a medium-size sauce pan. Add a little salt and the potato cubes. Cook for 2 to 3 minutes, until the potatoes are just cooked through; drain and leave them in a strainer to dry.

2. In a medium-size bowl, combine the turkey, corn, grated onion, parsley, Worcestershire sauce, mustard, thyme, salt, and pepper. Add the potatoes and mix well.

3. Heat the butter and 1 tablespoon of vegetable oil in a large, heavy skillet over medium-high heat. When the butter has foamed, add the hash mixture, flattening it slightly with a spatula. Let it cook for 15 minutes until it starts to brown on the bottom and become crusty. Turn it with a spatula, add another tablespoon of oil if it sticks, scrape up the browned bits, and cook for 6 or 8 minutes longer.

4. Pour the vermouth over the hash, and stir up all the browned bits on the bottom of the pan. Cook only 1 minute longer. Serve the hash on warmed plates, adding a poached egg on top of each serving, if desired. We like to eat toasted English muffins with our hash.

DID YOU KNOW? Most markets sell baked turkey breast in their Deli departments. Some also sell packaged "turkey rolls." Since these prepared products require a longer shelf life, many are heavily salted and preserved with chemicals. Be sure to ask whether the market sells sodium-reduced turkey if salt is of concern to your family. Read the label on the packaging to find out about added fillers, too.

Raspberry-and-Duck Salad with Raspberry Vinaigrette

Serves 4

Both the colors and combination of tastes in this dish are dramatic. Vibrant greens shot with ribbons of radicchio form the base of the salad. Add julienned strips of duck tossed with mushrooms, cracklings, and fresh raspberries in a raspberry vinaigrette, and this main course salad is a heavenly blend.

The duck for this salad is prepared in an unusual manner: It is skinned before being poached. I did this because I loathe eating fatty ducks, and I wanted to use the skin to make Cracklings (page 148). Some of the poaching liquid is also used in the vinaigrette.

FOR THE SALAD
1 4- to 4½-pound duck, split and skinned; reserve the skin for cracklings
1 cup chicken stock
Salt and pepper
1 small head Bibb lettuce, washed, dried, and torn (about 4 cups loosely packed)
1 small head radicchio, washed, dried, and cut into ½-inch strips (about 4 cups loosely packed)
1 large bunch arugula, washed, dried, and coarse stems removed (about 4 cups loosely packed)
4 ounces white mushrooms, wiped, trimmed, and thinly sliced
1 cup raspberries
Cracklings

FOR THE VINAIGRETTE
1 teaspoon green peppercorns in vinegar or brine, rinsed
¼ cup raspberry or red wine vinegar
6 tablespoons walnut oil
2 tablespoons poaching liquid
1 tablespoon chopped fresh tarragon *or* 1 teaspoon dried
Salt and freshly ground black pepper to taste

1. Preheat your oven to 350°F.
2. Place the duck, breast side up, in a flat pan. Pour over the chicken stock, season liberally with salt and pepper, cover with aluminum foil, and place in the oven for about 45 to 50 minutes, or until the breast meat is just cooked. Remove the pan from the oven and let the duck cool for 15 minutes, leaving it cov-

ered. Remove as much meat as possible, and cut it into thin strips.

3. While cooking the duck, cut up the skin and fat, and slowly sauté it in a large skillet over medium-high heat. When very crisp, discard the fat and blot the cracklings on paper towels.

4. In a large bowl, combine the lettuce, radicchio, and arugula, and toss. Add the duck, mushrooms, and cracklings.

5. PREPARE THE VINAIGRETTE In a small bowl, mash the green peppercorns. Add the raspberry vinegar, then whisk in the walnut oil. Whisk in the poaching liquid, tarragon, salt, and pepper. Pour the vinaigrette over the greens and toss. Add the raspberries and toss very gently. Serve at once. This salad wilts quickly.

Mushroom, Fennel, and Duck Stew

Serves 4

When I want roast duck, I prefer to eat it in fine restaurants where it is cooked so the skin is crispy and the bird is not fatty. At home, I like this wintery stew where the combination of the duck meat blends well with the braised fennel, mushrooms, and pearl onions.

Almost all the ducks in our markets are the Long Island variety, bred with a thick layer of fat to be juicy and tender. Once that layer is melted, not much meat remains, and an average roasted duck will feed only two people, unless it is cut up for a stew. Many supermarkets now sell fresh ducks along with excellent quality frozen birds. Use fresh and defrosted birds within a day or two.

6 ounces thick-sliced bacon, cut into ¾-inch strips
2 large shallots, peeled and finely chopped
1 large clove garlic, peeled and minced
3 large bulbs fennel, trimmed and quartered
12 ounces white mushrooms, wiped, trimmed, and
    quartered if large, whole if small
1 4- to 5-pound duck
2 cups chicken stock
12 ounces small boiling onions, peeled, with a
    small "X" in each root end *or* use frozen pearl
    onions
1½ teaspoons marjoram *or* 2 sprigs of fresh
    marjoram
1½ teaspoon dried thyme leaves
Salt and freshly ground black pepper to taste
½ cup medium-dry Madeira
2 teaspoons red wine vinegar
2 teaspoons cornstarch

1. Place the bacon in a large, heavy Dutch oven or casserole and turn the heat to medium. Cook the bacon uncovered for a few minutes until the pieces start to separate and the fat covers the bottom of the pot. Stir in the shallots and cook for 5 to 6 minutes until they are clear, then add the garlic and cook for 30 seconds longer. Add the fennel, stir to cover with the bacon drippings, and continue cooking, stirring occasionally to cook evenly, until the fennel has started to brown, about 30 minutes. Add the mushrooms to the pot and cook for 2 to 3 minutes longer. Set aside.

2. While the fennel is cooking, wash the duck, trim off any excess fat from around the neck and tail, reserving it for later (see Did You Know below). Cut off the legs and wings, discarding the wing tips or reserving them for later use with the heart, neck, and gizzard in stock. Chop the remaining carcass into small serving pieces. Remove any extra bones. Pat the pieces very dry on paper towels.

3. Preheat your oven to 325°F.

4. Place a large piece of duck fat in a large, heavy skillet and render it over medium-high heat until about 2 to 3 tablespoons of fat cover the bottom of the pan. Remove the remaining fat and discard, or retain it for another use. When the melted fat is very hot, add the pieces of duck, skin side down. Sauté them for 10 to 12 minutes, turning once, until they are light brown;

then transfer them to the pan with the fennel. Discard the rendered fat.

5. Adjust the heat to high; stir in the stock, onions, marjoram, thyme, salt, pepper, Madeira, and vinegar; bring the liquid to a boil; cover; and transfer the pan to the middle of the preheated oven for 1½ hours, until the duck is tender. Stir occasionally.

6. Remove the casserole from the oven and skim off the fat with a large spoon. Or let the duck cool, so the fat is more solid and remove from the top. Once the stew is degreased, place the casserole on top of the stove over medium heat. Dissolve the cornstarch in a little water, then pour it into the casserole, and mix well. Let the duck simmer for 3 or 4 minutes uncovered, then serve over buttered noodles. This stew may be prepared ahead of time and held over gentle heat for 45 minutes to an hour. Or prepare it up to 2 days ahead, refrigerate, then reheat it slowly.

Indian Game Hens Marinated in Yogurt and Spices

Serves 2

After 12 hours of marinating in yogurt and warm Indian spices, this split Cornish game hen bakes to incredible tenderness. Sure, it's low in calories and sodium, but the wonderfully intense aroma and taste never let you think about that.

Many markets only sell game hens in pairs. One bird will freeze beautifully if well wrapped. Or, double this recipe and serve 4. If your market only sells frozen game hens, defrost them slowly in the refrigerator and use them here without a problem.

1 1- to 1½-pound Cornish game hen
½ cup plain low-fat yogurt
1 small onion, peeled and grated
1 small clove garlic, peeled and crushed
2 tablespoons lime juice
1 teaspoon chili powder
1 teaspoon paprika
½ teaspoon cinnamon
½ teaspoon ground coriander seed
½ teaspoon ground cardamom
⅛ teaspoon ground clove
Pinch of ground red pepper
½ teaspoon salt, or to taste
1 tablespoon vegetable oil
½ tablespoon unsalted butter

AS A VARIATION: In place of Cornish game hens, use a skinned frying chicken cut into serving-size pieces and double the quantity of yogurt and spices. It will serve 4. Or, buy just enough chicken thighs to serve 2 and follow the recipe exactly. In either case, cut into a piece of chicken to be certain that it is completely cooked.

1. Split the Cornish game hen in half, removing the backbone and tail. Cut off the wingtips and pull off the skin. Set the hen aside in a nonaluminum baking dish.

2. In a small bowl, combine all the remaining ingredients except the butter and spread this mixture over the game hen. Cover and refrigerate for 12 hours, turning the bird 1 or 2 times.

3. Preheat your oven to 325°F.

4. Heat the butter in a medium-size, oven-safe skillet or casserole over medium-high heat. Scrape the yogurt mixture from the game hen and place it skin side down in the hot butter. Sauté the bird for 2 to 3 minutes, until lightly browned on the flesh side. Turn the bird back over, pour the yogurt mixture back over the game hen, and transfer the pan to the preheated oven. Bake for about 15 to 17 minutes, or until the meat is cooked through.

5. Remove the pan from the oven and transfer the game hen to heated plates. On top of the stove, bring the yogurt mixture to a boil over high heat. Cook for 1 to 2 minutes until it is slightly thickened, then spoon it over the game hen. Serve at once with saffron rice, if desired. Or, leave the game hen to cool, and serve it with the ORANGE, JICAMA, WATERCRESS, AND OLIVE SALAD (page 92) for a good combination of flavors and textures. It is wonderful at room temperature.

Caribbean Game Hens

Serves 4

The sunny flavors of the Caribbean—coconut, banana, ginger, red pepper, and saffron—are blended into the spicy sauce for this tropical dish. Slowly simmered Cornish game hens are a succulent and economical main dish, even for a party. With a very large casserole (or two), you can double or triple this recipe.

Fresh game hens will last 2 days in the coldest part of your refrigerator. They are often found in the Frozen aisle, and properly wrapped, they will last for up to 9 months in your freezer. The plastic wrap should have no holes or tears. If it does, rewrap the birds before freezing to prevent freezer burn.

1 coconut, broken into pieces; reserve the milk
Milk to combine with the coconut milk to make
   1½ cups
¼ teaspoon crumbled saffron threads
2 tablespoons vegetable oil
2 Cornish game hens, about 1½ pounds apiece
Salt and freshly ground black pepper
1 lime
1 small orange
1 tablespoon vegetable oil, if necessary
2 cups finely chopped onions
1½ tablespoons minced fresh ginger
1 very ripe banana, mashed
½ teaspoon red pepper flakes
Salt and fresh ground black pepper to taste

1. Preheat your oven to 325°F.

2. Place the coconut pieces, shell side down, directly on the rack in the oven. Bake for about 10 minutes, or until the coconut meat is easily removed from the shell with a sharp knife. Chop enough coconut into small pieces to make 1½ cups.

3. Combine the coconut milk and regular milk in a medium-size saucepan. Add the fresh coconut, bring the liquid to a boil, then reduce the heat and simmer the milk for 30 minutes. Strain the liquid through a fine strainer into a bowl, stir in the saffron, and set aside.

4. While the milk is simmering, cut the remaining coconut into very thin slices. Scatter them on a cookie sheet and bake them in the oven for about 25 minutes, until toasted and medium brown. Set aside.

5. Wash the game hens under cold water. Cut them in half along the breastbone. Cut the back in half, cutting along the ribs, and removing the backbone. Split the halves into quarters, removing any excess fat. Pat the pieces very dry with paper towels.

6. In a large, heavy casserole heat the oil until very hot. Place the pieces in the pot, skin side down, adding only enough pieces as fit comfortably in the pot without crowding. Cook for about 2½ to 3 minutes over medium-high heat, until the skin is lightly browned. Turn and cook the second side for 2 to 3 minutes. Transfer the browned pieces to a bowl and continue until all the game hens are cooked. Season with salt and pepper.

DID YOU KNOW? If you don't find saffron on the shelf with the other spices, ask at the front desk. Often this golden spice is kept under lock and key because it is packaged in small bottles and is relatively precious. Figure that the saffron in this recipe will add $1.00 to the cost of the dish. While powdered saffron is wonderful, and it dissolves almost instantly, don't use a powdered substitute that some markets sell. Although the dish will turn yellow, the warm flavor of this spice will be missing.

7. Remove the lime and orange zest and mince; set aside. Squeeze the juice from the fruit. There should be about 6 tablespoons.

8. If the oil has burned, throw it out and add 1 tablespoon of oil to the pot. When it is hot, stir in the onions and sauté them over medium heat for about 5 minutes until wilted, stirring often. Add the fruit juice, adjust the heat to high, and boil the liquid until it is reduced by half.

9. Turn the heat down to medium, and whisk in the coconut milk, stirring continuously to blend well. Stir in the ginger, mashed banana, red pepper flakes, toasted coconut, and salt and pepper. Return the game hens to the casserole, cover, and simmer them in the liquid for about 25 minutes, turning the pieces over once or twice. The meat should be cooked through by this time. Serve immediately or leave on very low heat for up to 2 hours. Serve with basmati rice or orzo.

Pheasant Pâté

Serves 12

This elegant, spicy pâté, with a mosaic of smoked ham and pistachio nuts, is one of my favorite hors d'oeuvres for holidays. For New Year's Eve, I bake the pâté at least a week in advance and then refrigerate it to allow the flavors to mellow. The pale pink pâté looks especially festive when presented on a bed of chicory with small bunches of red grapes.

Along with duck, squab, and other game birds, pheasants have come into the market, as well. While they are often sold frozen, I have purchased fresh birds in a number of markets—especially those that have Service Meat departments. A simple rule of thumb: Find out what day the store received its pheasants. If they are more than a day old, make another choice. Use all poultry within a day or two.

1 pheasant, skinned and boned (2 to 2½ pounds
  dressed weight), fresh or defrosted
1 pound ground veal
8 ounces pork fat
3 eggs, beaten
6 ounces thick-sliced smoked ham *or* Canadian
  bacon, diced
⅓ cup shelled pistachio nuts
½ cup finely chopped shallots
10 juniper berries, crushed
1 teaspoon ground thyme
¼ teaspoon ground nutmeg
1 tablespoon salt, or to taste
Freshly ground black pepper
½ cup Madeira
¼ cup brandy
12–16 ounces fatback, sliced about ⅛ inch thick
  and simmered for 2 minutes, patted dry (see the
  suggestion on page 195 for slicing fatback)
2 bay leaves

1. Preheat your oven to 350°F.

2. Reserve half of the breast meat for later. Add the remaining pheasant meat, ground veal, pork fat, and eggs to the bowl of a food processor fitted with a steel chopping blade and pulse until a somewhat smooth texture is reached. *Do not overprocess* or the pâté will become too uniform and compacted in texture. This may need to be done in batches if the processor is small.

3. Transfer the mixture to a large bowl and stir in the ham, nuts, shallots, juniper berries, thyme, nutmeg, salt and pepper, Madeira, and brandy with a wooden spoon. Cook a small amount of the pâté mixture in a skillet to taste for seasoning. The pâté should be highly seasoned.

4. Line a 9 × 5 × 3-inch loaf pan or 6-cup terrine with fatback slices, extending them so they may be folded back over the top of the pâté. Pack half of the mixture into the mold, patting it down into the corners. Cut the remaining half breast into thin strips and place them over the meat mixture. Add the remaining pâté mixture, place the bay leaves on top, and turn the pork slices back over the meat. Cover with a double layer of heavy foil, and punch a hole in the middle for steam to escape.

DID YOU KNOW? You may have to ask the butcher for pork fat for this recipe. When pork comes into the store, it is usually trimmed, and the fat is discarded. Give the Meat department a little time while you shop, and you will have it, often with no charge. Or, call in advance to be sure. However, if there is no fresh pork fat available, use fatback which has been simmered for 2 minutes, then blotted dry and minced.

5. Place the pâté in a larger pan and fill it with boiling water. The water should come half way up the side of the pâté mold. Bake in the preheated oven for 1½ to 1¾ hours. When it is done, the juices will run clear and the pâté will have shrunk slightly from the pan.

6. Remove the pans from the oven, lifting the pâté from the water. Place about 8 ounces of weight evenly distributed on the pâté. (Another loaf pan with a pound of dried beans inside will work well.) Let the pâté cool for an hour, then refrigerate it with the weight. Remove the weight after several hours. This pâté is best when made at least several days in advance. To serve, remove the pâté from the pan. Scrape off the fat, leaving the fatback lining, if desired. Cut into ⅓-inch slices and serve it with pumpernickel or dark whole grain breads, and Dijon mustard or CRANBERRY, PEPPER, AND ONION CONSERVE (page 85).

Jack Daniel's Roasted Pheasant on Braised Cabbage

Serves 2 to 3

Once, when cooking for a great American lady living near Venice, Italy, I deglazed the pan in which I had roasted a pheasant with her favorite libation, Jack Daniel's. To keep the bird tender and moist, I buried it under a mound of caramelized cabbage and onions while it cooked. The results were spectacular—if a little unusual. While the bourbon packs a good punch, the final addition of cream softens and balances the flavor. This is an easy dish to prepare for a special autumn dinner.

Since the pheasants that you find in a supermarket are usually pen or ranch raised, they never develop the strong "gamey" flavor of wild birds—nor are they as tough. Hanging a bird whole with feathers for several days tenderizes the meat and develops the flavor in young birds. This is done especially in Europe where strong tastes are more appreciated. Americans tend to prefer milder flavors, and many pheasants are sold already skinned and frozen. Freezing tenderizes them by breaking down the meat fiber and protects them from deterioration.

2 tablespoons unsalted butter
2 tablespoons vegetable oil
2 large onions, peeled and coarsely chopped
1 tablespoon unsalted butter
1 large green or white cabbage, approximately 2½ pounds, cored, tough ribs removed, and shredded
Salt and freshly ground black pepper to taste
7–8 juniper berries, crushed
1 pheasant, cleaned and skinned or plucked (approximately 2 to 2½ pounds dressed weight)
2 tablespoons Dijon mustard
1 medium onion stuck with 6 cloves
Flour for dredging
1 tablespoon unsalted butter
½ tablespoon vegetable oil
2 generous slices of fatback, blanched
½ cup Jack Daniel's or bourbon
1 cup heavy cream

1. In a large, deep casserole, melt 2 tablespoons of butter and 2 tablespoons of oil over medium-high heat. When it has foamed, add the chopped onions and sauté them over medium-high heat for 6 to 8 minutes, until lightly colored.

2. Add 1 tablespoon of butter and the shredded cabbage and continue cooking for 35 to 40 minutes, stirring occasionally, until the cabbage is caramelized and medium brown in color. Use a combination of uncovered and covered cooking. As moisture evaporates and the cabbage browns, cover the pan to prevent burning. When a lot of moisture forms on the cover of the pan and drops onto the cabbage, remove the cover, stir the cabbage to incorporate the liquid, and continue cooking. Repeat as necessary. Season generously with salt and pepper and stir in the juniper berries. Set aside.

3. Preheat your oven to 350°F.

4. Wash the pheasant under cold water and dry well. Season the cavity with salt and pepper. Paint the inside of the bird with Dijon mustard and place the whole onion inside. Tie the legs together and turn the wing tips under. Lightly dredge the pheasant in flour.

5. In a heavy skillet, heat 1 tablespoon of butter and ½ tablespoon of oil. When it has foamed, add the pheasant and brown it lightly on one side. Turn and continue cooking until all sides are colored. Do this quickly. It will take about 6 to 8 minutes.

6. Transfer the pheasant, breast side up, to the casserole with the cabbage. Place the slices of fatback on the breast, pack the cabbage around and over the bird, and cover the casserole. Place the pan in the middle of the preheated oven for 35 to 45 minutes depending on the size of the bird. Baste with the pan juices 1 or 2 times during this time.

7. Remove the pan from the oven, push the cabbage off the pheasant into the pan, and discard the fatback. Return the pan to the oven and continue cooking uncovered for 10 minutes more. Test for doneness by pricking the thigh. If the juices run clear, and the thigh moves easily in its socket, the bird is done.

8. Remove the pan from the oven, discard the onion, and drain the juices from the inside of the pheasant into the casserole. Transfer the pheasant to a heated platter, and leave it in the turned-off oven while finishing the dish.

9. On top of the stove, add the Jack Daniel's, adjust the heat to high and boil the liquid for 2 to 3 minutes, stirring often to prevent the cabbage from burning. Add the cream, turn the heat down to medium, and continue cooking for 3 to 4 minutes. Either present the bird whole and carve it at the table or cut it into pieces and serve it on the bed of cabbage. Serve with sautéed spinach or green beans.

NOTE: If pheasants are unavailable or not your favorite bird, substitute a small roasting chicken. Or use 2 Cornish game hens and roast for about 20 minutes. In both cases, skinning is not necessary, but be sure to brown the birds.

DID YOU KNOW? If you are given a pheasant by a hunter friend, be sure to probe any little dark spots with the tip of a knife. There may be birdshot there, which is tough on teeth and stomachs.

Roasted Squabs Stuffed with Porcini and Chestnuts

Serves 8

This dish reminds me of the fall in Tuscany when porcini mushrooms and squabs are both in season. Squabs (or pigeons) have a special flavor all their own that complements a well-seasoned stuffing. Here, porcini and chestnuts are combined with sausage meat, currants, and marsala. The roasted birds are served with a sauce made from deglazed pan juices and red grapes. Reminder: Provide extra napkins for this rustic dish; guests may want to pick up the bones with their fingers.

Because some forward-looking supermarkets are aware of the current interest in game birds, it is not unusual to find quail, pheasant, and squab in the Poultry department in season. In stores with a Service Meat Counter, they may be special ordered.

8 1-pound squabs, cleaned
Juice of 1 lemon
Freshly ground black pepper
2 ounces dried porcini mushrooms
1 tablespoon olive oil
1 6-ounce sweet Italian sausage, casing removed
1 large onion, peeled and chopped
2 medium-size stalks of celery, trimmed and chopped
24 chestnuts, freshly roasted, *or* 1 15½-ounce can unsweetened chestnuts, drained and chopped
½ cup currants
⅓ cup marsala
3 tablespoons finely chopped flat-leaf parsley
1 teaspoon salt or to taste
Freshly ground black pepper to taste
¼ cup toasted bread crumbs
3 tablespoons olive oil
2 sprigs fresh rosemary *or* 2 tablespoons dried rosemary (see Note)
8 slices bacon
1½ cups dry vermouth
1 tablespoon unsalted butter, at room temperature (optional)
1 tablespoon unbleached all-purpose flour (optional)
Salt and freshly ground black pepper to taste
48 seedless red grapes, stems removed, washed

1. Wash the squabs under cold water. Remove and discard any excess fat. Dry them well and squeeze the juice of the lemon inside the cavities. Season with a liberal amount of black pepper.

2. Place the porcini mushrooms in a bowl and cover them with warm water. Let them soak for about 25 to 30 minutes until soft. Transfer the mushrooms to a clean bowl, removing all the grit and fibrous pieces, and coarsely chop. Reserve until later. Pour the liquid through several layers of cheesecloth or a fine strainer lined with paper towels and transfer it to a saucepan. Bring the liquid to a boil, cook until the liquid is reduced to ½ cup, and set aside for use in the sauce.

3. In a large, heavy skillet, heat 1 tablespoon of olive oil until hot and fragrant. Add the sausage meat, breaking it into small pieces with a wooden spatula or spoon. Continue cooking over medium heat for 4 or 5 minutes, until the sausage is no longer pink. Stir in the onion and celery and cook over medium-high heat for 5 minutes until clear. Add the porcini, chestnuts, currants, marsala, parsley, and salt and pepper; stir to blend well. Raise the heat to high and let the liquid boil until it is almost completely reduced, about 2 to 3 minutes. Add the bread crumbs and mix well.

4. Divide the stuffing among the squabs. Tuck the wings back and tie the legs together. In a large, heavy casserole, heat 3 tablespoons of olive oil until fragrant. Add the birds a few at a time, making sure to keep the oil hot. Turn them to brown on all sides. Set the birds aside. Throw out the fat and add the vermouth, stirring up the browned bits.

5. Place 3 or 4 rosemary leaves on each bird and wrap with bacon slices; return them, breast side up, to the casserole. Turn the heat to medium, cover the pot, and cook slowly for 35 to 40 minutes, basting twice during this time. Birds are done when the thigh moves easily in the socket and the juices run clear when the thigh is pricked.

6. Remove the birds to a heated ovenproof platter. Discard the bacon. If the birds are not brown enough, run them quickly under the broiler. Skim off as much fat as possible from the casserole. Deglaze the pan with the vermouth scraping up any browned cooking bits; boil until almost completely evaporated. Add the reduced mushroom liquid, and return to a boil. If a thicker sauce is desired, combine the softened butter and flour and stir it into the liquid in small lumps.

DID YOU KNOW? It is far safer not to stuff a squab, turkey, or chicken ahead of time because of the possibility of salmonella poisoning. Rather, prepare the stuffing ahead, if you like, and refrigerate it. Fill the chest cavities close to cooking time or bake the stuffing separately.

Immediately turn off the heat. Season with salt and pepper. Stir in the grapes to heat them through. Place the birds on heated plates and ladle a large spoonful of the sauce over them. Serve with sautéed baby green beans and HOLIDAY CRANBERRY CARROTS (page 31).

NOTE: To refreshen dried rosemary leaves, place them in a small bowl with some hot water for about 2 minutes. Drain and blot dry.

Roasted Squabs Stuffed with Turnips, Olives, and Figs

Serves 4

The unusual combination of ingredients in the stuffing for these squabs adds an intriguing complex dimension to the final flavor. Sautéed turnips impart a hint of caramel sweetness that plays off the slightly salty olives, and the tangy lemon juice. It's a great dish for cold-weather dining.

Squabs are young birds that generally weigh between 14 ounces and a pound. They are small in size with plump, meaty legs and are much prized for their sweet eating by game fanciers.

FOR THE STUFFING
4 tablespoons unsalted butter
2 tablespoons vegetable oil
4 cups grated white turnips, about 6 medium turnips, peeled
2 small onions, peeled and finely chopped
8 ounces cultivated mushrooms, wiped, trimmed, and thinly sliced
1½ cups sliced pitted California black olives
2 tablespoons finely chopped flat-leaf parsley
½ cup coarsely chopped dried Mission figs
4 tablespoons fresh lemon juice
Salt and freshly ground black pepper to taste

FOR THE SQUABS
4 fresh squabs, dressed, livers reserved and cleaned
1 tablespoon unsalted butter
1 tablespoon vegetable oil
4 slices bacon
¾ cup Madeira
1 tablespoon unsalted butter
½ cup split pitted California black olives
1 tablespoon lemon juice

1. Preheat your oven to 400°F.

2. **PREPARE THE STUFFING** In a large, heavy skillet, melt the butter and oil over medium-high heat just until it has foamed. Add the turnips and cook them over medium heat until softened and lightly browned, about 10 minutes. Stir them often. Add the onions, mushrooms, and sliced olives and continue cooking until the mixture is fairly dry and the mushrooms are wilted, about 6 minutes. Add the parsley, chopped figs, lemon juice, salt, and a liberal amount of black pepper; stir; and cook for about 30 seconds longer. Set aside.

3. **STUFFING THE BIRDS** Dry the squabs and generously season the insides with salt and pepper. Fill each cavity with the prepared stuffing, tie the legs together, and turn the wing tips under (*or* truss each bird). There will be extra stuffing, which can be put into individual buttered soufflé dishes or custard cups, covered with foil, and baked with the squabs.

4. Melt 1 tablespoon of butter and oil in a large, low baking pan on top of the stove just until the butter foams. Place the birds breast side down over medium-high heat for 2 to 3 minutes to brown the skin. Discard the fat. Turn the birds breast side up and place 1 slice of bacon over each bird. Transfer the pan to the preheated oven and roast for 23 to 28 minutes. Prick the thigh; if the juices run clear and the thigh moves easily in the socket, the birds are done.

5. Remove the squabs from the oven, remove the bacon, untie or untruss, season with salt and pepper, and place the birds on a warm platter in the turned-off oven.

6. Strain the pan juices into a medium-size skillet, skim off as much fat as possible, add the Madeira, and bring the mixture to a boil over high heat. Boil until reduced by half. Mash the reserved squab livers into this mixture, and cook for 30 seconds longer. They will thicken the sauce. Add 1 tablespoon of butter, and the split olives. Taste to adjust the seasonings, adding more lemon juice, if needed. Serve the squabs on a bed of polenta or orzo. Spoon the sauce over them. Turn out the stuffing that has been baked in soufflé dishes and serve alongside.

Surviving the Supermarket: A Lighter Look at Food-Shopping Dilemmas

Most people responsible for purchasing food go to the supermarket at least a couple of times a week, whether for major shopping or just to pick up a couple of needed items. Sometimes this activity is leisurely; more often, it is done under pressure. Some shoppers go alone; others have a family in tow, or in the basket. Between changing displays and new products, improved technology and mix-ups, shopping does require a sense of humor. Whether a novice or an expert, you may experience some of the following supermarket snafus.

THE STOP-AND-STARE SYNDROME

Most often this occurs when moving from a metropolitan-size market to the suburbs with giant supermarkets. Invariably, the shopper is left pondering the wide choices of sizes and brands.

VISITING THE LAND OF THE LILLIPUTIANS

Rather than expanding aisles into non-existent floor space, some smaller markets build ever-higher shelves. The problem is trying to reach the jar on the top without toppling the jars on the two shelves below, or to pull out "your" color paper towels from under a pile. In super-large markets, maneuvering around the never-ending expanse of floor space makes roller skates a tempting solution.

THE SHOPPING-BASKET MIX-UP

Most likely to occur when you have done almost all of your shopping, carefully selecting the only perfect melon in sight and special ordering your meat. Some victims become irate and scream for their lost basket; others ask for assistance over the loudspeaker. The worst recorded example of this syndrome is the woman who checked out and wheeled her groceries to her car, only to discover that she had the wrong food and the wrong child.

DOUBLE TROUBLE

When mothers take their children shopping, often two tots fill one basket, dropping pieces of bagels or cookies along the way, while Mom drags another basket in tandem. Watch these trollies around corners or in crowded Produce departments where the couplings may come undone, followed by large sobs.

THE HOARDERS

These folks think that if an item is on sale or the weather is bad, they are the only ones who are entitled to a lifetime supply of the product. With baskets piled high, collisions are inevitable. It is, of course, never their fault. They also think nothing of making several trips to redeem a limited-quantity coupon.

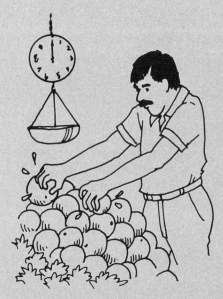

THE PINCHERS, POKERS, AND SAMPLERS

It's OK to gently feel produce and meat for intelligent buying, but some zealous shoppers persist in bruising and nearly destroying food. Others leave unwanted perishables or partially opened packages on grocery shelves to spoil.

THE ENDLESS END CAPS

The problem here is figuring out if the giant mountain of paper towels marked $.95 a roll on display at the end of an aisle is really a bargain. Items put on display *may* be marked at a promotional price. But, then again, they may not. The frustration is having stocked up on the item, only to discover that there is no savings.

THE DEMONSTRATION DILEMMA

A free taste of a new product often leads to increased sales. This is fine until the aisles are so crowded with demonstrators and people sampling that you can't move. Some families think that this is a great way to feed themselves for free, and stick around far longer than they are welcome to. And where do you put those toothpicks once you've taken a bite? On the floor to clog the wheels of baskets, right?

SINGLES NIGHTS/CONTESTS/LIVE ENTERTAINMENT

A little amusement never hurts when time is not pressing. But, when all you want to do is get in and out of the market in a hurry, these "new-age" entertainments are far from appreciated.

THE SHORT-LINE TWO-STEP

To make a faster exit, some shoppers rapidly switch from one check-out lane to the next, even if this means putting food back in their baskets and making other shoppers back up.

THE FRAGILE-FOOD COMPACTORS

Perishable and delicate foods are scattered throughout the store. It's a difficult puzzle fitting them into a basket without smashing the bread or bruising the berries. So where does the bread end up after it's bagged? On the bottom or crammed along the side of a bag.

EXPRESS-REGISTER CONCESSIONS

Often a misnomer, "express lanes" get more congested than other lanes when customers don't respect the limitation on the number of items, forget to have checks approved, or suddenly dart back for a forgotten item on the other side of the store.

ELECTRONIC CONFUSION

Now that laser-read UPC codes have replaced price markings on many items, you may become mesmerized by the light and noise as each item is scanned. Total pandemonium is likely to break loose if you question a transaction or the "system is down."

And that's just getting out of the market. . . .

·4·
MEATS: BEEF, LAMB, PORK, VEAL, AND GAME

INTRODUCTION

Something wonderful is happening in some supermarket Meat departments: along with familiar cases piled with cellophane-wrapped pieces of meat, new (or we should say "oldtime") Service Meat departments are making a comeback. In consumer-oriented stores, butchers have come out from behind glass walls and stand ready to talk to you with counters full of unwrapped specialty cuts of familiar meats, "value added" items (partially prepared or stuffed meats and poultry), and unfamiliar game meats. Customers need personalized—not automated—a.tention to decipher the many variables that can save time and money. When questions are answered and recipes offered, sales are brisker.

Butchering has changed over the years, and so has the meat in your market. The beef and pork industries are breeding leaner animals for our health-conscious society. Animals arrive already cut up. Beef is no longer aged as it once was, making the question, "Can I get a good steak anymore?" as valid in a supermarket as a butcher shop. (The answer varies with each market. Some markets sell great steaks.)

If no butcher is in sight and the clerk seems uninterested, an aware shopper with basic meat-buying skills is still far ahead of the game. Fortunately, food safety is still a primary concern of most every market. They make it a rule to use only USDA inspected meat, which means the animal was healthy and was processed in a sanitary packing house. In general, markets only sell the top two grades of meat: prime and choice, the latter having a higher percentage of internal fat.

There are some other important facts you should ascertain on your own for economical and healthful buying.

Find out either from the label or the butcher *which primal section* of the animal the piece of meat comes from.

Especially in beef and pork, cuts from the working parts—the chuck, shank, brisket, plate, flank, and round—are leaner, tougher, and more sinewy than the more tender rib, loin, and sirloin, from the middle or support section of the animal. Since the muscles in this area do little work, they de-

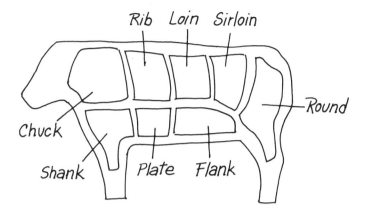

velop more marbling (internal fat) to keep the meat moist and juicy.

Where the meat comes from should determine *the most appropriate cooking methods.*

Tougher cuts will become tender with slow, *moist cooking*: braising, stewing, or simmering, or by being marinated first.

Tender cuts should be cooked with *dry heat* methods: broiling, frying, or barbecuing. But, since there is no additional moisture added to the meat, overcooking (past medium) is likely to produce dry meat. This is especially important with newer varieties of beef and pork bred to be lower in fat and cholesterol. For maximum flavor and juiciness, cook them to a lesser degree of doneness.

Lamb is butchered young, so the locomotive parts do not have a chance to toughen and most parts may be cooked with dry heat.

Veal never develops any internal fat to moisten it, so it is best cooked with moisture (except the thinnest cutlets).

Once you settle on a specific cut, look at the piece of meat itself.

Meat needs some *marbling* for tenderness and flavor. The marbling should run evenly through the meat. On the other hand, a thick layer of fat on the outside is not healthful, it is wasteful. Why should you pay for what will be discarded? Meat should be well trimmed, including tails from tougher adjoining muscle groups which will not cook the same as the whole.

Excess *bones* are another problem, especially with packaged meat. When you cannot see the underside, gently press the meat to feel for concealed or wider bones or gristle underneath.

Color may be an indicator of age and tenderness. The older an animal gets, the darker the meat becomes. Young beef is bright red. Top quality veal should be whitish pink—not dark rose. However, exposure to air and packaging can affect color, as well.

If the meat is wrapped, be certain that the *package is sealed*. Exposure to air leads to bacteria formation and quality deterioration.

One of the best sources of information about the meat you plan to purchase is the label already glued on the wrapped meat or affixed once the butcher weighs it. It tells you:

the weight
the price per pound
the cost of this package

1.56 lb $2.79 $4.35
NET WT.   PRICE PER LB.   TOTAL PRICE

BONELESS PORK LOIN
ROAST-RIB END

FEB 2
SELL BY

the kind of meat
the primal part
the specific cut of meat
the date it must be sold b

Other sources of information about meat cookery are:

Butchers can tell you about cooking times and temperatures, give you recipe ideas, and may suggest a less expensive or more appropriate cut of meat for a specific recipe.

Printed information cards and pamphlets are now frequently displayed on the meat cases. Pick them up for tips on cooking new recipes, nutritional information, and entertaining ideas.

Cookbooks and magazines are sold in many markets.

Since meat is extremely perishable, proper handling is vital.

Choose meat after staples and other less-fragile items.

Don't leave meat in a warm car for extended periods of time.

Refrigerate meat in the coolest part of the refrigerator as soon after arriving home as possible. If it is very warm, first place it in the freezer for about 15 minutes to cool it down fast.

Different cuts of meat vary in the length of time they remain fresh. As a general rule, the smaller the cut, the more perishable it is, because there is more surface-to-air exposure. Ground meats and organ meats should be used within a day or two.

If the meat will not be used within the time suggested (see tips throughout this chapter), then wrap and freeze it until ready to use. For short periods, it may be frozen in the store packaging if it is sealed.

Defrost meat on a plate in the refrigerator. Be sure to wash any plate used for defrosting or marinating before reusing it to serve cooked meat.

For cooking meat to perfection, a thermometer is a must. I feel the best available are the instant-read ones that often are merchandised in Meat departments. One ruined roast costs more in money and inconvenience than the price of a good thermometer.

One final bit of advice: Remember to remove your meat or fowl from the oven when the internal temperature measures 5 to 10 degrees below the desired temperature. Once outside, food will continue to cook those last degrees before serving. This is called the "carry-over cooking time," and it can make the difference between perfection and a near miss.

Brown Meat Stock

Makes about 6 quarts

A good, flavorful brown stock is the basis for many soups, stews, and sauces. With properly browned bones and vegetables and long, slow simmering, a rich caramel flavor will permeate the broth. When the stock is done, skim the surface of all fat, and refrigerate or freeze it.

When the stock is boiled until it is reduced in half, it becomes a *demi-glace*; when it is very thick and gelatinous it is a *glace de viande* or meat glaze. To make 1 cup (16 tablespoons) of meat glaze, you must boil down 32 ounces (4 cups) of stock. The flavor is very intense. A little of this "amber gold" added to any dish will dramatically enrich the flavor. It's worth saving bones and trimmings in your freezer until you are ready to make stock.

5 pounds beef bones with some meat (shin, marrow, ribs), cracked if large
3 pounds meaty veal shanks or knuckles, cracked if large
2 leeks or the green tops of 4 leeks, trimmed, rinsed free of sand, and split in half lengthwise
5 large carrots, washed and cut into quarters
3 large unpeeled onions, split with 1 clove stuck in each half
2 large celery stalks including leaves, cut into quarters
8 quarts or more cold water
1 cup warm water
1 large clove garlic, unpeeled and split in half
5 sprigs flat-leaf parsley
3 sprigs fresh thyme *or* 1 teaspoon dried
10 black peppercorns
1½ teaspoons salt (optional, see Note)

1. Preheat your oven to 400°F.

2. Place the beef and veal bones in a large, shallow roasting pan, and roast the bones for 45 minutes to an hour, turning occasionally, until browned. Pour off almost all the fat. Add the leeks, carrots, onions, cut side down, and celery to the pan and roast about 15 minutes longer, or until the vegetables have started to brown and caramelize.

3. Transfer the bones and vegetables to a very large stock pot, add the cold water, and bring just to the

BE SURE TO see page 375 for how to "doctor up" a canned broth.

boil. Adjust the heat down, let the soup simmer, and skim off any scum that rises to the surface during the first hour. In the meantime, deglaze the roasting pan with the warm water, scraping up all the browned cooking bits with a wooden spoon, and add this liquid to the stock pot.

4. Stir in the garlic, parsley, thyme, peppercorns, and salt and simmer slowly partially covered for at least 8 hours, adding water as necessary.

5. Strain the stock into a large bowl or bowls, cover, and refrigerate overnight. Remove the layer of fat on the surface, and refrigerate or freeze until needed. *Or* return the stock to the pot, bring it to a boil, and boil rapidly to reduce it to a *demi-glace* or *glace de viande*. As the stock becomes thick, adjust the heat to low and watch it carefully to make sure it does not burn. *Glace de viande* may be refrigerated for several months or frozen. I cut mine into cubes and store it in small Ziploc bags.

NOTE: The vegetables and meat have a certain amount of natural salt. If you plan on making *glace de viande*, I do not feel that any additional salt is needed.

Made-to-Be-Leftover Meat Loaf

Serves 8 to 10

DID YOU KNOW? When preparing a dish with raw ground pork, such as this meat loaf or any pâté, *do not taste it raw* for seasonings. Instead, heat a few drops of oil in a skillet and cook a small amount of the meat mixture until it is browned and cooked through. Let it cool slightly and taste. Correct your seasonings accordingly.

Now that we are eating "comfort foods"—those treasured preparations we grew up on that made us feel good—meat loaf has come back into style. Actually, in our house it never went out of style, especially because the leftovers make great sandwiches. This is one of our favorite versions to make for picnics and summer buffets, as the chopped olives, capers, and Worcestershire sauce add plenty of flavor even at room temperature. We slice and serve it on dark bread with grainy Dijon mustard. MARINATED THREE ONION SALAD (page 46) is the perfect cool-creamy salad to serve with this.

For meat loaf, I find the combination of ground veal, pork, and beef gives the best flavor. Some markets even sell it this way—usually 2 parts beef to 1 part veal and pork. Be sure to check the package for added fillers and/or spices, though.

1½ pounds lean ground beef
¾ pound ground veal
¾ pound ground pork
1 small onion, peeled and finely chopped
1–2 large cloves garlic, peeled and crushed
⅓ cup chopped flat-leaf parsley
3 tablespoons Worcestershire sauce
½ cup pimento-filled green olives, chopped
½ cup drained and puréed canned Italian
  tomatoes
2 eggs, beaten
1 cup oatmeal
2 teaspoons salt, or to taste
Freshly ground black pepper to taste

1. Preheat your oven to 350°F. Line the bottom of a 9 × 4 × 3-inch loaf pan with a piece of wax paper brushed with oil on both sides.

2. Combine all of the ingredients in a large bowl and mix just until blended. Cook a small amount of the meat mixture in a skillet to test the seasonings.

3. Fill the loaf pan with the meat mixture, smoothing the top to make it even. Place the meat loaf on a jelly roll pan (to catch any spills), transfer it to the oven, and bake for 1 hour and 20 minutes. The juices will run clear when it is done.

4. Remove from the oven, and drain the excess juices. Do not weight it down, as the meat loaf will become dry. Either let it stand for 5 minutes, slice, and serve or remove it from the pan, wrap, and refrigerate until needed. Meat loaf tastes better if it is served at room temperature rather than very cold. Serve with cornichons, if desired, mustard, and French bread.

HAMBURGER HINTS Ground beef is sold in every supermarket I have ever walked into. Because it is reasonably priced, it is used in many dishes from tacos to meat sauce. While "hamburger" is a good meat choice in most supermarkets, there are some facts you should be aware of for using ground beef to its best advantage.

What's in a Name? The name "hamburger," or "chopped," or "ground" beef means that this product is made from 100 percent beef. No water, binders, or fillers may be added. It must be at least 70 percent lean meat.

How Lean Is Lean?

Many markets now label their ground beef by the percentage of fat in the mixture, i.e., diet or super-lean (10 to 12 percent). The level of fat is not regulated by the USDA. It is determined by the market itself, so the name might be confusing, and the ratio of lean to fat differs from one market to the next. Other markets designate which primal part of the animal the meat comes from, such as the round or chuck, assuming that the customer knows which cut is less fatty. Still another practice markets use is to grind the trimmings and less popular parts of the animal with enough fat to make the determined ratio of fat to lean.

Which Is the Best Choice?

There is more than one "best" choice, depending on how you use ground meat. For strict fat-controlled diets, the leanest meat obviously has the least amount of fat. *But* since fat also gives flavor and moisture to meat, super-lean meat may easily become dry and crumbly, especially if it is overcooked. It is best broiled to no more than medium rare.

Ground meat with a higher fat content is less expensive. If the meat is drained after it has been cooked, the actual amount of internal fat is very similar, although the quantity of meat is somewhat smaller. A hamburger made this way will be juicier and have more flavor.

Where the ground meat is well cooked and well drained, for meat sauce or tacos, even the least expensive meat is a satisfactory choice.

How to Store Ground Meat

As discussed in the introduction to this chapter, the smaller the cut of meat, the more surface area there is to be contaminated, and the quicker it should be used. All ground meats (beef, veal, pork, turkey, lamb) are highly susceptible to bacteria. Ask when the meat was ground. It should be sold within 24 hours. And don't buy an opened package.

Once home, store the meat in the coldest part of your refrigerator for up to 2 days. If the original container is torn or damaged, rewrap the meat in airtight packaging. If you will not use the meat within 2 days, freeze it and defrost at a later date. It will keep for up to 3 months.

If ground meat is used for hamburgers, freeze it in patties. It will lose less moisture when defrosted. Otherwise, smaller packages are still better to prevent large ice crystals from forming within the block of meat. Always defrost meat slowly in the refrigerator with a plate underneath.

Because there is a high risk of bacterial infection from ground meat, eating raw ground meat or steak tartare is risky. For health's sake, it is wiser to select the piece of meat from a Service Meat counter, if available, or buy it from a butcher, have it ground, and use it quickly.

And, don't forget to look at other ground meats. Lamb is wonderful for many ethnic recipes. Pork adds great flavor. And, ground veal, turkey, and chicken are lower-calorie alternatives to beef.

Beyond Plain Hamburgers

Beyond burgers on the grill, there are many internationally flavored hamburgers you can make. The following variations are only the beginning. Be creative and make your own. The recipe serves one. Broil, grill, or sauté each of the following to your own favorite degree of doneness.

Oriental Burger

5 ounces ground beef
1 water chestnut, minced
1 tablespoon chopped scallion
1 teaspoon hoisin sauce
½ teaspoon soy sauce
¼ teaspoon ground ginger

Mexican Burger

5 ounces ground beef
1 teaspoon minced pickled jalapeño pepper
½ teaspoon salt
Freshly ground black pepper

TOP WITH
1 tablespoon sour cream
1 tablespoon purchased or homemade salsa
2 thin avocado slices

French Burger

5 ounces ground beef
½ teaspoon minced shallot or onion
⅛ teaspoon dried tarragon, crumbled
Freshly ground black pepper
1 ounce Roquefort cheese, flattened into a disk to
  fit between the patties
1 tablespoon Dijon mustard

1. Mix the beef with the shallot, tarragon, and pepper. Divide it into 2 parts, and flatten them into disks. Put the cheese between the meat and mash it gently together.

2. After turning the hamburger, brush it with Dijon mustard while the second side cooks.

Ukrainian Cabbage Meat Soup —A One-Dish Meal

Serves 6 to 8

This hearty meat soup is perfect for a chilly winter evening when family or friends can gather around for steaming bowls of an Old World classic. The slowly simmered sweet-and-sour broth is rich with onions, cabbage, and fork-tender meat. Serve it topped with dollops of sour cream mixed with freshly chopped dill and big slices of dark pumpernickel bread. Add boiled potatoes, if you like.

Inexpensive beef shin bones, with marrow intact, impart a wonderfully rich flavor to a soup or sauce. If you'd like additional marrow, ask your butcher to save the bones after they remove and grind the meat. The bones are very reasonable. Look to see that the marrow is white and fills the bone.

3 tablespoons vegetable oil
6 pounds beef with shin bones
Salt and freshly ground pepper to taste
4 tablespoons vegetable oil
3 large onions, peeled and finely chopped
4 large carrots, scraped and finely chopped
3 large stalks celery, trimmed and finely chopped
3 tablespoons vegetable oil
2 large cloves garlic, peeled and minced
1 large cabbage (approximately 2½ pounds), cored and shredded
1 12-ounce can tomato paste
6 cups warm water
⅓ cup chopped flat-leaf parsley
10 cloves
1 large bay leaf
1 teaspoon celery seeds
3 tablespoons red wine vinegar
3 tablespoons dark brown sugar
¾ cup golden raisins (optional)
Salt and freshly ground black pepper to taste
½ pint sour cream
3 tablespoons freshly chopped dill *or* 1 tablespoon dried

1. In a very large, heavy casserole, heat 3 tablespoons of oil until very hot. Pat the meat dry and sauté it for about 3 to 4 minutes on each side, or until it is a rich brown color. Brown the meat in batches, without crowding. Remove the meat to a bowl, season liberally with salt and pepper, and set aside.

2. Heat 4 tablespoons of oil in the casserole until hot, then add the onions, carrots, and celery. Sauté them over medium-high heat for 4 to 5 minutes until softened.

3. Pour in the last 3 tablespoons of oil and sauté the garlic and cabbage for 1 to 2 minutes, stirring frequently. Cover the pot, turn down the heat to medium, and let the cabbage cook for about 15 minutes until it is wilted. Uncover the pan, raise the heat to medium-high, and cook for 5 to 7 minutes longer, turning the vegetables often.

4. Stir in the tomato paste, water, parsley, cloves, bay leaf, celery seeds, vinegar, brown sugar, raisins, and a liberal amount of salt and pepper. Bring to a boil, cover, and adjust the heat down so that the liquid is just simmering. Cook slowly for at least 2½ to 3

DID YOU KNOW? When browning meat, it is essential that the pieces are not crowded. Otherwise, the meat will steam and turn an unattractive gray color. The outside will not be seared and the juices won't be locked in. You will not get the nice browned bits that are often used to flavor soups and sauces.

hours, or until the meat is very tender. Skim off any fat on the surface. Cut the meat into chunks, removing the bones, if desired. I usually serve a bone with the marrow to each guest.

5. To serve, combine the sour cream with the dill. Ladle the soup into large bowls and top with a generous dollop of the sour cream.

My Dynamite, All-Time Favorite Chili

Serves 6 to 8

This heady, southwestern chili is great over rice, but look at the two unique ways of serving it that follow this recipe. They raise chili to new heights. In my house, we make huge quantities of chili, often with venison, which is also appearing more and more in good markets. The chili is then frozen in serving-size portions, so the kids can defrost it in the microwave. They like it ladled over toasted sourdough bread or hard rolls.

3 tablespoons vegetable oil
1 large onion, peeled and finely chopped
2 large cloves garlic, peeled and minced
1 small hot green chile pepper, seeds and
   membranes removed, minced (optional)
1¼ pounds beef round, cut into ½-inch cubes
¾ pound ground pork
1 28-ounce can crushed Italian tomatoes
3 tablespoons red wine vinegar
2 tablespoons and 2 teaspoons ground chili
   powder, or to taste
2 tablespoons ground cumin
2 tablespoons Worcestershire sauce
½ teaspoon ground red pepper, or more, to taste
1 large green bell pepper, seeds and membranes
   removed, and chopped
2 teaspoons salt, or to taste
Freshly ground black pepper to taste
1 10-ounce can red kidney beans, drained
3 tablespoons *masa harina* or fine cornmeal, mixed
   with a little water into a smooth paste (see Note)

1. Heat the oil in a very large skillet or Dutch oven over medium heat. Stir in the onion, garlic, chile pepper, and cook, stirring occasionally, until the onion is tender, about 5 minutes.

2. Add the cubed and ground meat, and continue

cooking until the meat is no longer pink, about 4 to 5 minutes. Stir in the tomatoes, vinegar, chili powder, cumin, Worcestershire sauce, ground red pepper, bell pepper, salt and pepper. Bring the mixture to a boil, then reduce the heat to medium and cook, uncovered, stirring occasionally, until the meat is tender, about 45 minutes to an hour. The stew should be fairly thick.

3. Stir in the kidney beans and the *masa harina* and heat through. Taste and adjust the seasonings.

NOTE: If your market does not have *masa harina* or cornmeal with the Mexican foods or other flours, the chili may be thickened by cooking it longer.

Spaghetti Squash Chili

Serves 8

Served with tortilla chips, ripe black olives, sour cream, and sliced green onions, this is a southwestern fiesta in its own serving dish. Cooked spaghetti squash is combined with the chili, and then the whole mixture is presented in the squash shell and garnished.

1 recipe MY DYNAMITE, ALL-TIME FAVORITE CHILI (above), heated
1 spaghetti squash, approximately 3½ pounds, rubbed with oil

1. Prepare the chili as directed.
2. Preheat your oven to 350°F.
3. Place the squash directly on the middle oven rack and bake, turning the squash once, for 45 minutes or until the flesh begins to give and to feel tender when pressed. Remove from the oven and cut in half lengthwise. With a spoon, quickly scrape out the seeds. With a fork, scrape out the flesh into spaghettilike strands, leaving about a ½-inch-thick shell.
4. Mix the squash strands with the hot chili and spoon it back into the shells. Decorate with sour cream, sliced olives, green onions, and tortilla chips.

Individual Chili Strudels

Serves 8

These individual strudels are fun fare for a casual party. Since each role is a single portion, they are perfect for a buffet table. Prepare them ahead of time (they even freeze) and add the cheese and festive garnishes of tomato wedges, black olives, sliced green onions, and chopped jalapeño peppers (found in the International section) just before serving. Look at page 344, for tips about working with phyllo.

1 recipe MY DYNAMITE, ALL-TIME FAVORITE CHILI (page 177)
12 leaves phyllo
6 tablespoons (¾-stick) unsalted butter, melted
1 cup (4 ounces) coarsely shredded Monterey Jack cheese
Tomato wedges, black olives, sliced green onions, and chopped jalapeño peppers, for garnish

1. Prepare the chili as directed, and chill.
2. Preheat your oven to 400°F. Grease a 15½ × 10½ × 1-inch jelly roll pan.
3. Place 1 leaf of phyllo on a towel with the long edge in front of you, and brush lightly with melted butter. Place a second leaf on top, and brush again with butter. Top with a third leaf (*do not brush with butter*), and cut the stack in half crosswise.
4. Spoon about ¾ cup chili along the near edge of each phyllo stack, leaving about a 1-inch border uncovered on each side.
5. Holding the towel corners nearest you, flip the towel up, causing the phyllo to roll over on itself and cover the filling. (You can do both stacks with one

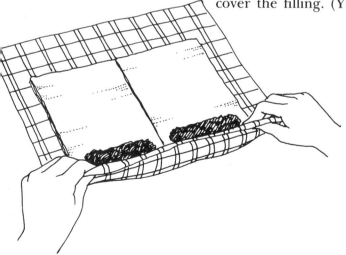

flip.) Turn the edges in over the filling and continue to roll 1 strudel at a time to the end. Carefully place each strudel on the greased pan, seam side down. Repeat 3 more times with the remaining chili and phyllo. Brush the strudel tops with melted butter, place the pan in the middle of the preheated oven, and bake for 12 to 14 minutes, until the strudels are crisp and golden brown.

6. If you have an attractive oven-safe serving platter, transfer the strudels to it, and sprinkle the cheese on top. (Otherwise, leave the strudels in the pan.) Return the strudels to the oven until the cheese melts, about 3 minutes. Remove the pan from the oven, garnish the strudels, and serve 1 strudel to each guest, placing some olives, onions, peppers, and tomatoes on each plate.

Belgian Beef Stew with Beer and Sauerkraut

Serves 8

A flavorful, slowly cooked stew is satisfying and economical. Many robust Belgian recipes use beer as the simmering liquid for the distinctive malty taste it adds while tenderizing the meat. In this dish, the flavors of the beer, tangy sauerkraut (which mellows during the long cooking), olives, and a touch of brown sugar, blend together into a hearty winter dish. Since stews taste better when made the day before, this one is ideal for a party or a busy household when preparing ahead is necessary.

Beef stew meat is readily available in your market. Look for cubes that have only a small amount of fat. Beef cut from the round is more expensive and leaner than stew meat from the chuck. Slow cooking tenderizes the meat and releases excess fat that rises to the surface of your stew. The greater amount of fat given off from cheaper cuts indicates there is less meat to serve. Stew meat should be refrigerated and used within 2 days of purchase. Otherwise, freeze it.

3 pounds lean stewing beef, cut into
   approximately 1½-inch cubes
Flour for dredging
3 tablespoons vegetable oil
2 tablespoons vegetable oil, if needed
2 large onions, peeled and thinly sliced
2 garlic cloves, peeled and minced
Salt and freshly ground black pepper to taste
1½ cups (12-ounce can) beer
2 pounds sauerkraut, rinsed and squeezed dry
2 teaspoons marjoram
2 tablespoons dark brown sugar
1 teaspoon celery seed
1 bay leaf
¾ cup pitted green olives, sliced
1 cup cream (optional)
½ cup finely chopped flat-leaf parsley for garnish

1. Preheat your oven to 325°F.

2. Dredge the meat in flour. Heat 3 tablespoons of vegetable oil in a heavy casserole with a cover or Dutch oven over medium heat until hot. Add only enough meat to cover the bottom of the pan without crowding and brown it on all sides, scraping and turning the cubes so they don't burn. Remove the meat with a slotted spoon to a bowl, and continue until all the meat is browned, adding fresh oil as needed.

3. If the oil has burned or more oil is needed, add the remaining 2 tablespoons of vegetable oil to the pot and, when it is hot, add the onions and cook for 6 to 7 minutes more, stirring frequently until they are light brown and soft. Stir in the garlic.

4. Add the meat, salt, pepper, beer, sauerkraut, marjoram, brown sugar, celery seed, bay leaf, and olives and stir to mix well. Cover and transfer the casserole to a preheated oven for 1½ hours. Stir occasionally.

5. After the meat is tender, remove the bay leaf, skim off any excess fat, and stir in the cream, if desired. Add the chopped parsley and serve with noodles or boiled potatoes. If you want to make this ahead for freezing, do not add the cream until after defrosting.

DID YOU KNOW? There are two ways of browning stew meat. One is to dredge the meat in flour, and then brown it. The second is to dry the meat very well, and brown it in very hot oil. (See HEARTY VEAL STEW WITH HAM AND ARTICHOKES on page 203.) The light flour coating on the meat thickens the sauce slightly in both cases. Otherwise, the sauce may be thickened later with a small amount of flour and water or boiled down to the right consistency.

Oven-Barbecued Chuck Steak

Serves 4

This fork-tender steak is not only easy to prepare, it utilizes the very reasonably priced blade (chuck) steak. Once the meat is seared, it is smothered with barbecue sauce, onions, sunchokes, and mushrooms and braised in a *very slow* oven. This is a good method to use with any of the less tender cuts of meat.

When buying meat with the bone in, be sure to let your fingers feel through the packages to find out how much bone there actually is. Turn the package over to look at the underside if you can see it. There can be a large difference from front to back and from one package to the next. Consider, too, how well the meat has been trimmed of fat. Remember that internal fat, or marbling, makes meat tender and adds flavor as it melts during cooking.

1 tablespoon vegetable oil
2 pounds blade (chuck) steak, patted dry on paper towels
1 cup SPICY TOMATO CHILI BARBECUE SAUCE (page 378) or purchased barbecue sauce
1 large onion, peeled and thinly sliced
8 ounces sunchokes, scrubbed and thinly sliced
6 ounces white mushrooms, trimmed, wiped, and sliced
Freshly ground black pepper to taste

1. Preheat your oven to 250°F.
2. In a heavy oven-proof skillet or casserole, heat the vegetable oil until hot but not smoking. Add the meat and brown it on the first side, about 3 minutes. Turn it and brown the second side.
3. Spread the barbecue sauce over the meat, add the sliced onion, sunchokes, and a liberal amount of pepper. Cover with foil or a tight-fitting lid and place in the preheated oven for about 2½ hours. Uncover, add the mushrooms, and allow the sauce to thicken for another 20 minutes, basting the meat occasionally. Serve with cornbread and MEXICAN COLE SLAW (page 28).

NOTE: If using a larger or smaller cut of meat, I estimate about 45 minutes cooking time for each ½ pound of meat *including* the final 20 minutes when the pan is uncovered.

Marinated Steak Teriyaki

Serves 4 to 5

A marinade not only tenderizes meat, it imparts flavor and is a preservative. For this Oriental-flavored flank steak, I found that several days (up to a week) in the spicy honey-soy-wine liquid actually improve the texture and taste, while one day is not enough. In general, marinating works best with thinner pieces of meat, chicken, and fish where the acidic liquid has a chance to penetrate completely. (This marinade, by the way, is equally wonderful for chicken breasts or shrimp.)

Teriyaki steak is great grilled on a hot barbecue. The meat quickly sears on the outside and remains rare inside. Flank steak is a very lean and economical cut, since there is no waste and it will keep in the refrigerator for up to 5 days. Frozen airtight, these steaks last for 6 months providing the temperature remains at 0 degrees or below.

⅓ cup soy sauce
3 tablespoons red wine vinegar
¼ cup honey
¾ cup vegetable oil
2 chopped scallions, including the green parts
2 large cloves garlic, peeled and crushed
1½ tablespoons ground ginger
1½ teaspoons ground coriander seed
2 teaspoons ground cumin
1½ teaspoons ground cardamom
Freshly ground black pepper
¾ cup pineapple juice
½ cup red wine
1 1¾- to 2-pound flank steak

1. In a medium-size mixing bowl, combine the soy sauce, vinegar, honey, and oil. Stir in the scallions, garlic, ginger, coriander, cumin, cardamom, and black pepper, and mix well. Add the pineapple juice and red wine.

2. Place the flank steak in a flat, nonaluminum roasting pan just large enough to hold the meat. Pour the marinade over the meat. Cover the pan and refrigerate for at least 4 or 5 days, turning the meat once a day.

3. Position the rack of a barbecue about 4 inches from the fire. When the charcoal briquettes are gray

and hot, remove the steak, pat it dry with paper towels, and place on the grill. Discard the marinade. Cook the steak for about 5 to 7 minutes on the first side, turn and cook another 5 or 6 minutes on the second side. Remove the meat from the grill, let it stand for 1 or 2 minutes, then cut it into thin diagonal slices across the grain of the meat. For the broiler, preheat the pan in the broiler for at least 10 minutes. Cook the meat close to the heat for the same length of time, leaving the door slightly ajar. Serve teriyaki with boiled rice and sautéed pea pods and water chestnuts.

Steak 'n' Stout

Serves 4

When I have a steak, I love it grilled: crunchy on the outside and deep pink inside. While this steak sears on the barbecue, the stout-brown sugar marinade reduces over mounds of onions into a caramelized glaze. Served together, it is a heavenly summer treat.

There are two reasons for buying meat with the bone in: the cooked meat is juicier and more flavorful, and, it is less expensive. When selecting cuts of meat with a bone in, look carefully at the ratio of bone to meat and how well the meat is trimmed. Sometimes a large "tail" is left on a porterhouse or T-bone. That piece is wasteful, since it is less tender than the rest of the steak. Even if you have it ground you are paying too much for it. Sirloin steaks cost less than steaks cut from the short loin (porterhouse, club, T-bone). Although less tender, they are fine in this barbecued version, especially since the meat is served sliced.

1 12-ounce bottle stout or dark beer
¼ cup firmly packed dark brown sugar
2 tablespoons cider vinegar
1 clove garlic, peeled and split
1 bay leaf
2½–3 pounds sirloin (or porterhouse or T-bone) steak, bone in steak, about 1¼ inches thick
3 tablespoons unsalted butter
1 tablespoon vegetable oil
4 large yellow onions, peeled and thinly sliced
Salt and freshly ground black pepper to taste

DID YOU KNOW? To test the heat of a charcoal barbecue, place your hand palm side down at cooking level. If you can keep it there for 2 seconds, the temperature is hot; 3 seconds is medium hot; 4 seconds is medium; and 5 seconds is low. Thicker foods require slower cooking temperatures to prevent burning.

SUPERMARKET SMARTS: Winter is a good time to buy and freeze steaks if you have the space, since they are less expensive than in the popular summer barbecue season. Wrap the steaks well, mark the date of purchase, and the amount of meat. They will last for at least 6 months.

1. Prepare the marinade by combining the stout, brown sugar, vinegar, garlic, and bay leaf. Place the steak in a glass or other nonmetal container just large enough to hold the meat and pour the marinade over it. Allow the steak to marinate at least 1 hour, turning after ½ hour. (The meat may marinate several hours.)

2. In the meantime, melt the butter and oil in a very large, heavy skillet just until the butter foams. Add all the onions and stir. Adjust the heat to medium-high and continue cooking for 30 minutes, stirring often, until the onions are wilted and lightly colored. Add about ½ teaspoon salt, or to taste, and freshly ground black pepper and set aside. (This first part of the onion preparation may be done ahead of time.)

3. Light a charcoal fire and place the rack about 3 inches from the heat. When the charcoal briquettes are very hot, remove the steak from the marinade and cook it for about 9 to 10 minutes on the first side. Turn and cook the second side for another 4 to 5 minutes for medium rare.

4. While the steak is barbecuing, add 1 cup of the marinade to the onions and turn the heat up to high. Allow the liquid to evaporate, stirring the onions often. This will take approximately 6 to 8 minutes.

5. When the steak is done, transfer it to a wooden slicing board and season it with salt and freshly ground black pepper to taste. Let it stand for 2 to 3 minutes, then slice it. Serve the onions on top of the steak or as a bed under the meat slices.

Sautéed Calves Liver Lebanese Style

Serves 2

This is one of the most delicious ways I have ever tasted liver. Thin strips are marinated in a garlic-mint mixture for about a half an hour and then quickly sautéed. Because the cooking time is so quick, all that garlic (3 cloves) is only warmed through and never gets a chance to become bitter. I serve the meat over mashed potatoes or cooked orzo to catch every drop of the sauce.

Properly prepared, liver is very tender. Of all liver sold, calves liver has the most delicate flavor and is the most expensive. Some markets sell "baby beef liver" at a price between beef and calf liver. Butcher friends of mine tell me this is most often from a full-

grown animal, so the higher price is not justified. Lamb liver tastes almost identical to calves liver, and the price is usually half, so the savings are great. Select dark-red-colored liver—without any discolored spots.

1 tablespoon minced garlic (3 large cloves)
1 teaspoon salt
¼ cup olive oil
1 teaspoon dried mint leaves, crumbled
Freshly ground black pepper
8–10 ounces calves liver, sliced ½ inch thick
2 tablespoons fresh lemon juice

1. Combine the garlic and salt together in a medium-size bowl, mashing the garlic with the back of a spoon. Stir in the olive oil, mint leaves, and plenty of pepper.

2. Cut the liver into 1 × 2-inch pieces and add it to the bowl with the garlic mixture, stirring to cover. Let the liver marinate for 30 minutes.

3. Heat a large, heavy skillet over medium-high heat. Add the liver-and-garlic mixture, stir, and turn the pieces just until the liver is cooked through, about a minute and a half. Remove the pan from the heat, stir in the lemon juice, and serve at once.

Moroccan Lamb in Peppers

Serves 4

Here is a chance to use the beautiful colored bell peppers we find in the Produce section. Why not use different colors and exchange the tops—a yellow pepper with a red cap? These individual serving containers are filled with an exotic combination of lamb, almonds, dried fruits, and spices.

We often read the term *Spring Lamb* in this country; it used to indicate a young animal. In fact, with modern breeding, we can buy very tender young lamb almost year round, since the shepherd hardly ever walks down the side of the mountain anymore. Another excellent option is frozen New Zealand lamb. The flavor may be slightly stronger than American lamb, but the meat is sweet and the price is often below fresh lamb. Properly stored, you can keep larger cuts of fresh lamb for 5 to 6 days in the refrigerator. Stew meat should be used within 2 to 3 days. Cook thawed meat within a day.

4 large bell peppers (about ½ pound each), red, yellow, or green
1 pound ground lamb
½ cup drained and chopped canned Italian tomatoes
½ cup dark raisins, soaked 20 minutes in warm water and drained
⅓ cup coarsely chopped pitted prunes
¼ cup slivered blanched almonds
1½ tablespoons vegetable oil
½ pound very well-trimmed lamb stew meat, cut into ¾-inch cubes, patted dry
1 small onion, peeled and finely chopped (about ½ cup)
2 cloves garlic, peeled and minced
¼ cup orange juice
2 tablespoons finely chopped flat-leaf parsley
1 teaspoon ground ginger
1 teaspoon ground cumin
¼ teaspoon ground red pepper
1½ teaspoons salt, or to taste
Freshly ground black pepper to taste
1 egg, beaten
½ tablespoon vegetable oil

1. Preheat your oven to 325°F.

2. Cut off the stem end of the peppers about ½ inch from the top and remove the seeds and white membranes. If the peppers do not stand up straight, slice a very thin layer off the bottom as well. Save the tops and set aside.

3. In a large bowl combine the ground lamb, tomatoes, raisins, prunes, and almonds. Set aside.

4. In a large, heavy skillet, heat the vegetable oil. When hot, add the lamb cubes and cook over medium-high heat, stirring often, just long enough to brown lightly on all sides, about 2 to 3 minutes. With a slotted spoon, transfer the cubes to a bowl with the ground lamb mixture.

5. Add the onions to the skillet and sauté over medium heat just until the onions are wilted, about 1½ to 2 minutes. Stir in the garlic, cook for 30 seconds, then add the orange juice. Bring the mixture to a boil. Stir up any browned cooking bits and cook over medium-high heat until the liquid has almost evaporated. Scrape the onions into the bowl with the meat mixture, add the parsley, ginger, cumin, red pepper, salt and pepper, and beaten egg, and mix quickly until just blended.

6. Brush the peppers and tops with the remaining oil and place them in an 8- or 9-inch pie plate or round baking dish. Divide the filling among the peppers, replace the tops and bake in the preheated oven until the peppers are tender when pierced with a fork and the meat juices run clear, about 1 hour to 1 hour 10 minutes. Serve with cooked pilaf or orzo seasoned

Javanese Lamb Stew with Peanut Sauce

Serves 6 to 8

The combination of peanut butter and molasses in this sauce is surprising. But, try it. I think you will be pleased with both the delicious results and the reasonable cost. Served in a large earthenware bowl, this lamb stew is inviting on winter buffet tables.

Like most stews, the flavors improve with gentle cooking and reheating—a boon to do-ahead party planning. Another entertaining idea: Double the recipe and freeze half for another night when unexpected guests arrive or you don't feel like cooking. (Be sure to check the Strategy Pages on Freezing.)

4 tablespoons vegetable oil
3 pounds well-trimmed lamb stew meat, cut into
    1½-inch cubes
2 large cloves garlic, peeled and crushed
6 tablespoons soy sauce
1½ tablespoons dark molasses
½ cup smooth peanut butter
⅓ cup dark brown sugar
4 tablespoons fresh lemon juice
¼ teaspoon ground red pepper
Salt and freshly ground black pepper to taste
½–¾ cup water
½ cup chopped peanuts
3 tablespoons chopped fresh coriander (cilantro)
    or chopped flat-leaf parsley, for garnish

1. In a large, heavy casserole, heat 2 tablespoons of the oil over medium-high heat until hot. Add just enough lamb to cover the bottom of the pan without crowding and brown on all sides. Remove the pieces with a slotted spoon to a bowl. Continue until all the meat is browned, adding additional oil as needed.

2. Add the garlic and, after a few seconds, the soy sauce, molasses, peanut butter, brown sugar, lemon juice, red pepper, salt and pepper. Stir, scraping up any browned cooking bits, and mix well. Stir in ½ cup of the water. Return the meat to the casserole, cover, and simmer until the meat is very tender, stirring occasionally, about 40 to 45 minutes. If the sauce becomes too thick, add the remaining water. A few minutes before serving, stir in the chopped peanuts. Sprinkle with the coriander or parsley before serving. Serve with steamed white or brown rice, or couscous, and SAUTÉED SNOW PEAS, RADISHES, AND CHERRY TOMATOES (page 51).

Braised Lamb Shanks with Glazed Lemon and Orange Slices

Serves 4

These slowly cooked lamb shanks are succulent and tender. The meat literally falls off the bone into the slightly sweet tomato sauce flavored with citrus slices, honey, and cinnamon. This dish is ideal for preparing ahead of time as the flavors improve with reheating.

Lamb shanks are easily found in your market. Even through the plastic wrap you can check that the bones have a little red in them. That lets you know that they are fresh and that the animal was not too old. As shanks come from the front legs, the working part of the animal, they have lots of connective tissue, which is tough. With moist cooking (braising), this breaks down and adds a rich flavor to the broth.

2 tablespoons olive oil
4 1- to 1¼-pound lamb shanks, patted dry
1 medium onion, peeled and finely chopped
1 large lemon, thinly sliced
1 navel orange, thinly sliced
1 28-ounce can Italian tomatoes, drained and
  chopped
¾ cup beef stock
⅔ cup hearty red wine
¼ cup honey
1 stick cinnamon
Salt and freshly ground black pepper to taste

1. Preheat your oven to 325°F.

2. In a large, heavy casserole, heat the oil until almost smoking over medium-high heat. Add the lamb shanks and brown them on all sides. This will take about 15 minutes. (If you cannot fit all the shanks in without crowding, brown 2 at a time.)

3. Stir in the onion, adjust the heat down to medium, and cook until the onion is wilted and pale, about 4 to 5 minutes.

4. Add the lemon and orange slices, tomatoes, stock, wine, honey, cinnamon, salt, and pepper and blend. Bring the liquid to a boil, stir to combine the ingredients, cover the casserole, and transfer it to the preheated oven.

5. Bake the lamb shanks until they are very tender, about 1 hour and 45 minutes. Remove the cover, skim off the fat, and return the pot to the oven, partially covered, for another 15 minutes, turning the shanks a couple of times during this time. Serve over cooked pasta or bulgur.

Rack of Lamb Persillade

Serves 2 to 3

Everyone seems to be delighted with rack of lamb. It is such a festive dish and very easy to make. It is as simple to cook 6 racks (if you have the pan and oven space) as one. The meat should come out of the oven slightly undercooked, as the "carryover cooking time" continues the roasting process for another 5 to 10 minutes before carving. Just remember that you will need help carving the racks into chops if you are serving individual plates. And, those plates need to be warm.

Racks of lamb are expensive, so look carefully at what you are buying, and make a friend of the butcher. He will help you select racks that have a large eye (center portion), since almost all the fat needs to be cut off. The mustard and flavored breadcrumbs in this recipe seal in the juices. The lamb is so juicy and delicious I serve it without a sauce. If you would like a sauce, BÉARNAISE SAUCE (page 278) is a classic.

1 rack of lamb (approximately 1½ pounds),
  trimmed with the chine bone removed
1 tablespoon olive or vegetable oil
⅓ cup homemade toasted bread crumbs
2 tablespoons finely chopped flat-leaf parsley
1 small clove garlic, peeled and finely minced
¼ teaspoon salt
Freshly ground black pepper
1½ tablespoons Dijon mustard
2 tablespoons unsalted butter, melted

1. Preheat your oven to 400°F.

2. Make sure the rack has been well trimmed (Frenched) and that all excess fat has been removed. Brush with the oil and place it fat side down in a heavy, low baking dish in the preheated oven for 15 minutes.

3. Meanwhile, combine the bread crumbs, parsley, garlic, salt, and pepper in a small bowl. Turn the rack over. Brush the mustard over the lamb and then apply the bread crumb mixture with a cupping motion of your hand. Drizzle the melted butter over the crumbs and continue to cook for another 10 to 12 minutes for medium-rare meat. Remove the rack from the oven, let it stand 3 to 4 minutes, then slice into chops, and serve with THOSE POTATOES! (page 54) and fresh asparagus or CREAMED SPINACH (page 411).

Noisettes of Lamb Florentine

Serves 8

This is a grand dish that befits a special occasion. Juicy panfried morsels of lamb on sautéed spinach and a toasty crouton are topped with a green-peppercorn-flavored cream sauce.

It is essential to have a helpful butcher who will prepare the meat ahead of time for you. While boneless rib chops are the most elegant choice for this dish, noisettes may be prepared from the less costly sirloin (see Note).

FOR THE CROUTONS
8 slices good-quality white bread, cut into 3-inch
  circles
6 tablespoons (¾ stick) unsalted butter, melted

FOR THE SPINACH
2 pounds fresh spinach, stems removed, washed and lightly shaken
Pinch of salt
3 tablespoons unsalted butter
1 clove garlic, peeled and minced

FOR THE LAMB
3 tablespoons unsalted butter
1½ tablespoons vegetable oil
8 noisettes of lamb, about 1¼ inches thick, patted dry
Salt and freshly ground black pepper to taste

FOR THE SAUCE
2 tablespoons finely chopped shallots
¾ cup dry vermouth
1 cup heavy cream
¼ cup green peppercorns packed in vinegar or brine, rinsed and drained
2 tablespoons finely chopped flat-leaf parsley for garnish

1. PREPARE THE CROUTONS Preheat your oven to 350°F.

2. Brush both sides of the bread with melted butter. Arrange the circles on a baking sheet and bake in the preheated oven until browned, about 10 to 12 minutes on each side. Keep warm.

3. FOR THE SPINACH Combine the spinach and salt in a large casserole or Dutch oven over medium heat and cook until tender, about 5 to 7 minutes. Transfer it to a strainer and drain, but do not squeeze.

4. Melt 3 tablespoons of butter in a medium-size saucepan over medium-high heat. Add the garlic and shake for several seconds. Add the spinach and sauté, stirring occasionally, 2 more minutes. Season with salt. Remove the pan from the heat and set aside.

5. FOR THE LAMB Heat 3 tablespoons of butter with the oil in a large, heavy skillet over medium-high heat just until the butter foams. Add the noisettes and cook, turning once, about 4 to 5 minutes on each side for medium-rare. Season generously with salt and pepper. Transfer the noisettes to a heated platter and keep them warm in a turned-off oven.

6. PREPARE THE SAUCE Discard all but about 1 tablespoon of fat from the skillet. Add the shallots and let them soften over medium-high heat, about 3 minutes. Pour the vermouth into the skillet, adjusting the heat to high, scraping up any browned bits. Boil the liquid until it is reduced by half. Add the cream and peppercorns, crushing the peppercorns with the back of a spoon. Boil the sauce until it is thickened, about 3 minutes.

7. FOR THE FINAL ASSEMBLY Arrange the croutons on individual plates. Stir the spinach for 1 minute over high heat to reheat. Divide it evenly over the croutons. Place the noisettes over the spinach and top each serving with a generous tablespoon of sauce. Sprinkle on parsley and serve. Serve with glazed carrots and CAULIFLOWER AND POTATO PURÉE (page 32) or steamed baby vegetables.

NOTE: Have the butcher prepare the noisettes from 2 boned rib chops, well-trimmed and tied together, or from a boneless sirloin. Remove all fat and tie each one into a neat circle. Noisettes should weigh about ⅓ pound. Flatten them gently with the palm of your hand before cooking.

Joanna's Country Pâté

Serves 8

I have always loved pâtés—especially for picnics when I bring along thin crusty loaves of French bread, Dijon mustard, and a bottle of a hearty red wine. What is remarkable is how many different kinds of meats (or poultry, vegetables, and fish) you can use to make them. This one reminds me of some of the rustic, garlicky versions you find in the French countryside.

Pâtés are really glorified meat loaves, which I also love (see MADE-TO-BE-LEFTOVER MEAT LOAF on page 171), with luxurious ingredients like brandy, Madeira, pistachio nuts, and extra fat added to them. For me, the trick to keeping a pâté moist and flavorful is not to weight it too heavily (usually 1 to ½ pounds is enough) once it comes out of the oven, so you don't squeeze out the moisture and seasonings.

1½ pounds lean ground pork
8 ounces ground pork fat
8 ounces ground veal
⅓ cup chopped flat-leaf parsley
½ cup chopped shallots (3 to 4 large), peeled and minced
2 large cloves garlic, peeled and minced
3 eggs, beaten
1 teaspoon ground thyme
¼ teaspoon ground nutmeg
¼ cup shelled pistachios
4 ounces smoked ham or Canadian bacon, cut into ¼-inch dice
10 juniper berries, slightly crushed
1¼ tablespoons salt, or to taste
Freshly ground black pepper
⅓ cup Madeira
⅓ cup brandy
16 ounces fatback, sliced ⅛-inch thick, simmered 2 minutes in water, drained, and patted dry *or* 14 ounces sliced bacon
2 bay leaves
Cornichons (small French pickles) and Dijon mustard as accompaniments

🛒 DID YOU KNOW? The easiest way to line a pâté mold is to buy the widest and most regular-shaped package of fatback available in the Meat department. Take it over to the Deli department and ask them to use the electric slicer to make ⅛-inch slices, slicing it *across the face* (producing wide sheets of fat). Slice just to the thick rind. The rind may be used for flavoring soups, such as minestrone. Extra fatback may be frozen for up to a year if wrapped airtight.

The difference between salt pork and fatback is that there are some lean streaks of meat in salt pork and it is brine cured. Fatback has no lean meat, and it is cured in salt. Fatback is actually saltier than salt pork. They are generally sold side by side in Cryovac packages. You can use them pretty much interchangeably, remembering to blanch the pieces to remove some of the salt.

1. Preheat your oven to 350°F.

2. Combine the pork, pork fat, veal, parsley, shallots, garlic, eggs, thyme, nutmeg, pistachios, ham, juniper berries, salt, pepper, Madeira, and brandy in a large bowl and mix well.

3. Test a small amount of the mixture by sautéing it in a skillet and, when it has cooled, tasting for seasonings. Pâtés should be highly seasoned.

4. Line a 9 × 5 × 3-inch loaf pan or pâté mold with the fatback or bacon, draping half of the slices over the edge to be used in covering the top of the pâté. If using bacon, line the pan with about ½ of the bacon and use the remainders to cover the pâté.

5. Pack the meat mixture into the mold. Place two bay leaves on top and fold over the fatback to cover the top of the mixture. Add additional slices of fatback or bacon, if needed, to insure that the top is well covered. Cover the top of the pan with a double layer of heavy foil, and punch 2 holes to let the steam escape.

6. Place the mold in a larger pan and fill the latter

with boiling water to a level half way up the side of the pâté. Bake in the preheated oven for 1 hour and 45 minutes. When it is done, the juices will run clear.

7. Remove the pan from the oven. Cover the pâté with a piece of cardboard or a second pâté mold (or loaf pan) the same size as the first, place about 1 to 1½ pounds of weight evenly distributed on the pâté. (Cans work well.) Let it cool for 2 hours and then refrigerate it until cold. Once it is cold, remove the pâté from the mold, wrap it in plastic wrap, and let it rest for at least 5 days to a week before serving to develop the flavors.

8. Remove the pâté from the refrigerator at least one hour before serving, wipe off any congealed juices, and remove the pork fat, if desired. When presenting the pâté whole, cut a few slices and place them on pieces of bread or crackers. Cut 2 or 3 cornichons into a fan shape by making several thin lengthwise slices almost to one end of each pickle. Spread them out on the pâté. Serve with additional cornichons, Dijon mustard, crackers, and French bread.

Pork Cutlets for Fall

Serves 8

When I think of pork chops, I think of cold-weather dining. Here, the boneless chops are served with a sauce using other wintery flavors: prunes, cranberries, chestnuts, and port.

To save money, buy chops in the summer—when they are usually cheaper—and freeze them. They will keep for up to 4 months. Store fresh pork chops in the coldest part of the refrigerator and use within 2 to 3 days.

2 cups canned or jarred whole unsweetened chestnuts *or* freshly roasted, if available
1½ cups tawny port wine
1½ cups pitted prunes, each one chopped in six pieces
1 cup cranberries
1 cup orange juice
8 boneless center-cut pork chops, 1 inch thick (about 4 to 5 ounces each)
Flour for dredging
2 tablespoons unsalted butter
1 tablespoon vegetable oil
Salt and freshly ground black pepper to taste
½ cup finely chopped shallots
¾ cup good beef stock or broth
Julienned orange rind, 4 cranberries split in half, and 1 tablespoon finely chopped flat-leaf parsley for garnish

1. Simmer the chestnuts in the port until just tender, about 10 minutes. Set them aside in a bowl to cool. With a fork, break the chestnuts apart into coarse pieces. Add the prunes and mix.

2. In the meantime, in a medium-size saucepan, simmer the cranberries in the orange juice until softened and split, about 5 to 7 minutes. Add them to the chestnut mixture.

3. Pat the pork dry and dredge lightly in flour. In a heavy skillet, large enough to hold all the meat comfortably, melt the butter and oil over medium heat. When the butter foams, add the pork and cook for 7 to 8 minutes on the first side. Turn and continue to cook for 6 to 7 minutes. Remove the cutlets to a warm platter and generously season them with salt and pepper.

4. If all the butter and oil have been absorbed, melt another 1 tablespoon butter and 1 tablespoon oil in the skillet. Add the shallots and sauté over medium-low heat until translucent and tender, about 4 to 5 minutes. Add the stock and turn up the heat, stirring to incorporate all the brown bits. Cook over medium-high heat until slightly reduced, 6 to 7 minutes.

5. Add the fruit mixture and continue to stir over medium-high heat. Return the pork and any accumulated meat juices to the pan and reheat for 2 to 3 minutes, turning the cutlets once. Place each cutlet on

DID YOU KNOW? When selecting pork chops, the center cut (as used above), is the most costly because it has the least amount of bone and fat. Chops that come from the rib end have a smaller amount of bone compared with the loin end.

a warmed plate, spoon over some sauce, and garnish with a few strands of julienned orange rind, a cranberry, and a sprinkle of parsley. Serve immediately.

Braised Loin of Pork in Cider

Serves 8

This is a lovely roast to serve in the fall when fresh apples and cider are plentiful. The combination of apples, turnips, and cream in the sauce complement the delicate flavor of the pork.

Pork is a good choice in the market, as the supply is plentiful, and the turnover is usually high. Fresh pork should be pale pink with solid white fat and red bones. Your butcher will bone out the loin, or you may do it yourself. Save the ribs and bake them with some SPICY TOMATO CHILI BARBECUE SAUCE **(page 378) for a low-cost second meal.**

1 4-pound boneless loin of pork (preferably from the center, tied
2 tablespoons unsalted butter
1 tablespoon vegetable oil
Salt and freshly ground black pepper
1 large onion, peeled and finely chopped
10 whole cloves
2 teaspoons dried sage leaf
2 cups apple cider, preferably fresh
5 juniper berries, slightly crushed
2 large Granny Smith or other tart apple, peeled and diced
1½ pounds turnips, peeled and diced
¼ cup heavy cream
2 tablespoons finely chopped flat-leaf parsley

1. Preheat your oven to 325°F.

2. Pat the roast very dry with paper towels. Melt the butter and oil in a deep casserole just until the butter foams. Add the pork and brown it evenly on all sides over medium heat, turning with wooden spatulas or spoons. This will take approximately 7 to 10 minutes. Remove the roast to a platter and season it liberally with salt and pepper.

3. If the butter and oil have burned, discard and replace them. Heat the new butter and oil, add the onion, and sauté it slowly over medium heat for about 4 to 5 minutes, or until light golden colored.

4. Stud the roast with the cloves and return it to

the casserole, fat side up. Sprinkle the sage on top of the roast and add the cider and juniper berries. Turn up the heat and bring the liquid in the pan to the boil. Cover the casserole with aluminum foil and the lid, and place it in the preheated oven.

5. After 1¼ hours, add the apples and turnips and baste the roast, basting 3 times in all during the cooking time. After a total of 2 hours, remove the lid, and roast for 15 minutes longer. Transfer the roast to a warmed platter, tent with aluminum foil, and return it to the turned-off oven.

6. Skim off any surface fat. Reduce the pan juices with the apples and turnips over high heat on top of the stove—about 15 minutes, stirring occasionally with a wooden spoon.

7. Add a small amount of pan juices to the cream to warm it, then stir it into the pan juices. Taste to adjust the seasonings.

8. Slice the roast and ladle large spoonfuls of the sauce over the meat. Sprinkle a little finely chopped parsley on top. Serve with HOLIDAY CRANBERRY CARROTS (page 31) and CREAMED SPINACH (page 411).

Pork Cathedral Style

Serves 8

For glamour and delicious flavors, this dramatic stuffed pork roast would make any cool-weather dinner party a special event. In order for each person to be served a juicy, tarragon-rice-filled chop, you definitely need to choose the meat carefully. Let the butcher know what you need a week ahead of time, because butchers frequently cut the center portion into chops.

The "eye," or meaty center, should be large and of a similar size so both loins cook evenly. Once the butchering is done, this recipe is really quite easy to make . . . and worth it!

2 loins of pork cut as follows:
Have the butcher cut the 5 center rib chops from 2 different loins into roasts. These should weigh about 3 pounds each once they are well trimmed, with the back and chine bones cracked, and the tops Frenched (trimmed to leave about 1 inch of bone exposed on each rib). This will include removing the small section of meat surrounded by fat at the top of the ribs.

FOR THE DRY MARINADE

1½ teaspoons ground coriander seed
1½ teaspoons ground sage
2–3 bay leaves, crushed
1½ tablespoon salt
¾ teaspoon freshly ground black pepper
8 crushed juniper berries
3 tablespoons rendered pork fat, duck fat, or
    vegetable oil

FOR THE STUFFING

3 tablespoons unsalted butter
1 tablespoon vegetable oil
4 ounces mushrooms, wiped, trimmed, and thinly
    sliced
4 large shallots, peeled and minced (about 1 cup)
2 medium carrots, scraped and shredded (about ¾
    cup)
¾ teaspoon salt
Freshly ground black pepper to taste
1½ cups cooked rice
2½ tablespoons finely chopped flat-leaf parsley
2½ tablespoons finely chopped fresh tarragon or 1
    tablespoon dried

FOR THE SAUCE

Cooking juices, from which all the fat has been
    skimmed, plus enough fine chicken stock to
    make 1½ cups
1 tablespoon chopped shallots
1 tablespoon chopped fresh tarragon
⅔ cup dry white wine
½ cup heavy cream
2 tablespoons chopped fresh tarragon
Salt and white pepper to taste
2 tablespoons flour combined with 2 tablespoons
    softened unsalted butter

1. MARINATE THE MEAT Mix all the ingredients
for the dry marinade together. Wipe the meat well
and pat the spice mixture on each piece. Place the
loins in a deep bowl, cover, and refrigerate for 16 to
24 hours. Turn the loins 3 or 4 times during this time,
redistributing any herbs that fall off.

2. PREPARE THE STUFFING In a large, heavy skillet, melt the butter and oil over medium-high heat

just until the butter foams. Add the mushrooms and stir until they separate. Add the shallots and continue cooking for another 3 to 5 minutes. Stir in the carrots. Combine the vegetables with the cooked rice, season with salt and pepper, and stir in the parsley and tarragon. Set aside.

3. PREPARE THE MEAT Scrape off the seasonings from the loins and dry well. In a roasting pan large enough to accommodate both loins, heat the oil until it is almost smoking. Place the loin meat side down, and when it is browned, turn to brown on all sides possible. It is easiest to do each loin separately and to add fresh fat if the first batch has burned. Allow the browned loins to cool slightly.

4. Preheat your oven to 325°F.

5. With a sharp knife, make a deep cut vertically into the meaty side of the roast cutting directly *in front of* each rib bone. Do this very carefully, following the direction of bone, or the final presentation will not work. Each cut will be about 4 inches long.

6. Fill each pocket with ¼ cup of the stuffing mixture.

7. Place both loins in the pan from which all but 2 tablespoons of the fat have been discarded. Interlock the ribs in the center of the pan. This will hold the loins up and keep the stuffing inside. Cover the meat with aluminum foil.

8. Return the pan to the heat, and when the pan begins to sizzle, transfer it to the preheated oven. Roast for about 25 to 30 minutes per pound, or 2 to 2½ hours, basting 3 or 4 times. The roast is done when the internal temperature reads 145°F on a meat thermometer and the juices run clear. Remove the pan from the oven, transfer the meat to a heated platter, and place in the turned-off oven.

9. PREPARE THE SAUCE In a small saucepan, combine the shallots and 1 tablespoon tarragon with the white wine. Over medium-high heat, reduce this mixture by half, then strain it into the chicken-stock and pan-juice mixture. Wipe out the pan, pour the liquid back into it, and bring to a boil, reducing it slightly. Add the cream, bring to a boil, and let the sauce thicken, about 5 minutes.

10. Turn off the heat, add the remaining tarragon and salt and pepper. Whisk in the prepared flour-butter mixture (*beurre manié*), heat the sauce, but do not let it boil. Taste to adjust the seasonings.

11. FOR THE FINAL PRESENTATION This dish is presented with the two loins locked together standing up to form a cathedral-like arch in the center with paper frills on each rib, if desired. The chops should be sliced between each rib so that the stuffing remains inside each chop (see illustration). Serve lightly sauced and pass the remainders at the table. Steamed broccoli florets, SAUTÉED JULIENNE OF LEEKS AND CUCUMBERS (page 40), and FRIED TURNIP CRISPS (page 59) go well with this dish.

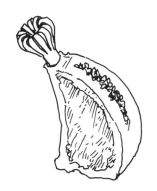

Veal and Sausage Meatballs

Makes 4 to 5 dozen meatballs

Using a mixture of pork and veal makes these meatballs delicious and juicy. Because they are chilled and then rolled in breadcrumbs, they have a crunchy golden coating. I like to serve them on a platter with cherry tomatoes along with cocktails. Dip both meatballs and tomatoes in CAPER MAYONNAISE. Without the coating, they may be cooked and added to tomato sauce for spaghetti or used for sandwiches.

In this recipe, I think that "sweet" sausages are a better combination with the other ingredients. "Hot" sausages contain pepper flakes along with the fennel seed and other seasonings used in the milder variety.

⅔ pound ground veal
3 Italian sweet sausages (about 12 ounces), casings removed
3 ¾-inch slices stale Italian bread, moistened with milk and squeezed dry
2 eggs
¼ cup freshly grated Parmesan cheese
3 tablespoons minced flat-leaf parsley
½ teaspoon salt
¼ teaspoon freshly grated nutmeg
Freshly ground black pepper
1 cup very fine stale white bread crumbs
Olive oil for frying
Lemon slices, flat-leaf parsley sprigs, cherry tomatoes, for garnish
1 recipe CAPER MAYONNAISE (page 370)

1. In the bowl of a food processor fitted with a steel chopping blade, combine the veal, sausage, Italian bread, eggs, Parmesan cheese, parsley, salt, nutmeg, and pepper and pulse with an on-off motion just until well blended, or mix by hand. *Do not overprocess.* Scrape the meat into a bowl, cover, and refrigerate for at least 1 hour.

2. Pour the bread crumbs into a flat dish, shape the meat mixture into 1-inch balls, and roll them in the crumbs.

3. Pour the olive oil into a large, heavy skillet to a depth of ½ inch and heat over medium-high heat until very hot, but not smoking. Add the meatballs slowly to keep the oil hot. Cook only as many as will comfortably fit in the bottom of the pan at one time without crowding, and fry them until golden brown on all sides, about 5 to 7 minutes. Continue with the remaining meatballs. Remove with a slotted spoon and drain on paper towels. Meatballs may be prepared ahead of time and kept warm in a 300°F oven for 30 minutes.

4. Arrange the meatballs on a serving platter or inside a hollowed-out French bread (page 438) or in WHOLE WHEAT CREAM PUFF SHELLS (page 313). Garnish with lemon slices, parsley, and tomatoes. Once cooked, the meatballs may be stored several days in the refrigerator or frozen.

DID YOU KNOW? When buying Italian sausages, make sure to check the label if you are allergic to MSG. Unfortunately, this flavor enhancer is used by many sausage companies.

There are some fat-reduced breakfast sausages in the market that are juicy and compare quite favorably with the more traditional sausages.

Hearty Veal Stew with Ham and Artichokes

Serves 8

In this version of veal stew, ham, mushrooms, and artichoke hearts enhance the delicate taste of the meat and the appearance of the dish. It is the kind of simple, comforting dish to make ahead and have ready to greet you on a cold night. It will keep for 2 days in the refrigerator or 3 months in the freezer.

By far the most reasonable and reliable veal in a market is stew meat cut from the chuck or round where slow, moist cooking in a sauce usually produces fine results. Buying veal in the supermarket is sometimes risky because what is sold may actually be young beef. Really top-quality veal is "nature" veal—fed only on milk until it comes to market at about 4 months. The meat should be very pale whitish-pink—not red or gray—with a small amount of pure-white fat.

3 tablespoons olive or vegetable oil
3 pounds veal stew meat, cut into 2-inch cubes and patted very dry
1 tablespoon olive or vegetable oil
1 large onion, peeled and coarsely chopped
1 large clove garlic, peeled and split
1½ cups dry white wine
¾ cup beef stock
3 tablespoons finely chopped flat-leaf parsley for garnish
1 teaspoon dried thyme
1½ teaspoons salt, or to taste
Freshly ground black pepper to taste
3 tablespoons unbleached all-purpose flour
6 ounces boiled ham, cut into ¼ × ¼ × 1-inch pieces
2 10-ounce packages frozen artichoke hearts, defrosted and patted dry
12 ounces small white mushrooms, wiped and quartered
⅓ cup cream (optional)
2 tablespoons finely chopped flat-leaf parsley for garnish

1. Preheat your oven to 325°F.
2. Heat 3 tablespoons of oil in a large, heavy skillet until almost smoking. Add just enough pieces of veal to cover the bottom of the skillet without crowding. Turn and brown on all sides. As the pieces brown,

transfer them with a slotted spoon to a large, heavy Dutch oven or casserole.

3. After all the meat has been browned, add the last tablespoon of oil to the skillet and, when it is hot, add the onion and sauté it over medium heat until it is golden, about 5 to 6 minutes. Add the garlic and cook for 30 seconds longer.

4. Pour the wine over the onions, turn up the heat, and bring the liquid to a boil, scraping up all the brown bits from the bottom of the pan. Add the beef stock, parsley, thyme, salt, and pepper and allow this liquid to simmer for 5 minutes.

5. Turn the heat on under the Dutch oven. Season the veal with salt and a generous amount of black pepper. Sprinkle the 3 tablespoons of flour over the veal and toss to coat it evenly. Cook over medium heat for 1 to 2 minutes to brown the flour. Stir the wine-stock mixture into the veal, and bring the liquid to a simmer. Add the ham, cover the pot, and place in the preheated oven for 1 hour 15 minutes.

6. Add the artichokes and mushrooms, stirring to cover the vegetables, and return the pot to the oven for an additional 30 minutes. The meat should be very tender. Remove the casserole from the oven, stir in the cream a little at a time, if desired, and sprinkle a little parsley on top for garnish. Serve with buttered noodles, parsleyed rice, or couscous.

Sautéed Veal Cutlets with Mustard, Capers, and Peppers

Serves 4

There is nothing more wonderful than juicy, tender veal cutlets with a scrumptious sauce or a little lemon juice squeezed on top. These cutlets are easily prepared in a few minutes. With the vibrant red-pepper strips, Dijon mustard, and capers, the finished dish is not only well seasoned, but very colorful.

Alas, buying the veal properly cut isn't always that easy in a market. You need to use your eyes and ask questions, especially if the meat is already packaged. Besides being the palest pink color, a cutlet should be a solid piece of meat thinly sliced *across* the grain of the meat. If it is sliced lengthwise, you may be buying pieces with connecting membranes. When cooked, the meat will separate into different sections.

2 tablespoons unsalted butter
2 tablespoons vegetable oil
1–1½ pounds boneless veal cutlets, sliced thin and
  pounded, if necessary
Flour for dredging
Salt and freshly ground black pepper to taste
½ cup dry vermouth
1 red bell pepper, peeled, seeds and membranes
  removed, cut into thin strips
2 tablespoons Dijon mustard
⅓ cup cream
Salt and freshly ground black pepper to taste
2 tablespoons small capers, drained
1 tablespoon finely chopped flat-leaf parsley for
  garnish

1. Heat the butter and oil in a large skillet over medium heat until very hot. Dust both sides of the cutlets in flour, shaking to remove the excess. (Do not stack the cutlets on top of one another, as they will become gummy and won't brown.)

2. Gently place the cutlets in the hot fat one at a time. The fat should sizzle as each piece is added, so allow a little time in between to keep the fat hot. Sauté only as many pieces of veal as will fit comfortably in the pan at one time. Sauté the cutlets until they are lightly browned on one side, then turn and brown the other side, about 1 to 2 minutes if the meat is cut very thin. As the cutlets are cooked, transfer them in a single layer to a heated platter in a warm oven. Season with salt and pepper. Repeat with the remaining veal, adding 1 tablespoon of fresh oil, if needed.

3. Discard any extra fat. Over medium-high heat, add the vermouth to the skillet, scraping up any browned bits at the bottom of the pan, and stir for about 1 minute. Add the red pepper and cook 30 seconds. Adjust the heat down to medium; stir in the mustard; then the cream, salt, and pepper; and cook for 1 to 2 minutes, taking care not to let the sauce boil. Add the cutlets to the sauce, turning once, then arrange them on a warmed serving dish, spoon over some sauce, and sprinkle the capers over them. Serve at once with a little chopped parsley sprinkled on top.

DID YOU KNOW? The terms *cutlets*, *medallions*, *scallops*, and *scallopini* are confusing. Actually, they are often used interchangeably. While medallions are usually small (1½-inch) circles of veal cut from the loin, the most expensive part, they may also be called "cutlets," or "scallops," or "scallopini," depending on the nationality of the butcher. Cutlets are usually cut from the different muscle groups in the leg.

For even cooking, the pieces should be about the same thickness. Flatten veal carefully. You don't want to make holes in the meat by brutally pounding it. Instead, gently spread the fibers by striking and pushing the center (or thickest part) outward with a meat pounder or the heel of your hand.

Venison Chestnut Pâté

Serves 8 to 12

For years, venison was eaten as a great delicacy in restaurants during game season, or in the home of hunters. Recently, supermarkets have become more adventuresome and have started to merchandise venison, pheasant, and quail, as well as other more exotic game. This is a cause to celebrate, and this well-seasoned pâté is perfect for a celebration. (Look on pages 151 to 153 for pheasant recipes.) The flavor of a pâté improves as it ages, so I make mine at least a week ahead of time. Or, I double the recipe and fill 6 mini-loaf pans for holiday gift-giving.

1¼ pounds ground venison
1¼ pounds ground pork (½ lean, ½ fat)
8 ounces venison, cut into strips ½ × ½ × 1½ inches
4 ounces pork fatback, rind removed, blanched, and cut into ¼ × ¼ × 1-inch strips
8 ounces chestnut meat, fresh-roasted or unsweetened from a can, crumbled
1 generous teaspoon ground cloves
1 generous teaspoon ground allspice
1½ teaspoons freshly grated nutmeg
2 large cloves garlic, peeled and minced
½ cup dried currants
½ cup Madeira
¼ cup cognac or brandy
2½ teaspoons salt, or to taste
2 tablespoons raspberry vinegar
Freshly ground black pepper to taste
3 eggs, slightly beaten
1 bay leaf
16 ounces fatback, sliced ⅛-inch thick, simmered for 2 minutes in water, and patted dry (see page 195)
Cornichons, for garnish

1. Preheat your oven to 350°F.
2. Combine the ground venison, ground pork, venison strips, fatback strips, chestnuts, ground cloves and allspice, nutmeg, garlic, currants, Madeira, cognac, vinegar, salt, and pepper in a large bowl and let the mixture stand for 1 to 2 hours.
3. Add the eggs and mix well. Fry a small ball of the mixture until cooked and taste for seasonings, adjusting as necessary. The pâté should be spicy.

4. Line a $9 \times 5 \times 3$-inch loaf pan or 6-cup terrine with fatback slices, extending them so they can be folded back over the top of the pâté. Transfer the pâté mixture into the mold, packing it down into the corners. Fold the fatback slices over the top of the pâté. Cover the top of the pan tightly with three layers of heavy-duty aluminum foil, and punch 1 or 2 steam holes in the top. Place the loaf pan or mold in another larger pan and fill the larger pan with enough boiling water to come halfway up the outside of the mold. Bake in the lower third of the preheated oven for 1 hour and 35 to 45 minutes or until the juices run clear.

5. Remove the pâté from the oven, lift the foil, and check to see if the pâté has shrunk slightly from the edges. Put the foil back on, place the pâté on a plate, and put a flat board or another loaf pan the same size on top. Weight it with 1 to 1½ pounds of cans, jars or pie weights for 2 hours, then refrigerate overnight. Remove the pâté from the loaf pan, wrap it tightly in plastic wrap, and refrigerate at least 5 to 7 days before eating.

6. Remove the pâté from the refrigerator at least 1 hour before serving. Place it on a platter lined with curly endive or parsley, and cut a few slices. Leave the rest of the pâté uncut, as it will be fresher if cut as needed. Serve with CRANBERRY, PEPPER, AND ONION CONSERVE (page 85) and dark-bread triangles, and garnish with cornichons (small gherkins) cut into fans.

Rabbit in Red Wine and Balsamic Vinegar Sauce

Serves 4

This rabbit, gently simmered with mushrooms and pearl onions in red wine, makes an autumnal feast once the rich balsamic vinegar and tangy crème fraîche are added to the sauce.

Until recently, if you found rabbit at all in your market, it was usually frozen. With the return of Service Meat counters, and an increased interest in game, fresh rabbit is more readily available. Ask your butcher to order it. (He can also cut it up for you.) You may find whole rabbits or a boneless saddle, which would be more expensive. Frankly, I think rabbit needs those bones to keep it juicy. The meat of this animal is lean and tender when slowly cooked, and the flavor is quite mild, like chicken.

1 2½ to 3-pound rabbit, dressed, and cut into eight
  pieces (see Note)
Flour for dredging
3 tablespoons vegetable oil
1½ tablespoons vegetable oil
1 medium onion, peeled and finely chopped
1 medium carrot, scraped and finely chopped
1 medium stalk celery, finely chopped
1 large clove garlic, peeled and minced
1½ cups hearty red wine, such as zinfandel
1 large bay leaf
⅓ cup finely chopped flat-leaf parsley
1 teaspoon dried thyme leaves
¼ cup balsamic vinegar
Salt and freshly ground black pepper to taste
1 tablespoon unsalted butter
1½ cups pearl onions, peeled
¼ cup beef stock
½ cup currants
8 ounces small mushrooms, wiped, trimmed, and
  quartered
6 ounces crème fraîche or sour cream

1. Dry the rabbit well with paper towels and dredge it in flour, patting to remove the excess flour. In a large, heavy casserole or Dutch oven, heat 3 tablespoons of oil until very hot but not smoking. Add only enough pieces of rabbit to fit comfortably in the bottom of the pan without crowding and brown them evenly in batches over medium-high heat, about 2 to 3 minutes on each side. Remove the pieces to a bowl with a slotted spoon, season with salt and pepper, and set aside.

2. Add 1½ tablespoons of oil to the pot, heat it until hot, and add the onion, carrot, and celery. Sauté them over medium heat until the vegetables are translucent and softened, about 6 to 7 minutes. Stir in the garlic and cook for 30 seconds longer.

3. Return the rabbit to the casserole and add the red wine. Turn heat up and bring the liquid to a boil, scraping up all the browned cooking bits. Stir in the bay leaf, parsley, thyme, vinegar, salt, and plenty of fresh pepper. Cover and cook over medium-low heat for 45 minutes. The liquid should only gently bubble on the surface.

4. While the rabbit is cooking, melt the butter in a

large, heavy skillet over medium heat just until it foams. Add the pearl onions and let them cook over medium-high heat until they start to brown, about 6 to 8 minutes. Add the beef stock and raise the heat, shaking the pan until the liquid has almost completely evaporated and coats the onions.

5. Stir the onions, currants, and mushrooms into the pot with the rabbit, turn up the heat, and boil the liquid gently uncovered for about 10 to 15 minutes longer to thicken the sauce. Remove the bay leaf, stir in the crème fraîche, and taste to adjust the seasonings. Serve with buttered noodles, polenta, or small boiled parsleyed potatoes.

NOTE: Read the box carefully when buying a frozen rabbit. Select only a "frying rabbit," not a "mature rabbit," which, unless stewed for a long time, will be tough. Frozen rabbits may be cut into more than 8 pieces. Don't worry, this recipe will work with larger or smaller pieces. And a slowly defrosted frozen rabbit (in the refrigerator with a plate underneath), will be fine eating.

Storage: Keeping Fresh Food at Its Best

It is a primary tenet of good cooks and great chefs alike, and is repeated many times in this book as elsewhere: The freshest possible ingredients are vital to eating well. Getting food to you in top condition is the supermarket's responsibility, and with the help of technology, foods can be delivered rapidly from around the world into your local market. The secret of keeping fresh food at its best, however, is choosing carefully when you buy, then storing it properly once at home and knowing how long it will last.

The freshest and best-quality food, poorly stored, will soon become mediocre. *How* food is stored goes hand in hand with *where* it is kept in the kitchen. *When* it was purchased and/or prepared is the third part of the equation. While some whole spices, dried beans and sealed cans and jars seem never to deteriorate, most foods have a "shelf life" within which you can expect optimum flavor, texture, and color. For a moderate time after that point has passed, the food probably will not be harmful to your body, but you cannot expect the final dish to be first rate.

PLASTIC CONTAINERS

There are many practical storage containers available today. In fact, some good ones are free, such as those the supermarkets themselves use. The reusable plastic half-pint, pint, and quart containers with snap-on lids culled from the Deli or Dairy sections, are fine for short-term reuse. Tupperware and Rubbermaid are but two of many manufacturers who make multi-sized and shaped containers in a heavier, more durable weight. My biggest reservation about plastic containers is that the plastic tends to absorb the flavors and colors of the ingredients stored. So a broccoli soup may end up with a haunting taste of peppered shrimp. Wash these containers with very hot water and air them well between uses.

The second objection I have to plastic is that the lids and containers often split, preventing a tight seal. In a refrigerator, this lets circulating air bring other smells to the stored food and causes food to dry out. In a freezer, exposed and improperly wrapped food is often ruined by the formation of ice crystals and by freezer burn. (Check in the Frozen Foods section of this book for detailed freezing tips.)

GLASS JARS

Before plastics, a lot of food was packaged in screw-top glass jars. If used for preserving, a rubber sealing ring was necessary. (Some of us still preserve fruits and sauces this way.) I find that empty glass jars from mustards, baby foods, jams, instant coffee, and peanut butter are perfect for storing small amounts of ground nuts, home-made relishes, and fresh vinegars. These recycled bottles and jars appeal because glass is impervious to color and odor and is transparent for easy identification. Scrub the lids and jars well and insert a piece of wax paper between the food and the screw top to form a tight seal. Use new corks available from hardware stores for narrow-top bottles.

HEAVY PLASTIC POUCHES

Under different storage conditions, the same food requires different treatment. Fish, for example, must be wrapped airtight without moisture for freezing, but should breathe in the refrigerator. Ziploc bags, a boon to storage, are heavy weight and ideal for freezing. Learn to push out all the air just before finally sealing the bag. Solids and liquids, such as soup, can both be stored in these pouches, taking up a minimum of storage space.

Plastic wrap, aluminum foil, and freezer paper are other essentials in the kitchen. The specific information on how best to store each item should be obtained from the supermarket department in which you shop. Make certain to ask. Savvy supermarkets are training personnel to know these key facts and manufacturers like Reynolds Aluminum provide useful storage pamphlets to markets. Look for them.

PREPARATION AND LABELING FOR STORAGE

Whichever type of storage container you choose, cleanliness is vital for food safety and longevity. This includes those largest of containers—your refrigerator and freezer. Always wipe up spills quickly and use an open box of baking soda, as suggested by the manufacturer, to keep the inside of a refrigerator odor-free. (It also sweetens a garbage disposal.)

How many times have you misplaced a choice morsel in the fridge because in haste you put it away without labeling? Make a practice of labeling and dating stored products. For frozen foods, indicating the approximate number of servings is helpful. A permanent, non-smudge marker prevents these notations from running off due to dampness.

Some perishables come with "sell by" or "use by" dates stamped on their packages. These include dairy products, breads, and even cereals. But what about remembering to mark the date of purchase on dried herbs, so that you don't wonder why the jar that says "rosemary" looks like brown twigs? Alas, your notation reminds you that it was bought over nine months ago, and sitting on the window ledge has given it a good suntan. Or mark a box of phyllo dough so you don't find brittle parchment when you're ready to use it. ·

STORING STAPLES

Rosemary in the window alerts us to *where* to store "nonperishable" foods. While it is convenient to have all your spices above the stove, and they are attractive displayed in full view, unfortunately, heat and sun shorten their vitality and diminish flavor. These items, along with grains, oils and vinegars, are best kept in a cool, dark pantry or cupboard. Even well-wrapped chocolate keeps for nine months under these conditions.

Incidentally, to preserve the wonderful summer harvest of fresh herbs, spread them on cookie sheets and air-dry them or place them in a turned-off oven. You will find they retain more flavor than store-bought varieties and can be stored in small jars (that emptied rosemary jar?) placed in the pantry.

STORING FRUIT

While in Europe, I learned to keep fruit in a bowl on the counter. Fruits taste fruitier at room temperature. They also continue to mature. So, if your family does not consume fruit quickly or you buy too much, by all means chill it when it's ripe. But take it out of the refrigerator at least an hour before serving.

One fruit (yes, it is a fruit) I try never to refrigerate is tomatoes. The flavor is dramatically better when the fruit is left out.

REFRIGERATOR

Storage

Perishables must be kept in a cold refrigerator. The coldest part is at the bottom, near the back. It is worth noting here (as I have in other chapters) that care must be taken to prevent poultry or meat from dripping juices that might cause food poisoning on other foods. Placing them on a plate is good insurance. Tightly wrapped foods often decay more quickly than those which are allowed to breathe. You will find tips about individual storage concerns with each recipe.

There are cheese and butter compartments, often on the door or in a drawer, where the temperature is slightly warmer. The trick in keeping cheese fresh is to recognize that once air is trapped within the package for a long time, it becomes stale and causes food spoilage. Cheese departments change the plastic wrap on their large blocks each time they cut off a wedge.

Unfortunately, we are prone to overbuying foods and then finding out that they do not last. It is best to use meat, poultry, and fish within a day or two of purchase. Use defrosted ingredients within a day. If after a couple of days your vegetables are in jeopardy of deterioration, try partially cooking them. Once blanched, they are fine when sautéed a day or two later. Older fruits can be made into compotes where appearances are less noticeable.

Organization

The top shelf is a good place to store flours, delicate oils, condiments, and coffees. Remember, however, if a refrigerator is opened and closed numerous times, the temperature inside rises and cold storage is impaired.

Vegetable and fruit bins are provided even in apartment-size refrigerators. They are often at the bottom where it is coolest. If your refrigerator has two drawers, separate lettuce from pears, cantaloupes, apples, and other fruits that give off ethylene gas causing rust-colored spots on greens.

I try to group similar types of ingredients together in the refrigerator. This helps me locate things faster.

FREEZER

Today, if we choose, we can stock our freezers with an entire meal, freshly prepared and frozen. There are hors d'oeuvres, entrées, sinful desserts, and exotic coffees from around the world. A freezer is also an ideal place to keep nuts; infrequently used flours; home-made soups, pastas, and fruit purées. Here, too, grouping by similar items is very helpful.

Dishes

Ice cube trays are terrific for making small-size portions of stocks, egg whites, and puréed and water-packed fresh herbs to pack in small storage bags.

"PRESENTS" AND PRESENTATION

And finally a little aside on the subject of storing: Today's super-markets are loaded with wonderful boxes, baskets, and containers of all sorts. Why not keep some of these in one corner of your pantry with the prettiest empty jars, some snippets of ribbon, a remnant or two of checkered or country-print fabric, and some decorative labels? No gift is so well received as the one you make and give yourself.

INTRODUCTION

Happily, Americans are discovering what most other cultures have known for a long time: how rich the harvest from our oceans and lakes can be. There are some good reasons for this:

Along with sole, flounder, salmon, and trout, less familiar fish are now sold in supermarkets. This includes inexpensive (but delicious) varieties that used to be thrown overboard as unsaleable, such as wolffish and skate.

Prepared items such as stuffed clams and calamari salad are offered to tempt us without cooking.

In progressive markets, fish are displayed unwrapped, in full view, on handsome iced counters much as they are in the finest fish stores—with all the expertise (cooking tips and recipes) included.

If this has not yet occurred in your local supermarket, it could happen soon, especially since *fresh* fresh fish is best (good-quality product properly handled), and markets are seeing the sales potential here.

As a smart consumer, you need to use your eyes and nose to check quality when buying seafood. I'd suggest taking a little extra time to really study the fish or shellfish you are contemplating. If it is unwrapped, check the *first* clue to freshness: a lack of fishy odor. While we often hear that clear eyes in a whole fish reveal its freshness, this may not be the best indicator. Withdrawing fish quickly from deep waters can result in eyes that bulge, and ice burn can produce clouded eyes. But, there is no hiding the fact that as fish gets older, it smells *fishy*.

Often, you can visually ascertain if the fish has been handled quickly and correctly by the purveyor and market:

With a whole, unwrapped fish, look into the gills or ask the clerk to show you. They should be bright red. As a fish ages, these turn brownish.

Even through plastic you can judge the overall appearance. Is it bright and does the flesh feel firm when lightly pressed? Good. Slime develops on fish with poor handling and time.

Bruises, too, are to be avoided. They are a quick port of entry for bacteria.

Fillets should be pearly with the muscle groups holding together. Edges should not be browned or curled.

When I'm choosing fish in the market, I don't hesitate to ask for a second or third fillet or fish if the first one is an uncomfortable choice for any reason. In packages, I look at each item and ask questions, as well. Fish can be opened and rewrapped by a clerk. As you ask more about fish, the seafood personnel will get to know you and vice versa. It is important to have confidence in their judgment and reliability, especially where plastic-wrapped or unfamiliar products are concerned.

Ask what are the best buys that day. Is there a more economical cut or size available? Fresh salmon tails, I've found, work just as well for a WARM SALMON MOUSSE IN A PHYLLO CROWN (page 232) and are usually less costly than fillets. Often, you can find out when the fish is delivered and be there for the best selection. Or ask to have your fish held aside. For party-quality whole fish, I special order it and discuss this choice with the department manager. And, if a clerk in the Seafood department says that the swordfish isn't great (and you should ask), don't gamble. No matter how great the sauce or the chef, the odds are against the final dish ever being wonderful if the raw fish isn't.

Careful handling on the part of the supermarket to assure freshness is only half of the picture. The other part of the responsibility begins with you the minute the fish leaves the store. This means watching where and how the fish is transported home. A long ride in a hot car is like partial cooking. Remember to ask for freezer bags and, where possible, pack the fish surrounded by other chilled items in your bag.

Once home, proper storage assures good, healthful eating. The sooner the fish or shellfish is cooked, the better.

Rinse it under cold water and rewrap in fresh, tightly sealed paper, not plastic. This is especially true of live lobsters, which suffocate in airtight bags.

Store fish in the coldest part of the refrigerator and let it breathe.

If you won't use it within two days, wrap the fish in

airtight covering (plastic wrap or paper) and freeze for up to 3 months.

If freezing a whole fish, gut it first.

Once any seafood is defrosted (even if sold as "fresh frozen") do not refreeze; use it immediately.

A revolution in fish eating has occurred. Today's lighter sauces no longer mask delicate flavors. Nor do we overcook fish. Instead, the Canadian Fisheries standard of 9 to 10 minutes cooking per inch of thickness has been widely adopted. Whether the fish is whole or in fillets, stuffed or grilled, this rule works wonders to produce moist, delicate, perfectly prepared fish.

We've all heard how healthful fish is for low-fat/low-cholesterol diets. Even fatty fish like salmon are now credited with helping us win the battle against clogged arteries and heart attacks. But, don't let the good news overshadow the fact that fish tastes good. For peak flavor and enjoyment, freshness is still the key. Beyond that, a fish can go from the fanciest LOBSTER TIMBALES WITH RIESLING BEURRE BLANC (page 234) to SWORDFISH STEAKS (page 253) cooked on the barbecue. With supermarkets upscaling and upgrading their Seafood departments, I think our choices are vast.

Avocado and Scallop Seviche

Serves 10 to 12

This colorful hors d'oeuvre is a boon to summer entertaining. It is prepared ahead of time and without a stove. Instead, the fresh lime juice cooks the scallops. The crunch of the slightly marinated mushrooms provides an interesting contrast to the soft scallop mixture.

Scallops are one of the best bets in a supermarket Fish department. They should look pearly and moist, without any yellowed edges. Their aroma should be sweet. Make sure to unwrap sealed trays of scallops as soon as you bring them home to avoid an ammonia smell.

½ cup fresh lime juice (about 4 limes)
3 tablespoons peanut or vegetable oil
20–24 green peppercorns, crushed
Salt and freshly ground black pepper, to taste
¾ pound sea or bay scallops, finely chopped
1 large ripe avocado, peeled
2 tablespoons fresh chives or scallions, chopped
30–40 small white mushrooms
¼ cup vegetable oil
2 tablespoons fresh lemon juice
1 medium clove of garlic, peeled and crushed
Salt and freshly ground black pepper to taste
Additional chives or scallions for garnish
   (optional)

1. Combine the lime juice, oil, crushed peppercorns, salt, and pepper together in a glass or ceramic bowl. Stir in the scallops, cover, and refrigerate them for at least 4 hours while they marinate. They should become opaque in this time.

2. Mash the avocado until almost smooth, then add it along with the chives or scallions to the marinating scallops (do not drain them) and mix it well. Set aside.

3. About half an hour before serving the scallops, remove the stems from the mushrooms and wipe them to remove any dirt. Combine the vegetable oil, lemon juice, garlic, salt, and pepper in a small bowl, and brush the insides of the mushrooms liberally with this mixture.

4. Just before serving, drain the caps and fill with the scallop mixture. Garnish with additional chives, if desired.

DID YOU KNOW? Haas avocados, the ones with the dark, almost black skins, have smaller pits and less moisture than the dark-green-skinned variety. The flavors are similar, and either variety will work in this recipe. An avocado will ripen faster in a closed paper bag at room temperature.

NOTE: Any remaining scallop mixture may be spooned onto endive leaves or wide strips of sweet red bell peppers.

Squid Caponata

Makes 8 ½-cup servings

Caponata is a tasty Sicilian dish, traditionally made with eggplant, tuna, anchovies, capers, onions, olives, and garlic in a tomato sauce and served as an hors d'oeuvre or first course. I've added delicately simmered squid for texture and color here.

It's easier to work with squid now since many supermarkets sell it cleaned. If this has not been done, the Seafood department might accommodate you if given some time. If you cannot find fresh squid, check in the Frozen Foods aisle. Squid is often frozen in the summer months when it is plentiful and, therefore, less expensive. Even the "fresh," clean squid in the Seafood department may be defrosted. Be sure to ask. When allowed to come to room temperature slowly, it's a good bet. But, it should be used quickly.

1 2-ounce can anchovies, drained and finely chopped
2 cups CHUNKY HOMEMADE TOMATO SAUCE (page 377)
¾ pound cleaned squid, including tentacles
¼ cup red wine vinegar
¼ cup fruity olive oil
2 large cloves garlic, peeled and minced
2–3 tablespoons coarsely chopped flat-leaf parsley
1 3½-ounce jar small capers, drained.
¾ cup oil-cured black olives
½ teaspoon salt, or to taste
Pepper to taste
1 tablespoon fruity olive oil
1 large onion, peeled and coarsely chopped

1. In a medium-size saucepan, preferably not aluminum, combine the anchovies and tomato sauce, and bring to a simmer. Partially cover the pan and cook over medium heat for 10 minutes. Remove the pan from the heat and set it aside uncovered.

2. Rinse the squid under cold water. Remove any of the spotted skin that remains on the outside of the tentacles and any cartilage or hard beak inside. Bring

AS A VARIATION: You might add cooked frozen artichoke hearts, diced and sautéed celery, steamed green beans, and, naturally, cubes of sautéed eggplant.

a skillet filled with cold water just to a simmer. Add the squid and simmer just until it turns white, about 30 to 45 seconds. Remove the squid, blot it dry, and cut it into ¾-inch rings. In a medium-size bowl, combine the squid with the wine vinegar, olive oil, garlic, parsley, capers, olives, salt, and pepper, and stir to blend. Set aside.

3. In a small skillet, heat 1 tablespoon of olive oil until fragrant. Stir in the chopped onion, lower the heat, and cook slowly until it is lightly colored, about 10 minutes. Add it to the tomato sauce.

4. Combine the tomato sauce with the squid mixture and serve at room temperature or refrigerate in a covered bowl. Serve on small plates with forks for an hors d'oeuvre or on luncheon-size plates with 3 small Bibb or romaine lettuce leaves for a first course.

Mini Shrimp Spring Rolls

Makes approximately 24 to 28

These crunchy two-bite morsels filled with spicy shrimp make a wonderful cocktail snack. Once you have mastered the technique of making the spring rolls, almost anything can be put inside. Spring roll wrappers are far thinner than the traditional egg roll wrappers. Check out the Oriental section for other spring roll ingredients. One half ounce of "tree ears" or dried Mo-er mushrooms can be substituted for the black mushrooms.

When the shrimp's appearance is not critical, as in these spring rolls or for chowders and stews, there are economical bags of small-size (salad) shrimp in the Frozen Foods aisle, which are sometimes already peeled and deveined. Also, check to see what is on sale. When using fish that is already cooked in a stew or chowder, add it toward the end of the cooking time, just to heat it through.

¾ pound (approximately 40) small shrimp, peeled
and deveined
½ 8-ounce can water chestnuts (approximately 15),
drained
1 ounce dried black mushrooms, soaked in warm
water until soft, stems removed, drained, blotted
dry, and coarsely chopped
½ cup thinly sliced scallions, including most of
the green parts
2 teaspoons soy sauce
1 tablespoon minced fresh ginger
1 tablespoon minced garlic
1 tablespoon dry sherry
2 teaspoons sesame oil
1 teaspoon salt
1 teaspoon sugar
1 teaspoon rice vinegar
12 spring roll wrappers *or* 24 phyllo leaves (see
Note)
1 egg white
Peanut oil for deep frying
GINGERY PEANUT DIPPING SAUCE (page 368)

1. Bring a small skillet half filled with water to a
simmer. Add a little salt, if desired, and stir in the
shrimp. Cook them over medium heat just until they
have turned pink. Drain and blot dry.

2. In a good processor fitted with a steel chopping
blade, place the shrimp, water chestnuts, and mushrooms, and pulse about 12 times until these ingredients are the size of small peas. Or chop by hand.
Add the scallions, soy sauce, ginger, garlic, sherry,
sesame oil, salt, sugar, and vinegar and pulse a few
more times just to blend.

3. Separate the spring roll wrappers carefully, and
cut them in half on the diagonal. Place a rounded
tablespoon of the filling in the middle of the long
edge. Brush the perimeter of the spring roll with egg
white. Fold the right corner over the filling, leaving
about ⅓ of the long edge exposed. Fold the left corner
over the folded right corner, and then roll into a small
cylinder (see illustration). Repeat this procedure until
all the filling is used.

4. Fill a wok or skillet with peanut oil to a depth
of 2 inches. Heat the oil to 350°F or until a cube of
bread dropped in becomes golden brown quickly.

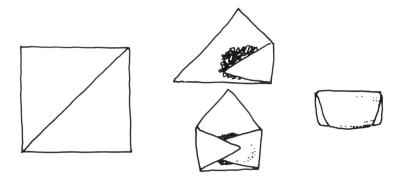

Gently drop in a couple of spring rolls. Add 1 or 2 more, if space permits, and cook just until golden brown on all sides, about 30 to 40 seconds. (If you are using phyllo dough, it will take about 20 seconds.) Remove the rolls with a slotted spoon and drain on paper towels. Continue with other batches until all the spring rolls are fried, making sure the oil is hot every time. Let the spring rolls cool for at least 10 minutes before serving. Serve with GINGERY PEANUT DIPPING SAUCE and/or hoisin sauce, found in the Oriental section.

NOTE: To substitute phyllo for spring roll wrappers (which is preferable to traditional, thicker egg roll wrappers), spread 1 leaf of phyllo with the long edge near you on a work surface, and brush very lightly with peanut oil. Place a second leaf over this. Using a ruler or straight edge, first trim the phyllo into a square, then cut the square in half on the diagonal as with the spring roll wrappers, and continue with the recipe.

DID YOU KNOW? Spring roll wrappers are about ¼ the thickness of egg roll wrappers. There are about 40 to a pound. They should be located in the Frozen Foods section of your market, since they are fragile and manufacturers prefer to ship them this way. If they are sold defrosted in the Produce or Dairy department, look to see that the surface does not have moisture on it, developed from deterioration. Keep unfrozen wrappers chilled and well sealed to prevent drying out. Don't be alarmed if the stack of wrappers seems stuck together when you unwrap them. Carefully pull them apart; they are actually far more sturdy than they seem at first glance. Tightly wrapped in plastic, wrappers may be frozen for a month.

Grilled Stuffed Trout

Serves 4

This recipe has an unusual combination of prunes and almonds in the spinach stuffing that is appealing not only for its intensity of flavor but for its low calorie count. I first tasted it at the cooking school of Sabine de Mirbeck in England. "Sweating" the vegetables (sautéing with a minimum of fat and then covering to let the steam continue to soften) is a secret for cutting fat in cooking.

The freshest trout is the one you catch yourself. Your next-best choice is to find a market with fresh farm-raised trout swimming in a tank. The seafood clerk can clean them and trim the gills. They will freeze beautifully this way for 3 to 4 months.

4 brook or rainbow trout (approximately 10 to 12 ounces), gutted and boned
Salt and freshly ground black pepper

STUFFING
1 pound fresh spinach, thoroughly washed and patted dry
1 teaspoon safflower or flavorless vegetable oil
1 large onion, peeled and finely chopped
2 ounces small white mushrooms, wiped, trimmed, and thinly sliced
2 ounces pitted prunes, finely chopped
2 ounces sliced almonds, toasted until lightly brown
Salt and freshly ground black pepper to taste

SAUCE
⅔ cup natural yogurt
2 tablespoons olive oil
2 tablespoons freshly snipped chives
Salt and freshly ground black pepper to taste

1. Rinse the trout under cold water and blot dry. Remove any remaining bones with tweezers. Generously season the fish with salt and pepper.

2. FOR THE STUFFING Remove the stems of the spinach, pat dry, and cut it into thin strips. Pour the oil into a large skillet and heat it over medium-high heat. Add the onion, cover, and let it sweat over gentle heat for 1 minute. Add the spinach and mushrooms, raise the heat to high, and cook for 2 minutes longer. Stir in the prunes and cook 1 minute more. Transfer

the stuffing to a flat dish to cool. When it is cold, combine it with the almonds and season to taste with salt and pepper.

3. Turn on the broiler and place a rack about 5 to 6 inches from the flame.

4. Stuff the trout with the spinach mixture, packing it well, and place the fish on lightly oiled foil on a cookie sheet or broiler pan. Broil for 4 minutes on each side. Turn off the broiler and leave the fish in for 4 minutes longer to rest.

5. **PREPARE THE SAUCE** Place the yogurt in a small bowl and whisk in the olive oil. Season well to taste, then add the chives. Pour the sauce into a gravy boat and pass it at the table.

6. Before serving the trout, remove the top skin from each fish. Arrange them on individual warmed serving plates with some steamed vegetables such as a few small boiled potatoes or broccoli florets.

Sweet and Sour Sole

Serves 6 to 8 as a first course

This unusual dish is called *Sogliole in Saor*, in Venice, Italy, where it is a specialty dating from the Middle Ages. While its background is old, the tastes are a contemporary mixture of tangy and slightly sweet flavors.

There are many varieties of sole available in this country. Any one will work for this do-ahead appetizer. (Look at the Smart Shopping tip at the end of this recipe for a surprising money-saving option.) When selecting recipes, I suggest you read them through. This recipe must be prepared in advance.

2 pounds sole or flounder fillets
¾ cup vegetable oil
Flour for dredging
Salt and freshly ground pepper to taste
3 large onions, peeled and very thinly sliced
1 cup apple cider vinegar
1 cup dry white wine
⅔ cup water
¼ cup yellow raisins
4 bay leaves
¼ cup pignoli (pine nuts)

Lemon sole is much sought after for its fine-textured meat and delicate flavor. It is often one of the most expensive varieties of fillets in the Seafood department. The name *lemon sole* is actually a marketing term, referring to a large blackback flounder weighing over 3 pounds. If there is a large whole flounder on the ice in the Seafood department, select this instead of lemon sole. It is the same fish and often dramatically less expensive. For example, I bought a flounder that weighed 3.09 pounds (at $3.29) for $10.17, and had the Seafood manager fillet it for me. The same amount of lemon sole fillets would have cost me $19.49 for about 1½ pounds of fish at $12.99 a pound! I knew my fillets were the freshest available, since I could look at the condition of the whole fish. I froze the bones and trimmings to make a fish stock on another day.

Fluke, halibut, petrale sole, plaice, sanddabs, gray sole, and Pacific turbot are all flat fish belonging to the flounder family.

1. Wash the fillets under cold water and pat very dry. Cut them into pieces no larger than 3 × 4 inches.

2. Add enough oil to cover just the bottom of a large skillet and heat until the oil is very hot and rippling on the surface.

3. Dredge just enough pieces of fish to fit in the skillet, shaking to remove excess flour. Cook for 2 to 4 minutes on each side, depending on thickness, until golden brown.

4. As the fish is cooked, transfer it with a slotted spatula to an earthenware or porcelain dish. Season with salt and pepper. Continue dredging, then cooking, the remaining fish, adding more oil as needed.

5. Add the remaining oil and onion slices to the pan, stirring to separate them. Turn down the heat to very low and continue cooking, stirring occasionally, until the onions are very soft and tender, about 15 minutes.

6. Add the vinegar, turn up the heat, and boil until the liquid is almost evaporated, about 5 to 7 minutes. Stir in the wine, adjust the heat to medium-low, and simmer for 20 minutes. Add the water and raisins and simmer 5 minutes longer.

7. Sprinkle the whole bay leaves and pignoli over the cooked fish and pour over the cooking liquid. Cover with heavy aluminum foil and let the fish marinate in a cool place for 12 to 24 hours.

8. Discard the bay leaves, carefully transfer the pieces of fish to an attractive serving platter, if desired, and serve at room temperature. I'd serve this as a first course or fish course for a substantial formal dinner. A small timbale of saffron rice and baby peas would be an attractive addition to each plate.

Individual Curried Scallop Strudels

Serves 8

This recipe is a great favorite among my friends who entertain, since the strudels can be prepared a day ahead and the portions are easily served to each guest. I love the crunchiness of the phyllo layers. Here I added a small amount of ground nuts and mustard between the layers for added flavor. Working with phyllo is quite easy, once you get the hang of it. And, lots of different fillings can be wrapped inside. For a Tex-Mex variation, see the INDIVIDUAL CHILI STRUDELS on page 179.

Of the hundreds of scallop species, only a few come to our markets. The most expensive are the *bay*, which are fished in shallow bays of water. They are small in size, about ½ to 1 inch, and are the sweetest for simple sautés. *Calicos* are similar to bays but come from deeper waters, and the flavor is not as rich. *Sea scallops* can measure up to 2 inches in diameter and, if very fresh, are spectacular when quickly grilled. For this recipe, any variety will work. If sea scallops are less expensive, buy them.

FILLING
¾ cup clam juice
1½ pounds sea scallops cut in ⅛ths or bay scallops
2 tablespoons unsalted butter
2 tablespoons flour
1 tablespoon freshly grated ginger
4 teaspoons curry powder (hot or mild)
½ teaspoon salt, or to taste
Freshly ground black pepper to taste
⅛ teaspoon ground red pepper
2 large cloves garlic, peeled and minced
2 tablespoons fresh lemon juice
1 12½-ounce jar Major Grey's chutney
⅔ cup thinly sliced scallions, including green parts
1 8-ounce can water chestnuts, drained and thinly sliced

STRUDEL
½ cup freshly toasted bread crumbs
3 tablespoons finely chopped walnuts
½ teaspoon dry mustard
½ teaspoon salt
12 phyllo leaves
8 tablespoons (1 stick) unsalted butter, melted
Paprika for garnish
24 pea pods, 16 cherry tomatoes, sliced scallions for garnish (optional)

1. MAKE THE FILLING Pour the clam broth into a medium-size skillet, add the scallops, and bring to a simmer. Poach the scallops until barely cooked, about 2 minutes. Drain, reserving the broth for later.

2. Dry the skillet. Melt 2 tablespoons of butter over

DID YOU KNOW? Scallops are a best bet for freezing. If they are properly frozen and defrosted, it is virtually impossible to tell them from fresh. When they are on sale, check the freshness code on the plastic container or ask when they came into the store. If not using them within 2 days of this date, freeze immediately. When the scallops are packaged in shrink-wrap trays, be sure to rinse them under cold water, drain, and freeze in airtight containers, leaving a small amount of space at the top for expansion.

medium-high heat, just until it foams. Add the flour and cook it until lightly colored, stirring with a wooden spoon. Whisk in the reserved clam broth, ginger, curry powder, salt, black pepper, red pepper, garlic, and lemon juice. The mixture will be thick. Cook over medium heat for 2 to 3 minutes, then remove the pan from the heat.

3. Before pouring the chutney from the bottle, heat it in a pan of water or (without the top) in a microwave, so that it pours more easily. Strain the chutney, reserving the liquid for later use. Cut the fruit into thin slivers. There will be about ½ cup fruit (mango) pieces. Add the chutney, scallions, water chestnuts, and scallops to the curry mixture.

4. Preheat your oven to 400°F and lightly butter a jelly roll pan.

5. ASSEMBLE THE STRUDELS Mix the bread crumbs, walnuts, mustard, and salt in a food processor fitted with a steel chopping blade and pulse a few times to distribute the nuts and mustard evenly, or stir the ingredients together in a bowl.

6. Place 1 leaf of phyllo with the long edge near you on a towel-lined work surface, covering the remaining phyllo with a dry towel. Brush the phyllo lightly with melted butter and distribute a generous tablespoon of crumb mixture over the entire leaf. Repeat with a second phyllo leaf, buttering and sprinkling with the crumb mixture. Add a third leaf, *do not* butter, and cut the pile of phyllo in half down the middle from top to bottom, using a sharp knife. Brush around the edges of each stack of phyllo with melted butter.

7. Place ½ cup of the filling along each of the lower edges of the strudel, leaving about 1 inch of phyllo free of filling on either end. Holding each side of the towel in a hand, flip the towel toward the back, causing the phyllo to roll over the filling. Continue to roll until about half of the dough is rolled, then turn the side edges in to form neat packets, and finish rolling. Using your hands or a spatula, transfer the strudels carefully onto the buttered jelly roll pan, placing them seam side down. Brush with melted butter and sprinkle with paprika. Continue with the remaining phyllo and filling.

8. Bake in the top third of the preheated oven until the strudels are golden brown, about 12 to 14 minutes.

Serve at once or leave in a turned-off oven for up to 45 minutes. Place one strudel on each plate with a fan-design of 3 lightly steamed pea pods and a couple of cherry tomatoes for garnish. Sprinkle a couple of scallion rings on top, if desired. Pass the remaining chutney and its liquid at the table.

Individual Red Pepper Salmon Mousses

Makes 8 ½-cup mousses

This is a contemporary variation of an old favorite. Twenty years ago, we were making and serving salmon mousse as a first course. What makes this version modern is that it's made without cream and mayonnaise. Puréed red bell pepper and low-fat yogurt update this classic and give it a pared-down new line. Add a little red salmon caviar and serve with the COOL AND TANGY WATERCRESS SAUCE on page 63 for an elegant entrée. It is important to buy the best quality *red* canned salmon for the mousse to look and taste good.

1 15½-ounce can "fancy" quality red salmon, drained with liquid reserved, large bones, cartilage, and skin removed
1 large red bell pepper, peeled, seeds and membranes removed, *or* ½ of a 7-ounce jar red peppers packed in water, drained and blotted dry
¾ cup plain low-fat yogurt
¼ cup minced scallions, white part only; reserve greens for garnish
¼ cup minced celery
¼ cup peeled, seeded, and minced cucumber
¼ cup finely chopped fresh dill
1½ tablespoons fresh lemon juice
¼ teaspoon salt
¼ teaspoon ground red pepper
1 package unflavored gelatin
Boiling water to combine with salmon liquid to make 1 cup
2 egg whites at room temperature
1 2-ounce jar red salmon caviar
1 recipe COOL AND TANGY WATERCRESS SAUCE or YOGURT CUCUMBER RAITA (page 277)

1. Lightly oil eight decorative ½-cup molds.

DID YOU KNOW? To soften gelatin so that it is evenly distributed, I first sprinkle the granules on a small amount of cold liquid and wait until it is absorbed. Then I combine this mixture with a hot liquid to melt it.

To determine how much gelatin you will need to solidify a liquid, you should estimate that 1 envelope of gelatin will gel 2 cups of liquid.

2. Place the salmon and red pepper in a food processor fitted with a steel chopping blade, and process until smooth. Add the yogurt, scallions, celery, cucumber, dill, lemon juice, salt, and red pepper and pulse just until combined, scraping down the sides occasionally.

3. Meanwhile, pour about ¼ cup cold water in a cup and sprinkle the gelatin on top of it. Do not stir. Once the granules are absorbed, combine the gelatin with the salmon liquid and boiling water and stir to blend. Allow the liquid to cool in the refrigerator until room temperature, then add it to the salmon mixture through the feed tube while the processor is running. Transfer the salmon mixture to a bowl.

4. Beat the egg whites until stiff but not dry. Fold them into the salmon, but do not overmix. Ladle the mousse into the prepared molds, cover, and refrigerate until firm, at least 4 to 6 hours.

5. To serve, invert the molds onto individual plates, shaking gently to loosen the mousses. Spoon some COOL AND TANGY WATERCRESS SAUCE or YOGURT CUCUMBER RAITA around each mousse. To garnish: Place a tiny spoonful of red caviar on top of each mousse and at 3 equally spaced spots on the sauce. From the remaining scallion tops, cut 8 narrow strips about 4 inches long and ⅛ inch wide. Tie each into a knot and place one on top of each mousse.

Warm Salmon Mousse in a Phyllo Crown

Serves 12 for a first course or 8 for a main course

This elegant warm salmon mousse is wrapped in a crown of golden flaky pastry and served with COOL AND TANGY WATERCRESS SAUCE, a pleasing contrast in color and temperature.

Salmon in every form from poached whole to ethereal mousses seems to be among everyone's favorite fish. Supermarket Seafood departments recognize this and reach out around the world to keep their ice-covered displays or cases full of fillets and steaks from the Atlantic and the Pacific oceans. To save money without compromising quality, I would ask for salmon tails and trimmings—a good choice here since the fish is puréed. Should you be counting calories, look at the recipe for INDIVIDUAL RED PEPPER SALMON MOUSSES (page 231). The salmon caviar and red bell pepper make them seem rich, while yogurt keeps the fat content low.

2 pounds fresh salmon, skinned and boned
4 egg whites
1½ cups heavy cream
¼ teaspoon freshly grated nutmeg
Pinch ground red pepper
Salt and white pepper to taste
1½ tablespoons finely chopped fresh tarragon *or*
    1½ teaspoons dried tarragon
1 tablespoon finely chopped flat-leaf parsley
2 tablespoons unsalted butter
8 tablespoons (1 stick) unsalted butter, melted
8 phyllo leaves
1 recipe COOL AND TANGY WATERCRESS SAUCE (page 63)

IMPORTANT: Have the salmon, egg whites, cream, and all equipment very cold.

1. Divide the salmon almost in half, reserving the smaller amount. Cut the larger amount into 3 to 4 pieces, place it in a food processor fitted with a steel chopping blade, and purée until smooth, scraping down the sides as needed. With the motor running, pour in the egg whites through the feed tube, blending well; then add the heavy cream. Add the nutmeg, red pepper, salt, pepper, tarragon, and parsley and pulse a few times just to blend. Remove the blade from the bowl, cover the bowl with plastic wrap, and refrigerate until ready for use.

2. Cut the remaining portion of salmon into small cubes. Melt 2 tablespoons of butter in a medium-size skillet just until it foams. Add the salmon and sauté over medium-high heat for 1 minute, stirring often. Allow it to cool.

3. Preheat your oven to 375°F and generously butter a bundt pan.

4. Brush 1 phyllo leaf with melted butter, covering the remaining leaves with a dry towel until ready to use. Fold the phyllo leaf into quarters lengthwise and drape it inside the buttered bundt pan with the long edge hanging over the outside edge of the pan. The inner edge should come just to the top edge of the center tube. Repeat with the remaining 7 leaves.

5. Fill the pan with half of the salmon mixture. Arrange the salmon cubes evenly over this and scrape the remaining mixture over the salmon, smoothing the mousse with the back of a spoon or a spatula. Cover the mousse with the extended phyllo leaves, gently pushing the leaves together at the center. Brush liberally with melted butter, and transfer the pan to the middle of the preheated oven. Bake until the top is crisp and golden colored, about 35 to 40 minutes. Remove the pan from the oven, invert it onto an oven-proof serving dish, lift off the pan, and return the mousse to the oven for 10 minutes for additional crispness.

6. Remove the mousse from the oven and let it stand for 5 to 7 minutes before slicing. Garnish with some fresh watercress sprigs, if desired. Cut it into wedges with a serrated knife, and spoon COOL AND TANGY WATERCRESS SAUCE around each slice.

Lobster Timbales with Riesling Beurre Blanc

Serves 6

I find that glamorous fare is available from your supermarket if you are a selective shopper. This dish is extravagant, elegant, and ethereally delicious—definitely an indulgence for a very special occasion. The pairing of lobster with sweet wine affords a wonderfully rich, complex combination of flavors. The essences of *all* the lobster and aromatic vegetables are distilled into this shimmery custard.

2 1½ pound live lobsters
Court bouillon or salted water for poaching
3 tablespoons unsalted butter
2 medium shallots, peeled and minced
1 medium carrot, scraped and minced
½ red bell pepper, seeds and membranes removed,
   and minced (about ¼ cup)
2½ cups heavy cream + liquid drained from the
   lobster shells to make 3½ cups liquid
2 whole eggs
3 egg yolks
¼ cup Late Harvest Riesling wine *or* white wine
⅛ teaspoon freshly grated nutmeg
Pinch of ground red pepper
Salt and white pepper to taste
Unsalted butter to grease custard cups
1 recipe LATE HARVEST JOHANNISBERG RIESLING
   BEURRE BLANC (page 281)
2 tablespoons unsalted butter
18 small scallions, trimmed to 5 to 6 inches, for
   garnish

1. Fill a pot large enough to hold both lobsters with court bouillon or salted water and bring to a boil. Add the lobsters, return the liquid to a boil and cook for 14 minutes longer. Remove the lobsters and let them cool slightly. Working with the lobsters in a large bowl to catch the juice, break off the tails and remove the meat. Twist off and crack the claws, removing as much meat as possible. Drain enough of the liquid from within the body of the lobster into the cream to make 3½ cups of liquid. Reserve the meat from 1 large claw to use in the sauce. Cover the lobster meat and set aside.

2. Discard the head. Break the emptied lobster shells into small pieces.

3. In the same pot that the lobster was cooked in, melt 3 tablespoons of butter just until it foams. Stir in the shallots, carrots, and red pepper and sauté them over medium-high heat stirring frequently, until softened, about 5 minutes. Add the cream and lobster shells, including the small legs, and bring the mixture just to a simmer. Cook very gently, partially covered, for about 25 minutes.

4. While the cream is simmering, transfer the lobster meat (except for the reserved claw) to a food processor fitted with a steel chopping blade and pulse until almost smooth. Scrape it into a bowl and set aside.

5. Preheat your oven to 325°F and butter six ¾-cup custard cups or a 6-cup ring mold. Bring a pot of water to a boil.

6. Line a fine strainer with a double thickness of cheesecloth or heavy-duty paper towels. Strain the vegetable-cream-lobster shells into a large measuring cup or bowl, pressing with the back of a spoon to extract all the flavor. In a large bowl, whisk the eggs and egg yolks together. Pour the wine into the cream mixture, then add the liquid to the eggs in a slow, steady stream, stirring continuously. (Do not overbeat or a foam will form on top.) Add the ground red pepper, nutmeg, salt, white pepper, and lobster meat and stir.

7. Ladle the lobster mixture evenly into the cups or mold, and set them into a baking dish large enough to hold them. Pour boiling water into the baking dish (it should come halfway up the side of the cups) and cover the custard with wax paper. Transfer the pan to the bottom third of your preheated oven and bake for 30 minutes, or until a knife inserted near the middle of the custard comes out clean. Carefully remove the baking dish from the oven and let the cups sit in the water while you prepare the beurre blanc and garnish.

8. Chop the reserved claw meat into fine dice and stir it into the beurre blanc.

9. Before serving, sauté the trimmed scallions in 2 tablespoons of butter just until wilted, about 2 to 3 minutes, and set aside. Loosen each custard with a sharp knife and invert it onto a heated plate. Spoon beurre blanc around the timbales. Place 3 scallions arched around each lobster timbale.

NOTE: To serve the timbales cold, replace the beurre blanc with COOL AND TANGY WATERCRESS SAUCE (page 63) and garnish with sprigs of watercress.

Court Bouillon for Poaching Fish

Makes about 1 gallon

Court bouillon is often used to enhance the flavor of a fish while it is being poached. It is easy to make, and once the fish has been poached (for example CHILLED WHOLE COD TONNATO on page 250) in it, it can be reduced and turned into a fish aspic. It can also then be frozen. If you are not poaching a fish but want fish stock, add the trimmings and bones from 3 or 4 lean white fish to the liquid instead of the whole fish.

12 cups (3 quarts) water
1 bottle dry white wine
¾ cup white wine vinegar
3 large onions, each stuck with 3 whole cloves
4 medium carrots, chopped
2 medium stalks of celery with leaves, chopped
1 bay leaf
1 teaspoon dried thyme leaves
6 sprigs flat-leaf parsley
6 black peppercorns
1 tablespoon salt

1. Combine all of the ingredients together in a large pot or fish poacher and bring just to a boil; then reduce the heat and simmer the liquid for 1 hour before adding the fish to be poached.

2. To turn the bouillon into aspic once the fish (or additional bones and trimmings) has been cooked and removed, strain it into a clean pot through several layers of cheesecloth placed over a colander or fine-mesh strainer. Simmer to reduce by about two thirds, skimming the surface if necessary. Chill until firm.

Providencial Clam Chowder

Serves 8 to 10

Like Providence, Rhode Island, this chowder is half-way between Manhattan and Boston: a creamy fish soup with tomatoes! What's more, it's easy and quick to make.

Some Seafood departments have shucked clams. These are great to add to chowders to save time. If your recipe calls for clam broth, buy it bottled where either juices or other canned fish products are sold. I'd steer clear of canned clams for chowder, since neither the taste nor the texture are the same as fresh.

Individually quick frozen or chopped clams will work, as well.

24 chowder clams, scrubbed in cold water
3 cups water
2 ounces salt pork, diced in ¼-inch cubes
3 medium carrots, scraped and finely chopped
   (about 1¼ cups)
1 large onion, peeled and finely chopped
1 large sweet green pepper, seeds and membranes
   removed, finely chopped
1 large clove garlic, peeled and minced
Salt and freshly ground black pepper
1 bay leaf
1 teaspoon dried thyme leaves, crushed
1 large red or all-purpose potato, peeled and diced
   (about 2 cups)
1 cup heavy cream
2 cups drained canned Italian tomatoes, finely
   chopped
2 tablespoons finely chopped flat-leaf parsley

1. Place the clams in a large pot, add water, and cover with a tight-fitting lid. Cook gently until the clams open, about 10 to 12 minutes. Remove the clam meat, chop coarsely, and set aside covered. Discard the shells. Strain the liquid through a double thickness of cheesecloth or a fine-mesh strainer lined with dampened paper towels and set aside. You should have about 6 cups of liquid.

2. Rinse and dry the pot. Add the salt pork and sauté it over medium heat, stirring constantly, until lightly colored, about 3 minutes. Stir in the chopped carrots, onion, green pepper, and garlic, cover and sweat them over medium-low heat until just tender, about 8 to 10 minutes. Season with salt and pepper.

3. Add the reserved clam broth, bay leaf, thyme leaves, diced potato, and chopped clams, and simmer for 40 minutes.

4. Stir in the cream, tomatoes, and parsley, and simmer for another 10 minutes. Taste for seasonings, and serve at once. This chowder may be prepared ahead of time and reheated. I would not suggest freezing it.

Tangy Cioppino

Serves 6 as a main course

Cioppino is a fish stew that is said to have originated in San Francisco. It is similar to bouillabaisse, from the south of France. As in most stews, ingredients may be substituted for one another. This recipe is meant as a guideline. Use it as a base and improvise from there, selecting what is the best the day you go marketing. I like this version because the addition of vinegar, oil, and garlic at the end really lifts the flavors. Generous bowls of cioppino, served with a crisp green salad, garlicky toasted French bread, and a chilled bottle of chardonnay, are great for a Sunday supper.

Oysters, mussels, and clams are difficult to buy when shrink-wrapped. Here, you must know that the Seafood buyer's sources are reliable. If the shellfish is on ice, touch any open shell to be sure it closes. When steamed, any clam, mussel, or oyster shell that remains shut should be discarded without being eaten.

1 pound littleneck clams, scrubbed
1 pound mussels, debearded and scrubbed
2 cups cold water
4 tablespoons olive oil
1 large green pepper, seeds and membranes
   removed, finely chopped
1 large onion, peeled and finely chopped
2–3 large cloves garlic, peeled and minced
1½ cups dry white wine
1 6-ounce can tomato paste
1 28-ounce can crushed Italian tomatoes
2 teaspoons dried basil
1 bay leaf
½ teaspoon red pepper flakes
¼ teaspoon crumbled saffron threads
½ cup chopped flat-leaf parsley
Salt and freshly ground black pepper
¾ pound monkfish fillets, cut into 1-inch cubes
¾ pound red snapper fillets, cut into 1½-inch
   strips
¾ pound medium shrimp, peeled and deveined
2 tablespoons red wine vinegar
5 tablespoons fruity olive oil
1 tablespoon finely minced garlic

1. Place the clams and mussels in a large nonaluminum pot, add the water, cover with a tight-fitting lid, and cook gently just until the shells open, 5 to 6 minutes. Remove the clams and mussels to a bowl and cover. Strain the broth through a double thickness of cheesecloth or a fine-mesh strainer lined with paper towels and reserve. Rinse the pot.

2. Add 4 tablespoons of olive oil to the pot and heat it until fragrant. Stir in the pepper, onion, and garlic, and sauté over medium heat until softened, about 7 minutes.

3. Pour in the wine, bring it to a boil, then stir in the reserved clam-mussel broth, tomato paste, crushed tomatoes, basil, bay leaf, red pepper flakes, saffron, salt, and plenty of pepper. Reduce the heat and gently boil uncovered until slightly thickened, about 20 minutes.

4. Add the monkfish, simmer for 2 minutes; then add the red snapper and shrimp, and simmer 3 minutes more. Return the clams and mussels to the pot. Combine the vinegar, olive oil, and minced garlic and stir this into the cioppino. Cover and simmer for 10 minutes. Serve at once with thin slices of French bread rubbed with garlic and brushed with olive oil, if desired.

NOTE: Cioppino may be made ahead and gently reheated.

Warm Mussel and Spinach Salad

Serves 2 to 4

This salad is a more substantial version of a classic spinach salad, tossed with a mustardy vinaigrette. Being served warmish, it seems more satisfying as a main course for lunch in either summer or winter.

Mussels are now being farmed and sold to supermarkets. These cultivated mussels are usually very clean and require little additional work. When storing them in the refrigerator, make sure to punch holes in the plastic bag to let them breathe. Or better yet, take them out of their wrapping, place them in a vegetable crisper, and cover them with a damp cloth or paper. It would be safer to cook them the first day and freeze them if not used within a day of purchase.

1¼ pounds fresh spinach
2 large cloves garlic, peeled and crushed
2 tablespoons Dijon mustard
2 tablespoons lemon juice
¾ cup fruity extra-virgin or top-quality olive oil
½ teaspoon salt, or to taste
⅓ cup minced red onion
1 tablespoon olive oil
1½ pounds mussels, scrubbed, beards removed
½ pound thick-sliced bacon, cut into ½-inch slices
2 tablespoons sherry or red wine vinegar
1½ cups (2 ounces) thinly sliced white mushrooms
1¼ cups garlic-flavored croutons
8 cherry tomatoes, split
Freshly ground black pepper to taste

1. Remove the stems from the spinach. Wash in several changes of water to remove the sand. Dry well (a salad spinner works well). Cut it into ¾-inch strips. This is easily done by rolling several leaves together lengthwise into a tight cylinder and cutting across the roll. This should make about 8 to 10 cups of spinach. Put the spinach in a large salad bowl.

2. PREPARE THE VINAIGRETTE Combine the garlic, mustard, and lemon juice in a medium-size bowl. Add the olive oil in a slow, steady stream, whisking continuously. Stir in the salt and the red onion. Set aside.

3. STEAM THE MUSSELS Pour 1 tablespoon of olive oil into a large pot with a tight-fitting lid and heat until fragrant; then drop in the mussels, cover, and cook just until the shells are open, about 4 minutes. Remove the mussels from their shells and add the meat to the vinaigrette.

4. While the mussels are cooking, begin sautéing the bacon in a medium-large skillet. Separate the pieces and cook until quite crisp. Remove the bacon with a slotted spoon to paper towels or a brown bag to drain. Discard the bacon fat, add the sherry vinegar, and deglaze the pan over medium-high heat for just a minute to incorporate all the browned cooking bits. Add this vinegar to the vinaigrette.

5. Add the mushrooms, crumbled bacon, and croutons to the spinach, turn the vinaigrette over the spinach, and quickly toss to cover evenly. Add the tomatoes and a generous amount of black pepper, and serve at once.

DID YOU KNOW? Reserve strained mussel broth and freeze it for later use in stocks, chowders, and stews.

Mexican Shrimp Baskets

Serves 6

Festive presentations certainly set the mood. They need not be elaborate or complicated. In this recipe, corn tortillas are deep-fried into individual south-western-style serving baskets. They are easily made ahead of time and are edible—that's part of the fun. Please, however, be *very* careful when you make them. Hot oil can cause a bad burn.

Peanut or vegetable oil for deep frying
6 corn tortillas
1 pound shrimp, peeled and deveined
36 medium-large pea pods, washed and strings removed
1 cup SALSA (page 57)
⅓ cup sour cream
1 tablespoon fresh lime juice
2 tablespoons vegetable oil
¼ teaspoon salt, or to taste
Freshly ground black pepper to taste
1 cup peeled and julienned jicama
6 cherry tomatoes
¾ cup thinly sliced scallions, including most of the green parts

1. Fill a small saucepan about 6 inches in diameter with enough oil to measure 2 inches in depth. Heat the oil to 350°F on a deep-fat-frying thermometer or test with a cube of bread. (If the bread cube turns golden brown when dropped in the oil, the temperature is correct. If it blackens almost immediately, the oil is too hot. Let it cool before continuing.)

2. Working with 1 tortilla at a time, drop it into the hot oil. Carefully push an empty can about 2½ inches in diameter (such as a soup can), weighted with dried beans, down into the center of the tortilla to form a cuplike shape. The oil will bubble up, so you may have to turn the heat down slightly. Let it cook for about 30 to 45 seconds. Using tongs and a pot holder, *carefully* remove the can with the tortilla basket from the oil, draining any oil back into the pot. Slide the basket off the can and let it drain upside down on a double layer of paper towels. Continue until all the tortillas have been used. You may wish to make a couple of extras, as they keep very well for several days and can be refreshed in a warm oven. Or use them to serve extra condiments (see Note at the end of the recipe).

🛒 SIZING UP SHRIMP:
While sizes do vary from market to market, New York's Fulton Fish Market uses the term "jumbo" or "prawn" for a count of up to 15 shrimp per pound. Sixteen to 20 are called "extra large," 21 to 30 are "large," and 31 to 40 are "medium." Most supermarkets carry three or four sizes with large and medium the most common. However, many Seafood departments have at least eight different sizes that can be specially ordered. Sizes are often interchangeable in a recipe. But, remember shrimp are made up of lots of water. Between peeling, deveining, and cooking, 3 pounds of uncooked shrimp will weigh only 1½ pounds when ready for eating.

3. Fill a large skillet halfway with water. Bring it to a simmer. Add salt, if you wish, and then the shrimp and simmer just until they turn pink. Remove them with a slotted spoon to a small bowl, cover, and let them cool in the refrigerator.

4. Blanch the pea pods for about 15 seconds in hot water, drain, and rinse them under cold water to stop the cooking. Blot them dry on paper towels.

5. In a small bowl, combine the SALSA, sour cream, lime juice, vegetable oil, salt, and pepper and stir to blend.

6. Place 6 shrimp and some jicama in each basket. Stand 3 pea pods upright in one corner of the basket. Spoon the salsa mixture evenly over the 6 baskets. Place 3 more pea pods in a fan-like arrangement on each plate with a cherry tomato where they come together. Sprinkle on scallion slices and serve.

NOTE: There are store-bought tortilla basket makers available in cookware boutiques.

Most shrimp—even in the Seafood department—have been previously frozen and then defrosted, unless they have been air shipped. Make sure to check, since refreezing fish is not a good idea. If there are no shrimp in the Seafood department, take a look in the Frozen Foods aisle. The flash-frozen (IQF —individually quick frozen) variety is a good choice as long as they are slowly defrosted in your refrigerator—not in a poorly supervised market freezer or on a pallet in a warehouse and then refrozen. Large bags (5 pounds or 2 kilos) of block-frozen shrimp, iced at sea at very cold temperatures, seem to survive shipping best, since they are sold directly to restaurants and markets.

When shrimp taste of iodine, they were old before they were shipped or have gone through temperature fluctuations. I'd avoid the tiny foreign canned varieties. Even after rinsing they taste of salt and chemicals.

Oriental Crab-Asparagus Salad in Rice Nests

Serves 4

🛒 **DID YOU KNOW?** What is surimi or imitation crabmeat? Right there, next to the crabs, may be a product marketed under the name "sea legs" or something similar. When king crab prices went sky-high, the Japanese started using inexpensive Alaskan pollack plus flavorings and coloring agents to produce this low-cost alternative. Soon there will be shrimp and scallop look-alikes, as well. While this is an economical substitution in many recipes, my hesitation is due to the additives and extra sugar. Be sure to ask about ingredients.

Here is another recipe where the final presentation is far more dramatic than the sum of its parts. The colors and flavors are vibrant: green scallions, red-bordered radishes, and golden fried rice sticks. The texture, too, is intriguing.

Live hard- and soft-shell crabs will seem calm on the ice. As long as they move, they are fine. Watch them scurry about as the temperature goes up. Be sure that the crab, and *all* seafood on display, is kept cool. If fresh crab is unavailable or you don't have time to pick the meat out of the shell, try the tinned varieties of crab available in the Seafood department. They are a boon to quick cooking and are often of the highest quality. The pasteurization guards against bacteria formation.

½ package Chinese rice sticks
Peanut oil for deep frying
1 pound thin asparagus, woody ends removed, and pared
1 pound lump or backfin crabmeat, preferably fresh, all cartilage removed
3 tablespoons sesame seeds, toasted 3 to 4 minutes until golden
1 cup thinly sliced scallions, white and light green parts
½ cup thinly sliced radishes
⅓ cup rice vinegar
¼ cup vegetable oil
1½ tablespoons lemon juice
½ teaspoon salt, or to taste
Freshly ground black pepper to taste
A few drops hot pepper oil, to taste

1. Break the rice sticks in half. Pour the oil into a wok or deep skillet to a depth of about 2 inches and heat it to a temperature of 375°F. Add the rice sticks, turning to cook evenly. This will take seconds if the oil is hot. Watch them carefully. When the rice sticks are golden brown, remove them with tongs or slotted spoons, and set them aside on paper towels to drain.

2. Bring a large pot of water to a boil. Add the asparagus and cook until just tender, about 2 to 3 minutes after the water returns to a boil. Remove the asparagus from the water, plunge them into cold water to stop the cooking, and dry on paper towels. Cool, then cut the spears on the diagonal into quarters and set aside.

3. In a bowl, combine the crabmeat, sesame seeds, scallions, asparagus, radishes, vinegar, and vegetable oil and toss. Add the lemon juice, salt, and pepper and taste. Add the hot pepper oil, if desired. Adjust the seasonings to taste.

4. Divide the fried rice sticks evenly among 4 plates and spread them into circles. Spoon the crab salad into the middle of each ring, and serve at once. Or line a large platter with the rice sticks and mound the crab salad in the middle. Garnish it with scallion rings, if desired.

Baked Salmon Fillets in Parchment

Serves 6

These salmon fillets are delicious right out of their puffed-up bags, with the julienned vegetables adding a touch of color. Of course, they may be dressed up with a sauce like CONFETTI BEURRE BLANC (page 279), as well. Baking "en papillote" (parchment paper) is easy. Simply remember to cut the parchment circles large enough so that the packets do not open up during the cooking. The fish may be prepared a couple of hours ahead of time and refrigerated.

Paler-colored Atlantic salmon—like those from Ireland, Scotland, or Nova Scotia—have long been considered the most flavorful by fish fanciers. With dwindling numbers of these prized varieties, salmon is now being farmed in Norway with great success and is readily available in many markets. Pacific salmon is abundant and is wonderful eating, as well. Of the western species, the king (chinook) red is most desirable. This is followed by the coho, sockeye, chum, and finally pink (which is usually canned) varieties.

4 tablespoons unsalted butter, softened
6 5- to 6-ounce fillets of salmon
Salt and freshly ground black pepper to taste
1 small zucchini, trimmed and cut into fine julienne
1 small yellow squash, trimmed and cut into fine julienne
1 small carrot, scraped and cut into fine julienne
12 small sprigs flat-leaf parsley

1. Preheat your oven to 375°F.

2. Cut six 14-inch circles of parchment. Spread a teaspoon of butter on one half of each circle.

3. Rinse the fillets and pat them very dry with paper towels. Place 1 fillet on the buttered half of each parchment circle and season generously with salt and pepper. Place an equal amount of the zucchini, yellow squash, and carrot on each fillet, along with 2 sprigs of parsley. Dot the tops of the salmon with the remaining butter.

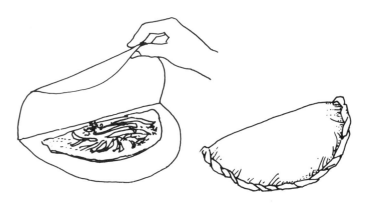

4. Fold the parchment paper in half and crimp the edges to seal completely. Transfer the packets to a jelly roll pan and place in the preheated oven for 13 to 14 minutes, until the paper has puffed. Remove and serve at once on heated plates with orzo or parsleyed small boiled potatoes.

Quick Paella with Monkfish

Serves 2 to 3

This saffron-flavored dish, with rice, olives, and sausages, is reminiscent of the classic Spanish dish paella. While this version uses fewer ingredients, the appeal is great for its ease of preparation, robust aroma, and colorful appearance.

Monkfish is often called "poor man's lobster." With increased popularity, the price has risen to where it is no longer a poor man's anything. Whatever the appellation, its firm flesh is perfect here. And since there are many singles and couples who like to "dine well at home," this recipe is for two hearty appetites to savor together. If you are having a party, see the

Note at the end of this recipe for the do-ahead party version that serves 8 to 10.

¾ pound monkfish fillets, cut into 1-inch cubes
¼ cup dry white wine
1 tablespoon olive oil
1 6-ounce hot Italian sausage, cut into ¾-inch
    slices
1 tablespoon olive oil
1 medium onion, peeled and chopped
1 large bulb fennel, trimmed and sliced into
    wedges
1 large clove garlic, peeled and minced
1⅓ cup chicken stock, heated
¼ teaspoon crumbled saffron threads
1 tablespoon olive oil
½ cup raw rice
1 teaspoon dried thyme leaves
½ cup drained chopped canned Italian tomatoes
½ cup oil-cured black olives
¾ cup frozen peas, defrosted
Salt and freshly ground black pepper to taste

1. Combine the monkfish with the wine in a flat glass or porcelain dish just large enough to hold the fish and set aside.

2. In a medium-large skillet, heat 1 tablespoon of olive oil until fragrant. Add the sausage pieces and sauté them over medium-high heat for 4 to 5 minutes, turning often to color all sides.

3. Add another tablespoon of oil, stir in the onion and fennel, and sauté them for 1 to 2 minutes. Stir in the garlic, cover, and adjust the heat to medium to sweat the vegetables until softened, about 10 to 12 minutes. Stir occasionally.

4. Add the saffron to the heated stock to soften. Add the last tablespoon of olive oil to the vegetable mixture and stir in the rice. Turn the heat up to high, pour in the hot broth and saffron, add the thyme, and stir to blend. Cover the pan and adjust the heat down so that the liquid slowly simmers.

5. After 15 minutes, add the monkfish, wine, and tomatoes and continue simmering uncovered until almost all the liquid has evaporated, about 5 to 7 minutes. Turn the fish pieces to cook evenly. Stir in the olives, peas, salt, and plenty of pepper and taste for seasonings. Simmer just 1 or 2 minutes longer. The paella may be served immediately. However, it will keep for at least ½ hour partially covered over very low heat.

NOTE: For party-size paella, use a very large, heavy casserole and proceed according to the directions above. Make the following substitutions in measurements:

Multiply the monkfish, wine, sausage, fennel, garlic, rice, chicken stock, tomatoes, olives, and peas by 4

Each addition of olive oil should be 3 tablespoons

Use 2 large onions

Double the amount of saffron and thyme

Stir-Fried Tuna with Gingered Vegetables

Serves 4

Many of us who grew up on canned tuna mixed with mayonnaise and a little chopped celery had no idea how wonderful fresh tuna is. In this recipe, I chose to stir-fry the fish because the cubes of tuna stay very moist and succulent when cooked quickly. They are well balanced by the color and the crunch of the carrots and pea pods in this Chinese-inspired dish.

While tuna has a good shelf life, look to see how the fish is stored. Is it resting directly on ice, or is there a piece of plastic or a metal liner protecting it from losing color and flavor? Are the steaks misted periodically to keep the edges from curling and the fish from drying out? Does the surface look pearly? Often, the age of the fish is less important than how it has been cared for.

1 ounce dried shiitake or other Chinese
   mushrooms (in the Oriental section) *or* 3 ounces
   fresh white mushrooms, wiped, trimmed, and
   sliced
¼ cup fresh lime juice (about 2 limes)
¼ cup soy sauce
⅓ cup dry sherry
2 tablespoons honey
1¼–1½ pounds fresh tuna steaks, cut into 1-inch
   cubes
½ pound pea pods, washed, strings removed,
   quickly blanched and drained
4 medium-size carrots, scraped
1 egg white
1 teaspoon cornstarch
4 tablespoons peanut oil
2 large cloves garlic, peeled and split
1 tablespoon finely diced fresh ginger
1 cup thinly sliced scallions (about 4), including
   most of the green parts
1 tablespoon sesame oil

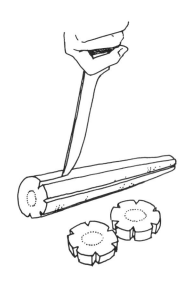

1. Place the mushrooms in a small bowl and pour
warm water over them. Let them soak until softened,
about 20 to 30 minutes, then drain, remove the coarse
stems, rinse away any sand, and cut into thick slices.

2. Make a marinade of the lime juice, soy sauce,
sherry, and honey and stir to blend. Add the tuna
and let it marinate for 2 hours, turning the cubes after
an hour.

3. Meanwhile, make a ¼-inch-deep cut down the
length of 1 carrot. Make a second cut ¼-inch to the
left and slice in at an angle to meet the first cut, removing a "V"-shaped wedge (see illustration). Repeat
these cuts in 4 or 5 more places equi-distant around
the carrot. Repeat with 3 remaining carrots.

NOTE: This step is optional. For a simpler method,
cut the carrot on the diagonal into long, oval-shaped
slices.

4. Steam carrots until almost tender—about 3
to 5 minutes. Drain and set aside.

5. Drain the tuna with a slotted spoon, and pat it
dry with paper towels. Reserve the marinade. Whisk
the egg white and cornstarch together in a medium-
size bowl, add the tuna, and toss to cover.

6. Heat 1 tablespoon of oil in a wok or skillet until hot. Working in batches, quickly stir-fry the tuna, tossing to cook all sides, about 1 to 2 minutes. The tuna will become light colored with a slight crispness on the edge. Remove the cooked tuna to a bowl with a slotted spoon. Repeat this process until all tuna is cooked, adding another tablespoon of oil as needed.

7. Wipe out the wok and heat 1 tablespoon of oil in it. Add the 2 split cloves of garlic, cook for a few seconds until lightly browned. Add the diced ginger and cook an additional 30 seconds. Stir in the pea pods, mushrooms, carrots, and marinade and cook over high heat to reduce the liquid by half. Return the tuna plus the scallions and sesame oil to the wok. Heat to blend the flavors. Serve at once over rice or lo mein noodles.

NOTE: Shrimp or swordfish work well in this recipe, too.

Chilled Whole Cod Tonnato

Serves 8 to 10

This cod recipe is ideal for entertaining, especially because it serves a crowd and tastes better if made the previous day. It is a variation on a classic Italian veal dish made with a tuna mayonnaise and served cold.

A whole cod is quite reasonable, especially compared with salmon. Dressed up with layers of cucumber "scales," it is a dramatic addition to any summer buffet table. And the fish certainly is obtainable. Speak directly to the Seafood manager and let him know what day you need it (a day before the party).

FOR THE TUNA MAYONNAISE (TONNATO SAUCE)

1⅓ cups mayonnaise, preferably homemade with extra-virgin olive oil or a combination of olive and vegetable oils

1 6½-ounce can imported tuna packed in olive oil

½ 2-ounce can anchovy fillets, rinsed and patted dry

¼ cup small capers

¼ cup fresh lemon juice

¾ cup olive oil

1 8-pound cod, whole, with head on, cleaned, gilled, and gutted with the center blood vein and air bladder (sound) removed
COURT BOUILLON to completely cover fish in poacher, (see recipe on page 237)
2 large cucumbers for garnish
Olive slices for garnish

1. MAKE THE TUNA MAYONNAISE Place the homemade mayonnaise in a medium bowl. In a food processor fitted with a steel chopping blade, combine the tuna, anchovies, capers, and lemon juice and process until a smooth paste is formed. With the processor on, pour the oil through the feed tube in a slow, steady stream. (If doing this by hand, mash the tuna, anchovies, capers, and lemon juice with a fork. Whisk in the oil in a slow, steady stream.) Fold the tuna mixture into the mayonnaise and blend well. Cover and refrigerate until needed.

2. POACH THE COD Place the fish on its side and measure the height at its thickest point. Figure 9 to 10 minutes poaching time per inch of thickness once the poaching liquid returns to a boil. The fish may be wrapped in a couple of layers of cheesecloth for easier handling—especially if a poaching rack is unavailable.

3. Fill a fish poacher or shallow pot large enough to accommodate the fish with court bouillon to cover the fish. Bring it to a boil and lower the fish into the pot. When the liquid returns to a boil, turn down the heat so that it never bubbles or boils. Time as directed above in step 2.

4. Once the fish is cooked, remove it from the liquid to a platter and let it cool for a few minutes. If cheesecloth has been used, carefully cut it open with a scissors. Skin the fish and remove the head if it has fallen apart—or if you do not wish to serve it. Slide the cheesecloth out from under the cod, using a wide spatula to help. It is not necessary to remove the skin on the under side. Leave the tail intact. Drain off and blot any liquid on the platter with paper towels, cover the fish loosely with foil, and refrigerate until cold.

6. ASSEMBLE THE FISH Make sure all liquid is removed from the platter. Generously spoon tuna mayonnaise over the cod and around it, reserving any remaining sauce to pass at the table once the cod is served. Smooth the sauce to cover any cracks in the fish, leaving the tail uncovered.

7. Wash the cucumbers. Run the tines of a fork along the length of the cucumbers to score the peel. Slice it in a food processor fitted with a very thin slicing blade, or by hand. Cut the slices in half and create scales on the fish by working from the tail toward the head. You can create gills, too.

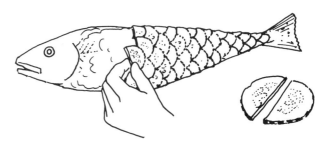

8. If the head has been discarded, stop the scale pattern about 2½ inches from the front end and re-create a head by changing direction of the scales and using an olive slice for an eye. Cover the fish loosely and refrigerate it for at least 4 to 6 hours or, preferably, overnight. For a garnish, lightly steam a pound of julienned carrots and toss with lemon juice, vegetable oil, chopped basil or parsley, salt, and pepper. Arrange the carrots around the fish. Serve with some crusty sourdough bread and a robust white wine, such as a Greco di Tufo. Finish the meal with a fresh fruit tart or some CHILLED WHITE WINE SOUFFLÉ WITH APRICOT SAUCE (page 288).

Sautéed Swordfish with Mustard and Pecan Coating

Serves 3 to 4

DID YOU KNOW? To barbecue swordfish steaks, make a marinade of ¼ cup fresh lemon juice, 1 cup olive oil, 2 large cloves of garlic, and ½ teaspoon freshly ground black pepper, and combine in a flat dish large enough to hold 6 servings of 1-inch swordfish steaks. Turn once to cover both sides, then refrigerate for 2 to 3 hours. Position the grill of the barbecue about 6 inches from the charcoal briquettes. When the fire is hot, place the steak on the grill, baste once, and with the aid of a spatula, turn after 4 to 5 minutes. Baste once again with remaining marinade and cook for another 3 to 4 minutes. Transfer the fish to a serving platter and serve with 1 or 2 swirls of RED PEPPER BUTTER (page 52) or herbed butter.

Swordfish is one of my family's favorite summer foods. We often barbecue these steaks well into the fall, as long as the grill will light. (See the Did You Know? below on grilling swordfish.) In this recipe, the crunchy coating and tarragon cream add a more elegant touch, while keeping the fish moist.

This large, firm-fleshed fish is found in warm waters around the world. In supermarkets and fish stores, swordfish steaks are sold fresh during the summer and fall months, with some of the best coming from local Eastern waters. Swordfish also freezes well. The Japanese ship frozen individually Cryovac-packed steaks and whole sides, which are then cut into steaks on a bandsaw in the market. Under these conditions, I'd prefer to buy the swordfish solidly frozen and then cook it when only partially defrosted to retain as much moisture as possible.

1½–1¾ pounds swordfish steaks, 1 inch thick (1 or 2 large steaks preferred)
Flour for dredging
¼ cup Dijon mustard
5 ounces (1½ cups) finely chopped pecans, *not* pulverized
1½ tablespoons unsalted butter
1½ tablespoons vegetable oil
½ cup heavy cream
1 tablespoon freshly chopped tarragon *or* 1 teaspoon dried
Salt and freshly ground black pepper to taste
Tarragon leaves, for garnish

1. Pat the steak(s) very dry. *Lightly* dredge 1 side of the fish with flour and spread half the mustard on top. Pat half the pecans over this, pressing them into the mustard coating. Turn the steak over and repeat the same process on the second side. Place on a plate, cover loosely, and refrigerate for 30 minutes.

2. Turn your oven on to low and heat a platter.

3. Melt the butter and oil in a large, heavy skillet over medium-high heat just until the butter foams. Add the swordfish and sauté for 4 to 5 minutes until well colored. Adjust the heat down if the pecans begin to burn. With a wide spatula, turn the fish and continue cooking the second side for 4 to 5 minutes.

ON SELECTING SAUCES FOR FISH DISHES: It's really personal preference, but I think spicy sauces such as SALSA (page 57) seem to cut through the richness of fatty fish like tuna, while butter and cream sauces go better with lean fish, such as flounder and other white fish.

In general, fattier fishes have a tendency to go rancid faster because of their oils.

Transfer the fish to the warmed platter and place in the oven.

4. Add the cream, tarragon, and any nuts that have fallen off the fish to the skillet, turn up the heat to high, scrape up all the browned bits in the pan, and boil for 2 to 3 minutes to thicken the sauce. Return the fish, and any liquids that have been exuded, to the pan. You may wish to cut the fish into 3 or 4 serving-size portions at this point if it has been cooked whole. Turn down the heat to low and cook 30 seconds more. Sprinkle a few tarragon leaves on each piece of fish and serve at once on heated plates.

Poached Red Snapper Fillets with Scallop Mousse in Cabbage Packets

Serves 2

These red snapper fillets are filled with a chive-flecked scallop mousse, wrapped in delicate green Napa cabbage leaves, and then poached in the oven. Served on a light tomato sauce, they are beautiful to look at and deliciously satisfying to eat.

2 large Napa cabbage leaves

FOR THE SCALLOP MOUSSE
½ pound sea scallops, very cold
2½ tablespoons heavy cream, very cold
1 egg white, chilled
2 teaspoons finely chopped fresh chives
Salt and pepper to taste

FOR THE FISH PACKETS
1 teaspoon unsalted butter
2 6-ounce red snapper fillets, skin removed, as flat as possible
½ cup dry white wine
½ cup fish stock or clam broth
½ cup white wine
½ cup fish stock or clam broth

FOR THE LIGHT TOMATO SAUCE
1 tablespoon unsalted butter
1 large shallot, peeled and minced
1 large ripe tomato, peeled, seeded, and finely
  chopped *or* ¾ cup drained, finely chopped
  Italian canned tomatoes
Salt and freshly ground black pepper to taste
2 teaspoons chopped fresh chives
Paprika, for garnish

1. PREPARE THE MOUSSE Bring a small skillet partially filled with water to a simmer. Drop in the cabbage leaves for about 30 seconds until they are just softened and pliable. Remove, plunge them into cold water, then blot them dry. With a sharp paring knife, slice away the raised rib on each leaf, taking care not to cut all the way through. Spread the leaves flat on a towel, cover with a damp towel, and set aside.

2. In a food processor fitted with a steel chopping blade, place the scallops, cream, and egg white, and process until very smooth. Stop the machine, scrape down the sides, add the chives, salt, and pepper and pulse a few times to blend.

3. Preheat your oven to 400°F and lightly butter a small baking dish.

4. STUFF THE FISH Place a fillet with the wider end of the fish on the rib-end of the cabbage. Season with salt and pepper. Place a rounded tablespoon of the scallop mousse on the wider end of the fish. Begin rolling the fillet up, including the cabbage leaf. About halfway, turn in the edges of the cabbage, and continue rolling to form a neat package. Place the fish in the baking dish. Bring the ½ cup of white wine and stock to a simmer in a small saucepan and pour it over the fish. If the baking dish is able to withstand direct heat, pour the liquid over the fish and bring it to a simmer on top of the stove. Cover with aluminum foil and transfer to the preheated oven for 15 minutes.

5. **PREPARE THE FISH DUMPLINGS (QUENELLES)**   In a small skillet bring the remaining white wine and stock to a simmer. Using a pair of teaspoons, scoop up 1 rounded teaspoon of the scallop mixture. Shape the top into a round form with the second spoon. Then, with the second spoon, scoop under the oval-shaped mound and let it fall gently into the simmering liquid. Continue with the remaining mixture, making about 5 to 6 more fish dumplings. Poach for about 2 minutes on the first side, then gently flip them over to the second side and continue cooking for another 1½ to 2 minutes. Once they are cooked, turn off the heat and leave the dumplings in the liquid.

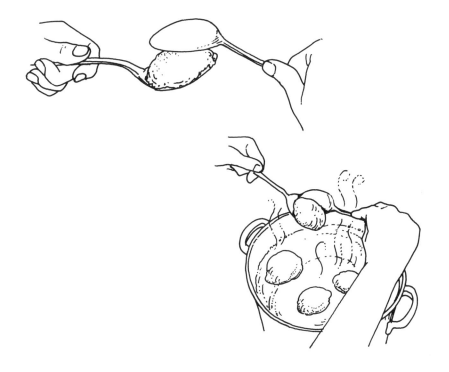

6. **PREPARE THE SAUCE**   In a small, nonaluminum saucepan, heat the butter until it has foamed. Stir in shallots and sauté over medium-high heat for 1 to 2 minutes, stirring occasionally, until just softened. Add the tomato, and continue cooking for another 2 to 3 minutes. Season with salt and pepper.

7. **FOR SERVICE**   Remove the fish from the oven, drain the packets on paper towels, but do not unwrap them. Divide the sauce between 2 heated plates. Add a serving of the red snapper, place 3 scallop dumplings alongside the roll, and sprinkle with chives and paprika. Serve at once. Steamed carrots and parsleyed new potatoes would be a nice accompaniment.

NOTE: This recipe may be doubled to serve 4.

Baked Flounder with Hazelnuts and Shrimp

Serves 4

The exquisite balance of flavors in this festive dish comes from the combination of sweet, delicately crunchy fish with hazelnuts and shrimp scattered on top.

A flounder is really a small sole. They are available the year around. When you are buying fish whole, it is best to make your selections from a Service Fish counter, so you can ask about the fish's age and condition. Here is where having a friend behind the counter is important. If wrapped in plastic, flounder may not be as fresh as you'd like. If the head has been removed, look at where the cut has been made. Edges yellow and curl with age.

FOR THE SAUCE
1 cup dry white wine
½ cup fish stock or clam broth
¼ cup dry vermouth
1 tablespoon red wine vinegar
2 tablespoons minced shallots
1 cup heavy cream
¼ cup hazelnut oil (see Note)

FOR THE FISH
4 1-pound flounders, head sliced off at an angle, gutted, gilled, dark skin removed, and white skin scaled only
Salt and freshly ground black pepper
1 tablespoon unsalted butter, at room temperature
10 tablespoons clarified butter
1 cup freshly toasted fine bread crumbs
24 small shrimp, peeled and deveined
3 tablespoons chopped fresh tarragon *or*
  2 teaspoons dried tarragon plus 1 tablespoon freshly chopped flat-leaf parsley
Salt and white pepper to taste
Pinch of ground pepper
20 hazelnuts, lightly toasted, and coarsely chopped

1. PREPARE THE SAUCE In a small saucepan, combine ½ cup white wine, the fish stock, vermouth, vinegar, and shallots and bring to a boil over high heat. Cook until the liquid has almost completely evaporated. Add the cream and hazelnut oil and boil gently until thickened slightly. Set the pan aside partially covered.

2. COOK THE FISH Meanwhile, preheat your oven to 425°F and butter a baking dish just large enough to hold the 4 flounder comfortably without crowding.

3. Wipe the flounder and season them inside with salt and pepper.

4. Brush both sides of the fish with clarified butter and place the fish in the baking dish, skin side up. Press the bread crumbs onto the top of each fish and drizzle the remaining butter over the crumbs. Pour ½ cup of the white wine around the fish, taking care not to moisten the crumbs. Transfer the pan to the middle of the preheated oven and bake for 13 to 14 minutes. Have ready 4 heated plates.

5. Once the fish is cooked and the crumbs are golden brown, remove the dish from oven and carefully transfer the fish to heated plates. (If the fish is not well colored after the proper cooking time, run it under a broiler for a very short period of time, watching carefully not to burn the crumbs.) Leave the fish in the turned-off oven lightly covered while finishing the sauce.

6. Stir the shrimp into the thickened sauce and cook just until pink, about 1 to 2 minutes. Add 2 tablespoons of the tarragon (or 2 teaspoons dried and crumbled), salt, and white and red peppers and taste to adjust the seasonings.

7. Remove the fish from the oven, blot up any liquid with a paper towel, place 3 shrimp on either side and put some chopped hazelnuts and a sprinkle of tarragon (or parsley) down the middle of each fish. Spoon the sauce evenly around each of the plates and serve at once.

NOTE: Hazelnut oil should be found next to the olive and vegetable oils if your market carries it. Or, perhaps, it will be in the Specialty Food section. If it is not there, ask for it. If enough customers ask for a product, eventually buyers get the idea. In the meantime, you could substitute walnuts and walnut oil, or 3 tablespoons softened unsalted butter and almonds or pecans.

DID YOU KNOW? In Europe and Asia, fish are often served on the bone. They maintain more flavor and moisture that way. If this is not to your liking, carefully split the fish along the center where the rib bones are attached to the backbone. Gently slide a knife along the upper ribs and then the lower ribs, forming 2 half fillets. Place to one side. Lift off the skeleton in 1 piece and discard. Place the 2 top fillets back over the lower whole fillet, and serve.

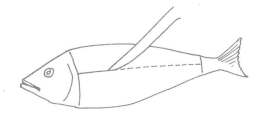

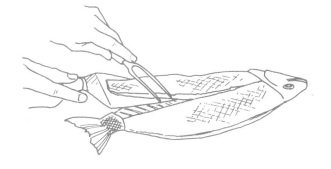

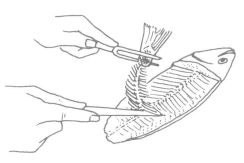

Whole Stuffed Sea Bass (or Red Snapper) en Croûte with Confetti Beurre Blanc

Wrapping small whole sea bass in pastry is dramatic and elegant. Using phyllo dough instead of home-made pastry makes the task easier and the finished dish much lighter. The best time of the year to buy sea bass is in the spring when they are plentiful and less expensive. Stop by or call the Seafood department manager or assistant as soon as you know what your needs will be. Give him time to special order the bass or snapper so that they are all the same size for even cooking. Good news: Most of the work for this festive dish can be done well ahead of time.

Serves 8

1⅓ cups raw rice
½ cup finely chopped flat-leaf parsley
2 large carrots, scraped and shredded
Salt and freshly ground black pepper to taste
4 tablespoons unsalted butter
1½ tablespoons vegetable oil
1¼ cups finely chopped onion
12 ounces mushrooms, wiped, trimmed, and thinly sliced
1 cup dry white wine
8 ¾- to 1-pound sea bass or red snapper, head and tails removed, boned, gilled, and scaled
Salt and freshly ground black pepper
16 tablespoons (2 sticks) unsalted butter, melted
28 phyllo leaves
1 recipe CONFETTI BEURRE BLANC (page 279)

1. Bring a large pot of salted water to a boil, add the rice, and boil until almost tender, about 7 minutes. Drain well and add the parsley, shredded carrots, salt, and pepper and mix.

2. Heat the butter and oil in a medium skillet just until the butter foams. Add the onions and sauté them over medium-high heat until they start to color, about 5 minutes. Add the mushroom slices and continue cooking for 2 to 3 minutes more, stirring frequently. Pour on the wine, raise the heat, and boil until the liquid has evaporated. Add the rice mixture to the skillet, stir, and cook for 1 to 2 minutes more. Set aside.

3. Preheat your oven to 400°F and lightly butter 2 jelly roll pans.

4. Wipe the inside of the fish, sprinkle with salt and pepper, and fill each fish with some of the rice mixture, dividing it evenly among all 8 fish.

5. Cut 7 phyllo leaves in half vertically. Place 2 of the half leaves horizontally on 1 of the jelly roll pans, and brush lightly with butter. Cover all unused phyllo with a towel. Place a second half leaf on top of each of the first, and brush again with a little butter. Place a third leaf on the others, and *do not* brush with butter. Center 1 fish on each of the piles.

6. Place 1 half leaf of phyllo on each fish, brush with a little butter. Repeat until there are 3 pieces of phyllo on each fish. Roll the extended edges of phyllo

DID YOU KNOW? When buying a whole snapper or sea bass, you can only count on about 35 to 40 percent edible fillets once the head, bones, and tails have been removed. However, the bones and trimmings are useful for making fish stock. Why not keep a bag in the freezer until you are ready to use them?

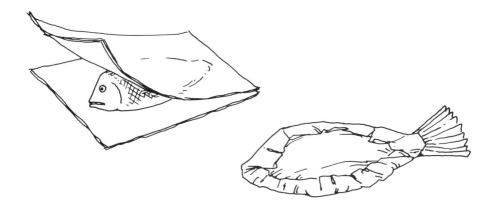

in toward the fish and brush the folded edges with a little butter.

7. To form the tails, brush the remaining half phyllo leaves lightly with butter, and fold them into fourths horizontally. Trim 1 long edge, and gather the uncut edge together in pleats. Place these at the tail end of each fish, and tuck under the crimped edge.

8. Using a wide spatula, carefully move the 2 wrapped fish over to ½ of the pan. Repeat the procedure with 2 more fish, either working on a clean, dry surface or in the jelly roll pan, if space permits. Prepare the remaining 4 fish in the same manner on the second pan.

9. Bake in the middle of the preheated oven for 15 to 17 minutes, or until well-colored. Place each fish on a warmed plate and serve at once, garnished with some greens, such as steamed broccoli florets or small green beans. Spoon some CONFETTI BEURRE BLANC around the fish. Pass the remaining sauce at the table.

Label Literacy: Extra! Extra! Read All About It

As an intelligent supermarket shopper, don't ignore the vital information available to you at no additional cost. I'm talking about being "label literate," and it can save you money and insure healthier eating. Increased consumer awareness of the effects of preservatives, fillers, coloring agents, as well as freshness of our foods has prompted governmental agencies, manufacturers, packers, and supermarkets to let us read more about what we are putting into our bodies. This is how it works:

LABELS ON THE PACKAGE

Dating on Fresh and Packaged Foods

"Sell by" or "pull by" dates indicate at what point the product must be taken off sale. If an item, such as meat, bread, or milk, is purchased by this date, the manufacturer, packager, or market has built in adequate time for the consumer to use the product safely at home. The date may be a date or simply the day of the week.

"Best if used by" dates are used on cans and packaged goods, such as cereals, snacks, and nuts, that are less perishable. This date often includes the year. Some refrigerated products use this or an "expiration" date, indicating that the manufacturer feels that after this time, the product should be discarded.

Another source of protection for the consumer is less obvious. It is the seven letter-and-number code on some labels. This is used mostly in cases of emergency or recall, and it identifies the exact facility, line, shift, and date at which the product was packaged.

Ingredient Information on Prepared and Packaged Foods

All the ingredients included in a product are listed in order of weight from the greatest to the smallest amount. This includes flavoring and coloring agents, identified as artificial or natural, and preservatives and their use (to prevent caking, to protect flavor, etc.).

Although some foods—such as pasta, ice cream, and peanut butter—used to be made according to a standardized formula listed with the Food and Drug Administration and were not required to identify the basic components, current interest in additives has prompted more and more manufacturers to list all ingredients, including different types of fat.

Nutritional Information

This is not required for most products. However, if a label boasts that the product is fortified or enriched with vitamins or minerals, the Food and Drug Administration requires supporting data to be printed on the package. Similarly, if a product is marketed as "low sodium" or "low fat," this must also be substantiated.

One recent trend to watch out for: labels marked "lite" or "light." These foods may be lower in calories, such as fruit packed in juice rather than sugar syrup. Or the flavor may be milder and the color paler, as in light olive oil, while the calorie count is the same as for the fruitier, dark-green varieties.

Smart manufacturers realize that aware consumers want to know these facts, so we are seeing an increased amount of nutritional information listing the number of calories, amount of protein, carbohydrates, fat, and sodium, as well as the percentage of USRDA (U.S. Recommended Daily Allowances) nutrients. In various departments throughout the market, if the package is not labeled, there are often pamphlets or cards, such as "Meat Nutrifacts" which give specific dietary information.

Weight

While a meat, fish, or poultry label will give the exact weight in pounds and tenths of pounds (1.3 pounds equals 1 and ³⁄₁₀ of a pound, or 1 pound, 4.8 ounces), a package or bottle label will indicate *net* (drained weight without liquid) or *volume* weight. Some packages indicate that while the box was full when packed, it will settle during shipping.

Storage and Serving Information

Keeping foods in top condition once they are in your home depends on you. Be sure to check the suggestions for refrigerating, freezing, or storing on a cool shelf.

Many manufacturers have test kitchens in which recipes and garnishing ideas are developed. This is a good source of primary information if the product is new to you.

Information "hot lines" are sometimes given for consumer problems and information.

SHELF INFORMATION

Unit Pricing

Unit pricing is indicated by small signs posted along the edge of each shelf, either above or below the item. It identifies each item by brand, size, and price, and is a useful tool for comparison shopping:

It tells how much each unit measures

- by weight, such as pounds or ounces for rice or hams
- by volume, such as a pint of milk or liquid detergent
- by length, such as feet for rolls of paper towels
- by quantity, such as number of napkins in each package

It indicates the cost per package and how much this is in standard measurements, i.e., by the pound or gallon. Thus, even if package sizes are different, you can ascertain if one is more expensive than the other.

However, even if two different manufacturers' products have the same unit cost, this does not guarantee that the quality will be the same.

Promotional and Sale Items

Some markets place a little flag or banner along the shelf when a certain item is specially priced.

AISLE INDICATORS

Don't ignore the overhead signs—especially if you are in a hurry. They will aim you in the right direction and allow you to skip unnecessary aisles.

Newer markets are installing electronic locators near the entrance or simplified guides on their carts to speed your marketing.

AT THE REGISTER: UNIVERSAL PRODUCT CODES

In markets where a computerized scanning system has been installed, the UPC code on bottles, cans, and packages including meats, is read by a beam of light. The grid of thin and thick lines on each package indicates the manufacturer and product. As the light passes over this mark, the computer reads the current price for the item in a data bank. All the information is then printed within seconds on your register receipt for future reference. In some cases, the machine also announces each purchase. Uncoded items are weighed at check out.

It will pay to watch as your foods are scanned. Sometimes there are errors and sometimes the changes in special prices are overlooked. The price posted may differ from the price charged at the register.

THROUGHOUT THE MARKET

Smart markets know that informed buyers are better buyers. They *want* to help you. Work at becoming an informed buyer. Look for consumer information brochures, hand-outs, hang tags, and warnings about certain products. There is a wealth of information available.

·6·
DAIRY PRODUCTS

INTRODUCTION	The familiar statement "I'm going to the market for a quart of milk" reminds us that most people buy dairy products in supermarkets. And with good reason. Since butter, eggs, and milk sell quickly, the supplies are normally very fresh. In recent years, dairy shelf space has been expanded to hold a multitude of yogurt products, familiar and lesser-known cheeses, and butter and margarine combinations. Although dairy products have always been popular, recent interest in calcium and newer fat-reduced varieties have sparked more interest in them.

WHAT'S IN A NAME

When selecting dairy products, it is important to read labels. Cheese is especially confusing. If cheese is made from milk with only enzymes and heat added, the Food and Drug Administration allows it to be labeled by its name alone, such as "cheddar" or "Swiss." However, "processed cheese food" is a combination of different cheeses with emulsifiers, water, and coloring agents added. "Cheese spreads" usually include vegetable gums and sweeteners, as well.

Low-fat, low-sodium, and low-cholesterol products should have labeling to back up their claims. If no comparison is given, read the ingredient list. When highly saturated vegetable fats, such as palm oil, replace dairy fat, the product is no healthier. Look for added salts, fillers, and chemicals.

BUYING FRESH

To assure freshness, almost every dairy product has a "sell by" date stamped on the package. You should look for it on each package. It may be on a foil wrapper, on the bottom of a cup of yogurt, on the crimped top of milk cartons, or on labels. In most cases, the milk, cheese, or yogurt you buy will be in good condition, and the date includes an adequate amount of time for home use.

However, if a distributor or market is careless, and storage temperatures have risen above 39° or 40° F, the cheese may be moldy or the cream almost soured. This happens often during promotions when "specialty items" are left out on display and ignored. Inspect each item as you pick it up. With cellophane-wrapped products and eggs in cartons, your eyes tell you the condition immediately. A strong indication of spoilage is a swollen carton or package. Even if the product is within code, make another choice.

Another fact to consider is that markets rotate their stock and push older products toward the front. If the carton of cottage cheese is eaten within a couple of days, an older date is of little consequence. However, for longer storage, reach toward the back for the freshest date.

HOME CARE

Dairy products last quite well with a little attention. Refrigerate them quickly after purchase, making sure containers are closed. Cheese needs to be tightly rewrapped after each use. Even with proper wrapping, soft cheeses deteriorate quickly, often within a couple of days. Hard cheeses may last a couple of weeks. Stronger cheeses are best kept in separate plastic containers so the odors don't travel. If a little mold forms on cheese, it can be scraped off, and the remaining piece is fine.

With the exception of butter and purchased frozen yogurt desserts, most dairy purchases are better not frozen. Cheese becomes crumbly, and sweet and sour creams separate.

Going to a neighborhood cheese shop is a wonderful experience. You can taste your way through the store, sampling a world of unusual and special dairy products. Supermarkets are trying to match that experience by expanding their inventory of imported and domestic items and bringing that old-fashioned feeling to the market. While you may still be frustrated looking for a wonderful Reblochon or Taleggio cheese, markets are listening to their customers. Beyond offering samples of new products, supermarkets are providing printed material, educating their clerks, and trying to make their Dairy departments more diversified.

Spicy and Crunchy Low-Cal Tofu Dip

Makes 2 cups

Who says tofu has to be unappealing? Try this oriental-style dip for cooked artichokes or raw vegetables and you may be surprised. It is low in calories, yet high in flavor and texture. You could also use it on a green salad with fresh crab or shrimp added for a light summer meal.

Tofu comes in soft and firm styles. I prefer the latter because it thickens the dressing. If you use part of the package, store the remaining tofu, covered, in a bowl of fresh water. Change the water every 2 days, and the tofu will last for a week.

1–2 medium cloves garlic, peeled
1 tablespoon minced fresh ginger
¼ cup soy sauce
2 tablespoons sesame oil
1 tablespoon rice vinegar
10 ounces firm tofu
1 6-ounce can water chestnuts, finely chopped
3 tablespoons thinly sliced scallions

1. Place the garlic and ginger in the bowl of a food processor fitted with a steel chopping blade and pulse until the garlic is cut into small pieces.
2. Add the soy sauce, sesame oil, rice vinegar, and tofu, and process until very smooth, scraping down the sides of the bowl as needed.
3. Add the water chestnuts and scallions, and process just until blended. Scrape the sauce into a bowl, cover, and refrigerate 1 hour. It will keep for 2 weeks.

DID YOU KNOW? Fresh ginger, cut into small pieces, keeps for weeks in the refrigerator when stored in a jar with some sherry to cover it.

Herbed Cream Cheese Dip

Makes 1 cup

As you look over the shelves in the Dairy department, you will find containers of cream cheese and herb dips with fancy labels and relatively expensive price tags. Nearby is plain cream cheese. Within minutes, you can make your own dip, and you can vary it to suit your taste. This is a good place to use up little bits of leftover herbs. Because I love basil, I often use it in this dip. But try experimenting with grated onion, grated Parmesan cheese, oregano, water-packed pimentos, or seasoning mixes, like Mrs. Dash.

Calorie- and fat-reduced cream cheese, Neufchâtel, and farmer cheese may all be substituted in this recipe.

¼ cup chopped flat-leaf parsley leaves
⅔ cup loosely packed basil leaves, chopped
1 large clove garlic, peeled and split
8 ounces cream cheese
½ teaspoon salt, or to taste
2–4 drops Tabasco sauce
1–2 tablespoons milk (optional)

1. Combine the parsley, basil, and garlic in the bowl of a food processor fitted with a steel chopping blade and pulse until the garlic is finely chopped.
2. Add the cream cheese, salt, and Tabasco and process until smooth. For a creamier consistency, add the milk and blend. Scrape the mixture into a bowl and serve with sturdy raw vegetables, such as carrots, celery, jicama, and red peppers. Or spread on toast, bagels, or sandwiches.

Vermont Cheddar and Maple Crackers

Makes 3 dozen puffs

From extra-sharp to mild, cheddar is the most widely consumed cheese in the world. Many of our American varieties are exceptionally good, especially those from Vermont and New York. Today, supermarkets are showcasing these regional cheeses, often by displaying a whole giant wheel with small samples alongside to tempt you—a smart move on their part. This is a good opportunity for you to taste a variety you are unfamiliar with.

Speaking of unfamiliar, the combination of cheddar cheese with maple syrup and pecans may strike you as unusual. It is, but it's also one of those great, easy hors d'oeuvres to throw together when guests arrive. You can make the mixture and keep it for 2 weeks in the refrigerator. It is especially good when served with sherry and port. For an open-faced sandwich, spread the cheese mixture on toast and top with smoked bacon.

2 cups shredded sharp cheddar cheese
2½ ounces chopped pecan pieces
⅓ cup mayonnaise
1 tablespoon maple syrup
½ teaspoon Worcestershire sauce
36 whole grain crackers, such as Wheatsworth, Triscuit, etc.

1. Mix the cheese, pecans, mayonnaise, maple syrup, and Worcestershire sauce together in a medium-size bowl. Spread the mixture by rounded teaspoonfuls evenly on crackers.

2. Place the crackers on a flat pan or cookie sheet and run it under the broiler until the cheese is hot, melted, and bubbling. Transfer the crackers to an attractive plate and serve at once. They will keep nicely in a warm oven for up to a half hour.

Puffy Asparagus and Cheese Gougère

Serves 8

This is an impressive hors d'oeuvre to make for spring when asparagus comes into the market. The pastry (*gougère*) is a giant cream puff circle, filled with chopped asparagus and Gruyère (or other Swiss cheese) and Parmesan cheese. The top is crunchy with bright green asparagus tips on top. When asparagus is out of season, substitute finely chopped broccoli and add ⅓ cup chopped parsley in step 5.

There are many kinds of Swiss cheese in supermarkets. While almost any of them will work in this recipe, Gruyère has a nutty, sweet, full flavor that most domestically produced varieties lack. Look for the name stamped on the rind in red. Gruyère is usually sold in square blocks and has almost no holes.

8 ounces fresh asparagus pared, woody ends removed
1 cup water reserved from cooking the asparagus
8 tablespoons (1 stick) unsalted butter, room temperature and cut into pieces
¼ teaspoon freshly grated nutmeg
¼ teaspoon dry mustard
Pinch of ground red pepper
½ teaspoon salt
Freshly ground black pepper
1 cup unbleached all-purpose flour
4 eggs
¾ cup (2½ ounces) shredded Gruyère cheese or imported Swiss cheese
1 egg yolk mixed with 2 tablespoons of milk
½ cup (1½ ounces) freshly grated Parmesan cheese

1. Preheat your oven to 400°F. Butter a round oven-safe metal pan (at least 10 inches in diameter) or a cookie sheet and run it under cold water or chill it for a few minutes.

2. Boil the asparagus in 1¼ cups salted water until just tender, about 3 minutes. Reserve the liquid. Plunge the asparagus into cold water, then drain and blot dry on paper towels. Cut off the tip plus about 1 inch of 8 asparagus spears and reserve them for the final garnish. Cut the remaining asparagus into ½-inch slices crosswise, and set aside.

3. Combine 1 cup of the asparagus cooking water, the butter, nutmeg, mustard, red pepper, salt, and pepper together in a heavy saucepan and slowly bring to a boil. If the liquid does not boil, the dough will not thicken correctly.

4. Remove the pan from the heat and stir in the flour. With a wooden spoon, beat until the dough forms a ball. Return the pan to low heat, stirring and flipping constantly to dry the dough slightly. This will take from 3 to 5 minutes. A slight film will form on the bottom of the pan.

5. Turn off the heat, add the eggs 1 at a time, beating to incorporate the first one before adding the next. Stir in the Gruyère cheese and chopped asparagus.

6. With a large spoon dipped into warm water to prevent sticking, drop large dollops of the batter onto the baking pan or cookie sheet forming a circle about 9 inches in diameter. There will be a space in the center. The gougère may be frozen at this point, before the egg wash (see Note below). Brush the top of the pastry carefully with the egg-milk mixture, taking care not to let any drop onto the pan. Sprinkle the Parmesan cheese over the top of the ring, reserving about 2 tablespoons.

7. Place the pan in the middle of the oven, and bake for 35 minutes until puffed and golden brown. Place the 8 asparagus tips on top, sprinkle with the remaining Parmesan cheese, and return the gougère to the oven for 5 minutes longer. Remove the pan from the oven, loosen the gougère, cut it into slices, and serve at once. Once removed from the oven, the pastry deflates quickly. This dish must be served right away.

DID YOU KNOW? It makes good sense to recycle the cooking liquid from vegetables, poultry, etc. In this recipe, you save the asparagus' vitamins and minerals, which otherwise would be thrown out with the water.

NOTE: Place the cookie sheet in the freezer. When the pastry is hard, slide the gougère off and store it in a Ziploc bag. To cook, place it on a buttered cookie sheet and in the preheated oven still frozen. Add 10 minutes to the cooking time.

Baked Chèvre on Fresh Red Pepper Sauce and Endives

Serves 4

This colorful first course celebrates the fact that we now find more high-quality imported cheeses in our supermarkets. Wonderful regional cheeses are also coming into their own. For years, I devoured goats' milk cheese (chèvre) in France and Italy, loving the tangy cream cheese-like flavor and lamenting that it was only available at specialty cheese stores. Now this first course, composed of a warm pillow of cheese on a bed of red pepper purée surrounded by endive leaves, is easy to assemble.

I have chosen a small Montrachet log for this recipe. You may see it, plain or with herbs or a smokey ash coating, sold in a plastic package. Other goat cheeses, such as Bucheron, come in larger logs, and still others in pyramid shapes, each varying slightly in taste and texture. Be sure to feel the cheese gently. It should be slightly firm in the center and softer— but not runny—on the outside.

⅓ cup fruity extra-virgin olive oil
1 5½-ounce log of chèvre (Montrachet), cut into 4 slices
1 tablespoon chopped fresh tarragon *or* 1 teaspoon dried
8 thin slices French bread, lightly toasted
1 clove garlic, split
2 tablespoons olive oil
⅓ cup fresh-toasted bread crumbs
¼ teaspoon salt
2 large red bell peppers, peeled, seeds and membranes removed
½ small clove garlic, peeled
1 tablespoon chopped fresh tarragon *or* 1 teaspoon dried
½ teaspoon salt
Freshly ground black pepper
16 endive leaves

DID YOU KNOW? When selecting a piece of cheese that has been plastic wrapped in the market, make sure that the oils are not separating, to insure that it has been properly refrigerated. Poor storage is the quickest way to ruin the flavor and texture of cheese. Once home, be sure to wrap any unused cheese airtight in plastic wrap. This wrapping should be changed each time the cheese is opened and exposed to air.

1. Preheat your oven to 400°F. Lightly oil a cookie sheet.

2. Pour the olive oil into a flat dish, and add the slices of chèvre, turning once to coat with the oil. Sprinkle on 1 tablespoon of tarragon and refrigerate for 15 to 20 minutes.

3. Rub the toasted French bread slices with the clove of garlic and brush lightly with olive oil. Set aside.

4. Combine the bread crumbs with the salt in a flat dish. Lift the slices of cheese from the oil and place them in the crumbs, turning to cover them all over. Place the cheese slices on the cookie sheet, reserving the oil, and bake them in the preheated oven for 8 minutes until golden brown and hot. Add the slices of bread after about 4 minutes to warm them along with the cheese.

4. While the cheese is baking, purée the red peppers and half clove of garlic in the bowl of a food processor fitted with a steel chopping blade, scraping down the sides as needed. With the machine running, add the olive oil through the feed tube in a slow, steady stream. Add the remaining tarragon, salt, and black pepper and pulse to blend.

5. Ladle the red pepper sauce evenly into the center of 4 luncheon-size plates. Place 4 endive leaves with the tips pointing out on each plate. Lift the warmed cheese with a spatula to the center of each plate, and place 2 slices of toast on either side. Serve at once.

Corny Cheesey Popovers

Makes 12 popovers

Using fine corn meal instead of flour is a new twist on popovers. I add a little cheddar cheese and some corn kernels and serve them with butter and jalapeño pepper jelly for a real eye-opening start to the day. For a south-of-the-border-style brunch, serve these popovers with MEXICAN RANCHERS' EGGS (page 282) or MY DYNAMITE, ALL-TIME FAVORITE CHILI (page 177).

Look for cornmeal near other flours. Both yellow and white have the same taste. There are different grinds, from fine to coarser stone ground, that will change the final texture of a dish from smooth to gritty.

Unsalted butter to grease a muffin tin
1¼ cups milk
3 tablespoons unsalted butter, melted
1 cup fine cornmeal
½ cup unbleached all-purpose flour
½ teaspoon salt
¼ teaspoon dry mustard
Generous pinch ground red pepper
½ cup corn kernels, frozen or fresh
4 eggs
½ cup shredded sharp cheddar cheese

1. Preheat your oven to 450°F. Butter a 12-muffin tin or 12 deep porcelain custard cups.

2. Combine the milk, melted butter, cornmeal, flour, salt, mustard, and red pepper, and beat until just smooth. Stir in the corn.

3. Add the eggs 1 at a time, beating just until each is incorporated. Using a ⅓ cup measure, fill the muffin tin with the batter, and sprinkle the cheese on top. With your finger or the handle of a spoon, gently stir each container of batter once or twice to cover the cheese.

4. Transfer the pan to the lower third of the preheated oven, and bake for 15 minutes, then, lower the temperature to 350°F for 20 minutes longer. *Do not open the oven while the popovers are baking.* Once they have "popped," remove the tin from the oven and test one to see if the centers are dried. If not, prick the others at this point with a toothpick, and return them to the oven for 3 or 4 minutes to let the steam escape. Once the popovers are done, immediately loosen them with a sharp knife and serve at once. (These popovers will not rise as high as those made with all-purpose flour.) If you have no jalapeño pepper jelly, try combining softened butter with a small amount of minced pickled jalapeño pepper.

Yogurt Cucumber Raita

Makes 2½ cups

In Indian cooking, a "raita" is a cooling sauce often made from yogurt and chopped raw vegetables. It is a nice foil for intensely spicy foods. This chunky version is not only delicious when used for a curry, but it is also a great sauce with grilled lamb, chicken, or falafel. I also spoon it over mixed greens or cool vegetables.

Because yogurt is a cultured product, it generally has a fairly long shelf life. Be sure to check the code. It is certainly safe for a week or 10 days in your refrigerator. But, yogurt does not freeze well.

2 large cloves garlic, peeled
Salt
1½ cups plain yogurt
1 medium-large cucumber, peeled, seeded, and coarsely chopped
1 large ripe tomato, peeled, seeded, and coarsely chopped
⅓ cup chopped fresh mint leaves
2 tablespoons finely chopped flat-leaf parsley (optional)
Salt and freshly ground black pepper to taste

1. In a medium-size bowl, mash the garlic with a little salt to create a paste, then stir in the yogurt and mix well.

2. Add the cucumber, tomato, mint, parsley, and salt and pepper and blend. Adjust the seasonings, if necessary. Refrigerate until needed.

DID YOU KNOW? If yogurt develops a little mold on top, simply scrape it off. The yogurt is usually fine to use.

Orange-Honey Yogurt Sauce for Fruit

Makes 1 cup

Here is an almost-instant sauce to serve with fruit. Spoon it over fresh fruit salads or use it for dipping cubes of melon or pineapple, whole grapes, cherries, or even squares of pound cake. The delicately sweet orange-honey flavors complement the slightly tangy yogurt.

When buying yogurt, be sure to read the labels carefully. Although plain yogurt—both those marked low fat and regular—is low in calories, when fruits with a lot of extra sugar are stirred in, the benefits are diminished. Remember to drain any extra liquid in the carton before using the yogurt.

3 tablespoons fresh orange juice
½ teaspoon ground cinnamon
1 cup plain yogurt
2 tablespoons honey

Combine the orange juice and cinnamon in a small bowl to dissolve the cinnamon. Add the yogurt and honey and mix well. Refrigerate until ready to serve.

Béarnaise Sauce

Makes 1½ cups

Béarnaise sauce remains a favorite to serve with roasted meats. It is a classic accompaniment for RACK OF LAMB PERSILLADE (page 190) and châteaubriand steak. The combination of wine, tarragon vinegar, and creamy butter is elegant and rich. Make it for special occasions.

When looking for the freshest butter, I buy "sweet" or unsalted butter, since salt is a preservative and can mask rancidity. To preserve freshness, refrigerate butter in a covered dish, away from foods with a strong aroma. The butter section of your refrigerator is usually several degrees warmer to make butter spreadable. That's fine for a few days. Otherwise, find a cooler shelf (around 39°F), and butter will last up to 2 weeks. Wrapped in another airtight layer of foil or plastic wrap, butter can be frozen for up to 9 months.

½ cup dry white wine
2 tablespoons tarragon vinegar
2 tablespoons finely chopped shallots
4 black peppercorns
2 tablespoons fresh tarragon leaves *or* 2 teaspoons dried
3 egg yolks
12 tablespoons (1½ sticks) unsalted butter, melted
½ teaspoon salt, or to taste
Pinch of ground red pepper
2 teaspoons finely chopped fresh tarragon leaves *or* ½ teaspoon dried

1. In a small saucepan, combine the wine, vinegar, shallots, peppercorns, and 2 tablespoons tarragon leaves and bring to a boil over high heat. Cook until the liquid is reduced in half. Strain and let it cool. Wipe out the saucepan.

2. Combine the egg yolks and wine mixture in the saucepan. Over *very low heat* (or in a double boiler), beat the mixture with a whisk until it is frothy and the yolks have thickened slightly. *Slowly* add the melted butter, beating constantly.

3. Add the salt, red pepper, and finely chopped tarragon leaves, and taste for seasonings. Serve warm. Keep warm in a double boiler or in a thermos until ready to serve.

Confetti Beurre Blanc

Makes about 2 cups to serve 8 to 10

Although many people have streamlined their diets, there are still those gala occasions when a *beurre blanc*, or light-colored butter sauce, is perfect, especially for fish dishes. In this version, the minced carrot, onion, green beans, and tomatoes are so colorful, they remind me of confetti. It is particularly delicious with BAKED SALMON FILLETS IN PARCHMENT (page 245) or WHOLE STUFFED SEA BASS EN CROÛTE (page 259). Spooned over blanched leeks, steamed asparagus, or chicken breasts, these simple-to-prepare foods become elegant.

The butter you find in your market is usually U.S. Grade AA (93 Score) or Grade A (92 Score), based on federal standards of evaluation. The best butter (AA) has an appealing flavor with a delicate aroma of fresh sweet cream. It must be smooth with a very even texture. Any salt is distributed equally. Grade A is made from slightly older cream, and the texture may be less even. Grade B (90 Score), is rarely sold in markets. It is made from slightly sour cream and has a more intense, slightly acidic taste.

1 tablespoon unsalted butter
2 tablespoons minced carrot
2 tablespoons minced onion
4 thin green beans, thinly sliced
2 tablespoons minced shallots
6 tablespoons tarragon vinegar
6 tablespoons dry white wine
20 tablespoons (2½ sticks) unsalted butter, chilled
and cut into pieces
3 plum tomatoes, peeled, seeded, and finely
chopped *or* ½ cup finely chopped canned Italian
tomatoes, well drained
Salt and white pepper to taste

1. In a medium skillet, melt 1 tablespoon of butter over medium-high heat. When it has foamed, add the carrot, onion, and beans and stir to coat with butter. Cook for 1½ to 2 minutes, or until the vegetables are slightly softened. Set aside.

2. Combine the shallots, vinegar, and white wine in a medium-size heavy, nonaluminum saucepan and bring to a boil. Continue boiling over high heat until the liquid has reduced to about 1 tablespoon.

3. Turn off the heat and whisk in about 2 tablespoons of butter, beating until the butter looks frothy and slightly opaque. Add 2 more tablespoons of butter, and whisk until smooth.

4. Return the pan to low heat, and continue whisking in the remaining butter 2 tablespoons at a time until all the butter has been used, making sure to incorporate each lump of butter before adding the next one.

5. Stir in the sautéed vegetables, tomatoes, salt, and pepper and taste for seasonings. This sauce may be prepared up to 30 minutes ahead of time and kept over warm (not boiling) water. Or transfer it to a thermos, and the sauce will hold for up to 3 hours.

DID YOU KNOW?
Whipped butter is fine for spreading on toast or seasoning vegetables. However, it contains about 30 to 45 percent air, so it is not appropriate to substitute it in baking.

Late Harvest Johannisberg Riesling Beurre Blanc

Makes about 2 cups

This is a very special sauce to make for a grand meal. The sweet late-harvest wine balanced with tarragon vinegar and shallots is truly exceptional. I serve it with LOBSTER TIMBALES (page 234), with some diced lobster meat stirred in. It would be appropriate to serve this sauce with grilled swordfish, roasted game birds, or slices of roasted veal. Drink the remaining wine with an elegant dessert.

Beurre blanc is an emulsified sauce thickened by butter being whisked into a base of reduced vinegar and wine or water. Hollandaise and béarnaise are similar in their preparation but build upon beaten egg yolks. There is nothing in this sauce to hide the taste of slightly old butter, so it must be very fresh. Unsalted butter allows you to season the sauce to your own taste.

¼ cup tarragon vinegar
½ cup Late Harvest Johannisberg Riesling
1 tablespoon minced shallots
8 ounces unsalted butter, chilled and cut into
  pieces
Pinch of ground red pepper
Salt and white pepper to taste

1. Combine the vinegar, wine, and shallots in a small, heavy, nonaluminum saucepan and bring to a boil. Continue boiling over high heat until the liquid has reduced to about 1 tablespoon, about 6 to 7 minutes.

2. Turn off the heat and whisk in about 2 tablespoons of butter, beating until the butter looks frothy and slightly opaque. Add 2 more tablespoons of butter and whisk until it is completely incorporated and smooth.

3. Return the saucepan to low heat, and continue whisking in the remaining butter in small amounts, making sure to incorporate each piece before adding the next. Add the red pepper and season to taste with salt and pepper. The sauce should coat the back of a spoon. It may be prepared 30 to 45 minutes ahead of time and kept warm over warm (not boiling) water. Be sure to look at it occasionally, whisking to prevent separation.

Mexican Ranchers' Eggs

Serves 8

These individual Mexican egg baskets are perfect for a brunch when most of the work done can be ahead of time. You can easily double or quadruple the ingredients to feed a crowd. Poach the eggs ahead of time. Then reheat and serve them in crunchy corn tortilla baskets, dressed with salsa, avocado slices, and Monterey Jack cheese.

The Mexican influence in food has filtered into supermarkets in a big way. Dairy departments now contain fresh salsa, Monterey Jack cheese with or without jalapeño peppers, and corn and flour tortillas.

FOR THE BASKETS
8 corn or flour tortillas
3 tablespoons vegetable oil

FOR THE EGGS
1 teaspoon vegetable oil
8 eggs
3 tablespoons white vinegar for poaching the eggs
1½ cups SALSA (page 57), or purchased
½ cup shredded Monterey Jack cheese with or without jalapeño peppers
1 large ripe avocado, peeled and cut into 16 thin slices
½ cup thinly sliced black olives for garnish (optional)
½ cup sliced scallions, including most of the green parts for garnish
3 tablespoons chopped cilantro (fresh coriander) for garnish
4–5 cups shredded iceberg lettuce

1. PREPARE THE TORTILLA BASKETS Preheat your oven to 400°F.

2. Make 4 incisions, from the edge in, about 2 inches long in each tortilla at equal distances (see illustration). Brush each tortilla lightly with oil on both sides. Place each one in an 8-ounce custard cup, overlapping the edges to form a cup-like shape. Place a second custard cup over the tortilla, and bake in the oven for about 10 minutes, until crisp and light brown. Remove from the oven and gently loosen the tortillas with a sharp knife. Return to a warm oven until needed.

3. POACH THE EGGS Lightly oil a large, nonalu-

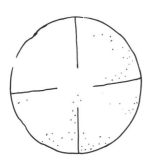

minum skillet or saucepan, fill it with water to a level of about 2 inches, add the vinegar, and bring to a boil. Reduce the heat so the water is just simmering. Break an egg into a custard cup or saucer and then slide it into the water. Using a spoon, turn the egg gently to wrap the white around the yolk. Cook only a few at a time, for about 3 minutes, until the white is set and the yolk is still soft in the center when touched lightly. Gently loosen, if necessary, and remove with a slotted spoon. If making the eggs ahead of time, slip them into a bowl of ice water to stop the cooking, then store them in fresh cold water in the refrigerator. They will hold for several days. Otherwise, blot gently with paper towels, and place each egg in a tortilla basket.

4. ASSEMBLE THE BASKETS Preheat your oven to 400°F. If the eggs have been made ahead of time and refrigerated, place them in a pan of salted water, and heat just until the water feels very hot to the touch, drain, and blot them, then continue with the recipe.

5. Pour about 2 tablespoons of Salsa over each egg, drizzle on the cheese, then spoon on another table-spoon of Salsa. Place the cups on a cookie sheet and warm them in the oven for about 5 to 6 minutes until the cheese is melted. Remove the pan from the oven, add the avocado slices, olives, scallions, and cilantro.

6. To serve, make a circle of shredded lettuce on each plate, and place 1 egg basket in the center. Serve immediately.

DID YOU KNOW? When poaching eggs, white vinegar in the water will help to keep the egg white from spreading. When boiling eggs, salt will keep a cracked shell closed, preventing the egg from running out. Boil eggs gently for the best results.

For added flavor, eggs may be poached in stock, beer, milk, cream, or white wine.

Frittatas

Frittatas are flat Italian omelets made with eggs and almost any other ingredient you may choose. They are a good way to use up leftovers, and they're a super supermarket dish to prepare, since the ingredient choices are only limited by your imagination. Try the unexpected—apples and cheese or Polish sausages and sauerkraut are given below.

Once you have mastered the cooking technique, any frittata is a snap. Making one large frittata is far easier than cooking 4 individual omelets—and a lot more festive. Slice them for dinner or cut them into squares for hors d'oeuvres. All it takes is a mixing bowl, a heavy 10-inch skillet, and a large plate. You can make a frittata in the morning and serve it at room temperature at night.

The recipes below will each serve 4 to 5 as a first course; cut into squares, they will serve 12 to 15 as an hors d'oeuvre.

BASIC FRITTATA TECHNIQUE

1. Break 5 eggs into a mixing bowl, add ½ teaspoon of water, and stir until just blended.

2. In a heavy 10-inch skillet, add 1 or 2 tablespoons of butter, margarine, or oil, as specified in the recipe, and sauté any ingredients which need to be cooked —times will vary according to the recipe directions.

3. Add the cooked ingredients to the egg mixture, along with any remaining ingredients and seasonings, and mix well. Wipe or rinse out the pan if any burned particles remain.

4. Heat the butter, margarine, or oil over medium-high heat, and when it is very hot, pour in the egg mixture. Shake the pan or use a spatula to distribute the ingredients evenly and adjust the heat to medium-low.

5. After 6 or 7 minutes, when the bottom is set (the top will still be moist), begin to loosen the frittata around the edge with a sharp knife or spatula. Gradually work the spatula toward the center to loosen the entire frittata. Shake to be certain it is completely detached.

NOTE: Frittatas that contain many ingredients or high-moisture foods, such as cheese and fruit, often take longer to cook.

6. Invert a plate which is just larger than the skillet over the pan. Using potholders or gloves, hold the plate and skillet together with both hands, and flip the skillet over so the frittata falls onto the plate. Slide the frittata back into the skillet, and gently pat it down if it is lumpy. Continue to cook for 3 to 4 minutes (or longer if needed because of the ingredients) until the second side is set. Shake to loosen if necessary.

7. Slide the frittata onto a serving plate and serve at once or let it cool to room temperature. Cut it into pie-shape wedges or squares.

ALTERNATIVELY, instead of flipping the frittata, you can place it in a preheated 400° oven and let it finish cooking for the remaining 3 to 4 minutes.

Kielbasa, Sauerkraut, and Caraway Frittata

Serves 4 to 5 as a first course

Although frittatas are Italian in origin, Polish sausage and sauerkraut make this a hearty and satisfying winter dish. Serve it with dark bread, and pass the German or French mustard for added tang.

5 eggs
½ teaspoon water
1½ tablespoons unsalted butter
1 cup sauerkraut, squeezed very dry
7 ounces kielbasa, cut into ¼-inch slices
1½ teaspoons caraway seeds
½ teaspoon salt, or to taste
Freshly ground black pepper to taste
1½ tablespoons butter

1. In a large mixing bowl, beat the eggs and water until well blended.

2. In a heavy 10-inch skillet, melt 1½ tablespoons of butter over medium-high heat. Add the sauerkraut and cook over medium heat for 4 to 5 minutes, stirring occasionally. Add the kielbasa, caraway seeds, salt, and pepper to the eggs, and stir to blend well.

3. Add 1½ tablespoons of butter to the skillet, and when it foams, pour in the egg mixture, shaking to distribute the ingredients evenly. Adjust the heat to medium-low.

4. After 6 or 7 minutes, begin to loosen the edges with a knife or spatula, gradually loosening the whole frittata. Invert a large plate over the skillet and, holding the plate and skillet together, flip the pan over, letting the frittata fall onto the plate. Cook the second side for 3 to 4 minutes longer. Loosen if necessary, before removing.

Swiss Cheese, Apple, Onion, and Almond Frittata

Serves 4 to 5 as a first course

Apples and cheese are often served together. Here the combination is savory with the addition of almonds and sautéed onions. Serve with a bottle of chilled chardonnay for a summer dinner.

5 eggs
½ teaspoon water
1 tablespoon unsalted butter
1 teaspoon vegetable oil
1 medium onion, peeled and chopped
2 medium Granny Smith or other tart green apples, peeled, cored, and chopped fairly fine
½ teaspoon nutmeg
⅛ teaspoon white pepper
½ teaspoon salt, or to taste
⅓ cup slivered almonds, lightly toasted
1½ tablespoons unsalted butter
1 cup shredded Swiss cheese

1. In a large mixing bowl, beat the eggs and water until blended.

2. In a heavy 10-inch skillet, melt the butter and oil over medium-high heat just until the butter has foamed. Add the onion and sauté it over medium heat until light brown, about 6 to 7 minutes. Add the apples and continue cooking until they are limp, about 4 to 5 minutes.

3. Scrape the onion and apples into the egg mixture. Add the nutmeg, white pepper, salt, and slivered almonds, and mix well.

4. Melt the remaining butter in the skillet over medium-high heat. When it has foamed, pour in the egg mixture, shaking to distribute the ingredients evenly. After about 1 minute, sprinkle on the cheese. Adjust the heat to medium-low. After *11 to 12* minutes, begin to loosen the edges with a knife or spatula, gradually working under the entire frittata. Shake to be sure it is detached. Flip the frittata, as above, and continue cooking the second side for an additional 5 to 6 minutes. Loosen, if necessary, before removing.

Spinach, Mushroom, Scallion, and Feta Cheese Frittata

Serves 4 to 5 as a first course

Spinach and feta cheese are favorite ingredients of Greek chefs. They work wonderfully in frittatas, as well.

5 eggs
½ teaspoon water
1½ tablespoons olive oil
4 ounces white mushrooms, trimmed, wiped, and thinly sliced
½ cup thinly sliced scallions, green parts included
4 ounces feta cheese, crumbled
1 10-ounce package frozen spinach, defrosted and pressed very dry in a strainer
3 tablespoons fresh dillweed, minced *or* 1 tablespoon dried
¾ teaspoon nutmeg
¼ teaspoon salt, or to taste
Pinch of ground red pepper
Freshly ground black pepper
1½ tablespoons olive oil

1. In a large mixing bowl, beat the eggs and water until well blended.

2. In a heavy 10-inch skillet, heat the oil until hot. Add the mushrooms, and sauté them over medium heat, stirring often, until just wilted, about 1 to 2 minutes. Add the scallions and continue cooking for 30 seconds longer. Scrape the mushrooms and scallions into the egg mixture.

3. Add the feta cheese, spinach, dillweed, nutmeg, salt, red pepper, and ground pepper to the eggs, and mix well.

4. Put the remaining oil in the skillet and heat over high heat until the oil is hot. Pour in the egg mixture and shake the skillet to distribute the ingredients evenly. Adjust the heat to medium-low. After 7 or 8 minutes, begin to loosen the edges with a knife or spatula, gradually working under the entire frittata. Shake the pan to be sure that it's completely free, then flip the frittata, as above, and continue cooking for 4 to 5 minutes longer. Loosen, if necessary, before removing.

DID YOU KNOW? Using a well-seasoned omelet pan will make frittatas and omelets a joy to make. These pans should never be exposed to soap or abrasive pads. Salt and warm water are all you need. Dry the pan right away and place oil on its surface.

Chilled White Wine Soufflé with Apricot Sauce

Serves 8

This delicate chilled dessert is light and airy—a perfect finale for a summer meal. My guests are often pleasantly surprised to find out that the soufflé is made from only wine, sugar, and eggs, with a little gelatin and cornstarch for body. It is easy to make and can be decorated glamorously with whipped cream and sugar-frosted grapes, or simply with fresh strawberries. The orange-apricot sauce provides a citrusy accent that complements the flavors of the soufflé.

FOR THE SOUFFLÉ
7 eggs, separated, at room temperature
⅔ cup sugar
2 tablespoons cornstarch
2 cups medium dry white wine
1 package unflavored gelatin
Pinch cream of tartar

FOR THE SAUCE
8 ounces apricot preserves
¾ cup orange juice
Grated zest of 1 lemon
¼ cup Grand Marnier

FOR THE DECORATION (OPTIONAL)
16–20 red or green grapes with a little stem left on
1 egg white
½ cup superfine sugar *or* processed granulated sugar
4 ounces heavy cream, whipped until stiff and lightly sweetened

PREPARE THE SOUFFLÉ   In a heavy saucepan, whisk the egg yolks and sugar together until well blended and pale yellow. Stir the cornstarch into the wine. Stir it into the eggs and bring the mixture to a boil over medium-high heat for 1 to 2 minutes.

2. Dissolve the gelatin in a little reserved wine or water. When it is softened, add it to the wine mixture and stir to blend well. Remove the pan from the heat and beat the mixture with an electric or hand mixer until cool and thick. This process may be speeded up by transferring the mixture into a metal or glass bowl and setting it in another bowl filled with ice while beating.

AS A VARIATION: Use fresh strawberries or raspberries, and substitute the STRAWBERRY SAUCE from the FLOATING ISLANDS recipe on page 291 for the Apricot Sauce.

3. Add the cream of tartar to the egg whites and beat until stiff but not dry. Using a rubber spatula or your hands, gently fold the egg whites into the wine mixture, mixing until just blended, and pour it into a 6-cup soufflé mold or glass bowl. Cover and chill the soufflé for at least 6 hours or overnight.

4. FOR THE SAUCE In a small, heavy saucepan, heat the preserves with the orange juice and lemon zest until melted. Let the mixture boil until slightly thickened. Remove from the heat, stir in the Grand Marnier, and let the sauce cool to lukewarm.

5. PREPARE THE GARNISH In a flat dish, beat the egg white just until frothy. Pour the sugar into another flat dish. Holding each grape by its stem, dip it into the egg, then into the sugar, forming a thin coating. Place on a plate to dry, and remove the stem.

6. Beat the cream until stiff. Using a pastry bag fitted with a decorative star tip, pipe small rosettes onto the soufflé. Place the frosted grapes on top. To serve, spoon a generous serving onto each plate, including a couple of grapes. Ribbon the sauce over the soufflé.

Soft Peach Mousse in Crêpe Flutes

Serves 6

This frothy light dessert not only looks glamorous, it will keep your waistline in good shape, too. Unsweetened frozen peaches and low-fat vanilla yogurt are the secret ingredients in the quick and easy preparation. The peach mousse has a hint of rum and orange juice to perk up the flavor.

My talented friend Carole Walter taught me to make these low-fat crêpes. Make them ahead of time; then, before serving, spoon in the mousse and add fresh raspberries and mint leaves for a delightful finale to any meal.

FOR THE MOUSSE
1½ envelopes (1½ tablespoons) unflavored gelatin
½ cup orange juice
1 20-ounce package frozen peaches without added
    sugar, almost completely thawed
¼ cup sugar
3 tablespoons light rum
16 ounces low-fat vanilla yogurt
½ pint fresh raspberries for garnish
Mint leaves for garnish

FOR THE CRÊPES
½ cup 1 percent or skimmed milk
1 egg
⅛ teaspoon vanilla
½ cup unbleached all-purpose flour
Nonstick vegetable spray such as Pam
1 egg white, lightly beaten
6 8-ounce Pyrex custard cups

1. PREPARE THE MOUSSE In a small saucepan, sprinkle the gelatin over the orange juice. Once the gelatin granules have softened, bring the mixture to a boil over medium heat, stirring until the gelatin has melted. Remove the pan from the heat and set it aside to cool while continuing with the recipe.

2. In a food processor fitted with a steel chopping blade, or in a blender, purée the frozen peaches with the sugar until completely smooth. Add the rum and orange juice-gelatin mixture and blend. Spoon the yogurt into the mixture and process just until combined. Scrape the mousse mixture into a medium-size bowl, cover, and refrigerate overnight until firm.

3. PREPARE THE CRÊPES Combine the milk, egg, and vanilla in a small bowl. Gradually whisk in the flour, stirring until smooth. It should be the consistency of heavy cream. If not, add a little more milk. Let the batter stand for 10 minutes.

4. Spray an 8-inch nonstick skillet with vegetable spray and heat over medium-low heat. Stir the batter. Fill a coffee measure (2 tablespoons) with batter, and pour it onto one side of the skillet, removing the pan from the heat with your other hand as you do this. Rotate the pan so the batter will spread evenly.

5. Return the skillet to the heat, and cook the crêpe for about 1 minute, or until the sides begin to brown and leave the sides of the pan. Loosen, if necessary, with a knife and lift up an edge carefully with your fingers. Flip the crêpe over. Cook 20 seconds on the second side. Flip the crêpe onto paper towels. Spray the pan for each crêpe. Proceed in the same manner for the remaining batter, separating the crêpes with wax paper or paper towels. (This recipe will make up to 8 crêpes.)

6. Preheat your oven to 350°F. Spray six 8-ounce Pyrex custard cups with nonstick vegetable coating.

7. Place a crêpe in each cup. They will form scalloped tart shells. Bake in the preheated oven for 15

OTHER SERVING IDEAS: Prepare the mousse, and transfer it to a decorative 4 or 5-cup soufflé dish or wine glasses. After it is chilled, add fresh berries and mint leaves in an attractive pattern and serve with crisp cookies.

Use the crêpe shells to serve a dessert of fresh fruit salad or ice cream. Try presenting purchased chicken salad from the Deli section or TARRAGON CHICKEN SALAD (page 120) in this decorative way.

minutes or until golden brown. Remove the cups and let the crêpes cool for 5 minutes. Remove the shells carefully and invert. Brush the bottoms of the shells with beaten egg white. Place the inverted shells directly onto the oven rack. Bake for 1 to 2 minutes or until the shells are very crisp. Watch closely so they do not burn. Remove and let cool.

8. TO SERVE Place a crêpe shell on each plate. Using a large spoon or ice cream scoop, divide the mousse among the cups. Add raspberries and mint leaves and serve.

Floating Islands with Two Sauces

Serves 6

The soft meringue "islands" that are floating in this dessert are made from egg whites, while the yolks become the custard sauce. I like the addition of the slightly tangy strawberry sauce that perks up the taste and adds a beautiful color contrast.

When selecting eggs at the market, always check the carton for breakage. If eggs crack on the way home, use them at once in dishes where they are completely cooked, like custards or cakes. Uncracked eggs will keep in a refrigerator for several weeks.

FOR THE MERINGUES AND CUSTARD SAUCE
2½ cups milk
¾ cup confectioners' sugar
5 eggs, separated, at room temperature
Pinch of cream of tartar
¼ cup confectioners' sugar
1½ teaspoons vanilla extract

FOR THE STRAWBERRY SAUCE
2 pints fresh strawberries, washed
3 tablespoons confectioners' sugar
1–2 tablespoons framboise or kirsch (optional)

1. TO PREPARE THE MERINGUES AND CUSTARD SAUCE
Pour the milk into a 10-inch skillet and stir in the confectioners' sugar. Over low heat, bring the milk to a simmer.

2. In the meantime, combine the egg whites with the cream of tartar in a medium-size bowl and beat until soft peaks begin to form. Add ¼ cup of confectioners' sugar, a little at a time, and continue beating until stiff peaks form.

3. With a large spoon, drop generous spoonfuls of egg white onto the warmed milk, and let the meringues poach over low heat for about 3 to 4 minutes, until firm on the bottom. Using a slotted spoon or two forks, carefully turn the meringues over, and continue cooking for another 3 to 4 minutes. Remove the meringues with a slotted spoon to a platter and refrigerate them for at least 1 to 2 hours.

4. Let the milk cool slightly. Gradually beat in the egg yolks, and stir continuously with a wooden spoon over medium-low heat until the custard thickens enough to coat the spoon lightly, about 5 to 6 minutes. Remove the pan from the heat, stir in the vanilla, and beat the sauce for 1 to 2 minutes to cool. Pour the sauce through a fine strainer into a bowl, and refrigerate until needed.

5. TO MAKE THE STRAWBERRY SAUCE Reserve 6 to 12 (depending on the size) of the nicest berries to be used as garnish. Hull the remaining berries, add the sugar, and purée them in a processor fitted with a steel chopping blade or in a blender. Pass the purée through a fine sieve and add the optional framboise or kirsch, if desired. Refrigerate until needed.

6. FOR THE FINAL ASSEMBLY In a shallow serving bowl or on individual plates, spoon out the custard sauce. Place the meringues on top of the sauce (divided equally if served individually), followed by generous spoonfuls of the strawberry sauce. Garnish with the remaining whole berries.

Mandarin Velvet Caramel Custard

Serves 8

This custard ring, presented with mandarin segments and chocolate leaves, always wins raves because of its perfectly smooth texture and hint of orange flavor. These few supermarket ingredients become an elegant finale to the finest meal.

Check the code on milk cartons to guarantee freshness. Use it within 5 days.

FOR THE CARAMEL
½ cup granulated sugar
3 tablespoons water

FOR THE CUSTARD
1½ pints (3 cups) milk
5 eggs
4 egg yolks
½ cup sugar
¼ teaspoon salt
½ teaspoon vanilla extract
1 teaspoon orange extract
24 chocolate leaves, page 297, for garnish (optional)
24 canned mandarin orange segments, drained, for garnish (optional)

1. LINE THE MOLD Place the sugar and water in a small saucepan and bring to a boil. Boil the syrup, swirling but not stirring it, until it has turned a rich amber brown, about 6 to 8 minutes. Watch carefully so that it does not burn. If any sugar crystals start to burn on the side of the pan, wash them down with a wet brush.

2. Using a pot holder to protect your hands, quickly pour the caramel into a 6-cup ring mold and tilt the mold so the caramel covers all sides. As the caramel cools, it will crack. (To clean the saucepan easily after pouring the caramel into the mold, refill it with hot water and bring it to a boil. This will dissolve any remaining caramel.)

3. FOR THE CUSTARD Preheat your oven to 325°F.

4. Scald the milk in a saucepan and set it aside.

5. In a large mixing bowl, blend the eggs, yolks, and salt. Slowly whisk in the sugar, and continue mixing until the eggs are light yellow and frothy, about 2 to 3 minutes. Beat in the milk in a slow steady stream. Add the vanilla and orange extracts.

6. Pour the mixture through a fine strainer into the caramel-lined ring mold. Place the ring mold into a larger pan (*bain-marie*), and transfer the pans to the lower third of the preheated oven. Pour enough boiling water from a kettle into the larger pan to come halfway up the side of the ring mold. Bake until a knife inserted *near* the center of the custard comes out clean, about 40 to 45 minutes. While the custard is cooking, the water should never show any bubbles on the surface. Adjust the temperature down, if necessary.

7. Remove the custard from the oven. Allow it to

cool for about 1 hour, then cover and refrigerate it until cold.

8. To unmold, run a sharp knife around the outside and inside of the mold. Agitate the pan to be sure the custard is loose. Holding a serving dish over the mold, invert them, shaking slightly to make sure the custard has dropped onto the dish.

9. Add ¼ cup water to the mold, and boil on top of the stove to melt the remaining caramel. Strain this over the custard. Before serving, if desired, place chocolate leaves around the outside of the custard, and mandarin orange segments between the leaves and the custard. Add some leaves around the inside of the ring, as well, with some more mandarins (see illustration). Serve each portion with some chocolate leaves, mandarins, and caramel syrup.

Cherries in the Snow

Serves 12

This white chocolate-and-coconut mousse, with its warm cherry sauce, is a winter favorite of my guests and children—especially my son Ben, who helped create and name it. It proves that while white chocolate may not actually be chocolate (because it has no cocoa solids in it), it sure has appeal to many chocolate- or sweet-lovers. Look for white chocolate in the imported-candy section. It is usually sold in 3½-ounce bars. One high-quality Swiss chocolate company mixes crunchy bits of nougat with its white chocolate bars. This may be used, although the mousse will not be as pristine white.

Whenever possible, I try to buy heavy cream that is labeled "pasteurized" rather than "ultra-pasteurized," although markets usually stock the latter because the shelf life of an unopened carton is 6 to 8 weeks instead of 1 week. I think it whips better without the risk of the cream turning to butter. The terms "heavy cream" and "whipping cream" are often used interchangeably. However, by general standards of identity, heavy cream must have at least 36 percent milkfat, while whipping cream may have only 30 percent fat. "Light" or "table" cream has between 18 and 30 percent fat, while "half and half" is a combination of cream and milk and has between 10.5 and 18 percent milkfat.

FOR THE MOUSSE

3 cups (1½ pints) heavy cream, chilled
10½ ounces (3 bars) white chocolate
4 egg whites, at room temperature
Pinch of cream of tartar
½ cup shredded coconut
2 tablespoons white crème de cacao
4 ounces heavy cream, whipped, for garnish
13 frozen pitted black cherries, defrosted and blotted dry, from a 12-ounce package (reserve the remaining cherries and juice for sauce), for garnish
¼ cup shredded coconut for garnish

FOR THE SAUCE

Cherries reserved from the mousse (above)
⅔ cup white crème de cacao

1. PREPARE THE MOUSSE In a chilled large bowl, whip the heavy cream until stiff.

2. Melt the chocolate in the top half of a double boiler over barely simmering water. Remove it from the heat, and stir in about ¾ cup of the whipped cream. This will smooth out the chocolate. Set it aside to cool.

3. Beat the egg whites with the cream of tartar until stiff but not dry.

4. Using a rubber spatula, fold the chocolate into the cream, then add the ½ cup coconut, crème de cacao, and finally the egg whites. Scrape the mixture into a 6-cup soufflé dish, cover lightly, and refrigerate until firm, about 3 hours.

5. Whip the remaining cream until stiff. (Since the mousse is sweet, no additional sugar is needed for this cream.) Fill a pastry bag fitted with a star tip and pipe a decorative border around the outside edge and a rosette in the center. Place 12 cherries around the outside and 1 in the center. Sprinkle on the ¼ cup coconut. Cover the mousse lightly with foil or plastic wrap, and refrigerate until needed.

6. TO PREPARE THE SAUCE Combine the reserved cherries and their juice with the crème de cacao in a small saucepan and bring the mixture just to a boil. Lower the heat and simmer for 2 to 3 minutes. Allow the sauce to cool to lukewarm.

7. To serve, place a large spoonful of mousse on

DID YOU KNOW? The rotary egg beater was invented in 1870, providing a real boon to cooks who wished to beat eggs or cream into airy lightness. Before that date, whipping was accomplished by a variety of whisks, much like the ones we use today, or even a wooden rod.

Today's cooks have electric mixers to make this chore easier. However, I find that switching back to a whisk toward the end of beating heavy cream or egg whites makes them lighter and gives me better control to prevent overbeating.

each plate and ribbon some of the warmed cherries in the center.

NOTE: This recipe may also be prepared in individual mousse dishes or wine glasses.

Deceptively Decadent Cheesecake

Serves 8 to 12

Why is this deceptive? Because this rich, creamy-tasting confection is actually made with cottage cheese, a low-calorie alternative to ricotta cheese. It bakes in a gingersnap crust and is served with juicy ripe fruit spooned on top.

While some cottage cheese is labeled "low fat" (1 or 2 percent), cream-style cottage cheese has only 4 percent fat. (I prefer that tiny bit extra in this dessert.) It is a good source of low-fat protein at a modest cost. Try substituting it for more caloric cheeses like ricotta and feta. Newer cartons in the market are sealed to prevent shoppers from opening and peeking inside, a reassuring safety precaution. Check the code on the carton. In your refrigerator, cottage cheese will usually last a couple of weeks.

FOR THE CRUST
20 gingersnaps, finely ground
2 tablespoons unsalted butter or margarine, melted

FOR THE FILLING
1½ pounds regular or low-fat cottage cheese
½ cup sugar
4 eggs
1 teaspoon vanilla extract
Grated zest of 1 lemon
1 pint fresh strawberries, washed, hulled, and split

1. PREPARE THE CRUST   Preheat your oven to 350°F.
2. Combine the cookie crumbs with the melted butter in a small bowl. Spread them in the bottom of a 9 × 1½-inch springform pan. Press down gently with your fingertips or palms, spreading the crumbs evenly across the bottom and about a quarter way up the side of the pan.
3. Bake the crust in the preheated oven for 8 minutes until slightly crisped. Remove the crust from the oven, and set it on a rack to cool. Leave the oven on.

4. TO MAKE THE FILLING Place the cottage cheese in the bowl of a food processor fitted with a steel chopping blade, and process, scraping down the sides as needed, until completely smooth, about 3 minutes.

5. Add the sugar, eggs, vanilla, and lemon zest and process just to blend.

6. Place the springform pan on a cookie sheet and pour in the cheese mixture. Bake in the middle of the preheated oven until a knife inserted near the center comes out clean, about 45 minutes. Turn off the oven, prop the door slightly open, and let the cake stay in the oven for 15 minutes longer.

7. Remove the cheesecake from the oven and let it cool on a wire rack for 1 to 2 hours. Cover lightly with foil, and refrigerate the cake until chilled, at least 2 to 3 hours. Run a sharp knife around the edge of the cake, and slip off the side of the pan. Arrange the berries on top, cut into slices and serve. Fresh or frozen blueberries could be used, as well.

NOTE: One-half cup golden raisins and/or toasted slivered almonds would be a delicious addition to the cake if calories are not so important.

Ricotta-Almond Torte

Serves 8

This torte is a majestic finale for a grand cool-weather meal. The creamy ricotta filling, flavored with crème de cacao and amaretto liqueur, rests in a toasted almond crust. The chocolate leaves and caramelized almonds add visual glamour. (If your supermarket doesn't sell crème fraîche, check at the end of this recipe for instructions on how to make your own.)

The quality and texture of ricotta cheese varies dramatically with different brands available in supermarkets across the country. Some are quite dry, while others are soupy. If yours is too moist, turn it into several layers of cheesecloth, tie the corners together, and suspend it over the sink or a bowl overnight. Once opened, ricotta cheese only lasts 4 or 5 days in the refrigerator. Do not freeze it.

TOASTED ALMOND CRUST

1 teaspoon unsalted butter
1¾ cups ground toasted almonds
¼ cup sugar
4 tablespoons (½ stick) unsalted butter, melted and cooled
⅔ cup sugar
¼ cup water
20 whole almonds for garnish

RICOTTA FILLING

2¾ cups whole-milk ricotta
¼ cup plus 2 tablespoons sugar
1 tablespoon crème de cacao
1 tablespoon amaretto liqueur
1 teaspoon vanilla
1 cup crème fraîche *or* lightly whipped cream
3 tablespoons grated chocolate

CHOCOLATE LEAVES

3 ounces semisweet chocolate
21 camellia or other waxy nonpoisonous leaves with stems, washed and patted dry (see Note)

1. FOR THE CRUST Preheat your oven to 375°F. Butter a 9 × 3-inch springform pan. Grease a small baking sheet.

2. Combine the ground almonds, ¼ cup sugar, and butter in a large bowl and mix. Press the almond mixture into the bottom and sides of the prepared pan. Bake for 10 minutes in the preheated oven, remove, and cool on a wire rack.

3. Combine the ⅔ cup sugar and water in a small, heavy saucepan and cook over low heat until the sugar is dissolved. Increase the heat to medium-high and cook until the sugar is caramelized. The mixture should be rich, medium brown. Remove the pan from the heat and quickly dip and swirl the whole almonds in the caramel, placing them on the prepared baking sheet. Set them aside for garnish. Quickly pour the remaining syrup over the crust, rotating the springform pan to spread it evenly. Let the crust cool for about 30 minutes.

4. FOR THE FILLING Combine the ricotta, sugar, crème de cacao, amaretto, and vanilla in a food processor fitted with a steel chopping blade, and process until smooth and creamy. *Do not overprocess.* (This mix-

🛒 **DID YOU KNOW?** To make crème fraîche: For each ½ pint of pasteurized *not ultra-pasteurized* cream, add 1 tablespoon of buttermilk to the cream in a screw-top jar, shake gently, and leave in a moderately warm spot—about 70°F —such as your kitchen counter— for 24 to 36 hours. Although ultra-pasteurized cream *may* set up, because the cream has been heated to a high temperature, the enzymatic action may have been destroyed, and the cream will not thicken.

ing may also be done by hand with a wire whisk. Make sure that the cheese is very smooth.) Transfer the cheese to a mixing bowl and gently blend in the crème fraîche. Fold in the chocolate. Scrape the cheese mixture into the prepared crust. Cover and freeze the torte for at least 2 hours. (If frozen more than 2 hours, the torte may need to be softened in the refrigerator before serving.)

5. FOR THE LEAVES   Melt the chocolate in the top of a double boiler, stirring until smooth. Using a spoon or spatula, generously coat the *underside* of the leaves. Refrigerate or freeze the leaves on a cookie sheet or flat plate until set.

6. Just before serving, loosen the crust from the pan using a sharp knife. Remove the sides of the pan. Gently peel the leaves from the chocolate, starting at the stem end. Arrange the leaves around the outside, reserving 3 for the center. Place the almonds close to the leaves.

NOTE: You may use each leaf several times, providing it does not break. As the chocolate hardens, peel off the leaf, and carefully transfer the chocolate leaf to a dish in the freezer or refrigerator. Make sure the leaf is clean before coating it again.

Chocolate Chip Angel Food Cake

Serves 12

Angel food cakes made from scratch bear little resemblance to the packaged variety containing powdered egg whites and other ingredients that may have been sitting on the shelf for a long time. Homemade versions are far moister and usually not as cloyingly sweet. Try one for yourself, following the directions carefully. I know you will be pleased with the results. This angel food cake, with tiny chocolate bits suspended throughout, may be decorated with a mixture of confectioners' sugar and cocoa sifted over the cake and served with fresh sliced berries or peaches. Or, for a splurge, split and frost it with the heavenly mocha whipped cream frosting at the end of the recipe.

FOR THE CAKE
12 egg whites at room temperature
1½ teaspoons cream of tartar
½ teaspoon salt
¾ cup granulated sugar
1½ teaspoons vanilla extract
½ teaspoon almond extract
1 cup sifted cake flour
¾ cup granulated sugar
1 cup mini chocolate chips

FOR THE FROSTING
2 tablespoons instant coffee
1 tablespoon hot water
¼ cup unsweetened cocoa
1½ cups sifted confectioners' sugar
2 cups (1 pint) heavy cream, chilled

1. PREPARE THE CAKE Preheat your oven to 350°F.

2. In a large bowl, combine the egg whites, cream of tartar, and salt and beat with an electric mixer until just foamy. Add ¾ cup granulated sugar, a tablespoon at a time, beating continuously to completely incorporate the sugar. Beat until soft peaks are formed.

3. Add the vanilla and almond extracts.

4. Combine the flour and confectioners' sugar and sift about ½ cup of the mixture over the egg whites. Using a rubber scraper, gently fold them in just until the flour is no longer visible. Continue adding the sugar-flour mixture by half-cupfuls, each time gently folding it in. Add the chips, and gently fold them in. Pour the batter into an ungreased 10-inch tube pan, and gently cut through the batter with a knife in several places to remove air pockets. Place the pan in the lower third of the preheated oven and bake until the top springs back when lightly pressed with your finger, about 40 to 45 minutes.

5. Remove the cake from the oven and invert the cake in the pan on a bottle neck or inverted funnel to cool completely, about 1½ hours. Once the cake is

🛒 DID YOU KNOW? While some supermarkets pride themselves on selling eggs delivered right from the farm, angel food cake and meringue recipes work better with eggs that are at least 3 or 4 days old. Use eggs that are freshly separated (not defrosted egg whites) in this recipe for the tallest cake. Save the yolks for BÉARNAISE SAUCE (page 278), or MANDARIN VELVET CARAMEL CUSTARD (page 292).

A pinch of cream of tartar in egg whites has the same effect as beating them in a copper bowl. They both stabilize the egg whites once beaten. As a general rule, use ⅛ teaspoon of cream of tartar for each egg white, except with meringues, when the ⅛ teaspoon is enough for every 2 egg whites.

cool, loosen it with a sharp knife or spatula and place onto a serving dish.

6. TO PREPARE THE FROSTING While the cake is cooling, combine the coffee with the hot water and stir to mix completely. Set it aside to cool. Sift together the cocoa and confectioners' sugar. Set aside.

7. In a large chilled bowl, beat the cream with an electric mixer just until it starts to thicken. Add the coffee and sift in the cocoa-sugar mixture, beating continuously with a wire whisk just until the cream is the consistency of a frosting. Take care not to overbeat.

8. With a long serrated knife, cut the cake in half horizontally. Carefully place the top half to one side. With a metal spatula, spread about ⅓ of the frosting over the middle of the cake. Replace the top, and press down gently. Spread the remaining frosting over the top and sides of the cake. Refrigerate until needed. To serve, use a special angel food cake cutter or a serrated knife, and carefully cut the slices without exerting pressure on the cake.

Stocking a Baker's Pantry

Stocking a baker's pantry in this age of expanded supermarkets is far easier than ever before. In fact, because most of us find storage space at a premium, I would not buy large quantities of any items that are regularly stocked in a market. Unless you do a lot of baking, let *their* shelves hold those cumbersome bags and boxes of specialty flours, nuts, and chocolates until you need them.

But a totally empty pantry is not advisable, either. If you get the urge to bake late at night, like I do, especially when the weather is dreary, then provisions should be handy. To save time, I group them in the pantry together. My bare-bones list of baking essentials includes:

- unbleached all-purpose and whole wheat flour
- granulated, dark brown, and confectioners' sugar
- baking soda and baking powder
- vanilla and almond extract
- ground cinnamon and ginger and whole nutmeg
- whole and slivered almonds and walnut pieces
- jar of jelly or preserves (raspberry, apricot, currant)
- raisins
- 3-ounce bar of premium-quality bittersweet chocolate
- packets of dry yeast
- envelopes of unflavored gelatin
- flavorless vegetable oil

I also have the following nonfood items:

- wax paper, plastic wrap, aluminum foil, paper towels, and parchment paper
- sandwich and gallon-size Ziploc bags
- toothpicks and string
- dried beans for pie weights

When it comes to commercial freshly baked goods, we shun two-day-old bread. With homemade confections, attention to *freshness* is just as vital, although we have a longer grace period with baking staples before they begin to spoil.

Wherever possible, check for freshness code dates on packaged nuts, cereals, or dried fruits.

Look to see that all boxes, cellophane bags, and jars are sealed in the store and show no sign of deterioration.

At home, cool to cold storage is usually best. Butter, delicate flours, and nuts belong in the refrigerator for short-term storage, in the freezer if stored longer than a week. Keep spices, sugars, and extracts in a cool, dark place.

Buy small amounts of fragile seeds and dried fruits if using them for a special recipe.

Keep all packages tightly closed. Plastic bags over bags of flour and/or sugar deter pests and keep brown sugar moist.

Label refrigerator- or freezer-stored foods—e.g., "1 cup ground walnuts with sugar, 4/17/88" for future reference.

Be a *quality* and *price conscious* shopper here, as you are throughout the store.

Packaging costs money. Consider the quality of products sold in fancy boxes, clear bags, or loose in the Health (bulk) Food sections. There is a price code marker on the edge of each shelf giving the net price per pound. If the Bulk Food section is well tended and has a good turnover, this is a good place to save money, providing the quality is high. Whole shelled walnut halves, for example, may be priced the same as broken pieces. If you are willing to sift through the bin, you will have a nice saving. Store these products in airtight bags or clean jars at home.

Sometimes bigger is better. But, only if you will use the product within a reasonable period of time. Because it is less costly to pack in larger containers, almost twice the amount of orange marmalade costs about ⅓ more. But, if the jar is left to take up shelf space for months and eventually goes bad, the savings are lost.

Look at generic products. Buy a can of the market's brand of mandarins and one from a well-known supplier. Compare the two for size, color, uniformity, broken pieces, etc., and decide if the difference makes the savings economical or wasteful. Sometimes large manufacturers ship a product of the same quality in both generic and fancy-labeled packaging.

Be *adventuresome*. Take the time to explore new possibilities to add to your baked goods. Do some creative tasting. But, be sure to read labels to avoid preservatives and hidden sweeteners.

The Cereal and Grain sections of the market are expanding because these carbohydrates are a good source of sustained energy in this pressure-filled world of ours. Breakfast foods are important. They also add fiber to our diet and are easily incorporated into muffins and cookies.

Nuts and seeds add texture and flavor.

Convenience packaging, like chopped dried fruits or shredded coconut, makes baking easier.

Think about the *presentation* and *packaging* for your baked goods. Supermarkets are a good source for inexpensive and recycled containers.

Doilies, gift ribbons, and festive baskets are all sold in the market.

Tins and jars from mustards, jams, or crackers are excellent containers for your own storage.

Use inexpensive disposable aluminum trays, which come in the right sizes to bake in, to give brownies and tarts as gifts.

Look at the professionally baked products in the Bakery for inspiration. Ask questions.

Finally, let your market work with you to meet your needs. Call ahead and give your market the time to order larger quantities of items you may need. Don't risk finding depleted shelves. Most of the time, however, supermarkets have everything you need when you want it—even late at night and on weekends.

·7·
STAPLES: FLOUR, SUGAR, NUTS, AND CHOCOLATE

INTRODUCTION

In this day of prebaked, prepackaged convenience foods and upscale supermarket bakeries, one might argue that baking is less popular than it used to be—that time limitations have wiped out this homey art. Why then have grocery aisles expanded with more varieties of flour, nuts, and luxury-quality chocolate than ever before? Pick up almost any food magazine, and the answer is there, if not on the cover, then throughout the pages and in the beautiful photographs.

Baking is one of the most creative and therapeutic endeavors in the entire cooking repertoire. It connects us from one generation to the next, and it is an experience to share with young and old. The same simple ingredients—flour, sugar, butter, nuts—available in every market, produce special confections unique to each country. And it is a sensual, satisfying experience, the perfect retreat from a pressure-filled day. Even though just a few aisles over from the Staples section there are cookies with names such as "Like Home" and "Grandma's Best," they cannot begin to compare with the fresh-from-the-oven, homemade ones with their diet-wrecking aromas and tastes.

There are some extraordinary supermarket Bakeries today, offering scrumptious brick-oven baked breads, fresh fruit tarts, and cookies. (Others, unfortunately, still sell the same mass-produced average-tasting fare that they have for the past 20 years.) But nowhere can you buy the satisfaction of baking from scratch without doing it yourself. Dazzlingly glamorous creations, the kind no market and few bakeries could ever offer without a giant price tag, are yours to be had from this section.

With a little time and practice, fresh, professional-quality baked goods can be yours. I'm not suggesting that you attempt to make everything from scratch. Most of us don't have that kind of time. But, a pile of frozen tart shells will enable you to make quickly a heavenly apricot tart (page 76) when you find the fruit in the market. Your own refrigerated cookie dough and even frozen waffles will taste better than store-bought ones.

I urge you to invest the time to wander up and down these aisles slowly and find out how your market is reflecting the growing fascination with baking. Discover the Health Food section where nuts and seeds are sold in bulk. When I see new products, my mind races forward to envision contemporary combinations: a whole yam (including the healthful skin) puréed and combined with rye flour into chewy, sweet DAY AFTER THANKSGIVING SWEET RYE AND YAM MUFFINS (page 318) or IRISH OATMEAL HERMITS laced with coconut and dried fruits (page 327).

Look for hazelnuts, marzipan, and candied fruits on the shelves in the fall for holiday sweets. Cornmeal and wheat flours; sourdough bread starters; improved, preservative-free packaged mixes; even miniature fluted-foil and colored-paper cups in which to serve candies and tiny hors d'oeuvres like a professional are some of the many options we have. But some items seem impossible to find in a market. Cake flour is frequently missing, supplanted by mixes. Slower-selling items rob the market of vital space. If you don't find what you are looking for, ask the manager. Some ingredients are in more than one section. Chocolate, for example, is often found in the Baking section and in a separate Candy department. Or, write to the market's Consumer Affairs department. Smart stores are listening to their valued customers.

Although it is not as obvious with baking staples as with produce or fish, ingredient freshness is still very important. Delicate flours, nuts, and chocolates do not last forever. Take a look at the Strategy Pages just preceding this chapter entitled "Stocking a Baker's Pantry" for some suggestions for more successful supermarket baking.

One final note. I always use *unbleached* all-purpose flour, as I consider it more healthful. When I measure flour, I use the spoon and sweep method: spooning the flour into my measuring cup and then leveling it with a spatula or knife. Where eggs are used, they are standard (USDA) large, unless otherwise indicated.

Basic Pâte Brisée Made in the Processor

Makes one 11-inch tart or two 8-inch tarts

This all-purpose pastry is ideal for savory dishes as well as sweets. It is extremely easy to make in a food processor and may be prepared up to 5 days in advance and refrigerated until ready for baking. The texture is light and flaky.

When working with pastry, I find that a large aluminum sugar shaker filled with flour makes it easy to sprinkle small amounts of flour on the dough or bread. You will find them with the nonfood items.

1⅔ cups (7½ ounces) unbleached all-purpose flour
2 tablespoons sugar
¼ teaspoon salt
9 tablespoons (1 stick plus 1 tablespoon) chilled unsalted butter, cut into small pieces
3 tablespoons solid vegetable shortening or lard, chilled
4–5 tablespoons cold water

1. Place the flour, sugar, and salt in the bowl of a food processor fitted with a steel chopping blade. Add the butter and shortening and bury them under the flour. With on-off motions, process until the mixture resembles small peas. Add a scant 4 tablespoons of water and process just until the dough begins to pull into a ball. If it seems very dry, add additional water by the teaspoon, as needed. But don't overprocess.

2. Remove the dough from the processor. Pat with flour and flatten into a disk about ¾ inch thick. Wrap it in plastic wrap and let it rest in the refrigerator for at least 2 hours.

3. Preheat your oven to 400°F.

4. Remove the dough from the refrigerator, unwrap it, and place it on a lightly floured board or pastry cloth. Massage the dough gently with your fingertips until it begins to soften and be workable, turning it over a couple of times. Dust lightly with flour. Using a lightly floured rolling pin, roll it into a circle measuring about 14 inches in diameter and ⅛ inch thick. If using a pastry cloth, flip the dough into the pan. If not, roll the dough back onto the pin or fold it into quarters, position it over the pan, and carefully ease the dough into the tart pan, working to flatten the bottom, then gently pushing the dough well into the corners and against the sides with your thumb and fingertips. Trim off excess dough by rolling the rolling pin over the top of the pan, or by using a knife. Cut excess dough into decorative shapes and bake them on a cookie sheet along with the tart. Or refrigerate and use it later for little tartlets.

5. Place a piece of aluminum foil shiny side down on the crust. Smooth the foil against the edges, prick it well with a fork (through the foil), and fill the pan with dried beans or pie weights (see Note). Transfer the pan to the middle of your preheated oven and bake until the crust is pale-beige-colored, set, and starts to pull away from the edge of the pan, about 12 to 15 minutes.

6. Carefully remove the foil and beans. Discard the foil, reserving the beans or weights for future use. Prick the bottom of the crust again with a fork, and lower the heat to 350°F. Return the tart shell to the oven and continue cooking for another 10 to 15 minutes until light-gold-colored. Check from time to time, pricking any air bubbles, if necessary. Remove the pan from the oven and let the tart shell cool on a rack.

NOTE: Pie weights are small aluminum pieces used to keep pastry flat while baking. They are sold in packages along with other baking supplies in markets that stock cooking equipment. I personally think that dried beans, such as Great Northern or kidney, are a less expensive and a better choice. The weights, being metal, get far hotter than the beans. Beans can be reused (but not eaten) many, many times before being discarded.

Walnut Pastry Crust

Makes one 11-inch crust

This buttery-rich nut crust is one of my favorite pastries for making fancy desserts in a hurry. Add a dense layer of chocolate, plenty of raspberries, strawberries, or plums to this cookielike sweet crust and a glamorous confection is yours. (See page 348 for RASPBERRY CHOCOLATE TART **and some suggestions for dramatic decorations.)**

If you are chopping nuts in a food processor, take them directly from the freezer (where it is best to store them) and pulse them with an on-off motion, rather than running the machine continuously. Otherwise, you might get a nut butter. If the recipe calls for sugar, add a tablespoon to the nuts as they are

chopping; this will prevent them from clumping together. Fresh walnuts in shells are usually available during the fall. However, canned or bagged shelled nuts are found all year.

2 cups unbleached all-purpose flour
12 tablespoons (1½ sticks) unsalted butter, chilled, cut into small pieces
1 egg
1 tablespoon milk
1 teaspoon vanilla extract
2 tablespoons sugar
¼ teaspoon salt
¼ cup finely chopped walnuts

1. Combine the flour, butter, egg, milk, and vanilla in the bowl of a food processor fitted with a steel chopping blade. With an on-off motion, process until the butter is the size of small peas.

2. Add the sugar, salt, and walnuts and process just until the dough starts to pull together. *Do not overprocess.* Remove from the bowl, pat into a ball, flatten into a disk about ¾ inch thick, and dust with flour. Cover with plastic wrap and refrigerate for at least 2 hours or overnight.

3. Preheat your oven to 375°F.

4. Remove the dough from the refrigerator and gently massage it until it is workable, turning it over a couple of times, and starting to flatten it with your fingertips. Dust the dough with a little flour. Lightly flour a rolling pin and board, and quickly roll the dough into a circle measuring about 14 inches in diameter and about ⅛ inch thick. If the dough sticks, add a small amount of flour and loosen with a dough scraper or long, thin-bladed knife. (I prefer to work on a pastry cloth, as I can turn the cloth quarter turns and roll the dough more evenly. It also makes it easy to flip the dough over into the tart pan.)

5. Carefully roll the dough over the pin or fold into quarters and position it over the pan. Unroll, and ease the dough into the prepared tart pan, working to flatten the bottom, and then gently pushing the dough well into the corners and against the sides with your thumb or fingertips. Trim off any excess dough by rolling the rolling pin over the tart pan or trimming with a knife. Excess dough may be cut into decorative

DID YOU KNOW? You can freeze pastry crusts in the tart pan uncooked or already cooked. Make sure that the pastry is double wrapped. I use plastic wrap or wax paper for the first layer, and a Ziploc bag for the second. Squeeze all the air out. The uncooked and cooked tarts may be frozen first, removed from the tart pan, and then carefully stacked for easier storage. Uncooked pastry should be slowly defrosted before baking, but should still be chilled. Return it to the tart pan for baking. The cooked shells should be reheated without defrosting at 350°F for 5 to 7 minutes to recrisp them. The crusts will keep for at least 6 months if they are properly wrapped and your freezer is kept constantly below 0°F. As a rule, unbaked pastry has a slightly longer shelf life.

shapes (like leaves or apples) and baked alongside the tart. Once baked, glaze them and place them on finished tarts for decoration.

6. Tear off a piece of aluminum foil large enough to cover the tart and place it, shiny side down, on the dough. Prick the dough well with a fork (through the foil), and fill with pie weights or dried beans. Place the pan in the middle of the preheated oven and bake until the crust begins to pull away from the pan, about 15 minutes. Carefully remove the aluminum foil and beans or weights, saving the beans for another use. Remove the sides from pan (optional), prick the pastry with a sharp knife or fork if it swells up, and return the crust to the oven for another 6 to 8 minutes until golden. Remove the tart shell from the oven and let it cool on a rack.

Whole Wheat Cream Puff Shells (Pâte à Choux)

Makes about thirty 2½-inch puffs

Who said cream puffs can only be used to serve sweets? These savory shells are perfect for a cocktail party or elaborate tea, when finger foods and individual servings are especially appreciated. I find the more substantial whole wheat flavor appealing when the puffs are filled with TARRAGON CHICKEN SALAD (page 120). Or, make mini versions to hold single VEAL AND SAUSAGE MEATBALLS (page 201).

Another way to make your market work for you: Bake these puffs and fill them with a prepared salad (like turkey or tuna) from the Take-Out department that you have "doctored up." Drizzle a little shredded cheese on top, heat for a minute or two, and let your guests be impressed with your talents. Be sure to look at the chapter on prepared foods for suggestions on how to dress up some of these time-saving Take-Out items.

¾ cup low-fat milk
6 tablespoons unsalted butter, cut into cubes
½ teaspoon salt
⅛ teaspoon white pepper
½ cup unbleached all-purpose flour
¼ cup whole wheat flour
3–4 extra-large eggs at room temperature
1 extra-large egg combined with 2 tablespoons milk, for egg wash

1. Preheat your oven to 400°F.

2. Combine the milk, butter, salt and pepper in a heavy, medium-size saucepan and bring it to a full boil. Remove the pan from the heat and add both flours all at once, stirring with a wooden spoon until smooth.

3. Return the pot to medium heat and continue stirring and flipping the pastry to dry it out, about 5 to 7 minutes. A slight coating will form on the bottom of the pan and the dough will be smooth and slightly shiny. Make sure it does not burn.

4. Remove the pan from the heat and begin adding the eggs, one at a time, completely incorporating each egg before adding the next. A good test to determine if a fourth egg is needed is to pinch off a small amount of the dough between your thumb and index finger. Separate your fingers slowly. If the dough breaks into two parts, it is too dry and another egg is necessary. It should form a "U" shaped strand between the two fingers.

5. Butter 2 cookie sheets and then quickly run them under cold water, shaking to leave just a few drops on each pan *or* line the pan with parchment paper. Fill a pastry bag fitted with a plain number 4 tip and squeeze the dough into small mounds about 1½ inches in diameter and height, about 2 inches apart (see illustration). Brush carefully with the egg wash, taking care not to let it drip onto the cookie sheet, or the puffs will not rise properly.

6. Immediately transfer the pan to the upper third of your preheated oven and bake until puffed and a rich amber color, about 25 minutes. Remove the cookie sheets from the oven and with a spatula transfer the puffs to a rack to cool.

7. Once the puffs are cooled, carefully split them in half horizontally and remove any uncooked dough from the center with a spoon. Cooled cream puffs may be frozen in Ziploc bags for 2 to 3 weeks.

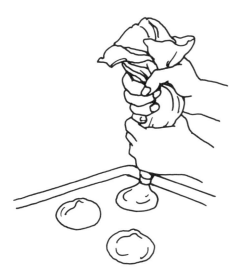

AS A VARIATION: For sweet cream puffs, use only all-purpose flour and add 1 teaspoon of sugar and ⅛ teaspoon nutmeg to the boiling milk, butter, salt and pepper in step 2. Fill with vanilla ice cream, fresh fruit, and top with THE ULTIMATE RASPBERRY CHOCOLATE SAUCE (page 417).

Heavenly Blues

Makes 50 to 60 dollar-size pancakes

The talented cook and author Marion Cunningham first served me these melt-in-your-mouth little morsels at Bridge Creek, the breakfast restaurant in Berkeley, California. They are sinfully delicious with warm maple syrup poured over them. To gild the lily, I borrowed Rose Levy Beranbaum's (founder of The Cordon Rose Cooking School) idea of adding solidly frozen fresh blueberries directly to the pancakes when on the griddle. They stay plump and juicy that way. This works well for other frozen berries and pieces of fruit like peaches and cherries as long as they will have adequate time to cook through.

4 eggs
½ teaspoon salt
½ teaspoon baking soda
4 tablespoons cake *or* 3½ tablespoons unbleached
   all-purpose flour (see Note)
2 cups sour cream
3 tablespoons sugar
Solid vegetable shortening for greasing the griddle
   or skillet
2 cups blueberries, frozen very hard

1. Mix the eggs, salt, baking soda, cake flour, sour cream, and sugar together in a large bowl and beat with a wooden spoon until smooth. This can be done in a food processor or blender, as well.

2. Heat the griddle or skillet until very hot. Add just enough shortening to cover with a thin film. Drop small spoonfuls of the batter measuring about 2½ inches in diameter when spread out onto the hot griddle. When a few bubbles appear on top of the pancakes, drop a few berries onto each pancake, and quickly turn and cook the second side briefly. Serve with maple syrup or confectioners' sugar. The batter keeps for up to one week when covered and refrigerated.

NOTE: In this recipe, substituting all-purpose for cake flour will not make much of a difference in the final results. When larger amounts of all-purpose flour are substituted for cake flour, reduce each cup of all-purpose flour by 2 tablespoons. While the results will be satisfactory, they will not be identical. Cake flour is milled from softer, spring-summer wheat and is

DID YOU KNOW? Freezing blueberries when they are plentiful is easy. Pick over the berries discarding any that are unsuitable. Rinse them and blot them as dry as possible. Spread the berries on a jelly roll pan and place them directly in the freezer for about 1 hour or until frozen solid. Then, quickly transfer them by cupfuls to Ziploc bags, gently squeezing out all the air, and place in the freezer. They will keep for 4 to 6 months. Small freezer containers just large enough to hold each batch of berries will also work. Leave a small amount of head room and make sure that the containers are very dry.

about 9 percent protein. All-purpose flour is a combination of harder, winter flour and summer flour and is 12 to 13 percent protein. Do not use cake flour in a recipe calling for all-purpose. It won't work.

Crispy Cream of Wheat Griddle Cakes

Makes 8 slices, serves 2 to 4

These breakfast slices, crunchy on the outside and creamy inside, are simple to make and a nice alternative to pancakes or hot cereal for breakfast. Using the convenient packaged Cream of Wheat, the cereal is made the night before and chilled. Then it's sliced and cooked in 5 minutes the next morning, or a few days later. Butter and maple syrup are fine toppings, but, sautéed apples with cinnamon sugar would be even better. Lots of ingredients, like chopped nuts, drained cooked corn kernels, wild rice, or wheat germ, could be stirred into the Cream of Wheat before it is refrigerated for added flavor and texture.

2⅓ cups low-fat milk
½ teaspoon salt
½ cup Quick Cream of Wheat, *not* instant
½ cup lightly toasted fresh bread crumbs
2 tablespoons unsalted butter
2 tablespoons vegetable oil

1. Line a 6 × 3 × 2-inch individual-size loaf pan with a large piece of plastic wrap.
2. Combine the milk and salt in a small saucepan and bring to just below the boil over medium-high heat. Slowly add the Cream of Wheat, stirring constantly. Continue cooking for about 2 to 3 minutes longer, stirring constantly, until the mixture has thickened.
3. Scrape the cereal into the loaf pan, let it cool slightly, then fold the wrap over and refrigerate until firm, at least 4 hours or overnight.
4. Remove the pan from the refrigerator, lift out the loaf of Cream of Wheat, and peel off the plastic wrap. With a sharp knife, carefully cut the loaf into 8 even slices.
5. Place the bread crumbs in a flat dish, and pat each slice of Cream of Wheat with them.
6. In a large skillet, heat the butter and 1 tablespoon of the oil just until the butter has foamed. Add

DID YOU KNOW? Fresh bread crumbs are easily made in a food processor. It's a good use for stale bread. Lightly toast the slices, without the crust if very thick, and then let them cool. Tear them into pieces, and place them in the processor fitted with a steel chopping blade. Remove the plastic insert in the feed tube to let any steam escape (which would cause the crumbs to become soggy), and process by pulsing to the size desired. Try using leftover rye or wheat crumbs for a subtle flavor difference. Store fresh bread crumbs in a cool place or refrigerate them in a closed container.

the slices, fry for 1½ minutes or until browned on the first side, turn, add the remaining tablespoon of oil, and continue cooking the second side for another 1½ to 2 minutes, until well colored. Serve at once with maple syrup, preserves, or VERY BERRY COMPOTE (page 414).

Wild Rice, Pecan, Buttermilk Waffles

Makes 12 waffles, serves 4 to 6

These crunchy waffles are loaded with texture, taste, and old-fashioned goodness. Wild rice used to be a scarce autumn product, but it has recently risen in popularity and availability. You can make these waffles ahead of time and leave them in a warm oven for at least 45 minutes. Or let them cool on a rack and freeze them in Ziploc bags. They reheat better than the store-bought varieties! Serve them with VERY BERRY COMPOTE (page 414) ladled over the top. All those crunchy indentations will catch the tangy juice.

Breakfast has made a big comeback in recent years, especially on weekends. There is something very satisfying about pancakes, hot cereals, and waffles. We know that they are a good source of sustained energy. Markets have reflected this trend with every variety of breakfast bar and frozen breakfast food imaginable. Alas, many of them are sugar, salt, and chemical rich, and nutrient poor.

2 cups unbleached all-purpose flour
2 teaspoons baking powder
2 tablespoons sugar
½ teaspoon salt
2 cups buttermilk
2 egg yolks
6 tablespoons (¾ stick) unsalted butter, melted and cooled slightly
¾ cup chopped pecans
½ cup cooked wild rice, cooled
2 egg whites

1. Heat an electric waffle iron (see Note).
2. Sift together the flour, baking powder, sugar, and salt into a large bowl.
3. In a small bowl, combine the buttermilk and yolks. Pour in the melted butter, and stir until combined.

Add this mixture to the dry ingredients, stirring only until the batter is well blended.

4. Add the pecans and wild rice and stir.

5. Beat the egg whites until they form soft peaks. Gently fold them into the batter.

6. Ladle about ⅓ of the batter onto the heated waffle iron, covering about ⅔ of the surface. Close and let the waffles cook for 7 to 8 minutes. The red indicator light will usually go off by this time, and the waffle will have stopped steaming. Test for doneness by carefully lifting the top. If it opens easily, and the waffle falls off without sticking, it is done. If there is resistance, let the waffle cook for another minute. Remove and serve at once, or leave in a warm oven for up to 45 minutes.

NOTE: Waffle irons should be properly seasoned. Newer electric models come with directions in the box. Many also have a Teflon coating. Once an iron is seasoned, you should only wipe the pan clean; do not wash it. You should not need to grease it further, since the batter has plenty of butter already in it.

Day-After Thanksgiving Sweet Rye and Yam Muffins

Makes 12

These muffins are a moist and delicious by-product of our Thanksgiving table when there is often an extra yam left over. Recently, we puréed one—nutrient-rich skin and all—in the processor and combined it with rye flour and sour cream. Served with a combination of cream cheese and strawberry preserves, these muffins are a festive morning-after treat.

It is better to refrigerate or freeze specialty flours like rye and whole wheat in airtight bags to keep them fresher tasting and free of pests. Given a choice, I'd buy the smallest bag possible if I weren't planning on using it quickly.

Unsalted butter for greasing the muffin tin *or* 12 muffin liners
1¾ cups rye flour, preferably stone ground
2½ teaspoons baking powder
½ teaspoon baking soda
½ teaspoon salt
1 cup mashed baked yam, fibrous tip and burned spots removed, but skin left on (approximately 1 large yam) (see Note)
2 eggs
¼ cup dark molasses
¼ cup orange juice
4 tablespoons (½ stick) unsalted butter, melted and cooled slightly
2 tablespoons caraway seeds
1 cup sour cream
¾ cup currants or chopped prunes (optional)

1. Preheat your oven to 375°F. Grease or line a 12-muffin tin.

2. Place the rye flour in a medium bowl. Sift the baking powder, baking soda, and salt into it.

3. In a large bowl, combine the mashed yam, eggs, molasses, orange juice, melted butter, caraway seeds, and sour cream and stir to blend well. Toss the currants or prunes with the dry ingredients and mix in the wet ingredients with a wooden spoon until just combined. The batter will be quite stiff.

4. Fill the muffin tins evenly with the batter. Bake in the middle of your preheated oven for 25 to 30 minutes, or until a toothpick or knife comes out clean when inserted in the middle of a muffin.

5. Remove from the oven, loosen with a small knife, if necessary, and gently turn muffins on their sides to cool.

NOTE: I mash my potato in a food processor.

DID YOU KNOW? Although sour cream contains 18 percent milkfat, it has only 25 calories per tablespoon, making it lower in calories than butter and most salad dressings. A newer lower-calorie option is sour half-and-half, with 10.5 percent milkfat. Both will keep in your refrigerator for at least a week after purchase. Sour cream should be smooth and thick with a slightly tangy taste and only a minimum of separation, if any. Do not freeze sour cream. When adding it to foods, it is best to do so just before serving.

Almost-Irish Soda Bread

Makes one 8-inch round loaf

Irish soda bread has long been one of my favorite quick breads. Its sweetness and slightly crumbly texture make it perfect for a snack in the afternoon or for a family dessert, instead of rich cake or cookies. I lightly butter warmed slices and spread on some apricot preserves. The addition of wheat germ and toasted sesame seeds gives it a more substantial, nuttier flavor, and the buttermilk adds a nice tang. I know it's not authentic, but it certainly tastes good.

4 cups unbleached all-purpose flour
1 teaspoon baking soda
1 teaspoon baking powder
2 teaspoons salt
⅓ cup sugar
1 cup toasted wheat germ (see Note)
⅓ cup sesame seeds, lightly toasted
6 tablespoons (¾ stick) unsalted butter, at room temperature
1 cup golden raisins
2 cups buttermilk
½ cup unbleached all-purpose flour

1. Preheat your oven to 350°F. Butter and flour a round 8-inch cake pan.

2. Sift together the flour, baking soda, baking powder, salt, and sugar into a large bowl. Add the wheat germ and sesame seeds.

3. Using a pastry cutter, two knives, or your fingertips, cut in the butter until the mixture is the consistency of fine cornmeal. Add the raisins.

4. Pour in the buttermilk and mix with a wooden spoon or your hands just until all the ingredients are mixed. The dough will be sticky.

5. Turn the dough out on a floured board and knead the dough for about 1 to 2 minutes, adding small amounts of the ½ cup of flour, until it is smooth and no longer sticky. Form the dough into an 8-inch ball, and put it in the prepared cake pan, flattening it slightly. With a sharp knife, score an "X" across the top extending beyond the edges.

6. Bake for 75 to 80 minutes in the lower third of your preheated oven. The bread is done when it has shrunk away from the edges of the pan and makes a hollow sound when tapped on the bottom. Remove the pan from the oven, turn the bread out of the pan,

🛒 DID YOU KNOW? What do you do with leftover buttermilk? A couple of tablespoons makes a tangy addition to creamed vegetable soups. Stir it in after the soup is heated. Use buttermilk in place of whole milk in waffles (see page 317), pancakes, or biscuits. There is also a good powdered buttermilk available in many markets. It keeps a long time on the shelf and combines with other liquids in baking to add the buttermilk flavor.

and let it cool on a rack for at least 1 hour. Once completely cooled, the bread may be sliced with a serrated knife and toasted, if desired. Serve with softened butter and apricot preserves, or softened cream cheese and orange marmalade.

NOTE: Wheat germ is the outer layer of the wheat that is removed during the milling process. When it is toasted, it becomes nutty and slightly sweet in flavor. While it was once found only in health food stores, it is readily available in jars and boxes with most other cereal products in the market. With all the discussion of fiber's benefits, this deliciously crunchy addition to breads, cookies, and other baked goods is even good for us.

Dilled Potato Bread

Makes 1 large loaf

Every time I make this beautiful golden-brown braided loaf, I remember the wide-eyed amazement of my children as they watch it rise in the oven. Homemade bread is one of the nicest pleasures in life, and this potato-dill loaf doesn't last long in our house, it is so delicious. Eat it plain or try it thinly sliced, lightly toasted, and spread with some chive-flecked cream cheese with thinly sliced smoked salmon on top. Cut into small canapés, it is an elegant accompaniment for cocktails.

1 cup milk
1 teaspoon sugar
1 package active dry yeast
12 tablespoons (1½ sticks) unsalted butter, at room temperature
½ cup sugar
1 tablespoon salt
2 eggs, beaten, at room temperature
¾ cup freshly mashed potatoes
3 tablespoons freshly chopped dillweed *or* 1 tablespoon dried
5½–6 cups unbleached all-purpose flour
Vegetable shortening for greasing a cookie sheet
1 egg beaten with a few drops of water

1. In a small saucepan, heat the milk until it measures 110°F to 115°F on a thermometer or until a few drops feel warm when placed on your wrist. Stir in the 1 teaspoon of sugar, sprinkle the yeast over the milk, stir, and let it stand 8 to 10 minutes in a warm, draft-free place (a turned-off oven works well) until the mixture has swollen and has small bubbles on the surface.

2. In the meantime, cream the butter until light in color. Add the ½ cup of sugar, salt, and eggs and beat until smooth. Add the yeast-milk mixture and stir until blended. Add the potatoes and dill and mix well.

3. Begin adding the flour, a cup at a time, stirring with a wooden spoon. Continue adding the flour until a soft dough is formed, working flour in with your hands when it becomes difficult to stir. Turn the dough onto a lightly floured board and begin to knead. Continue adding flour until a stiff dough is obtained. Knead for another 10 to 12 minutes until the dough is smooth and elastic.

4. Set the ball of dough into a lightly oiled bowl, turn once, and cover with a slightly dampened towel. Let it rise in a warm, draft-free place until doubled in size, 2 to 3 hours. Punch down the dough and divide it into three equal parts.

5. On a lightly floured board, roll each part into a rope about 1¼ inches in diameter and about 14 to 16 inches in length. Place the three ropes side by side and braid them together, pulling slightly as you braid the strands (see illustration). Pinch the ends together, tucking them under, and place the loaf on a lightly greased cookie sheet. Cover with a damp towel and let it rise in a warm, draft-free place until doubled in size, about 1½ to 2 hours.

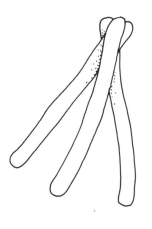
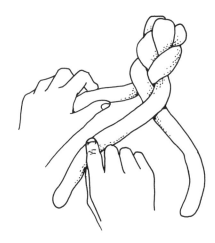

6. Preheat your oven to 350°F.

7. Brush the bread dough with the beaten egg and water and place in the preheated oven for 30 to 35 minutes until well browned on top and hollow-sounding when tapped on the underside. Cool thoroughly on a rack before cutting.

8. Once the bread is completely cooled, it may be wrapped in aluminum foil or plastic, placed inside another plastic or Ziploc bag (remember to squeeze out all the air), and frozen for up to a month. Reheat before serving.

Cranberry Holiday Braid

Makes 1 large loaf

This butter-rich yeast bread, braided with a cranberry-orange filling, looks especially festive if decorated with pine boughs (well rinsed and dried) around it and extra cranberries sprinkled on the greenery. It's wonderful for breakfast and good enough to pass for dessert, as well.

When choosing preserves, jams, and jellies, look for labels where the fruit is listed first. That tells you that there is more fruit than sugar or any other ingredient. Sealed jars of preserves will keep in a cool pantry for at least a year. Once opened, they should be refrigerated.

DOUGH
¾ cup milk
1 teaspoon sugar
1 package active dry yeast
1 cup unbleached all-purpose flour
12 tablespoons (1½ sticks) unsalted butter, at room temperature
6 tablespoons sugar
2 eggs, at room temperature
3–3½ cups unbleached all-purpose flour

FILLING
1 cup (12 ounces) sweet orange marmalade
1½ cups (6 ounces) fresh or frozen cranberries, coarsely chopped
1 stick cinnamon

¾ **cup confectioners' sugar, sifted**
2 tablespoons orange juice
1 teaspoon vegetable oil
7–8 cranberries, for decoration

1. FOR THE DOUGH In a small saucepan, heat the milk until it measures 105°F to 115°F on a thermometer or until a few drops feel slightly warm when placed on your wrist. Stir in 1 teaspoon of sugar, sprinkle the yeast over the milk, stir, and let it stand 8 to 10 minutes in a warm, draft-free place until the mixture has swollen and has small bubbles on the surface. Stir in 1 cup of the flour, cover with a dry towel, and allow it to rise in a warm, draft-free place (a turned-off oven works well) until doubled in size, about 1 to 2 hours.

2. In a large bowl, cream the butter and sugar until light and fluffy. Punch down the risen sponge and stir it into the butter-sugar mixture with a wooden spoon. Add the eggs one at a time. Stir in about 2½ cups of flour and blend well. Once the dough starts to pull away from the sides of the bowl and is too stiff to mix with a spoon, begin to knead by hand. Turn it out onto a lightly floured board and begin adding the remaining flour by ½ cupfuls until the dough is smooth and no longer sticky. Knead the dough for about 10 minutes or until very smooth and elastic.

3. Place the ball of dough in a lightly oiled bowl, turn once, cover it with a dry towel, and set it in a warm place to rise until almost doubled in size, 45 minutes to 1½ hours.

4. MAKE THE FILLING Combine the marmalade, cranberries, and cinnamon stick in a medium-size saucepan, cover, bring to a boil over medium heat, and continue cooking for 5 minutes, stirring occasionally. Uncover and continue boiling gently for 5 minutes more, stirring frequently. Remove the cinnamon and set the mixture aside to cool.

5. Punch down the dough. On a lightly floured board, roll it out into a rectangle approximately 10 × 14 inches and ¼ inch thick.

6. Spread the filling in a thin layer down the center third lengthwise, leaving a small border at the top and bottom. Cut the outer thirds into 7 diagonal strips approximately 1½ inches wide, so that they are at-

DID YOU KNOW? Cranberries freeze beautifully. Wrap them in an airtight bag, squeeze out excess air, and they will keep for almost a year. When adding them to a recipe, do not defrost. They will be much juicier that way.

Recently, the cranberry industry changed their standard bag size. Whereas we used to buy a 16-ounce bag (which contained 4 cups), we now get only three quarters of that. Make sure to check amounts given in older recipes.

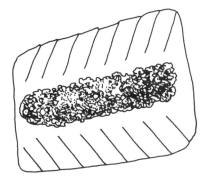
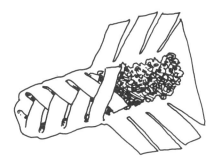

tached at the filling side. Lace strips alternately over one another and tuck the ends under (see illustration). Lightly grease a cookie sheet and transfer the braided bread to it. Cover it with a slightly dampened towel and let it rise in a warm place until doubled in size, about 30 minutes to 1 hour.

7. Preheat your oven to 350°F.

8. Bake the risen bread in the middle of the preheated oven for about 35 minutes until it is a rich golden color on top and when lightly pressed with your finger, the indentation springs back up. Transfer it to a rack to cool.

9. PREPARE THE GLAZE While the bread is cooling, combine the confectioners' sugar and orange juice in a small bowl and stir until smooth. Add the vegetable oil and stir. Brush the glaze generously over the cooled loaf and place the extra 7 or 8 cranberries evenly down the middle where the bread is braided. Let the bread cool completely before cutting it. It may be sliced and reheated, if desired.

Lemon Shortbread Cookies

Makes 18 pieces

I have always loved shortbread cookies for their firm, wonderful-to-dunk-in-tea texture. This slightly festive version with its lemon glaze and rectangular shape is an appealing addition to a plate of cookies served with custard, ice cream, or sherbet. The combination of crunch with soft is most satisfying.

Fresh lemons are always available in the market and infinitely superior to bottled lemon juice. Fresh-frozen lemon juice, near the condensed orange juice and lemonade in the freezer, is a reasonable substitute in a pinch. But, don't use dried lemon rind in

a jar. The flavor and texture are very different from fresh.

12 tablespoons (1½ sticks) unsalted butter, at room temperature
⅔ cup confectioners' sugar, sifted
½ tablespoon grated lemon zest
1 tablespoon fresh lemon juice
1¾ cups unbleached all-purpose flour
½ teaspoon salt

GLAZE
⅓ cup confectioners' sugar, sifted
1 tablespoon + 1 teaspoon fresh lemon juice

1. Cream the butter with a wooden spoon until fluffy and light in color, about 2 to 3 minutes. Add the confectioners' sugar and blend well. Stir in the lemon zest and lemon juice. These first steps can be done by hand or with an electric mixer.

2. Sift the flour and salt into the butter mixture and blend with your hands or a wooden spoon into a smooth dough.

3. Preheat your oven to 325°F.

4. Press the dough into an 8 × 8-inch cake pan and quickly smooth it with your hands or the back of a wooden spoon. Roll a small, straight-sided glass over the surface to make the dough as even as possible. Score the dough halfway through into 6 equal strips horizontally, then into thirds vertically. A short ruler and sharp paring knife will help. Prick each rectangular piece 3 or 4 times with a fork (see illustration).

5. Place in the lower third of the preheated oven and bake until the cookie is set when touched and light brown around the edges, 45 to 50 minutes. Remove the pan from the oven and set it on a wire rack to cool. Cut through the rectangles where the dough was scored and run a sharp knife around the outside.

6. FOR THE GLAZE Mix the confectioners' sugar with the lemon juice. Brush on the warm shortbread. Allow the cookies to cool. *Do not cover until completely cooled.* Shortbread cookies may be stored in the baking pan for at least a week.

NOTE: Supermarkets sell disposable aluminum baking pans in just the right size in which to make these shortbread cookies and then give them as a gift.

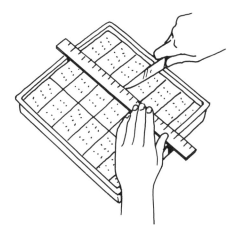

DID YOU KNOW? When working with pastry brushes, always smell them before use to guarantee that they were put away clean. Rancid tastes are easily transmitted this way and can ruin your best efforts. Wash brushes in warm, soapy water, then rinse well. If this does not do the trick, soak them in some hot water with a little bleach added. Rinse very well.

Irish Oatmeal Hermits

Makes 2 dozen 3½-inch cookies

These cookies could be called "true grit," for the crunchy toasted oatmeal and chewy coconut and dried fruits they contain. They are the result of foraging in the Staples aisles with my children, where we decided to experiment with ingredients we don't usually have on hand. The toasted Irish oatmeal, found in cans, lends a healthy nuttiness to these hermits, and the mixed fruit bits are a fast and helpful addition—much easier than chopping everything by hand. After consuming quite a few, we pronounced them a success.

1 cup Irish oatmeal, not the quick-cooking variety
12 tablespoons (1½ sticks) unsalted butter, at room temperature
½ cup firmly packed light brown sugar
2 eggs
1 teaspoon orange extract
¾ cup shredded coconut, sweetened or unsweetened
1 cup unbleached all-purpose flour
1 teaspoon salt
1 teaspoon baking powder
1 teaspoon baking soda
1½ teaspoons cinnamon
1½ teaspoons ground coriander seed
1½ cups chopped mixed dry fruits

1. Preheat your oven to 325°F.
2. Spread a thin layer of the oatmeal in a flat pan and toast it in the preheated oven until lightly browned, about 15 minutes. Set it aside to cool.
3. In a medium-size mixing bowl, cream the butter until light and fluffy with a wooden spoon or electric mixer. Stir in the brown sugar, then the eggs, orange extract, and coconut.
4. Sift the flour, salt, baking powder, baking soda, cinnamon, and coriander into the bowl, and mix well. Add the oatmeal and fruit and stir to blend.
5. Drop the mixture by rounded tablespoonfuls onto a lightly greased cookie sheet, leaving about 3 inches between each cookie. Or, line the pan with parchment paper. Bake in the middle of your preheated oven until lightly colored around the outside and puffed in the middle, about 12 to 14 minutes. Do not overbake. Remove the pan from the oven and let the cook-

DID YOU KNOW? To keep brown sugar soft: Once the bag has been opened, either transfer the sugar to an airtight container or carefully fold the plastic inner bag down and clamp closed. I have purchased small colored wire clothes pins which are excellent for this purpose. If sugar does become hard, place a piece of soft bread or an apple slice in the bag, close it tight, and leave it for a few days. The moisture from the bread or apple will soften the sugar.

ies cool on the cookie sheet for 5 minutes before transferring them to a rack. Store in airtight tins. They will last at least 1 week.

Molasses Spice Cookies

Makes about 4 to 5 dozen

Supermarket shelves are crammed full of old and new cookie varieties. Yet nothing can quite match the aroma and flavor of the fresh-from-the-oven variety.

These buttery, spicy cookies are bursting with flavor. They are wonderful to serve with NUTMEG-SCENTED CANTALOUPE SHERBET (page 81) or custards. When first out of the oven, these cookies are soft and chewy. After cooling on a rack, they become crisper. You can choose the texture you prefer—crisp or soft. By adding a piece of soft bread to the storage tin, you can soften crunchy cookies.

12 tablespoons (1½ sticks) unsalted butter
1½ cups sugar
¼ cup dark molasses
1 egg
2 cups unbleached all-purpose flour
2 teaspoons baking soda
1 teaspoon ground cinnamon
1 teaspoon ground ginger
½ teaspoon ground clove
¾ teaspoon salt
Shortening for greasing cookie sheets
½ cup sugar, for coating balls of dough

1. In a medium-size saucepan, melt the butter over low heat. Set it aside and let it cool to room temperature.

2. Stir the sugar, molasses, and egg into the butter.

3. Combine the flour, baking soda, cinnamon, ginger, clove, and salt and sift them into the butter mixture. Mix well. Cover and chill in the refrigerator until dough is firm, about 45 minutes.

4. Preheat your oven to 375°F. Lightly grease 2 cookie sheets.

5. Form the dough into 1-inch balls, rolling each ball in granulated sugar before placing it on the cookie sheet. Leave about 2 inches between each cookie. Bake in the middle of the preheated oven for 8 to 10 minutes, or until the cookies are golden brown and the

DID YOU KNOW? To measure molasses easily, lightly film the measuring cup with a little flavorless vegetable oil. When you pour out the desired amount of molasses, it will all slip into whatever you are baking, instead of sticking to the cup. No spatulas and no scraping needed.

tops are cracked. They will still be soft. Remove the pan and transfer the cookies with a wide spatula to wire racks to cool. Store in an airtight tin. (Add a piece of soft bread if you prefer softer cookies.)

Pogachel

Makes about 32 cookies

These simple hard biscuits are not too sweet and are perfect for dunking in cocoa, tea, or sherry. Sometimes I serve them along with rich fruit compotes, or strawberries soaked in Grand Marnier, savoring each soaked crumb. I learned to make them just as my Hungarian great-grandmother made hers, by hand. When I was teaching my daughter to make them, we tried a batch in the food processor. My great-grandmother must have been smiling as we discovered that the handmade batch had a finer, more delicate texture compared with the twentieth-century version.

8 tablespoons (1 stick) unsalted butter, at room temperature
¾ cup sugar
1 egg
2 tablespoons sour cream
2 cups unbleached all-purpose flour
2 teaspoons baking powder
½ teaspoon salt

1. Preheat your oven to 350°F. Lightly flour 2 cookie sheets.
2. In a medium-size bowl, cream the butter and sugar together until fluffy and light in color. Beat in the egg and the sour cream.
3. Combine the flour, baking powder, and salt, and sift them into the bowl with the butter mixture. Knead the mixture by hand into a smooth dough.
4. Lightly flour a wooden board or counter. Carefully roll out the soft dough to an even thickness of slightly more than ¼ inch. Using a round cookie cutter or a glass about 2¼ inches in diameter dipped in flour, cut out the cookies. Gently transfer them to a cookie sheet with a spatula dipped in flour. Gather up the scraps, reroll the dough, and repeat. Prick the center of each cookie in 2 places with a fork. Bake in the middle of the preheated oven until lightly browned

🛒 DID YOU KNOW? *Where you bake your cookies in the oven makes a difference. If too close to the heat source, they can burn on the bottom before the top is cooked. Good heat circulation produces even baking. Cookie sheets should be at least 2 inches narrower than the width of the oven. If 2 sheets are used, try to stagger them so that they are not right on top of one another. It helps to rotate their position in the oven, as well.*

around the edges, 18 to 20 minutes. Remove the pan and transfer the cookies to wire racks to cool.

Chocolate Pecan Icebox Cookies

Makes about 4 dozen

Those rolls of prepared cookie dough calling to you from the Dairy case have nothing over these easy-to-prepare cookies. Besides having no preservatives, these pecan slices have plenty of crunch and flavor, thanks to the chocolate, orange zest, and a nip of bourbon. You can make the dough up to a week in advance, wrap it in plastic wrap, and slice and bake as desired. Or, make 2 batches and freeze one. It will be there waiting for you 4 months later. Remember to defrost the dough slowly in the refrigerator until it can be easily sliced. And, when you slice, remember that cookies should be uniform in size and thickness to bake evenly.

8 tablespoons (1 stick) unsalted butter, at room temperature
1 cup firmly packed dark brown sugar
1 egg
2 tablespoons bourbon *or* freshly squeezed orange juice
1 tablespoon grated orange zest
2½ cups unbleached all-purpose flour
½ teaspoon baking soda
1 teaspoon salt
½ cup chopped pecans
½ cup mini chocolate chips

1. In a medium-size bowl, cream the butter and sugar together until light and fluffy. Beat in the egg, bourbon, and orange zest.
2. Combine the flour, baking soda, and salt and sift into the butter mixture. Blend well. Stir in the pecans and chocolate chips.
3. Shape the dough into a roll about 2 inches in diameter. Wrap it tightly in plastic wrap or wax paper and refrigerate overnight or for up to 1 week.
4. Preheat your oven to 350°F.
5. Using a sharp thin-bladed knife, cut the dough into ¼-inch slices and place them on ungreased cookie sheets. Bake in the middle of the preheated oven until lightly browned and set, about 15 minutes. Remove

DID YOU KNOW? Baking soda is not only a leavener. Place an opened box in your refrigerator to keep it smelling fresh, replacing it every 3 to 4 months. Pouring a little down the garbage disposal sweetens the sink, too. Baking soda will also extinguish small kitchen fires.

the pan from the oven and transfer the cookies to wire racks to cool. Store in a jar with a loose-fitting lid to maintain the crispness. They will keep for up to 1 week or they may be frozen (see Did You Know?, page 332).

Chocolate-Dipped Butter Walnut Crescents

Makes 18

The delicate texture and toasted-nut flavor of these crescents has made them a family favorite for generations. Inspired by a passion for chocolate and finding the high-quality imported and domestic bars available in supermarkets, I began dipping the cookies. I found that coating each cookie halfway made them particularly attractive. Alternatively, after the cookies have cooled, dust them with confectioners' sugar rather than dipping them in chocolate. Or use a small tipped pastry bag to make a thin lattice pattern of chocolate over each one.

Choose the variety of chocolate you like—from extra bitter to milk chocolate. But, read the labels and buy only *real* chocolate. If you wrap the bars in a double layer of paper or foil, they will keep well in a cool pantry for at least 9 months. The gray "bloom" that develops on chocolate that gets too warm will not affect the taste and will disappear if the chocolate is melted for baking.

8 tablespoons (1 stick) unsalted butter, at room temperature
½ cup confectioners' sugar, sifted
1 teaspoon vanilla extract
¼ cup finely ground walnuts, firmly packed
1 cup unbleached all-purpose flour
½ teaspoon salt
3 ounces bittersweet chocolate

1. Preheat your oven to 350°F.
2. In a medium-size bowl, cream the butter until light and fluffy. Stir in the confectioners' sugar. Add the vanilla and walnuts and mix well.
3. Sift the flour and salt into the first mixture and stir until smooth.
4. Lightly flour a cookie sheet. Scoop up enough dough to form a 1-inch ball. Roll each ball between your palms into a 3-inch cylinder, form it into a cres-

cent, and place it on the cookie sheet about 2 inches apart.

5. Transfer the cookie sheet to the middle of your preheated oven and bake until the edges of the crescents are golden brown, about 13 to 15 minutes. Remove the pan from the oven and transfer the cookies to a rack to cool.

6. Melt the chocolate in a small saucepan over low heat or in the top of a double boiler. Let it cool slightly, and then dip one end of the cooled crescent in the chocolate. Place the cookies on wax paper to harden.

Prince Albert's Cakes

Makes 32 squares 2½ × 3 inches

These glorious fruit-filled squares with their flaky cookie crust and sweet glaze are royal indeed. England's Queen Victoria liked to bake them for her husband, Prince Albert, and their nine children, when in their private apartment at Windsor Castle. They appeal to all ages and are the perfect sweet for late-afternoon tea or a large holiday open house. This is a princely confection, well worth the effort, and all the ingredients are found in the market.

I am grateful to Rona Deme, the charming proprietress of Country Host, for helping me to modify her bakery-size recipe into this smaller version.

FOR THE FILLING
2 cups raisins (golden and dark mixed *or* either one alone)
1 cup currants
½ cup candied diced lemon peel, finely chopped
2 tablespoons unsalted butter
¼ cup unbleached all-purpose flour
¼ cup water
¼ cup sweet sherry

FOR THE PASTRY
2 pounds (6½ to 7 cups) unsifted all-purpose flour
2 cups sugar
2 teaspoons salt
1 cup (½ pound) solid vegetable shortening or lard
½ pound (2 sticks) unsalted butter
⅔–¾ cup milk

FOR THE GLAZE
¾ **cup confectioners' sugar**
3 **tablespoons hot water**
½ **teaspoon vanilla extract**
½ **teaspoon flavorless vegetable oil, such as safflower**

1. FOR THE FILLING   Combine the raisins, currants, lemon peel, and butter in a medium-size saucepan and add just enough water to cover. Bring the mixture to a boil, then turn down heat, and simmer for 10 minutes. While the fruit is simmering, mix together the flour and water and gradually stir it into the fruit mixture.

2. After the fruit has thickened, stir in the sherry. Remove the pan from the heat and spread the fruit out on a dish to cool completely while preparing the pastry.

3. PREPARE THE PASTRY   Place the flour, sugar, and salt in a large bowl and cut in the shortening and butter, until it is the size of small peas. Gradually add the milk, mixing until a smooth, soft dough results. Vary the amount of milk as necessary.

4. Preheat your oven to 350°F.

5. Roll out half the pastry to fit a pan that measures $18 \times 12 \times 1$ inches. It will be easier to roll the pastry on an apron or non-terrycloth dish towel dusted with flour. Flour the rolling pin to keep it from sticking to the dough. When the desired size is reached, roll the dough and cloth around the rolling pin. Unroll the dough and cloth so that the cloth is on top and the dough on the pan. Remove the towel and patch the pastry as necessary. Using your thumb or a knife, cut the edges of the pastry off even with the top of the pan.

6. Spread the fruit mixture evenly over the pastry.

7. Roll out the remaining pastry, and fit it into the pan on top of the fruit. Press the dough edges together to seal, and prick the top of the pastry in several places. Bake in the middle of the preheated oven for 45 minutes or until the pastry is golden brown. Remove the pan from the oven and let it cool.

8. MAKE THE GLAZE   In a small bowl, mix the sugar and water together until smooth. Stir in the vanilla and vegetable oil and blend well. If the glaze stiffens, add a few drops of hot water and stir to smooth it

DID YOU KNOW? If you like to bake, a wide, heavy rolling pin is a valuable addition to your kitchen. It makes rolling out pastry far easier and faster. Check to see if your market has a Cookware boutique.

When storing boxes of dried fruits, make sure they are tightly closed. I slip a Ziploc sandwich-size bag over mine. If they do dry out, soak them for a few moments in warm water or a little sherry, port, or brandy until softened, then drain before using.

out. When the pastry is cool, brush the top crust with the glaze. When the glaze dries, cut the pastry into 32 squares. When storing these squares, cover them loosely with foil. Otherwise, they get soggy.

NOTE: Don't get discouraged if the dough breaks when you transfer it to the pan. It is a large amount and can be unwieldy and slightly sticky. Happily, patching and smoothing it out does not adversely affect the final taste or appearance. If this happens with the bottom layer, simply flatten the dough with your fingertips. For the top, gather the dough back into a ball, dust it lightly with flour, and reroll it. For small cracks, add a piece of the dough and smooth it with your fingertips.

Excess dough scraps can be stored in the refrigerator, wrapped in plastic, for 1 week. I reroll them to make tartlet shells to fill with LEMON CURD (page 90) or for sugar cookies.

Chocolate Carrot Brownies

Makes 16 squares

These brownies are chewy and somewhat reminiscent of a fruitcake. The shredded carrots, orange zest, and raisins add a distinct flavor and a unique texture. These squares will stay moist for at least a week, if stored well sealed. They are not fragile; we take them along on picnics and pack them in school lunches.

Unsalted butter to grease the baking pan
8 ounces bittersweet chocolate
8 tablespoons (1 stick) unsalted butter
¾ cup unbleached all-purpose flour
½ cup sugar
1 teaspoon salt
3 eggs
1 cup finely shredded carrots, approximately 3 medium
6 ounces pecans or walnuts, chopped
Grated zest of 1 orange
1 teaspoon vanilla extract
⅓ cup golden raisins (optional)
Heavy cream, for topping (optional)

1. Preheat your oven to 350°F. Line an 8 × 8-inch baking pan with aluminum foil, then lightly butter it.

2. Melt the chocolate and butter in a double boiler or over very low heat. Stir to blend, then remove from the heat and set aside.

3. Sift the flour, sugar, and salt together into a large bowl.

4. With a wooden spoon, beat the eggs into the chocolate mixture one at a time. Pour the chocolate into the flour mixture and blend well. Stir in the carrots, pecans, orange zest, vanilla, and raisins. Pour the batter into the prepared baking pan and place it in the middle of the preheated oven. Bake until a knife or toothpick inserted in the center comes out clean, about 30 minutes. Remove the pan from the oven and let the brownies cool on a rack. Cut into 16 squares and serve with soft whipped cream, if desired.

Curried Corn Nut and Sunflower Seed Nibble

Makes 1½ cups

This "nibble" is addicting. We make big bowls of it in the fall, for open houses and cocktail parties. It is both economical and festive, ideal to make and package in jars for hostess presents. Use the variety of curry powder that suits your palate.

Look in the Health Food, or bulk food, section for the corn nuts and sunflower seeds in larger quantities. They are also found in cellophane packages with other prepackaged nuts on display in the supermarket.

1 cup corn nuts
½ cup sunflower seeds
2 teaspoons sugar
2 teaspoons vegetable oil
1 teaspoon curry powder, mild or hot
½ cup dark raisins

1. Preheat your oven to 350°F.

2. Combine the corn nuts, sunflower seeds, sugar, and oil in a small, oven-safe bowl and toss to blend.

3. Transfer the bowl to the preheated oven and bake for 10 minutes.

4. Remove the nuts from the oven, toss with the curry powder, and stir in the raisins. Let the mixture cool. Store in airtight containers.

Cocoa Pecans

Makes 1 pound

This kind of glazed nut treat is often sold in expensive food boutiques although it is really very easy to make. You can use the general principle of dipping nuts into egg whites and add any combination of sweet or savory coating you desire—coconut and cocoa; or Parmesan cheese, ground red pepper, and nutmeg. The shiny nuts are very tempting. Packed in empty mustard jars or colorful tins, they make nice gifts.

1 tablespoon vegetable oil to grease cookie sheets
1 egg white
1 pound pecan halves
⅓ cup sugar
3 tablespoons unsweetened cocoa powder
½ teaspoon salt
½ teaspoon cinnamon
¼ teaspoon ground cloves

1. Preheat your oven to 350°F. Lightly oil 2 cookie sheets.

2. Place the egg white in a deep bowl and add the pecans. Toss to cover evenly.

3. Combine the sugar, cocoa, salt, cinnamon, and cloves in another bowl. Transfer the pecans to this bowl and toss to cover with the sugar mixture.

4. Distribute the nuts evenly among the cookie sheets, keeping them in 1 layer. Bake in the preheated oven for 15 minutes. Remove and let cool. Store in airtight containers.

🛒 DID YOU KNOW? Cookie sheets and baking dishes are usually buttered when baking time is short, as with cookies, where the butter will add flavor and not burn, or where the batter covers the butter, as with cakes. For longer baking with exposed pans, a flavorless vegetable oil is recommended.

Date and Nut Meringue Kisses

Makes about 100 Pieces

These delicious candy nibbles from my Great-Aunt Ann are an easy and unusual confection to offer either with other desserts, with cheese, or with a cup of tea in the afternoon. They are slightly crunchy on the outside—thanks to the toasted coconut—and chewy and nutty inside. Supermarkets now sell pitted and chopped dates—a time-saving convenience for those of us in a hurry. But many markets only stock them from the fall through the holidays.

Unsalted butter to grease a cookie sheet
1 pound pitted soft dates, coarsely chopped
½ pound walnuts, coarsely chopped
½ teaspoon grated orange rind
3 egg whites
Pinch of salt
⅔ cup superfine or processed sugar
2 cups moist shredded coconut

1. Preheat your oven to 250°F. Butter a cookie sheet or line a cookie sheet with parchment paper.

2. Place the dates, walnuts, and rind in a bowl, mix well, and form into small balls about ¾-inch in diameter.

3. In a large bowl, place the egg whites and salt and whisk only until the whites are foamy. Slowly add the sugar, a teaspoon at a time, and continue beating for 30 seconds longer until you have a stiff but not dry meringue.

4. Toss half the date/nut balls in the meringue, coating them with your fingers; then roll them in coconut. Place them on the prepared cookie sheet. Repeat until they are all enrobed. Bake in the preheated oven for 30 minutes, or until light brown in color and nearly dry to the touch. Remove the pan from the oven and let the candy cool. Store in a dry area.

NOTE: For best results, choose a dry day to prepare these. If they become tacky during storage, dry them for a few minutes in a 200°F oven.

Crunchy Chewy Caramels

Makes 64 squares

Dulce de Leche is a traditional Argentinian dessert made by slowly boiling milk and sugar until it has thickened into a caramelized pudding. My friend Erica Loutsch, who spent most of her youth in Argentina and Paraguay, says that today many Latins slowly boil an unopened can of sweetened condensed milk for 2 to 2½ hours and produce the same ambrosial results in less than half the time. I borrowed Erica's idea, using the familiar can of sweetened condensed milk. But I opened the can before cooking to make these candies, adding two of my favorite baking staples: sesame seeds and pine nuts (pignoli).

Some progressive supermarkets have started carrying both hulled and unhulled sesame seeds in bulk in their Health Food section. If you can find the latter, try them. They have a more pronounced, nuttier flavor. Unfortunately, both of these baking staples are usually only sold in very small jars or boxes, making them more expensive because of the packaging. But, because they are perishable even when sold in bulk, buy them in smaller quantities.

1 teaspoon unsalted butter to grease a baking pan
1 14-ounce can sweetened condensed milk
½ cup light corn syrup
4 tablespoons (½ stick) unsalted butter, at room temperature
½ cup lightly toasted sesame seeds
½ cup lightly toasted pine nuts

1. Butter an 8×8-inch square baking pan.

2. In a small, heavy saucepan, combine the sweetened condensed milk and corn syrup and bring it to a boil. Continue boiling the mixture over high heat for 10 to 15 minutes, stirring constantly.

3. Stir in the butter and boil until the mixture reaches the soft ball stage on a candy thermometer (238°F to 240°F), stirring constantly. It will take about 35 or 40 minutes cooking time all together. The mixture will be a rich caramel color and quite thick.

4. Remove the pan from the heat, stir in the sesame seeds and pine nuts, and scrape the mixture into the baking pan. Using a spatula or wooden spoon, spread the candy evenly in the pan and let it cool.

5. When almost cooled, cut it into 1-inch squares with a sharp knife. To remove the candy from the pan, run hot water over the back of the pan until the caramels lift out. Recut as necessary and store in an airtight tin.

DID YOU KNOW? Pine nuts have been used in cooking for thousands of years. They were used in Imperial Rome and by early American Indians. Because their oil can turn rancid quickly, they should be stored in the freezer if not used right away. To toast pine nuts and sesame seeds, pour a shallow layer into a flat baking pan and place in a preheated 350°F oven until lightly colored, about 7 to 10 minutes. Shake the pan occasionally during toasting.

Mandarin Cranberry Sorbet

Serves 8 to 12

This refreshing, richly berry-colored sorbet is beautiful to look at when garnished with mandarins and cranberries, and is an ideal palate refresher between the courses of a substantial meal or as a lighter dessert with cookies.

Canned fruits in light syrup or their own juices are perfect for making homemade sorbets. Sorbets and other fruit concoctions in which ingredients are puréed, offer an opportunity to buy less-expensive brands of fruit; the less-than-perfect size does not affect the final presentation, as long as the quality is not inferior.

⅔ cup sugar
⅔ cup water
1 12-ounce package cranberries, fresh or frozen
4 11-ounce cans whole mandarin segments in light
   syrup, drained
1½ tablespoons grated orange zest
2 tablespoons cognac (optional)

1. Place the sugar and water in a small saucepan. Over medium heat, bring the liquid to just below the boiling point. Set the syrup aside to cool.

2. For garnishing, set aside 6 cranberries and 12 nice mandarin segments (or a couple extra for mistakes). Add the remaining cranberries, mandarins, sugar syrup, zest, and cognac to the bowl of a food processor fitted with a steel chopping blade and purée until smooth. Pour the mixture into a shallow glass or metal dish and freeze until solid, about 6 to 10 hours.

3. Return the frozen mixture to the bowl of the food processor and process, starting with an on-off motion, until the mixture is smooth. Return it to the shallow dish and refreeze for another hour or until firm.

4. Remove the sorbet from the freezer and let it stand at room temperature for about 10 minutes. Serve in small scoops. On one scoop, place one mandarin segment split in half lengthwise and opened out to form the wings of a butterfly, and a half of a cranberry as the body.

Spicy Pumpkin Mousse

Serves 6

Pumpkins are native to the New World. They were brought back to Europe by Christopher Columbus. There they were used in vegetable dishes (see PUMPKIN AND PORCINI, page 53) and pasta. This lightly spiced mousse recipe is ideal for Thanksgiving—you can easily double the quantities of the ingredients—or anytime a flavorful do-ahead dessert is wanted. This mousse would be delicious served in ready-to-fill chocolate cups now sold in many markets.

Supermarket shoppers are used to buying cans of puréed pumpkin, not realizing that their Halloween Jack-o'-Lantern may be easily cut up, baked, and puréed, as well (see how below). If canned pumpkin is a staple in your house, buy an extra can or two between October and December. At other times, it may not be stocked.

1¾ cups fresh or canned pumpkin purée
1 teaspoon cinnamon
½ teaspoon freshly grated nutmeg
½ teaspoon ground ginger
½ teaspoon salt
⅛ teaspoon white pepper
Grated zest of 1 orange
3 tablespoons Grand Marnier or triple sec
1 package unflavored gelatin
2 tablespoons fresh orange juice
4 egg yolks
⅓ cup sugar
¼ cup heavy cream
1 teaspoon vanilla
1 cup heavy cream
6 ginger snaps, crumbled for garnish

DID YOU KNOW? To make pumpkin purée, lightly oil a jelly roll pan or cookie sheet, and preheat the oven to 325°F. Wash the pumpkin and scrape out the seeds; cut the pumpkin into large chunks and place it shell side up in the oven. Bake for an hour or until the flesh is easily scraped from the skin. Purée in a food processor fitted with a steel chopping blade, or pass through a food mill. Once cooled, the purée may be frozen for up to 3 months.

1. In a large bowl, combine the pumpkin, cinnamon, nutmeg, ginger, salt, pepper, orange zest, and Grand Marnier and stir to blend very well.

2. Dissolve the gelatin in the orange juice in a small bowl.

3. Combine the egg yolks and sugar in a small bowl and beat until thick and lemon colored.

4. Scald the ¼ cup cream and vanilla in a small saucepan. Add the softened gelatin to the pan and stir until entirely dissolved. Pour this mixture into the egg yolks, beating continuously.

5. Scrape the cream-egg mixture into the pumpkin and stir until smooth.

6. Whip the remaining 1 cup of cream until stiff. Reserve about ⅓ cup for the garnish. Fold the cream into the pumpkin mixture and when incorporated, scrape the pumpkin mixture into a 2-quart mold or 6 individual ramekins. Cover and chill several hours or overnight.

7. To serve, pipe the reserved whipped cream in rosettes on top of the mousse for decoration and drizzle the ginger snap crumbs over this in a design.

Caramel Curls with Apricot Cream

Makes 16

These lacy, crunchy caramel rolls are so delicious I often eat them just as they cool. Or I fill them with custard or cream whipped with a little instant coffee and mini chocolate chips. In this party version, the gingery apricot cream provides a stunning contrast in flavor and texture to the curls. Since crispness is important, avoid making them on humid days. Also, fill them just before serving for the same reason.

Dried apricots are often found in boxes, bags, and loose in the Health Food bins of your market. While bags and boxes are often about the same price, some bulk dried fruits are less costly and fresher. Why pay for the packaging? If this department is well cared for (covered containers, well stocked), buy the amount of apricots needed, seal them in a plastic storage bag, and keep them in a cool pantry or refrigerator until needed.

Shortening for greasing 2 cookie sheets

FOR THE CARAMEL CURLS
¼ cup light corn syrup
4 tablespoons (½ stick) unsalted butter
⅓ cup firmly packed light brown sugar
¼ teaspoon ground ginger
½ tablespoon brandy
½ cup unbleached all-purpose flour

FOR THE APRICOT CREAM
5 ounces dried apricots
1 tablespoon finely grated fresh ginger
¾ cup light cream
**2 tablespoons superfine sugar (or regular sugar
 processed in a food processor)**
1 tablespoon brandy
1 pint heavy cream

1. MAKE THE CARAMEL CURLS Preheat your oven to 350°F and generously grease 2 cookie sheets with shortening.

2. In a medium saucepan, combine the corn syrup, butter, brown sugar, ginger, and brandy and bring it to a boil. Remove the pan from the heat, slowly stir in the flour, and mix well.

3. Drop the batter by generous rounded teaspoonfuls onto the prepared cookie sheets. They will measure about 2½ inches once they flatten before baking. Bake only about 4 at a time, since they spread to about 5 inches in diameter. Bake in the middle of the preheated oven for 8 to 9 minutes, or until dark golden color.

4. Remove the pan from the oven and let the cookies cool on the cookie sheet for about 1 to 2 minutes, then lift off one at a time with a cake spatula or your fingers. Wrap each cookie around a clean broom handle or a metal cannoli form, and hold for a few seconds until firm, then carefully slide the curl off and let them cool on a cake rack before filling. If cookies become too brittle to bend, put them back in the oven for 15 to 30 seconds.

5. PREPARE THE APRICOT CREAM Place the apricots and ginger in the bowl of a food processor fitted with a steel chopping blade. First use on-off motions, then process until quite smooth. Add the light cream, sugar, and brandy, and process until very smooth.

6. Using a chilled bowl and beaters, beat the heavy cream until very stiff. Fold in the apricot mixture.

7. Fill a pastry bag fitted with a wide decorative tip (6B) and pipe the cream into both ends of the caramel curls. Serve as soon as possible.

AS A VARIATION: These cookies may be served plain or slightly bent over a rolling pin. Two flat cookies may be sandwiched with a few drops of melted chocolate.

NOTE: These curls become soggy if refrigerated. Once they are made, store them in a dry place. The apricot cream may be made ahead of time and refrigerated. Assemble the curls just before serving.

Strudel with Caramelized Brazil Nut Filling

Serves 10 to 12

Strudel dough or phyllo is widely used in Austrian and Hungarian baking and throughout the Middle East. Making this pastry is time-consuming and demanding. Happily, it is sold frozen and, sometimes, even fresh in almost every supermarket. Use it for making festive hors d'oeuvres, main courses, and desserts—like this sinful, giant nut roll. Within the flaky crust, you will find a wonderfully intense, spicy combination of flavors—apricots, apples, rum, cinnamon, lemon, and more—which are beautifully balanced by the softly whipped unsweetened cream served on top. What a heavenly combination!

½ cup golden raisins
½ cup chopped apricots
⅓ cup dark rum
2 tablespoons unsalted butter
1 large Granny Smith or other tart apple, peeled, cored, and finely chopped
¾ cup firmly packed dark brown sugar
2 tablespoons lemon juice
Grated zest of 1 lemon
1½ teaspoons cinnamon
½ teaspoon ground cloves
½ teaspoon salt
1 pound shelled Brazil nuts, coarsely chopped
4 tablespoons unsalted butter, melted
8 phyllo leaves
6 tablespoons toasted bread crumbs
Confectioners' sugar for dusting
3 whole shelled Brazil nuts, for garnish
1 cup heavy cream, lightly whipped

1. Combine the raisins and apricots with the rum and set aside.

2. Melt the butter in a large, heavy skillet just until it foams. Stir in the apple and let it cook over medium heat for about 5 minutes until softened, turning to cover with butter. Add the brown sugar, lemon juice, lemon zest, raisin-apricot mixture (including the rum), cinnamon, cloves, and salt and mix well. Turn up the heat and boil gently until the mixture is thickened and slightly reduced, about 5 to 6 minutes.

3. Add the Brazil nuts and stir to blend. Set aside.

4. Preheat your oven to 400°F. Lightly butter a cookie sheet or jelly roll pan at least 14 inches in length.

5. On a clean work surface, spread a large, dry towel horizontally. Place one leaf of phyllo with one long edge close to you on the towel and brush about a 1-inch strip of the upper edge lightly with butter. Place the lower edge of a second leaf of phyllo along the buttered upper edge of the first sheet, overlapping about ¾-inch. Brush both sheets lightly with butter and sprinkle about 2 tablespoons of bread crumbs evenly over this. Place the third sheet of phyllo over the first and repeat the above procedure. Do the same with the fifth and sixth leaves of phyllo. Place the seventh and eighth leaves on top of the phyllo layers, but do *not* brush with butter.

6. Transfer the nut mixture to the lower edge of the phyllo, forming it into an even cylinder, and leaving a 1½-inch border on each side. Holding the towel by the lower edge, flip it, causing the phyllo to roll over on itself. Turn in the side edges of phyllo sheets and continue to roll. When the strudel is about ⅔ rolled, brush across the top and sides with butter; then finish rolling.

7. Carefully transfer the strudel to a cookie sheet, seam side down, by lining up the edge of the towel with the cookie sheet and rolling the strudel onto it. Brush the top and ends with butter and bake in the middle of the preheated oven for 15 minutes, or until crisp and golden colored.

8. Remove the strudel from the oven and let it stand at least 10 minutes before serving. Dust with confectioners' sugar. Garnish with the 3 remaining Brazil nuts, and use a serrated knife to cut it into slices about 1 inch wide. Serve with unsweetened whipped cream.

NOTE: Once the strudel has been made, it can be covered with buttered aluminum foil and refrigerated for up to a couple of days. Place it directly into a preheated oven and allow a couple extra minutes to brown. If the foil sticks to the pastry, do not remove it. It will come off easily after a few minutes in the oven. This strudel can stay in a turned-off oven for several hours after baking.

SOME PHYLLO FACTS: When buying frozen phyllo, open the cardboard box and look inside. The roll of phyllo should be tightly sealed in plastic. If it isn't, or the sheets look dry and broken, check another box. Make sure to defrost slowly according to the package directions. Quickly defrosted phyllo develops moisture and the sheets then stick together. If fresh phyllo is available, buy it instead. Phyllo keeps for months in a refrigerator without spoiling if tightly wrapped. But refreezing causes it to become brittle. When working with phyllo, keep the unused portion covered with a towel. Air is the enemy of phyllo since it dries out quickly. However, don't panic if you have to patch, it will not show in most preparations.

Tuscan Pineapple Upside-Down Cake

Serves 8

Mita Antolini is a farmer woman who lives in the hills of Tuscany in a tiny hamlet called Cortona. Electricity and telephone service only recently reached her home. One afternoon she made this special treat for us in her old wood-burning stove. To my surprise, it turned out to be the best pineapple upside-down cake I'd ever tasted. The texture of the cake was unique—kind of firm but light at the same time. I tried to re-create the effect of Italian durum wheat flour by adding a little whole wheat flour to this batter.

¾ cup sugar
3 egg yolks
Grated zest of 1 lemon
1 20-ounce can sliced pineapple packed in its own juice, drained, juice reserved
2 tablespoons brandy
1 teaspoon vanilla extract
1¼ cups unbleached all-purpose flour
½ cup whole wheat flour
1½ teaspoons baking soda
8 tablespoons (1 stick) unsalted butter, melted
7 tablespoons sugar, strained to remove lumps
1 cup chopped walnuts and almonds
3 egg whites, at room temperature

1. Preheat your oven to 375°F.

2. In a large bowl, combine the sugar, egg yolks, lemon zest, ¼ cup reserved pineapple juice, brandy, and vanilla and stir to blend well.

3. Sift in the white and whole wheat flours and baking soda and mix until very smooth. Add the melted butter and mix to blend.

4. Place the sugar in a heavy, oven-safe 10-inch skillet (see Note). Heat it over medium-high heat until the sugar melts and lightly caramelizes. Immediately remove the pan from the heat and rotate it to cool it slightly. (Sugar will continue to cook once off the heat, so be careful not to over-brown it over the heat. Any remaining sugar crystals will melt while you are rotating the pan.)

5. Place enough slices of pineapple to cover the bottom of the skillet—about 7 or 8. Sprinkle the chopped nuts over the pineapple.

6. Beat the egg whites into soft peaks and fold them

into the batter. Pour the batter over the pineapple, and spread with a spatula.

7. Place the skillet in the top third of the preheated oven and bake until the cake is lightly browned on top and the center springs back when gently pressed, about 20 to 25 minutes. Remove the cake from the oven, run a knife around the inside edge of the skillet, and invert it onto a plate. Let it cool on a cake rack.

NOTE: A seasoned cast-iron or other heavy skillet would be ideal to bake this cake. If your skillet is not oven-safe, caramelize the sugar first in a skillet, then pour it into a 10-inch cake pan.

Mexican Chocolate Cake

Serves 8 to 12

This cake is a celebration of south-of-the-border flavors: dark rich chocolate, almonds, espresso, black pepper, and cinnamon. There is very little flour, so it is dense, like a torte. A little goes a long way, even for chocoholics. The cinnamon-laced whipped cream spooned on top provides a nice complement to the flavors. And, make it a fiesta. Add some colorful ribbons—magenta, turquoise, yellow—serpentined around the base. *Olé!*

FOR THE CAKE
8 ounces bittersweet chocolate
12 tablespoons (1½ sticks) unsalted butter, at room temperature
¼ teaspoon salt
1 teaspoon finely ground black pepper
1 tablespoon instant espresso (not granular)
2 teaspoons cinnamon
1 teaspoon vanilla extract
¾ cup firmly packed dark brown sugar
3 eggs
¾ cup unbleached all-purpose flour
1 cup finely ground toasted almonds

FOR THE GLAZE
6 ounces bittersweet chocolate
1 egg
1 egg yolk
3 tablespoons unsalted butter, at room temperature

FOR THE FINAL DECORATION
12 whole blanched almonds for garnish
½ cup heavy cream
¼ teaspoon cinnamon
¼ teaspoon sugar

1. Preheat your oven to 375°F. Butter a 9 × 1½-inch straight-sided cake pan with a removable bottom, or springform pan.

2. PREPARE THE CAKE Melt the chocolate in the top of a double boiler or over very low heat. Set it aside to cool.

3. Cream the butter until light and fluffy. Add the salt, pepper, espresso, cinnamon, vanilla, and brown sugar, and beat until well blended. Add the eggs one at a time, beating after each addition.

4. Stir in the chocolate and add the flour, mixing only until it is blended. Fold in the ground almonds. Scrape the batter into the cake pan. Bake in the bottom third of the preheated oven until a toothpick inserted in the center comes out with a little moist batter on it and the cake is set, about 25 to 30 minutes.

5. Remove the pan from the oven, slide off the sides of the pan and let the cake cool on a rack for at least 30 minutes. With a sharp, thin-bladed knife, separate the bottom of the pan from the cake. Once it is cooled, brush the cake gently with a pastry brush to remove any crumbs.

6. PREPARE THE GLAZE Melt the chocolate in the top of a double boiler or over very low heat. Stir in the eggs, mixing well. Add the butter and stir thoroughly. Allow the glaze to thicken for 5 to 10 minutes off the heat.

7. Pour the glaze on top of the cooled cake. Smooth the top of the cake and allow some of the glaze to run down the sides. Smooth the sides with a metal spatula, then swirl the top into a design. Place the whole blanched almonds evenly around the outside of the top.

8. Transfer the cake to a serving dish or cake stand and let it stand at least a couple of hours to set the glaze. Serve with softly whipped cream flavored with cinnamon and sugar.

DID YOU KNOW? Some of the most dramatic presentations are actually some of the simplest. In this Mexican Chocolate Cake, blanched almonds are a stark contrast against the shiny dark glaze. Place the cake on a broad platter. Then, cut 14-inch lengths of ¾-inch ribbon, the kind sold in most markets for making gift packages. Slip about 1 inch under the cake, and notch the other end. This ribbon is stiff, and will twist nicely on the plate or even on top of the cake. Or, tear the ribbon into thin strips (it splits this way easily) almost to the end to form a pom-pom effect.

Raspberry Chocolate Tart

Serves 8

This is the recipe for the wonderful tart I described with the WALNUT PASTRY CRUST. It's so special that my daughter Nicole thinks of it as her birthday "cake." The marriage of buttery walnut pastry with rich chocolate, crowned with a profusion of firm, juicy raspberries, is magical. Add some chocolate leaves and caramelized walnuts, and this dessert will win applause. (Note that I have combined bittersweet and milk chocolate because the berries and the added sweetness of the milk chocolate seems to be a better combination to me. If you prefer, all dark chocolate may be used.)

FOR THE TART
1 recipe WALNUT PASTRY CRUST (page 311), baked and cooled
3 ounces imported bittersweet chocolate
3 ounces imported milk chocolate
2½ tablespoons unsalted butter
1½ pints raspberries or 1½ quarts uniform-size strawberries, split

FOR THE GLAZE
4 ounces red currant jelly
2 tablespoons sugar

FOR THE CHOCOLATE LEAVES (See Note on two ways of decorating this tart)
2–3 ounces imported bittersweet chocolate
16–24 waxy, nonpoisonous leaves, such as camellia, orange, etc.

FOR THE CARAMEL WALNUTS
½ cup vegetable oil
8 walnut halves
½ cup sugar
¼ cup water

🛒 SOME SEASONAL VARIA-TIONS: Alternate fruits for this tart are in order, since raspberries in December are often not to be found. (Although markets are flying them in from Chile, where it's summer, they are usually too pricey or too mushy.) Substitute well-drained canned mandarins or apricot-glazed banana slices in the dead of winter. Sliced plums, available in late summer, are a knock-out choice, too.

1. ASSEMBLE THE TART   Melt the chocolate in the top of a double boiler. Remove the insert from the heat and stir in the butter. Spread the chocolate over the inside of the baked and cooled Walnut Pastry Crust. Place the raspberries in an orderly fashion over the chocolate before it is set.

2. PREPARE THE GLAZE   Combine the currant jelly and sugar in a small saucepan, and bring it to a boil

over high heat. Cook for about 3 minutes, or until the sugar dissolves and the glaze coats a spoon. Brush the outside and top edge of the tart shell. (I do not feel it is necessary to glaze raspberries. I would glaze strawberries, and there is enough glaze here to do it. Store extra glaze in the refrigerator.)

3. MAKE THE CHOCOLATE LEAVES   Melt the chocolate in the top of a double boiler. Wash the leaves and dry them well. Brush the underside with chocolate, and transfer them to the freezer for a few minutes. Carefully peel off the leaf, holding on to the stem end (see illustration). Return the leaves to the refrigerator or freezer until needed.

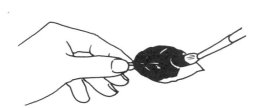

4. FOR THE CARAMEL WALNUTS   Heat ½ cup oil in a small saucepan until hot. Drop the walnut halves into the oil for about 30 to 45 seconds, or until lightly colored. Remove them with a slotted spoon, and drain on paper towels.

5. In a small saucepan, combine the sugar and water and bring to a boil. Once the sugar is dissolved, add the walnut halves and adjust the heat down to maintain a slow boil. Cook for about 10 to 12 minutes, until the nuts are shiny and coated, then remove them with a slotted spoon to a lightly buttered piece of wax paper to cool.

6. FOR THE DECORATION   Either place 8 walnut halves evenly spaced around the outside edge of tart, with 2 chocolate leaves on either side of each walnut *or* place 8 chocolate leaves evenly spaced around the outside edge of the tart with the stem edge pointed toward the center of the tart. Place 8 more leaves slightly overlapping the first leaves, working toward the center. Place the final 8 leaves in the same way, again overlapping slightly. You should have eight even sections of the tart. Place 4 walnut halves equally spaced around the outside. Place the remaining 4 walnut halves in the middle on the rows of leaves which do not already have a walnut (see illustrations). If desired, serve with softly whipped heavy cream.

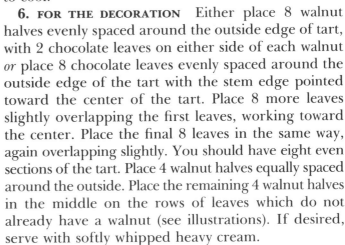

Queen Victoria's Christmas Trifle

Serves 10 to 12

This grand dessert can be made almost entirely with staples from the pantry and in a very short time. In Victorian England, trifles were often served in elaborate pedestal dishes as the flamboyant finale to a holiday meal. They are just as appropriate today in simple or elegant glass bowls, especially since this version may be made ahead of time for a dozen yuletide revelers. For another colorful addition, try canned or fresh fruit salad often found in salad bars.

2 cups CRÈME BRÛLÉE custard sauce (see page 107)
1 small sponge cake *or* 1 package ladyfingers
½ cup sweet sherry
¼ cup brandy
Grated zest of 1 lemon
2 ounces slivered almonds, toasted until light brown
1 cup raspberry or strawberry preserves
2 small bananas, sliced
1½ cups fresh or canned pineapple in own juice, cut into bite-size pieces
12 1¼-inch macaroons *or* amaretti cookies, crumbled
1 pint heavy cream, whipped until stiff, sweetened with sugar

1. Pour the custard in the bottom of a deep compotier or trifle dish. Slice the sponge cake into 3 × 1 × 1-inch pieces and arrange them over the custard and against the sides of the dish. Moisten the cake with the sherry and brandy.

2. Sprinkle the lemon zest and almonds evenly over this.

3. Spoon on the preserves and distribute the bananas, pineapple, and crushed macaroons.

4. Using a pastry bag fitted with a star tip, pipe heavy cream in a decorative design over the top.

5. To serve, spoon the trifle from the bottom of the dish to combine all ingredients.

NOTE: Victorian trifles were often decorated with angelica or candied flowers and fruit. It is quite difficult to find these today. Chocolate bits, maraschino cherries, and more nuts, would all make attractive garnishes.

DID YOU KNOW? Ladyfingers and sponge cakes may be located with Packaged Baked Goods, in the Produce department near berries, or even with Frozen Foods. Use them with any fresh or frozen fruit, custards, or ice cream for a quick dessert idea.

The Ultimate Decadent Orange-Chocolate Dacquoise

Serves 8 to 12

This is, perhaps, the most beautiful and delicious *dacquoise* I've ever tasted—and I've tasted many, since I am passionate about this meringue-and-buttercream dessert. It is well worth the effort and proves again what extraordinary foods are available from your supermarkets, since the ingredients are all right there. The chocolate-dipped orange segments will be the first visual seduction. But, taste the orange-chocolate buttercream: The balance of flavors between the bitter, sweet, and sour is out of this world and is heightened by an imperceptible amount of salt (½ teaspoon). The yolkless Swiss buttercream is far lighter than creams using the whole egg, so the flavors are even more intense. Finally, there is the crunchiness of the meringue layers. What a way to go!

Butter and flour for cookie sheets
FOR THE MERINGUE LAYERS
6 extra-large egg whites (1 scant cup), at room temperature
Pinch of cream of tartar
½ cup sugar
1⅓ cups (6 ounces) ground almonds

FOR THE CHOCOLATE-DIPPED ORANGES
1 navel orange
3 ounces imported bittersweet chocolate
1 teaspoon vegetable oil

FOR THE ORANGE-CHOCOLATE BUTTERCREAM
6 extra-large egg whites (1 scant cup), at room temperature
1½ cups superfine sugar (or processed regular sugar)
1 pound unsalted butter, cut into pieces, at room temperature
6 ounces imported bittersweet chocolate, plus chocolate left over from dipping the orange pieces
1 tablespoon orange extract
Grated zest of 1 orange, reserved from above
2 tablespoons Grand Marnier
½ teaspoon salt

1. MAKE THE MERINGUE LAYERS Preheat your oven to 250°F. Generously butter and flour 2 cookie sheets. Shake the excess flour from the sheets. Trace 3 circles about 8 inches in diameter on them.

2. Place the egg whites in a large bowl, add the cream of tartar, and using a wire whisk, beat until they stand in soft peaks. Gradually add ¼ cup sugar and beat the egg whites until stiff. Add the remaining ¼ cup sugar to the ground almonds, reserving ⅓ cup of the sugar-nut mixture for later use. Fold the remaining sugar-nut mixture into the egg whites.

3. Fill a pastry bag fitted with a plain (number 3) tip with the egg white mixture, and pipe circles following the patterns on the cookie sheets, working from the outside toward the center. Smooth any missed spaces with a metal spatula. Pipe or spoon any extra egg white mixture in dollops around the circles on the cookie sheets.

4. Bake the meringues in the middle of the preheated oven until they are firm and lightly colored, about 55 to 75 minutes. Rotate cookie sheets for even cooking. Remove the pan from the oven after 55 minutes. Press lightly with your fingertip. The meringue should be firm to the touch. Run a long, thin-bladed knife or spatula carefully under the meringues. If not firm, return them to the oven and check again in 5-minute increments. Meringues vary widely in moisture. They can take as long as 1 hour and 20 minutes to cook. They will become crisper on racks. *Note:* the use of 2 ovens for baking the meringues is ideal because you won't have to rotate the cookie sheets during baking.

5. Once the meringues are loosened, carefully transfer them and the extra dollops to cooling racks to harden. Meringues may be made the night before and left out uncovered in a cool, dry spot.

6. FOR THE ORANGE SEGMENTS Remove the zest, mince it, fold it in wax paper, or cover it in a custard cup, and reserve for later use.

7. Peel the orange and remove as much pith as possible. Carefully separate it into segments without breaking the membranes.

8. Melt the chocolate in the top of a double boiler and stir in the vegetable oil. Allow it to cool slightly, then dip each segment halfway into the chocolate. Let extra chocolate drip off each segment and back into the pan, then place the segments on wax paper to harden. (The design will be more attractive if all segments are dipped and placed in the same direction.) Use 8 of the nicest segments for the garnish. Once the chocolate has hardened, cover the segments lightly with plastic wrap and refrigerate until needed.

9. PREPARE THE BUTTERCREAM Place the egg whites in a large metal mixing bowl and set it *over* (not touching) a pot of boiling water. Using a wire whisk, gradually add the sugar and beat until the mixture is slightly thickened and measures 105°F on an instant-read or candy thermometer.

10. Immediately remove the bowl from the water and begin beating with an electric mixer. Continue to beat while gradually adding the butter. Beat until the mixture is room temperature and thickened, about the consistency of stiff filling—about 10 to 15 minutes. The buttercream will look ugly, and you will think that it won't come together. Keep beating; it will!

11. Meanwhile, melt the chocolate in the same double boiler as used for the garnish, including any leftover dipping chocolate. Add the orange extract, zest, Grand Marnier, and salt and stir to blend. (The chocolate may seize up slightly, but it will smooth out again when the buttercream is added.) Stir in ½ cup of the buttercream and beat until the chocolate is smooth. Scrape the chocolate mixture into the bowl of buttercream and mix well. Cover and refrigerate for 10 to 20 minutes.

12. ASSEMBLE THE DACQUOISE Keep the nicest meringue layer for the top. On a cake plate or 8-inch cardboard circle and turntable, if you have one, put a small amount of buttercream in the center to anchor the dacquoise and place the first meringue over it. Spread a generous quarter of the filling over it, making it a little thicker toward the outside.

13. Gently place the second meringue on top, pushing down *slightly*. Spread another fourth of the filling as before. Add the final meringue layer, and use another generous fourth of buttercream to cover the top and sides. A long metal spatula helps in icing.

14. Crumble the extra dollops of meringue into a bowl and combine them with the sugar-nut mixture. Using a cupping motion with your palm, pat this around the sides of the dacquoise. Arrange the chocolate-dipped orange segments in the center of the top, and

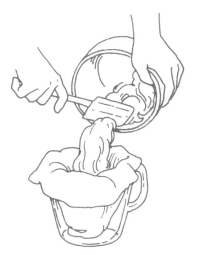

DID YOU KNOW? Filling a pastry bag is much easier if you twist the bottom of the bag and stuff some of the fabric down into the tip, sealing off the opening. Rest the pastry bag in a tall Pyrex measuring cup and open the top of the bag over it while filling the bag, so both hands remain free. When the bag is about ⅔ full, hold the top closed, position the pastry bag, and untwist the bottom.

pipe the remaining buttercream through a pastry bag fitted with a star tip, making rosettes on the outside edge. Refrigerate, uncovered, until an hour before serving.

NOTE: Meringues are like sponges, they absorb moisture like mad. So choose to make this dessert on a cool, low-humidity day. Otherwise, there is no crunch. If the meringues start to sag, quickly refresh them in a warm oven and let them cool on a rack.

A Well-Stocked Cupboard

The Staples aisles—canned vegetables, dried beans and rices, oils, vinegars, and prepared sauces—are expanding in today's supermarkets. Years ago, for example, our choice was a can of tomatoes or tomato paste and maybe two different brands. Today we choose from puréed, whole peeled, crushed, Italian, Spanish, and other varieties of the same product. With products packed in cans, jars, aseptic boxes, and even tubes, how do you select from the proliferation of new products? How much should you buy? What is the best way to organize stocking your cupboard? It requires thought and careful selection to utilize your space most effectively. Again, as in "Stocking a Baker's Pantry," less is usually best; let the market's shelves work for you.

Except in convenience stores, most large supermarkets have their aisles labeled overhead or at eye level, for example AISLE 4—CANNED VEGETABLES AND RICES. Newer stores have even installed electronic aisle finders at the entrance where you can punch your needs into a terminal. These indicators are useful for quickly locating products. If you shop at the same store most of the time, chances are you don't even look at the signs. But you may actually be cheating yourself by skipping certain aisles. Someday when you have time, take a slow walk up and down the Staples section. Stop and examine the varied products there.

PACKAGING

There are many kinds of packaging available today. The same product is frequently in more than one of these. Be sure to compare prices after determining that the quality is equal.

Cans

The contents will last for months and even longer when kept cool. Once the can is opened, transfer the food to a clean glass or plastic container and refrigerate. A little dent is usually not harmful, but bulging or rounded bottoms indicate bacterial activity, which can be fatal if consumed by people or animals.

Jars

These should be vacuum sealed, so if the seal is broken, make another choice. The storage time varies with the ingredients, but try to keep them in a cool, dark place. Once opened, some prepared sauces like mustard and ketchup are shelf-stable for months. Others, like delicate oils, should be refrigerated. Whole spices, such as nutmegs and peppercorns, last indefinitely.

Tubes

Tubes are a good choice for mustard, tomato paste, or other ingredients where a small amount is used and the rest is stored. Be sure the bottom end is well crimped and there are no small cracks or punctures. Once the tube is opened, refrigerate and store it for a month or two.

Cardboard Boxes

Boxes need to be sealed when purchased and show no signs of any pests. Check that the bottom is tightly glued. Boxes need not be resealed, but they should be closed. If there is a plastic or paper liner inside, as for cereals and crackers, roll this down. The contents will last well in a cool, dry place.

Aseptic Boxes

Be sure these are not dented or broken. They keep tomato sauces, milk, and juices fresh for up to a month in a cool place. Check freshness codes. If the box can be sealed tightly once it has been opened, place it in the refrigerator for up to a week. Otherwise, transfer the contents to a clean glass or plastic container first.

Plastic and Cellophane Bags

Bags should be sealed at the time of purchase. Because they are clear, it is easy to determine the quality of what is inside. Once they are opened, twist and seal them with a tie. Dried beans and rice keep well in a cool, dry cupboard. For spices in bags, seal or tie the bag to protect the spice from the air and store in a cool, dark place.

Fabric Bags

These are fine for imported rice and grains as long as they do not get wet or develop holes or tears. Be sure to close them before storage.

LABELS

Beyond the wide variety of shapes and sizes available for canned and bottled products, there are many attractive and inviting labels to capture your attention and your food dollars. Before making a selection, *be sure to read* what is written on the package.

Origins

Tomatoes, for example, are shipped from Italy, Spain, and the U.S. More specifically, the tomatoes from the San Marzano region of Italy are considered the best by many cooks. Yet, some clever manufacturers print "San Marzano-type." There is a difference.

Form

Look to see if the tomatoes are peeled and whole, crushed, puréed with basil, or made into a sauce. Some recipes ask that the tomatoes be drained first and then crushed. Crushed tomatoes affect the consistency of the dish.

Additives

"Hidden" sugars, especially in cereals and packaged mixes, are a real liability to health. Words that end in "ose" are all forms of sugar. They are often combined with honeys and corn sweeteners. Ingredients are listed in the order of greatest use in a food, i.e., the first ingredient listed is in the greatest quantity and the last the smallest.

Many canned and packed products contain salt. Newer no-salt products are now merchandised alongside salted alternatives instead of in a Health Food section.

BHT, BHA, and EDTA are all chemical preservatives and should be avoided.

Dietetic/Health Foods

Be sure to compare prices among products. Sometimes the same product merchandised as dietetic because it has no salt or is juice-packed will be substantially less expensive if sold with the regular canned goods rather than in the Diet Foods section. Fruit cocktail and tuna, for example, are often sold in both sections. Some dietetic products are a real boon, and others are filled with chemicals and taste it.

HOW MUCH TO BUY

While many unopened cans and bottles last a long time, why clutter up your cupboard with extras that will be used only occasionally?

Buy what you need, and let the supermarket warehouse what you can pick up easily. Unless you use a lot of a certain product quickly (or have a cellar), buying a case on sale will rob your precious storage space.

Buy smaller rather than larger sizes, unless you will use the remainders up quickly. A large can of garbanzo beans costs only 30 percent more than a smaller one. But, if the remainders go bad in the refrigerator, there is no savings. Delicate oils quickly turn rancid, and mustards and vinegars lose their bite.

Develop an inventory-control habit. Once a staple that you use often is opened and removed from your shelf, be certain to add it to your week's shopping list.

Whenever trying a product for the first time, buy only enough for one meal, no matter how tempting it looks. Better to buy more later than to be stuck with something you won't use.

STORAGE

To insure that your purchases are accessible and easily found in your cupboard, a personal system is a boon. I use the following method:

Group foods the way the market does: all soups and stocks together, tomato products, rices and dried beans, spices, etc.

Wipe products clean after each use before putting them away.

Label open packages with the name and date.

A turntable is useful for bottled condiments and oils and vinegars.

WHAT TO KEEP ON HAND

This is a personal choice and depends on your own style of cooking. Most supermarkets are well stocked with these provisions, and I try not to put away items that are easily purchased. I generally have the following items in case I need to improvise:

- 2 boxes of pasta—a longer one, such as spaghetti, and an extruded variety, such as elbows or penne
- long-grain and Arborio rices
- 2 varieties of dried beans or legumes, such as split green peas or Great Northern white beans
- polyunsaturated vegetable oil, virgin and extra-virgin olive oil, and a nut (hazelnut/walnut) oil
- red wine, herb (tarragon), fruit (raspberry), and balsamic vinegars
- condiments such as Dijon mustard, ketchup, mayonnaise, Worcestershire, Tabasco, and soy sauce
- beef, chicken, and clam broth
- whole and crushed Italian tomatoes, tomato paste
- can of olive-oil-packed tuna
- jar of oil-cured olives
- seasonings and dried spices: kosher or coarse salt, pouring salt, black peppercorns, basil, bay leaves, chili powder, cumin, curry powder, ginger, dry mustard, whole nutmeg, oregano, ground red pepper, rosemary, sage, and thyme

·8·
STAPLES: OILS, VINEGARS, BEANS, TOMATOES, PASTA, RICES, AND GRAINS

INTRODUCTION

Don't be a modern-day Mother Hubbard! An empty cupboard is an invitation to culinary disaster, while a few well-chosen staples will always provide a backup when drop-in guests, a long day at the office, or bad weather send you foraging for "just about anything" to eat. Many basic necessities of our food life, such as soups, pastas, and vinaigrettes, start with the ingredients kept in our cupboards. Sometimes those cans work wonders.

Canned tomatoes are the perfect staple to keep on hand. In fact, except for the few months of the year when the fresh varieties are truly outstanding, I prefer the San Marzano-region Italian ones for all my sauces, soups, and stews. Combine tomatoes with onions, garlic, tomato paste, and herbs, and a CHUNKY HOMEMADE TOMATO SAUCE (page 377) is ready in a short period of time. Grab another staple, pasta, and you are well on your way to satisfying large appetites. Since this sauce freezes beautifully, it may be used as the basis for other sauces, such as in a SQUID CAPONATA (page 222) where it becomes a marinara.

As you peruse the aisle with oils, vinegars, and condiments, notice how contemporary cooking has influenced our choices in the supermarket. Rich green and gold extra-virgin olive oil and delicate nut oils, once found only in specialty food boutiques, have recently appeared on the shelves. Raspberry, balsamic, and rice vinegars likewise are no longer as hard to find. Wasabi and mole sauce, too, are available to add their special touch to dishes. As Americans have fallen in love with ethnic cuisines, they want to buy authentic provisions in the same place they find most of their food—the supermarket. Originally these new foods were merchandised in Gourmet Foods sections, (where they were difficult to locate). They are now sensibly placed alongside similar products.

Our awareness of ethnic cuisines has increased our consumption of carbohydrates and legumes; and rice, grain, and pasta aisles reflect this with more and newer varieties. In many cultures, we find that meat is used sparingly, more in the form of a condiment or flavoring, as for a pasta sauce mixed with the carbohydrate pasta; this is a good source of sustained energy and *not* fattening. Look for bulgur (cracked wheat) to make HEARTY BULGUR PILAF (page 388) with sausages, chestnuts, raisins, and pine nuts; or orzo (the rice-shaped pasta) to make DOMED COLD ORZO SALAD WITH SHRIMP (page 385). CHICKEN, PECAN, AVOCADO, AND WILD PECAN RICE SALAD (page 386) with chicken, tomato, avocado, and a chick-pea, sesame, soy vinaigrette bursting with flavor and texture. There are so many exciting dishes that are easy to prepare, it is worth investigating and experimenting with them.

Mrs. Dash and other salt-free seasonings found near the herbs and spices add flavor but eliminate sodium or calories. Mix them with curry powder and mayonnaise for juicy broiled fish (page 370). Salsa, mustards, and chutneys may be combined into your own flavorful original creations.

Supermarkets are trying to meet the demand for a wider selection of convenience foods to make your job easier. Look at the proliferation of prepared canned, bottled, and packaged foods available. When you are considering buying any item to feed yourself, your family or friends, really read the label on that product. If the bottled Alfredo sauce has starch, sugar, and preservatives, remember that it won't taste like your own, and the chemicals won't nourish your body. I am not against convenience. When I don't have the time to make stock or mayonnaise, I buy them. I have doctored up a bottled spaghetti sauce. We all make compromises at certain times. Just select carefully. There are plenty of good choices available to you in these aisles.

Mustard Vinaigrette

Makes 1 cup

This is our "house dressing." It can be changed to suit a salad ingredient or to reflect your preference in vinegars and oils. We use it for the GREEN BEAN AND NEW POTATO SALAD OF VERNON on page 36, and on tossed greens. Red wine or sherry vinegars can replace the lemon juice. Delicious walnut or hazelnut oils are elegant additions to salads with cheese or bitter greens. The herbs, too, may be changed.

Along with the new "designer label" jars of vinegar and oil, mustards have spread out on the shelves, too. Since I use a lot of Dijon mustard in my cooking, I buy it in ample quantities, reading labels carefully to find a product made in France (where there is governmental control of ingredients), without any flours or sugars. Often, a large, simple jar contains a perfectly respectable mustard for about half the cost of the smaller, fancier bottle. Although mustard won't spoil, it will lose its bite. So, if you use it slowly, buy smaller jars. Refrigerate mustard after opening.

2 tablespoons Dijon mustard
1–2 cloves garlic, minced very fine or crushed
4 tablespoons lemon juice
¾ cup olive or vegetable oil, *or* a combination of both
2 tablespoons chopped flat-leaf parsley, *or* fresh dill
Salt and freshly ground black pepper to taste

1. Place the Dijon mustard in a small bowl. Add the garlic and lemon juice, and stir to blend well.

2. Slowly add the oil in a steady stream, whisking continuously to form an emulsion. Stir in the parsley, salt, and pepper, and taste to adjust the seasonings.

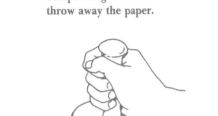

DID YOU KNOW? An easy way to crush garlic is to place the peeled and split clove(s) inside a piece of folded wax paper and pound it into a pulp with a meat pounder or flat-bottomed glass. Scrape the garlic into the bowl and throw away the paper.

Roquefort Vinaigrette

Makes about ¾ cup

DID YOU KNOW? The word *vinegar* comes from the French *vin aigre* or soured wine. Most vinegars have between 5 and 7 percent acidity. They will last for a very long time if sealed. However, once opened, vinegars react with the air, and they lose their bite after about six months. To reduce the acidity of vinegars in a vinaigrette, add a tablespoon of water, milk, or even stock.

This is another easy salad dressing, and one that goes especially well with stronger-flavored greens, like chicory and arugula. I like it combined with Boston lettuce, endive, arugula (or watercress), thinly sliced scallions, walnut pieces, and tiny slices of orange.

½ tablespoon Dijon mustard
2 tablespoons red wine vinegar
½ cup olive oil
1 tablespoon chopped fresh dill
2 ounces Roquefort cheese, crumbled
Salt and freshly ground black pepper to taste

1. In a small bowl, combine the mustard and vinegar.

2. Slowly add the oil in a steady stream, whisking continuously to form an emulsion. Add the dill and crumbled cheese. Stir in salt and black pepper, and taste to adjust the seasonings.

Puréed Chick-Pea Vinaigrette

Makes 2 cups

This is a wonderfully thick and spicy sauce to spoon on everything from the CHICKEN, PECAN, AVOCADO, AND WILD PECAN RICE SALAD (page 386) to steamed asparagus or sautéed veal cutlets. The combination of oriental flavors—rice vinegar, soy sauce, and sesame oil—with puréed chick-peas is that satisfying.

For purists, freshly cooked chick-peas (garbanzos) can't be beat. But for people in a hurry, the drained canned variety works wonderfully well here. Both dried and canned legumes stored in a cool pantry will keep at least a year.

1½ cups cooked or canned chick-peas (garbanzos), drained
1 large clove garlic
⅓ cup rice vinegar
2 tablespoons soy sauce
¼ cup sesame oil
¼ cup vegetable oil

DID YOU KNOW? Oils keep best in cool, dark cupboards. The more fragile oils such as walnut, hazelnut, and sesame go rancid very easily. Store them in the refrigerator and only buy small quantities. Always smell or taste an oil before using it. What a shame to ruin a dish by adding rancid oil.

1. Place the chick-peas, garlic, vinegar, and soy sauce in the bowl of a food processor fitted with a steel chopping blade and process into a smooth purée, scraping down the work bowl as needed.
2. With the motor running, pour the sesame and vegetable oils through the feed tube in a slow, steady stream. The vinaigrette will be creamy and thick. Scrape it into a screw-top glass jar and refrigerate until needed.

Spicy Old Bay Tomato Dressing

Makes 1 cup

This tangy dressing is reminiscent of the creamy Louis sauces often used with crab or shrimp salads. Sometimes the spice section of the market is stocked with tins or jars which have already combined ingredients to produce a unique tasting product. Old Bay seasoning is one, most often used in seafood preparations. Try this dressing with a combination of shrimp, blanched pea pods, cubed jicama, and diced red pepper. Use it for the PAPAYA, AVOCADO, AND CHICKEN SALAD (page 94) as well. With any prepared package or bottle, be sure to read the list of ingredients and add salt at the end if needed.

1 tablespoon capers, drained
1 large clove garlic, peeled and split
3 tablespoons tomato paste
1 egg, at room temperature (see Note at end if not using a processor)
1 tablespoon tarragon vinegar
¼ teaspoon dry mustard
1½ teaspoons Old Bay seasoning
½ teaspoon dried tarragon, crumbled
½ cup vegetable oil
8–10 drops Tabasco sauce
Freshly ground black pepper to taste
3 tablespoons finely chopped shallots

1. In a food processor fitted with a steel chopping blade, place the capers, garlic, tomato paste, egg, and vinegar, and process until smooth.

2. Add the mustard, Old Bay seasoning, and tarragon and pulse just to blend.

3. With the machine running, pour the oil through the feed tube in a slow, steady stream to form an emulsion.

4. Add Tabasco sauce and pepper to taste, then stir in the chopped shallots. Transfer to a glass screw-top jar and refrigerate for at least 3 hours.

NOTE: If making this salad dressing by hand, use only the yolk of the egg. Mince the capers, garlic, and shallots as fine as possible and whisk the ingredients together in a nonaluminum bowl. Remember to add the oil slowly, as with the processor version. A blender will work in place of a food processor.

Sweet and Tangy Oriental Vinaigrette

Makes 2 cups

We are always looking for new vinaigrettes for salads in our house. I first used this gingery sweet and spicy version on ORIENTAL BROCCOLI SALAD (page 24). But, it is also good on simple mixed greens, a pasta salad, or a composed salad with turkey, orange slices, almonds, and scallions.

In this recipe I use a combination of oils because sesame oil alone is too assertive, and the pepper oil adds a good bite. The hoisin sauce (from the Oriental section) thickens the dressing and adds a nice sweetness. Keep empty olive oil and sauce bottles to store your own preservative-free dressings—in the refrigerator, of course. Soy sauce, because it is fermented, need not be refrigerated. If kept closed, it will last a very long time. Any crystals, or even a bit of mold, may simply be removed, and the remaining soy is fine.

⅓ cup hoisin sauce
½ cup rice vinegar
2 tablespoons freshly chopped ginger
2 tablespoons soy sauce
2½ tablespoons honey
12–24 drops hot pepper oil
½ cup sesame oil
⅓ cup vegetable oil

1. Blend the hoisin sauce, vinegar, ginger, soy sauce, and honey together in a small bowl. In a slow, steady stream, whisk in the hot pepper, sesame, and salad oils.

NOTE: This recipe is better made ahead to allow the flavors to develop. It keeps well tightly covered in the refrigerator for a couple of weeks.

Mustard Custard

Makes 1½ cups

This piquant dipping sauce for crudités (raw vegetables) or Jarlsberg fingers is another one of Barbara Soyster's gifts for making and giving. It is also wonderful spread on sandwiches. I use it as a base for my GINGERY PEANUT DIPPING SAUCE (at the end of this recipe) served with MINI SHRIMP SPRING ROLLS (page 223).

English-style dry mustard is made from yellow mustard seeds which are ground into a fine powder. It is intensely spicy. A tin will keep its bite for at least 6 to 9 months if stored in a cool spot away from sunlight.

½ cup (2 1½-ounce tins) loosely packed English-style dry mustard
½ cup white wine vinegar
¼ cup dry vermouth
¾ cup sugar
2 eggs, well beaten

1. In a small bowl, mix together the mustard, vinegar, and vermouth and let it stand covered overnight.

2. The next day, add the sugar and beaten eggs and mix well.

3. Transfer the mixture to the top of a double boiler and cook over boiling water, stirring constantly with a spoon or whisk, until thickened, about 3 to 5 minutes. Remove the insert from the heat and continue stirring until the steaming stops. This sauce is best if refrigerated overnight before serving at room temperature. It keeps for months in the refrigerator. For a hotter sauce, increase the dry mustard to ¾ cup.

Gingery Peanut Dipping Sauce

Makes ¾ cup

¼ cup MUSTARD CUSTARD (above)
2 tablespoons dry sherry
5 drops (or more) hot pepper oil
1 tablespoon minced fresh ginger
2 teaspoons rice vinegar
1 teaspoon soy sauce
¼ cup chunky peanut butter

1. Combine all the ingredients in a small saucepan and heat gently over low heat, stirring constantly until the mixture has thickened, about 2 to 3 minutes. Allow the mixture to cool to lukewarm, and serve with MINI SHRIMP SPRING ROLLS (page 223). Or serve it with roasted pork or a cold meat salad.

Basic Whole Egg Mayonnaise

Makes about 1¼ cups

Homemade mayonnaise is one of the great pleasures in life. The taste may be delicate (if it is made with a flavorless oil) or gutsy (when a fruity olive oil is used). In any case, it is superior to most commercial varieties and will last more than a week in the refrigerator if stored in a screw-top glass jar.

Making mayonnaise is easy, especially in the food processor or blender. It is one of those versatile staples of cooking that changes color and flavor easily to suit the surroundings. Take a look at some of the variations listed at the end of this recipe, then try your own combinations. Also, be sure to note that if making this sauce by hand, you should use only the egg yolk and have all ingredients at room temperature.

1 egg, at room temperature
Pinch of salt
1 tablespoon lemon juice *or* white vinegar
1 teaspoon Dijon mustard *or* ½ teaspoon dry mustard
⅔ cup vegetable oil
⅓ cup olive oil

1. Place the egg, salt, lemon juice, mustard, and ¼ cup oil in the food processor fitted with a steel chopping blade. Process 3 to 4 seconds to mix well.

2. With the motor running, add the remaining oil through the feed tube, pouring in a slow, thin stream. The mixture should thicken immediately. Taste to adjust the seasonings, then transfer the mayonnaise to a glass screw-top jar, and store in the refrigerator. If the mayonnaise is too thick, add a little warm water to thin it.

TRY THESE VARIATIONS:

Russian Dressing

For salads and spreading on sandwiches:

To a cup of mayonnaise, add 3 to 4 tablespoons of ketchup or chili sauce, 1 tablespoon minced onion, and 2 teaspoons minced fresh parsley.

Thousand Island Dressing

For salads and spreading on sandwiches:

To 1 cup of mayonnaise, add 2 tablespoons of ketchup, 2 tablespoons minced celery, and 2 tablespoons minced green pepper, 1 finely diced hard-cooked egg, and 1 tablespoon minced sweet pickle.

Red Pepper Mayonnaise

For grilled scallops and chicken breasts:

To 1½ cups mayonnaise made with lemon juice and vegetable oil, add 2 large red bell peppers that have been roasted, peeled, seeded, patted dry, and puréed (*or* 2 jarred peppers packed in water and also puréed), 3 to 4 drops Tabasco sauce, and 1½ to 2 tablespoons extra lemon juice to taste.

Green Mayonnaise

For cold poached fish:

To 1 cup of mayonnaise made with mostly olive oil, fold in 1½ tablespoons minced fresh parsley, 2 teaspoons fresh snipped chives, 2 teaspoons minced fresh tarragon (*or* ½ teaspoon dried and crumbled), and 1 to 1½ teaspoons extra lemon juice or white vinegar to taste.

Curried Mayonnaise

For broiled fish steaks and dipping raw vegetables:

To ½ cup mayonnaise, add 2 teaspoons Mrs. Dash or other citrus-herb blend without salt, 1 teaspoon curry powder (hot or mild), ¼ teaspoon dry mustard. Spread on fish and sprinkle with toasted bread crumbs. Broil at least 6 inches from the heat for 5 minutes (if steaks are 1 inch thick), turn, spread mayonnaise and crumbs on second side, and cook another 5 minutes.

Caper Mayonnaise

For VEAL AND SAUSAGE MEATBALLS on page 201:

To 1½ cups of mayonnaise made with olive oil, add 2 tablespoons of crushed capers, 1 to 2 tablespoons anchovy paste, and some freshly ground black pepper.

Tapenade

Makes 3 cups

One often finds this kind of olive dip in the south of France, where it is usually served with a large tempting basket of raw vegetables. Although the horseradish is not part of the classic version, I like the tang it imparts. Beware, tapenade is addicting on a lazy summer afternoon. The warm colors and wonderful fragrances of Provence seem to come back to me with each bite.

You can find oil-cured olives in 6½-ounce jars in the Staples section. Look either next to canned olives or where other Italian and Greek specialties are located. If you don't find them there, check in the Deli section where they are sometimes sold loose.

1 6½-ounce jar black oil-cured olives, pitted
1 2-ounce can anchovies, drained, rinsed in warm
   water, and patted dry
1 tablespoon Dijon mustard
3 eggs, at room temperature
3 tablespoons lemon juice
1½ tablespoons prepared white horseradish
1½ cups olive oil
8 whole olives, for garnish

1. Place the olives, anchovies, mustard, eggs, lemon juice, and horseradish in the bowl of a food processor fitted with a steel chopping blade and process until smooth, about 10 seconds.

2. With the machine running, pour in a few drops of the oil through the feed tube. The first few drops should begin to emulsify the mixture before the remaining oil is added. Pour in the rest of the oil in a very slow, steady stream. The mixture will resemble a mayonnaise. If a thicker consistency is desired, refrigerate for 2 to 3 hours before serving.

3. Transfer the tapenade to a serving bowl and garnish with the olives around the edge. Serve with a basket of fresh vegetables, such as fennel, endive leaves, carrots, and red peppers, and/or thin slices of French bread brushed with olive oil, dusted with crumbled dried basil, and toasted until lightly colored. Tapenade will last for a couple of weeks under refrigeration.

Hearty Eight-Bean Soup

Serves a crowd

My dear friend Barbara Soyster volunteered this recipe as a unique gift-giving idea. Purchase a variety of eight dried beans and barley, usually packaged in one-pound bags. Set out 9 bowls, pots, or kitchen containers and empty each bag into one bowl. Reach in and take a generous handful (about ½ cup) of each and put it into a plastic food storage bag with a twister. Continue making packages of mixed beans until all beans are used. Tie the Eight-Bean Soup recipe to the top closure using a pretty ribbon, and you have a Gift from the Hearth! By all means, substitute other favorites, such as black beans, cannellini beans, green split peas, etc.

½ cup Great Northern beans—all beans are dried
½ cup pinto beans
½ cup Michigan pea (Navy) beans
½ cup lima beans
½ cup black-eyed peas
½ cup red kidney beans
½ cup garbanzo beans (chick-peas)
½ cup lentils
½ cup barley
3 quarts water
1 ham hock, optional
1–2 celery stalks, preferably with leaves attached
1 large carrot
Several sprigs of flat-leaf parsley
1 large garlic clove, minced
1 teaspoon dried thyme leaves
2–3 bay leaves
2 medium onions, peeled and coarsely chopped
1 28-ounce can crushed Italian tomatoes
1 tablespoon fresh lemon juice
1 tablespoon balsamic vinegar
1 teaspoon chili powder
1½ teaspoons coarse or kosher salt, or to taste
Freshly ground black pepper to taste

1. The night before, sort through the beans and remove any unwanted material. Rinse well. Place the beans in a large bowl. Add enough water to cover the beans by 3 inches. Let them soak overnight or for 8 hours.

2. In the morning, drain the beans well. Place them in a large stockpot or soup pot. Add 3 quarts of water and the ham hock and bring the liquid to a boil. Reduce the heat and simmer slowly for 2 hours, removing any surface foam occasionally.

3. Tie the celery, carrot, and parsley firmly together with kitchen string and add them to the soup pot.

4. Add the garlic, thyme, bay leaves, onions, tomatoes, lemon juice, vinegar, chili powder, salt, and pepper and stir to mix well. Simmer slowly for at least another half hour, adding more water if necessary.

5. At the end of the cooking time, remove the vegetable bundle, ham hock, and bay leaves. (Pieces of ham may be returned to the soup, if desired.) Serve with a wonderful tossed salad and hearty bread.

DID YOU KNOW? Most soups and stews may be served immediately after cooking or refrigerated or frozen for future use. They improve in taste, however, if refrigerated for a day or two before serving so flavors have a chance to blend. It's economical to make big batches of stews and soups and freeze them in serving-size portions.

Pumpkin Black Bean Soup

Serves 8

Many people love a hearty black bean soup, including me. Served with thick slices of bread, it is the perfect winter's lunch or supper. In this version, the puréed pumpkin adds a slight sweetness which nicely balances the tangy sherry vinegar and produces a rich, satisfying combination of flavors. I serve the soup in a whole pumpkin carved into a tureen, with the toasted seeds in place of croutons. It is festive enough for any great meal.

When buying dried beans, be sure to compare prices in different sections of the store: the dried legumes versus the ethnic foods. Sometimes there is a pretty big difference in price between brands. The quality is about the same. If substituting canned beans, drain and rinse them well. You will need about 4 1-pound cans. Since the quality varies widely—with some brands the beans are almost mashed because they are overcooked and overprocessed—you will have to do a little experimenting.

1 pound black beans, washed and picked over for foreign objects
1 teaspoon salt
¾ cup canned Italian tomatoes, drained
1 cup canned pumpkin or puréed fresh
6 ounces boiled ham, diced in ⅛-inch cubes *or* meat from a leftover ham bone
2½–3 cups beef stock
3 tablespoons unsalted butter
1½ cups finely chopped onions
3 large cloves garlic, peeled and minced
1 tablespoon ground cumin
1 tablespoon salt, or to taste
Freshly ground black pepper to taste
3–4 tablespoons sherry or red wine vinegar
½–1 cup medium sherry
1 large fresh pumpkin, optional

1. Place the beans in a heavy saucepan and cover with boiling water to a level of about 2 inches above the beans. Add the salt and return the liquid to the boil. Turn down the heat and simmer, partially covered, for about 2 to 3 hours, or until the beans are tender. Add more water if the beans become dry.

2. Stir in the tomatoes and transfer the mixture in batches to a food processor fitted with a steel chopping

DID YOU KNOW? "Cooking sherry," because of the addition of salt, can be sold in supermarkets which otherwise do not permit the sale of alcoholic beverages. I recommend that you do not buy it. Less expensive California or imported sherries are fine for this recipe, however.

blade. With a few on-off motions, process until the beans have started to smooth out but are still somewhat chunky. You can also do this in a blender. Return the beans and tomatoes to the saucepan and stir in the pumpkin, ham, and 2½ cups of the stock.

3. Melt the butter in a heavy skillet over medium heat just until it foams. Stir in the onions and sauté them for 8 to 10 minutes, or until lightly colored. Add the garlic and cook 30 seconds more. Add the cumin, salt, and pepper and stir to mix well. Add this to the bean mixture and stir in the vinegar.

4. Bring this mixture to the boil, reduce the heat, and simmer for 15 to 20 minutes longer. Stir in the sherry and taste to adjust the seasonings. If the soup is too thick, add additional stock or sherry.

5. To serve, cut the lid off the pumpkin in a scalloped or zigzag pattern. A "sugar pumpkin" has fewer seeds and heavier meat. Remove the seeds. An old-fashioned ice cream scoop with a pointed front works well for this job. Toss the seeds with 2 tablespoons of vegetable oil and toast for 7 to 9 minutes on a cookie sheet in a preheated 400°F oven or until well colored. Remove the pan from the oven and sprinkle the seeds lightly with salt, if desired. Fill the pumpkin with the soup, and use the toasted seeds in place of croutons. The pumpkin will keep the soup warm.

Split Pea Soup with Kielbasa

Serves 8

A steaming bowl of split pea soup is a great favorite in our house—especially during the fall and winter months. The ham and kielbasa (Polish sausage, found in the Meat department) make this thick soup more substantial—and perfect for a casual Sunday supper. It is an easy supermarket soup to make, because the ingredients are readily available and the preparation is uncomplicated. Try doubling the recipe and freezing it in 2- or 4-cup containers.

1 pound dried split green peas
6 cups water
4 cups chicken stock
⅓ cup salt pork, diced in ¼-inch cubes
½ cup chopped carrots
½ cup chopped celery
½ cup chopped onion
1 small bay leaf
2 ham hocks (see Note)
1½ teaspoons ground cardamom
Salt and freshly ground black pepper to taste
1½ cups diced kielbasa

1. Place the split peas in a colander or strainer. Rinse under cold water and discard any sediment.

2. Place the peas in a large, heavy saucepan or stockpot with the water and chicken stock. Cover and bring the liquid to a boil for 2 minutes. Turn off the heat, leave the lid on, and let the peas soak for at least an hour, or until very tender.

3. In a heavy skillet, sauté the salt pork over medium heat for 5 minutes, stirring occasionally, until it is opaque but not brown. Add the carrots, celery, and onion and continue cooking until tender, another 6 to 8 minutes.

4. Add the vegetables and bay leaf, ham hocks, cardamom, salt, and pepper to the pot with the peas, and return to a boil. Adjust the heat to low and simmer the soup until the meat begins to fall off the bones, 1½ to 2 hours.

5. Remove the ham hocks and bay leaf from the soup and pull the meat off the bones. Discard the bones and bay leaf.

6. Chop the ham into fine pieces and reserve them until the soup is finished. Transfer the soup to a food processor fitted with a steel chopping blade. With an on-off motion, purée the soup until it is slightly chunky. Return the soup to the pot, add the ham and kielbasa, and simmer for at least 10 minutes to warm the meat. Taste to adjust the seasonings. Serve with peasant bread cut into hearty slices.

NOTE: If you cannot find ham hocks, a leftover ham bone with some meat on it, or even a smoked turkey leg may be substituted.

STOCK OR BROTH? The terms are usually used interchangeably. If time does not permit making your own, you can enrich a canned broth by simmering it for about 10 to 15 minutes with some diced or sliced aromatic vegetables—an onion, a couple of carrots, and a stalk of celery—along with some parsley sprigs and a bay leaf. This is most acceptable when you are using it with hearty vegetables, meats, cream, and other strong-flavored ingredients. For delicate, clear soups, check page 170 for the homemade stock recipe.

Sautéed White Beans with Pork and Sage

Serves 8 to 10

There are only a few ingredients in this dish, and it's wonderfully simple to make. But, don't let the ease of preparation fool you. This northern Italian classic is the perfect accompaniment for roast leg of lamb—especially in spring. I like the flavor of the lamb drippings as they combine with the beans. Be sure to pass a fine-quality olive oil at the table when you serve them. White beans are very porous and absorb liquids like mad. Additional salt and pepper are also a good idea.

If time is short, the beans may be cooked, drained, and refrigerated in a covered bowl for up to 4 days ahead of time. Drizzle them with a little olive oil to prevent drying out. Or, some brands of canned beans, well rinsed, will do in a pinch, although the texture may be softer. You will need two 19-ounce cans, drained.

1 1-pound bag white kidney beans (cannellini-
  type)
1½ cups ¼-inch cubes diced salt pork
½ cup extra-virgin olive oil
2 teaspoons finely chopped fresh sage or rosemary
  leaves
Kosher or coarse salt and freshly ground black
  pepper to taste

1. Cook the beans according to package directions, drain, cover, and leave on a very low heat. (Or drain and rinse canned beans.)

2. While the beans are cooking, place the salt pork in a small pan, cover with boiling water, and simmer gently for about 10 minutes. Drain and blot dry.

3. In a medium-size saucepan, heat the olive oil until hot, fragrant, and almost smoking. Stir in the salt pork, lower the heat, and sauté until cooked through but not browned or crisp, about 10 to 13 minutes. Add the drained white beans and sage, stirring to coat evenly. Season with kosher salt and a generous amount of black pepper. If you are using canned beans, continue cooking until the beans are heated through.

NOTE: Leftovers are marvelous with a splash of red wine vinegar. Serve at room temperature as a salad.

Chunky Homemade Tomato Sauce

Makes 2 quarts

This tomato sauce is not only quick and easy to make with cupboard staples, it is also delicious and freezes beautifully. If you choose the flavorful Italian tomatoes, it is guaranteed to bring raves. Besides saucing pasta, I use it over STUFFED CHICKEN BREASTS ITALIANA (page 126), and as a basis for SQUID CAPONATA (page 222). Good-quality canned Italian tomatoes are generally superior to fresh tomatoes for sauces and stews except in the summer when the vine-ripened ones are available.

3 tablespoons olive oil
1 large onion, peeled and chopped
1–2 large cloves garlic, peeled and minced or crushed
2 28-ounce cans *crushed* Italian tomatoes, undrained (some imported cans come larger; the extra ounces will not make any difference in this recipe)
1 tablespoon dried basil or oregano *or* 3 tablespoons freshly chopped
1 teaspoon dark brown sugar
1 6-ounce can tomato paste
Salt and freshly ground black pepper, to taste

1. In a large, heavy saucepan, preferably nonaluminum, heat the oil until hot and fragrant. Stir in the onion, and sauté it over medium-high heat until soft but not brown, about 5 to 6 minutes. Stir in the garlic and cook for about 30 seconds longer.

2. Add the tomatoes, basil, sugar, tomato paste, salt, and pepper. Simmer, partially covered, over medium-low heat for *at least* 40 minutes, stirring occasionally with a wooden spoon, before serving.

NOTE: This sauce may be prepared and eaten immediately or stored in a tightly covered container in the refrigerator for up to 5 days. It freezes well when stored in an airtight container. Make sure to leave some head room for expansion.

HAVE YOU TRIED? Today there are improved jarred spaghetti sauces. Some are quite good and don't contain a lot of sugar, salt, and starches. Be sure to *read the label*, don't just admire the design. To dress up bottled sauces, add freshly chopped basil, oregano, or parsley. Fresh garlic, sautéed chopped onions and peppers, or a dash of olive oil and red wine vinegar will all liven up these prepared products. Refrigerate any leftovers in a tightly closed container.

There are also some fresh-pasta manufacturers who currently supply sauces like Bolognese, Alfredo, and Puttanesca in plastic 1-pint containers. These sauces are found in the refrigerated sections of the market near packages of fresh pasta. Some are terrific and real time-savers. Ingredients and freshness are, again, the key. Buy and taste before using them for party fare.

2 cups sliced mushrooms sautéed quickly in a little olive oil and added near the end of the simmering.

1 pound ground lean hamburger meat browned in the skillet before the onions are added. Add 2 thin strips of orange zest, about 1 × 3 inches each, during the simmering and stir in ½ cup heavy cream just before serving to make a Bolognese sauce—the meat sauce of Bologna, Italy.

Spicy Tomato Chili Barbecue Sauce

Makes 1 cup

This tangy, spicy barbecue sauce is easy and quick to prepare and not loaded with preservatives, either. After the first time, perhaps you will double or quadruple the recipe since it keeps for a couple of months when refrigerated in a screw-top jar. It is wonderful brushed on grilled shrimp or a pork roast during the last few minutes of cooking. But our favorite uses are for roasted chicken or OVEN-BARBECUED CHUCK STEAK (page 182). I always make extra chicken or brisket to serve at room temperature the next day.

½ cup tomato ketchup
⅓ cup orange juice
¼ cup Worcestershire sauce
3 tablespoons dark brown sugar
2 tablespoons chili powder
1 large clove garlic, peeled and crushed
1 large lemon, ends removed and thinly sliced
1 stick cinnamon

1. Combine all the ingredients in a small saucepan and bring the mixture to a boil over medium-high heat. Reduce the heat to medium-low, partially cover, and simmer for 25 minutes, stirring occasionally.

2. Strain if desired, or use with lemon slices for basting.

Tuna Niçoise Sauce

Makes 2½ cups

A Niçoise salad is usually made with tuna, small black olives, green beans, tomatoes, and boiled potatoes. Using the tuna in the vinaigrette and tossing it on a pasta salad is a variation on this theme. Or ladle this sauce on boiled new potatoes. "Niçoise" evokes the French Riviera, and Nice, the town famous for its little olives.

Tuna in olive oil is either sold with Italian products or other canned fish. It has a substantially richer flavor than the water-packed variety. Even tuna in vegetable oil is, for me, superior in taste. If you plan on breaking up the tuna into flakes for a salad, less expensive grades are a better buy than "solid pack" tuna. The meat is the same quality.

1 6½-ounce can imported tuna in olive oil, undrained
1 tablespoon Dijon mustard
5 tablespoons red wine vinegar
1 large clove garlic, peeled and minced or crushed
2 tablespoons finely chopped flat-leaf parsley
2–4 tablespoons lemon juice
1 cup extra-virgin olive oil *or* ½ olive oil and ½ vegetable oil
Salt and freshly ground black pepper, to taste

1. In a small bowl, mash the tuna with a fork, and stir in the mustard, vinegar, garlic, parsley, and 2 tablespoons of lemon juice.

2. Slowly pour in the oil in a steady stream, whisking constantly. Add salt and plenty of pepper and taste to see if it needs additional lemon juice and seasonings. Set aside while preparing Pasta Salad Niçoise (which follows).

DID YOU KNOW? "Extra-virgin olive oil" refers to the acidity of the oil. As long as the level is less than 1 percent, an olive oil may be called "extra virgin." It may be the result of the first cold pressing or the first and second pressings. It usually tastes very fruity and varies in color from rich green to pale green-gold. Use it for foods where the flavor can be appreciated.

Pasta Salad Niçoise

Serves 4

1 pound corkscrews or other dry pasta (penne, elbows, medium-size shells)
1 tablespoon olive oil
½ pound young green beans, tips removed, steamed until just tender
2 eggs, hard cooked, peeled, chilled, and quartered
¾ cup tiny Niçoise olives, if available, or oil-cured black olives
1 small red onion (or ½ large), peeled and thinly sliced
2 medium-size ripe tomatoes, cut into eighths
1 recipe TUNA NIÇOISE SAUCE (page 379)

1. Bring a large pot filled with 5 or 6 quarts of salted water to a boil. Add the pasta and cook until just tender. Drain the pasta and toss it with the olive oil. Refrigerate the pasta until cool but not cold.

2. Mound the pasta in the center of a large bowl. Place the green beans, eggs, olives, onions, and tomatoes in attractive groupings to cover the pasta. Take a moment to let your guests admire your design. Just before serving, pour half of the Niçoise Sauce over the salad and toss to distribute it evenly. Pass additional sauce and a peppermill at the table.

DID YOU KNOW? To keep the yolks in the center of hard-cooked eggs, turn the eggs over about halfway through the cooking time. It makes deviled eggs, etc., more attractive.

Spaghetti alla Puttanesca

Serves 4 as a first course, 2 to 3 as a main course

DID YOU KNOW? Smaller packages of herbs and spices being marketed in cellophane bags may be more economical, since many of us never use a whole bottle of a ground herb or spice before its maximum flavor is lost, about 3 to 6 months. Whole spices last indefinitely. To increase shelf life, store seasonings in a cool, dark spot or refrigerate them.

In Italian, a *puttana* is a "lady of the night." While this sauce tastes as if it has been slowly simmered for a good part of the night, it actually takes only half an hour to make—ideal for the working wives or husbands who rush home, prepare this aromatic favorite, and let their spouses think they have been tending the hearth. You can also make the sauce in advance, like the night before, and reheat it when needed.

Crushed Italian tomatoes make preparing sauces easier and quicker when a smoother texture is appropriate. For larger chunks, or when less liquid is important, buy whole peeled tomatoes.

3 tablespoons olive oil
1 large onion, peeled and chopped
1 green bell pepper, seeds and membranes
   removed, chopped
2 large cloves garlic, peeled and minced
1 28-ounce can crushed Italian tomatoes
1 2-ounce can anchovies, drained and chopped
16 pimento-stuffed green olives, sliced
1 tablespoon capers
¼ cup chopped fresh basil leaves *or* 2 teaspoons
   dried
¼ teaspoon dried red pepper flakes
Freshly ground black pepper to taste
12 ounces (¾ pound) spaghetti

1. In a large, heavy skillet, heat the oil until hot and fragrant. Add the onion and green pepper, and sauté them over medium-high heat for 5 to 7 minutes until soft. Add the garlic and cook 30 seconds longer.

2. Add the tomatoes and anchovies and simmer for 10 minutes.

3. Stir in the olives, capers, basil, red pepper flakes, and black pepper and simmer for an additional 20 minutes.

4. While the sauce is cooking, prepare the spaghetti (or other pasta of your choice) according to the package directions. Drain the pasta and pour the sauce over it, tossing to distribute evenly.

A PASTA PRIMER

There is nothing quite as satisfying as a plate of pasta—or as versatile. Recipes for pasta are found throughout this book. PASTA SALAD NIÇOISE (page 380), FETTUCCINE WITH ASPARAGUS AND LEMON CREAM (page 22), and CONVENIENT VEGETARIAN LASAGNA (page 412) show you only some of the many possibilities. A recipe for making homemade pasta in a food processor is given, too.

Traditionally served as a separate first course, pasta has become just as popular as a salad and, of course, everyone loves to make a meal of it. It can be flat, round, wide, narrow; shaped into twists, shells, or tubes; cut into squares and filled; or left in long sheets to layer. In today's nutrition-conscious world, pasta is one of our most enjoyable health foods, high in carbohydrates, a source of sustained energy, yet not high in calories—unless it is sauced with lots of cream, butter, or oil.

There should be some balance between pasta size, shape, and sauce. A light sauce calls for a lighter strand of pasta, while a heartier, more rustic sauce seems appropriate with a heavier shell or tubular shape. But mix and match to your own preference. Pasta assumes an infinite number of personalities.

Types of Pasta

There are three general types:

- dried pasta (either imported or domestic)
- fresh pasta (prepared commercially and sold in markets by weight or prepackaged)
- homemade pasta—the freshest of all

Amount Needed

One pound of dry pasta will feed 6 to 8 as a first course or 3 to 4 people as a main course.

To Cook

1. In a large pot, bring 5 to 6 quarts of water to a rapid boil for each pound of pasta. If you have more than 2 pounds to cook, use more than 1 pot for easier draining. Adding salt to the water is optional. It is incorporated into the final flavor of the pasta, and I prefer this, unless the sauce and other ingredients are very salty, e.g., feta cheese or anchovies. In this case, I think unsalted pasta balances the flavors of the dish.

2. Add all the pasta at once, stirring to separate the strands.

3. Cover the pot to return the water quickly to the boil, then uncover, and start timing. If enough water is used so the pasta can swirl around, if the water boils rapidly enough, and if the pasta is separated by early stirring, it will not stick together. Do not add oil to the cooking water. If you do, your carefully prepared sauce will slip off the cooked pasta. And do not rinse cooked pasta unless you want it chilled for a salad.

NOTE: For pasta salads, drain, rinse, and drain again. Mix the pasta with part of the dressing/sauce. Add more sauce just before serving. Pasta salads are best served at room temperature.

Timing is of the utmost importance. In general, the

fresher the pasta, the shorter the cooking time. Your aim should be to reach the al dente stage—tender but firm to the bite—and no more. While close clock-watching is inherent to your success, tasting for doneness just as the cooking time is approached is imperative. Then drain quickly in a colander.

- homemade pasta cooks in 30 to 50 seconds
- fresh (commercial) pasta cooks in a minute or so (according to package directions)
- dried pasta generally cooks from 6 to 12 minutes (according to thickness and cut of pasta and box directions)

To Sauce

Use a moderate amount of sauce, approximately 1½ to 2 cups per pound. You will need a larger amount for thicker sauces. Toss well. If you like, top with about ½ to 1 cup additional. It is unattractive to have pasta swimming in a pool of sauce because you have been overzealous and generous. Yet remember, pasta is porous and absorbs sauce quickly, so some sauce should be reserved and kept warm in the event you need more.

And just a reminder from pasta experts: Refrain from ladling sauce over a mound of cooked pasta. Instead, combine it with pasta by tossing several times to coat the strands or shapes thoroughly. Serve hot on warm plates.

Quick Homemade Fettuccine

Makes 1 pound of pasta

Making pasta in a food processor is quick and easy. So easy, in fact, that my children do it themselves. The long kneading and incorporating of flour are avoided, while the fun part (for us) of rolling the dough through a hand-crank pasta maker is retained. The results are a good-quality fresh pasta, which I serve often because it is so simple. I first learned this method from an Italian friend, Lorenza de' Medici, whose family had been making pasta by hand for centuries before she added this twentieth-century touch.

3 large eggs, at room temperature
2¼ cups unbleached all-purpose flour

1. Break the eggs into a glass measuring cup with a pouring spout, making sure all the white is removed from the shells.

2. Place the flour in a food processor fitted with a steel chopping blade, and process for about 10 seconds.

3. With the motor running, pour the eggs into the work bowl through the feed tube, allowing the measuring cup to rest on the feed tube for several seconds to make sure all the egg is added to the flour. Continue processing for about 45 to 50 seconds, at which time the dough should be the consistency of coarse cornmeal. Stop the machine and scrape down the sides of the bowl. Continue processing for about 15 to 20 seconds longer. The dough should just start to come into a ball and 2 pieces should stick to one another if pinched together. If the dough feels sticky, add a teaspoon more flour and process a few seconds. If it is very dry, add up to a teaspoon of water and process.

4. Remove the dough from the processor, divide it in half, and flatten it into 2 small rectangles, of a size to fit through your hand-crank pasta maker. Cover 1 rectangle with a clean, slightly dampened towel while working with the other. With the rollers set on the widest setting, feed the dough through. Fold it into thirds, flatten with your fingertips, and pass it through the machine twice more, or until the dough is smooth and the edges are even.

5. Adjusting the machine to ever-narrower settings, continue to pass the dough through until it is as thin as needed, usually the thinnest or next to thinnest setting. Take care not to pull or stretch the pasta. The easiest way to hold the strip is to drape it between your left thumb and forefinger, while cranking with the right hand.

6. Cut the pasta strip in half horizontally. Change the rollers to the fettuccine cutter, and pass the pasta through. Spread the fresh pasta on clean, dry towels and lightly dust with flour, tossing to separate the strands, or hang it over a pasta drying rack or kitchen chair. Repeat with the second rectangle.

7. Fresh pasta gradually dries when left out. This affects the cooking time but not the taste, tenderness, or quality. Within an hour after it has been prepared, it will take only a minimum of cooking time—as little as 30 seconds. This increases to 5 or 7 minutes after a few hours. Always taste pasta to determine when it reaches the *al dente* stage.

NOTE: When preparing fettuccine for a dish in which the pasta will cook further in a sauce, such as all'Alfredo, drain the pasta when slightly firm, so that it does not become too soft with the added cooking time.

Domed Cold Orzo Salad with Shrimp

Serves 8 to 12

I had been making this handsomely domed salad with its mosaic of peppers, shrimp, onions, peas, and olives for years before I discovered *orzo*, the rice-shaped pasta that is wonderful in soups, pilafs, and as an accompaniment to roasted meats or poultry. Now, I often combine orzo with rice or use it alone.

After chilling, this salad is easily unmolded into a dramatic spring or summer main course. For festive individual servings, choose large, firm red, yellow, or green peppers (or any other color in the market that day). Cut off the stem end in a zigzag pattern and remove the seeds and membranes. Fill each pepper with some salad, replace the tops, and serve.

2 cups raw orzo or rice, or a combination, cooked separately and drained well
1 10-ounce package frozen tiny peas, quickly cooked and drained
1 6-ounce can pitted black olives, thinly sliced
2 large red bell peppers, seeds and membranes removed, finely chopped
¾ pound medium-small shrimp, peeled, deveined, and cooked, cut into thirds (reserve a few whole for garnish)
1 medium red onion, peeled and finely chopped
½ cup finely chopped flat-leaf parsley
¾ cup extra-virgin olive oil
6 tablespoons red wine vinegar
1–2 cloves garlic, peeled and minced (optional)
Salt and freshly ground black pepper to taste
Cherry tomatoes and olive slices for garnish

1. In a large mixing bowl, toss together the cooked orzo (and/or rice), peas, olives, peppers, shrimp, onion, and parsley.

2. Pour the olive oil over the salad, and mix well.

3. Add the vinegar, garlic, salt and pepper, and taste to adjust the seasonings, adding more vinegar or oil sparingly, as needed. Don't make the salad too moist.

4. Spoon the rice salad into a mixing bowl, packing it down slightly, cover, and chill thoroughly.

5. Unmold the salad onto a serving platter and garnish with cherry tomatoes and black olives. Split the reserved shrimp in half lengthwise and place them on top for decoration.

Chicken, Pecan, Avocado, and Wild Pecan Rice Salad

Serves 6 to 8

Thanks to the rice, avocado, and the Middle Eastern-inspired PURÉED CHICK-PEA VINAIGRETTE (page 365), this chicken salad is a sophisticated variation on the mayonnaise classic. Serve it for a summer lunch or dinner. As an easy picnic idea, I'd bring along pita breads and let guests make pocket sandwiches.

Wild Pecan Rice is a new variety of brown rice from Louisiana marketed under the brand Konriko. It contains neither nuts nor wild rice. But the texture is firm and slightly chewy, and the flavor is somewhat reminiscent of pecans. Look in the Staples aisles near the ever-popular long-grain white rice to find this and other new rices. Opened boxes of rice should be closed and stored in a cool place. That way, they will keep fresh for at least 6 months.

1½ pounds boneless skinless chicken breasts *or* leftover chicken cut into cubes
3 cups chicken stock
1 7-ounce package Wild Pecan Rice
3 ounces (1 cup) pecan halves, lightly toasted and coarsely chopped
1½ cups thinly sliced scallions, including most of the green parts
12 cherry tomatoes, cut in half
1–2 large, ripe avocados
Salt and freshly ground black pepper to taste
1 recipe PURÉED CHICK-PEA VINAIGRETTE

1. In a large skillet, place the chicken breasts in the stock and bring the liquid just to a boil. Turn the heat down to low and poach the breasts until just cooked, about 15 minutes. Remove the chicken, let it cool, and cut it into ¾-inch cubes.

2. Cook the Wild Pecan Rice according to the package directions, making sure all the water has evaporated. When it is cooked, set it aside to cool.

3. In a large bowl, combine the rice, chicken cubes, chopped pecans, and scallions. Add the cherry tomatoes. Peel the avocado and cut it into ¾-inch cubes, adding it to the salad. Pour on the vinaigrette and toss to blend. Add freshly ground black pepper to taste. Serve on Boston lettuce leaves.

Curried Rice Salad

Serves 4

This cool, refreshing rice salad is a perfect lunch for a hot summer day. It is like a combination of my favorite condiments from a large curry dinner: raita (yogurt and cucumber sauce), mango chutney, chopped nuts, currants, and rice, all blended together.

Look for packages of aromatic, long-grain basmati rice, which are new to supermarket shelves. In India, the rice is called the "queen of fragrance," for the milky, floral aroma it gives off during cooking. If you can't find it, brown rice is a delicious alternative.

1 teaspoon salt
1 cup basmati or brown rice
1 cup plain low-fat yogurt
2 tablespoons curry powder, hot or mild
½ cup currants
½ cup sunflower seeds
1 cup peeled and thinly sliced cucumbers, quartered with seeds removed
1 cup thinly sliced scallions, including most of the green parts
½ cup dry roasted peanuts
¼ cup finely chopped Major Grey's chutney
½ Granny Smith or other tart apple, peeled, cored, and diced
Salt and freshly ground black pepper to taste
Boston lettuce leaves, for garnish (optional)

1. Following the package directions, bring the quantity of water indicated to a boil in a heavy saucepan. Add the salt and rice and simmer, covered, until all the water is absorbed. Drain the rice and transfer it to a large bowl to cool.

2. Once it is cooled, stir in the remaining ingredients: yogurt, curry, currants, sunflower seeds, cucumber, scallions, peanuts, chutney, apple, salt, and pepper and taste for seasonings. Serve on Boston lettuce leaves, if desired.

NOTE: For a more substantial salad, add 1 cup cooked shrimp or turkey cubes.

Hearty Bulgur Pilaf

Serves 8

Bulgur, or precooked cracked wheat, has long been a staple throughout the Middle East. In this dish, the grain is combined with the raisins, pignoli, and chestnuts, and baked into a golden ring—an ideal side dish for an autumn's feast.

Bulgur lasts for a very long time in a dry cupboard and is quick to prepare. Look for sizes from coarse to fine in many markets. Finer grinds seems to work better for stuffing, while a coarser grind is more appropriate when used in a pilaf. But you can use the size that appeals to you, or mix them. The nutty taste of bulgur adds flavor and good nutrition to pilafs, soups, and salads. Sometimes bulgur comes packaged with a premixed spice packet. If your market does not sell bulgur alone or you are inclined to experiment, use the grain and save the spices for another use (like mixing them with low-fat yogurt for a baked-potato topping).

1 teaspoon vegetable oil (optional)
1 6-ounce Italian sweet sausage, casing removed (optional)
2 tablespoons unsalted butter
1 teaspoon vegetable oil
¾ cup chopped onion
1 cup bulgur (fine or coarse grind)
8 chestnuts, roasted, peeled, and chopped *or* canned in water, drained, and chopped
⅓ cup golden raisins
¼ cup pignoli nuts, toasted
1¾ cups chicken stock, heated
Unsalted butter to lightly grease a 5-cup ring mold

 DID YOU KNOW? If you want to serve this pilaf or other rice dishes individually on a plate, pack the pilaf or rice into a ½-cup measure or ramekin, cover with a wide spatula or cake server, and invert onto the dish, slipping the spatula out once the cup is positioned.

1. In a small skillet, heat the oil until hot but not smoking. Add the sausage meat, breaking it into small pieces with a spatula, and cook until browned. Set aside. (Omit this step if not using sausage.)

2. Preheat your oven to 325°F. Butter a 5-cup ring mold. If you are not using sausage meat, a 4-cup mold will be sufficient.

3. In a large, heavy skillet, melt the butter and remaining teaspoon of oil over medium-high heat just until it foams. Stir in the chopped onion and sauté it just until it is translucent and soft, about 5 or 6 minutes. Add the bulgur, chestnuts, raisins, pignoli, and heated chicken stock. Bring the liquid to a boil, then reduce the heat to medium-low, cover, and let it cook for about 15 minutes, fluffing the bulgur every 5 minutes, until the liquid has evaporated.

4. Spoon the pilaf into the buttered ring mold, smoothing it to make it even, cover with foil, and bake in the preheated oven until lightly browned around the edges, about 15 minutes. Remove the pan from the oven and run a sharp knife around the outside and inside edges. Place a serving plate over the mold, invert, shake gently to be sure the ring is loosened, and let it stand for 1 to 2 minutes before removing the mold. Fill the center with a green vegetable, such as minted green peas sautéed with finely chopped scallions or steamed broccoli florets.

Risotto alla Parmigiana

Serves 6 to 8

Risotto is a creamy rice dish with a little al dente (toothy) spot remaining in each grain. It has been cooked in Milan, Italy, since the late sixteenth century, and prepared as it is below, it is often called "alla Milanese." Risotto is traditionally served as a separate pasta course. But, contemporary cooks now serve it with simple grilled meats, fish, and poultry, too. Once mastered, this dish may be prepared with everything from chicken livers and fresh vegetables to squid.

Short-grained, oval-shaped Arborio rice, which slowly absorbs the right amount of liquid to remain creamy and firm at the same time, is found on supermarket shelves in boxes or in white fabric bags. Either will do, but, I have found that the bags seemed to have fewer broken grains of rice.

3 cups beef broth or stock, preferably homemade
3 cups water
4 tablespoons unsalted butter
2 tablespoons vegetable oil
1 small onion, peeled and finely chopped
2 cups raw Arborio rice
½ teaspoon saffron threads, crumbled
⅔ cup freshly grated imported Parmesan cheese
2 tablespoons unsalted butter
Salt and freshly ground black pepper to taste

1. Bring the broth and water to a simmer in a medium-size saucepan and keep hot.

2. In a large, heavy skillet or saucepan, melt the butter and oil just until the butter foams. Add the onion and slowly sauté it over medium heat until it is translucent and tender, but not browned, about 5 to 6 minutes.

3. Add the rice and stir for 2 to 3 minutes to coat it evenly with butter.

4. Add approximately ½ cup of the simmering stock to the pan, stirring frequently to prevent sticking. Stir in the saffron.

5. Continue adding broth, a half cup at a time, stirring until it has been absorbed before adding the next amount. It should take about 25 to 30 minutes until the rice will be al dente (slightly firm to the bite). Turn off the heat.

6. Stir in the Parmesan cheese, additional butter, salt, and pepper and taste to adjust the seasonings. The risotto will be kind of lumpy. Serve immediately and pass a peppermill at the table.

Microwaved Risotto with Julienned Vegetables

Serves 4 as a first course, 6 to 8 as a side dish

Judy Murray, a talented cooking teacher who specializes in microwaving, and I developed this quick method of preparing risotto. It is a colorful variation on the classic RISOTTO ALLA PARMIGIANA (page 389). The sunchokes (also called Jerusalem artichokes and available in the Produce department) add a nutty, sweet flavor. The vibrant carrots, zucchini, and yellow squash add a crunchy-tender contrast to the creamy rice.

2 tablespoons unsalted butter
½ cup chopped onion
2 cups chicken stock, heated
¼ teaspoon crumbled saffron threads
1 cup Arborio rice
2 tablespoons unsalted butter
⅓ cup light or heavy cream
½ cup finely julienned carrots (approximately
   2 × ¼ × ¼ inches)
½ cup finely julienned zucchini (approximately
   2 × ¼ × ¼ inches)
½ cup finely julienned yellow squash
   (approximately 2 × ¼ × ¼ inches)
½ cup peeled and thinly sliced sunchokes
⅔ cup freshly grated Parmesan cheese
Freshly grated black pepper to taste

1. Place the 2 tablespoons of butter in a 2-quart glass casserole and microwave on high power for 30 to 45 seconds to melt. Add the onion, cover, and microwave on high power for 2½ to 3½ minutes or until the onion is softened.

2. Stir the saffron threads into the hot stock. Add the rice to the butter mixture and stir well, coating each grain. Add the hot stock, and stir. Cover and microwave on high power 5 to 6 minutes or until the liquid is boiling.

3. Reduce the power to medium (50 percent), and microwave an additional 8½ to 10 minutes, or until all the liquid is absorbed. Remove the casserole from the oven, stir in the 2 tablespoons of butter and the cream, cover, and let it stand while finishing the vegetables.

4. In a 1-quart casserole, combine the carrots and 2 tablespoons of water. Cover and microwave on high power for 2 minutes. Add the julienned squashes and sunchokes in with the carrots, cover, and microwave for 2 to 2½ minutes on high power, or until the vegetables are tender-crisp. Drain and stir them into the risotto.

5. Add the grated Parmesan cheese and black pepper to taste, stir, and serve.

NOTE: To make this recipe without a microwave, use the RISOTTO ALLA PARMIGIANA recipe (page 389) as a

DID YOU KNOW? While the number of microwave ovens has increased dramatically over the last few years and there has been a proliferation of special microwave products, experts in the field say that our own oven-safe glass bowls and plastic wrap or wax paper work fine in most cases. Take a class in this new "wave" of cooking to learn how to do more than reheat coffee.

guide. Double the quantity of stock used. Sauté the onion in a large, heavy skillet, add the rice, and begin adding the heated stock. After about 15 minutes, stir in the remaining vegetables and continue adding stock until the rice is creamy, but slightly al dente. Add the cream and Parmesan cheese and plenty of ground black pepper.

Wehani Rice Pudding

Serves 8

Wehani and other hybrid brown basmati rices are finding their way to supermarket shelves. Their flavor, intensely nutty, has a chewy texture reminiscent of brown, white, and wild rices all together. When combined with the apricots and rum in this custard pudding, it makes a rich, dense dessert, perfect for a cool autumn evening. The sliced oranges and julienned zest used to garnish the ring add a touch of seasonal color to the plate (see Did You Know? for an easy way to julienne the zest).

1 cup Wehani or other brown basmati rice (see Note)
2–2½ cups water
½ cup currants
⅓ cup finely chopped dried apricots
¼ cup dark rum
3 cups water
1 cup milk
1 cup heavy cream
¼ cup sugar
3 egg yolks
¾ teaspoon salt
½ teaspoon orange extract
¼ teaspoon ground coriander seed
Unsalted butter to grease a 5-cup ring mold
Zest of 2 navel oranges, cut into thin strips, for garnish
2 navel oranges, peeled, thinly sliced, and cut in half, for garnish

1. Combine the rice and water in a small saucepan and bring to the boil. Reduce the heat to a simmer, cover, and cook until all the water has evaporated, about 30 minutes. Uncover and set aside.

2. Meanwhile, combine the currants and apricots with the rum in a small bowl.

3. Preheat your oven to 350°F. Butter a 5-cup ring mold. Bring the 3 cups of water to the boil.

4. Scald the milk and cream in a saucepan. Combine the sugar and egg yolks in a large bowl, and beat until light in color. Add the scalded milk and cream to the yolks in a slow, steady stream, beating constantly with a wire whisk. Stir in the salt, orange extract, and coriander. Add the rice and currant-apricot mixture.

5. Ladle the liquid into the buttered mold, distributing the rice evenly. Place the ring in a larger pan or skillet and pour enough boiling water around the mold to come halfway up the sides. Carefully transfer the pans to the lower third of the preheated oven and bake until a knife inserted near the center of the pudding comes out clean, about 60 to 70 minutes. The edges will pull away slightly from the mold, and the top will be browned.

6. Remove both pans from the oven and let the pudding stand for about 20 minutes in the water. Run a sharp-bladed knife around outside and inside edges, shaking the mold to be sure the pudding is completely loosened. Wipe off any water. Place a large plate over the mold and carefully invert. Remove the mold, cover the pudding lightly with foil, and refrigerate for 1 to 2 hours, or until cool but not cold.

7. To serve, sprinkle the julienned orange zest over the pudding. Slice the oranges and layer them evenly around the outside.

NOTE: If neither Wehani nor other brown basmati rice is available, substitute ½ brown and ½ wild rice, cooked according to package directions, then combined.

🛒 **DID YOU KNOW?** In the Kitchen Tools section of your market, look for a citrus zester. It makes removing the outside colored portion of the skin easy. If possible, make sure the edges of the holes are sharp.

South-western Clam Puffs

Makes about 36 small puffs

Do you have a mini-muffin tin? If so, use it to make these amusing little southwestern-flavored clam cups. You can keep almost all of the ingredients in your cupboard and toss them together for this hors d'oeuvre in no time. Serve the baked puffs in tiny fluted cups, and decorate the tray with colorful flowers and greenery for a festive offering.

If you don't have a tin, simply leave the bread

rounds flat, or check near the cracker section of the grocery store. There might be a tin or a package of mini pastry shells. As these prepared products vary widely in quality and taste, it's best to test before serving them to guests.

3 tablespoons unsalted butter, melted
12–18 thin slices fresh white or wheat sandwich bread
3 tablespoons vegetable or olive oil
1 medium onion, minced
2 small cloves garlic, peeled and minced
¼ cup minced flat-leaf parsley
2 teaspoons dried oregano
Pinch dried thyme leaves, crumbled
Pinch dried basil leaves, crumbled
1 cup dried bread crumbs (approximately)
2 6½-ounce cans minced clams, not drained
1 6-ounce can corn kernels, well drained
1 pickled jalapeño pepper, seeds removed and minced
Salt and freshly ground black pepper to taste
½ cup finely shredded Monterey Jack or Muenster cheese
Pimento for garnish

1. Preheat your oven to 350°F. Brush the mini-muffin tin with the melted butter.

2. Using a 2½-inch glass or cookie cutter, cut out 36 circles from the bread, and press them gently into the muffin tin so that the bread conforms to the base of each muffin cup. Reserve the trimmings for fresh bread crumbs, if desired, or discard. Place the muffin tin in the preheated oven and toast the bread until lightly browned, 5 to 8 minutes. Remove the tin from the oven and set aside. Leave the oven on.

3. In a medium-size skillet, heat the oil over medium heat, then add the onion, stirring occasionally just until translucent, about 5 minutes. Stir in the garlic, parsley, oregano, thyme, and basil and cook for 1 to 2 minutes longer.

4. Add half the bread crumbs, clams and their juice, corn, jalapeño pepper, salt, and pepper and mix well. Add additional bread crumbs just until the mixture holds together. Continue cooking for 1 minute. Taste to adjust the seasonings.

DID YOU KNOW? Canned minced clams have a much softer texture than fresh or frozen clams. They are fine in this sort of mixture, but best not used in stews or soups. Finely chopped fresh or frozen clams with a little broth will certainly work in this recipe.

5. Divide the mixture evenly among the toast cups, pressing the mixture to mound slightly. Sprinkle with the cheese. (Clam puffs may be prepared ahead and refrigerated for one day.)

6. Transfer the shells to a jelly roll pan lined with aluminum foil for easy cleanup and bake in the preheated oven until bubbly and golden, 12 to 15 minutes. Top each puff with a tiny piece of pimento and serve at once.

Keeping Frozen Food at Its Best

Storing fresh and already frozen foods correctly will provide you with a treasure chest full of convenient top-quality foods in excellent condition. To accomplish this, consider the following:

Foods to be frozen need to be as fresh as possible. Freezing will not destroy bacteria or make old food taste better. If you will not use the food within the appropriate time, don't take a chance. It is far safer to freeze it and then defrost it at a later date.

Your freezer should be set at 0°F or below to maintain the optimum quality of foods. A hanging freezer thermometer will help verify this. Another test is a container of ice cream. If it becomes soft, turn down the thermostat.

When adding foods to your freezer, place only the amount that will freeze completely within 24 hours. Packages should be as flat as possible and be placed in the area which will allow the quickest freezing. For upright freezers, foods are best in a flat layer on the shelf with space between each item. For chests, against the walls is best. In refrigerator-freezer combinations, where the door is opened frequently, the back is cooler. After foods are solid, they can be placed in another section.

Cleanliness and order are important. Especially with non-frost-free models, freezers must be defrosted and cleaned regularly for maximum efficiency. Over-iced conditions wear out the motor. An orderly plan for storing different foods in different sections will help you locate what you have on hand, and what needs to be restocked. Rotate packages of food so that older ones are used first.

Foods must be wrapped airtight to retain their flavor, texture, and appearance. Freezer-burned foods exposed to air may be safe to eat, but the quality will be inferior. There are several options for good protection:

CONTAINERS AND WRAPS

Sealed heavy-gauge plastic Ziploc bags with the air squeezed out are excellent for fruits and vegetables first frozen on trays (page 315), puréed herbs and stocks frozen in ice cube trays, cooled servings of stews, and as extra protection around already wrapped food. They take up a minimum of space.

Rigid plastic containers in many sizes with tight-fitting snap-on lids are useful for stews, purées, and tray-frozen fruits and vegetables. Leave about 1 inch of headspace for expansion of the water in foods.

Aluminum trays with foil-cardboard lids or covered with freezer paper are good for heat-and-eat items that can go from the freezer to the oven. They also protect baked goods.

Freezer-wrap paper sealed with tape is especially useful for fresh meat, poultry, and fish. The shiny plastic-coated side should be next to the food for protection. Be sure to fold it as close around the food as possible and seal tightly.

Aluminum foil is not recommended, as it cracks and tears easily where it is folded. If using foil, place the item inside a plastic bag, as well.

Most plastic wraps are also too thin to protect food adequately.

DEFROSTING

When defrosting foods, do so slowly. On a plate in the refrigerator is the best place. Use them within 1 day. To retain the most moisture in foods, only partially defrost before cooking.

Partially defrosted foods that still have some ice crystals can be refrozen. However, the texture and flavor may be impaired. Prepared foods should not be refrozen.

WHAT TO FREEZE

When deciding what will freeze well, consider the following general guidelines. Other suggestions are found with specific foods in the recipes.

Dairy

With the exception of butter and separated eggs, which will keep for 9 to 12 months, it is best not to freeze dairy products. You can freeze hard cheese, but it becomes crumbly. Soft cheeses change texture. Cream separates.

Meats

These will freeze very well when wrapped properly. Larger cuts of meat, such as roasts and steaks, will last far longer than smaller pieces. Beef roasts last up to 9 months, pork for 6 months. Ground beef lasts up to 3 months, and ground pork up to 2 months. With processed and cured meats, such as ham and corned beef, the texture and taste change. Game meats will last for 8 to 12 months depending on the cut.

Poultry

Poultry freezes very well. It must be frozen within a day of purchase. Then it will last at least 6 months.

Fish

The fattier the species, such as bluefish or mackerel, the shorter the time it will keep, up to 3 months. Less fatty fish, such as sole, will last for up to 6 months. Breaded frozen fish products will keep only 3 months or have an expiration date on the package.

Vegetables

These are best when cleaned, pared, and blanched to retain their color, texture, taste, and vitamins. They should retain their crispness. The cooking time will vary with the size and density of each vegetable. Blanch by submerging them in boiling water for a short period of time, steaming them over boiling water in a covered pot, or microwaving them according to the manufacturer's instructions. Potatoes, beets, and lettuces do not freeze well. Other vegetables will last for up to 9 months in the freezer.

Bakery

Most purchased baked products will last at least 2 to 3 months. Unbaked and partially baked products have an expiration date stamped on the package. Fruitcakes and homemade cookies will keep from 10 months to a year.

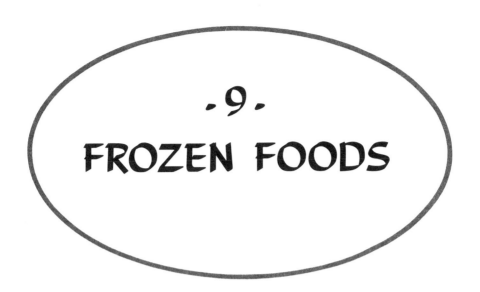

FROZEN FOODS

INTRODUCTION

For years, I was a "periphery shopper," buying primarily the fresh foods—produce, meat, dairy—that lined market walls. Occasionally I navigated up and down the Staples and Frozen Foods aisles for orange juice concentrate, peas, frozen berries out of season, or ice cream. But, as a serious cook, I was convinced that everything made from scratch was best, including puff pastry.

That viewpoint changed abruptly one day about a year ago when I was working on a project emphasizing convenience foods and I looked more closely at the Frozen Food aisles. I discovered a whole world of preservative-free, top-quality ingredients and pre-pared products that did not compromise the quality of dishes. They simply made the cooking process easier and quicker.

Some enterprising companies have done a remark-able job of improving frozen foods. They are supply-ing supermarkets with high-quality entrées, desserts, and hors d'oeuvres, that can be heated in both tra-ditional and microwave ovens. Well-known chefs have jumped on the bandwagon, too, recognizing how im-portant saving time has become in our lives. Some of these heat-and-eat products are very good; but they tend to be very pricey, too. Familiar frozen slice-and-bake cookies now share space with upscale, mouth-wateringly delicious varieties. There are quiches made from wholesome ingredients and a vast array of foods marked "all natural." In using these items, the trick is to read the labels—some are misleading—and taste the product before using it for guests.

With all frozen foods, it is important that the market monitor the condition of the freezer cases. A constant temperature below 0°F is essential to preserve the quality of foods. Packages should be sealed, airtight, and in good condition.

Some of my favorite frozen foods that I find con-venient include:

Puff Pastry

Select the all-butter variety, if possible. It produces wonderful results in a minimum of time when you follow the directions. A boon to entertaining, from CRISP CHEESE PALMIERS (page 403) to MEDITERRANEAN TOMATO TART (page 405).

Vegetables

In soups and purées, flash-frozen vegetables are a real time saver. WINTER SQUASH, APPLE, AND WALNUT SOUP (page 410) and CORN AND SHRIMP CHOWDER (page 408) are made in minutes. I'm really enthusiastic about baby peas, which are almost always superior to the fresh ones in the Produce aisle; and spinach is another good buy, especially for saving time. On the other hand, I shy away from vegetables prepared in sauces. They often have preservatives and end up being soggy or salty.

Fruits

Individually quick-frozen berries, melons, and summer fruits are a good buy especially in winter when they are more reasonable than out-of-season varieties sold fresh. THE ULTIMATE RASPBERRY CHOCOLATE SAUCE (page 417) is a good test of this. Fruits packed in sugar syrup are usually overly sweet and the texture is inferior.

Ice Creams and Sorbets

Markets are reflecting the national craze for designer ice creams. There are many wonderful flavors and brands available to use straight from the carton or as part of other desserts. Children are especially fond of ICE CREAM MIX-INS (page 417).

Every day new, more creative frozen products appear in the Frozen Foods aisles. Some will be wonderful. Unfortunately, there is no way to tell except by tasting. I still avoid prepared foods that have preservatives and flavor enhancers. But in our fast-paced world, isn't it nice to know that this industry is on our side, trying to help us eat better with quicker preparation?

Crisp Cheese Palmiers

Makes 3 dozen

With the aid of frozen puff pastry tucked away for unexpected guests, these delicate crunch morsels with a touch of Parmesan—ideal for cocktails—can appear magically from the oven. The real work has been done for you. For the flavors to be their best, use the best quality Parmesan cheese available.

When buying prepared puff pastry, there are two types to consider. One is relatively reasonable but is made with vegetable shortening. The other one is at least twice the price and worth every penny, since it is made from pure butter. It rises to great heights and is truly a gift for making fabulous confections in a matter of minutes.

½ pound puff pastry
6 tablespoons grated Parmigiano-Reggiano
Pinch of ground red pepper

1. Follow the package instructions for preparing the puff pastry. Lightly dust a work surface and rolling pin with flour. Carefully flatten the pastry and cut it in half lengthwise. Rewrap the second half and use it for another dish like MEDITERRANEAN TOMATO TART (page 405). Roll the pastry into a rectangle approximately 5½ × 15 inches, and make a light indentation lengthwise to indicate the middle.

2. Combine the cheese and red pepper, and spread about 4 tablespoons of the mixture over the pastry. With your fingertips, gently push the cheese into the pastry.

3. Bring both long edges to the middle, and push down gently. Sprinkle 2 more tablespoons of the cheese over the pastry, gently press it into the pastry, and then bring the 2 sides to the center. Cover the pastry with plastic wrap or foil, and refrigerate for about ½ hour, or until firm. (See illustration.)

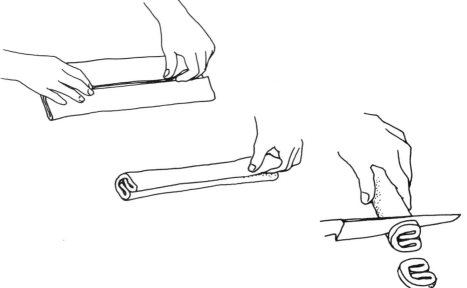

4. Preheat your oven to 375°F. Line 2 cookie sheets with parchment paper or aluminum foil with the dull side up.

5. Cut the roll into ⅜-inch slices and place each piece flat on the pan with about 2 inches of space around it. If the pastry becomes soft and sticky, return it to the refrigerator until firm. (If you only have 1 cookie sheet, store the uncut half in the refrigerator while the other bakes.) Transfer the pan to the middle of the oven and bake until golden brown, about 15 minutes. With a spatula or knife, carefully turn the palmiers and continue baking for 5 minutes longer.

6. Remove the pan from the oven, loosen the palmiers, let them cool slightly, then serve. They may be served at room temperature. Place the palmiers on a tray lined with a doiley.

Mediterranean Tomato Tart

Serves 8 as first course, 16 as an hors d'oeuvre

This flat tart with a sauce redolent of tomatoes and anchovies is reminiscent of the flaky open-faced snacks called "pissaladières" one finds in the south of France.

The advantage here is that frozen pastry and handy staples make this impressive hors d'oeuvre or first course a breeze to make—even ahead of time. The sauce can be spread over the pastry and left in the refrigerator for at least 2 days. Remember to cover it lightly, though.

½ pound frozen prepared puff pastry, defrosted according to the manufacturer's directions
1 tablespoon olive oil
½ cup finely chopped onion
¼ cup finely chopped green bell pepper
1 large clove garlic, peeled and crushed
3 tablespoons tomato paste
½ cup canned tomato sauce
1 teaspoon dried basil
½ teaspoon dried oregano
1 tablespoon small capers
½ tablespoon anchovy paste or mashed anchovies (about ½ of a 2-ounce can), drained and rinsed
1 teaspoon sugar
Salt and freshly ground black pepper to taste
1 teaspoon olive oil

1. On a lightly floured board, roll the puff pastry out with a floured rolling pin into a rectangle measuring about 5 × 14 inches. Place the pastry on the cookie sheet, roll up the edges slightly to form a little border, and return the pan to the refrigerator while preparing the tomato sauce.

2. In a large, heavy skillet, heat the olive oil over medium-high heat until fragrant, about 1 minute. Add the onion and sauté it until translucent, about 5 to 6 minutes. Stir in the green pepper and continue cooking for 2 minutes more. Add the garlic and cook for 30 seconds longer.

3. Stir in the tomato paste, tomato sauce, basil, oregano, capers, anchovy paste, sugar, salt, and pepper; bring the mixture to a boil; then reduce the heat and simmer it for about 15 minutes. Remove the pan from the heat and let it cool for about 15 minutes.

4. Preheat your oven to 400°F and line a cookie sheet with baking parchment.

5. Spread the tomato sauce evenly over the pastry and place the pan in the middle of the preheated oven. Bake for about 7 or 8 minutes, until the pastry has begun to puff. Turn the heat down to 350°F and continue baking until the crust is golden brown, about 12 to 15 minutes. Remove the pan from the oven, brush 1 teaspoon of olive oil over the filling, and let the tart sit for a few minutes before cutting it into 8 or 16 servings.

A Southern Salad

Serves 6

This is a salad I make for friends from the South, and it always elicits a chuckle for the familiar fare —ham, black-eyed peas, and yams—combined in this unconventional manner. It's a great buffet dish with leftover ham. The black-eyed peas are a snap, since they are easily defrosted and cooked. Although there are frozen yams, I would boil a couple of fresh ones for a better texture.

2 medium yams (about 1 pound), peeled and cut into 1-inch cubes, (approximately 4 cups of cubes)
1 10-ounce package frozen black-eyed peas, cooked according to the package directions until just tender, and drained
8 ounces ham, cut into ½-inch cubes (approximately 2 cups)
1 cup chopped celery
½ cup chopped red onion
½ cup coarsely chopped flat-leaf parsley
⅔ cup mayonnaise
2–3 tablespoons spicy mustard (American, German, or French)
Salt and freshly ground black pepper to taste

1. Bring some salted water to a boil in a medium-size saucepan, add the cubes of yam, and cook until just tender, about 5 minutes. Drain, and place them in a large bowl.

2. Add the peas, ham, celery, red onion, and parsley. Combine the mayonnaise and mustard in a small bowl, pour it over the salad, and toss gently. Season with salt and pepper, toss again, and serve.

Colorful Corn Salad

Serves 4

This is a quick, pretty, and fun salad to throw together in a hurry. There is virtually no preparation, but the combination of corn, olives, onion, and cheese is delicious. It's ideal for a picnic or any quick meal.

2 teaspoons whole-grain mustard
2 tablespoons cider vinegar
¼ cup vegetable oil
¼ cup mayonnaise
1 tablespoon sugar
½ teaspoon celery seeds
1 teaspoon salt, or to taste
Freshly ground black pepper to taste
1 stalk celery, trimmed and cut into ¼-inch dice
½ large red bell pepper, seeds and membranes removed, cut into ¼-inch dice
1 medium red onion, peeled and finely chopped
½ cup pitted black olives, sliced
3 cups corn kernels, fresh or defrosted frozen
4 ounces Monterey Jack cheese, cut into small cubes
2 tablespoons chopped flat-leaf parsley
Few drops Tabasco sauce (optional)

1. Combine the mustard and vinegar in a large bowl. Add the oil in a steady stream, whisking continuously until blended. Stir in the mayonnaise, sugar, celery seeds, salt, and pepper.

2. Add the celery, pepper, onion, olives, corn, cheese, and parsley. Toss well, add Tabasco sauce, if desired, and taste to adjust the seasonings. Line the bowl with lettuce leaves for garnish, if desired.

AS A VARIATION: Serve this salad in cooked artichokes, or in the baked shells of potatoes.

Corn and Shrimp Chowder

Serves 4 to 6

Most everyone loves a good cup of chowder. This one—made with corn, green pepper, and shrimp—is a snap to make with the aid of a food processor. It is light, too, because half-and-half is used instead of heavy cream.

Frozen kernels are a boon to corn aficionados and are infinitely superior to the canned varieties. For this soup, it is so quick simply to open a package. I like yellow corn here, but there are white kernels and even packages labeled "tiny sweet yellow kernels" to choose from, as well. Since most of the kernels are puréed in this chowder, the least expensive package is the best buy here.

2 tablespoons unsalted butter
1 medium onion, peeled and finely chopped
1 medium green bell pepper, seeds and
   membranes removed, finely chopped
2 cups corn kernels, defrosted frozen or fresh
2 cups chicken stock
1 cup half-and-half
1 cup corn kernels, defrosted frozen or fresh
¾ pound medium shrimp, peeled, deveined, and
   cut into ¾-inch slices
1 teaspoon salt, or to taste
Freshly ground black pepper to taste
¼ cup freshly chopped cilantro leaves + extra
   leaves for garnish

1. In a large, heavy skillet, melt the butter over medium-high heat. When it has foamed, stir in the onion and let it soften for about 3 to 4 minutes. Add the pepper and continue cooking for another 3 to 4 minutes.

2. Purée 2 cups of corn in a food processor fitted with a steel chopping blade, and scrape the purée into the skillet. Stir in the chicken stock and half-and-half, and let the mixture simmer for 2 to 3 minutes.

3. Stir in the remaining corn, shrimp, salt and pepper, and cilantro and gently simmer until the shrimp are just cooked through. *Do not overcook the shrimp.* Taste for seasonings, then ladle the soup into bowls. Garnish with a few cilantro leaves in each bowl.

DID YOU KNOW? Frozen chopped green bell pepper may be used in this soup in place of the fresh. Be sure to seal the bag tightly once it has been opened for maximum shelf life.

French Pea Soup

Serves 6

This is one great pea soup! It is simple to make and has no cream. The peas are cooked in the French manner—with butter and lettuce leaves providing the moisture—and then puréed. Little bits of ham added at the end provide a nice balance to the sweet taste of the peas. It is equally as appealing served hot or at room temperature when the weather is warmer.

Of all vegetables available frozen, peas are my favorite. In fact, except for a couple of weeks in the late spring or early summer when sugar snap peas may fleetingly grace the grocers' shelves, I buy the frozen ones exclusively. It's worth paying more for the ones marked "tiny." They are more tender and sweeter. Larger-size plastic bags of tiny peas are a good value since you can return the extras to your freezer.

6 tablespoons (¾ stick) unsalted butter
¼ cup finely chopped shallots
1 small Boston or Bibb lettuce, washed, cored, shaken of excess water, and cut into thin strips
1½ pounds frozen tiny peas, defrosted and drained
2 teaspoons salt, or to taste
2 teaspoons sugar
3 cups chicken stock
2 cups water
3 ounces boiled ham, cut into fine julienne (optional)

1. In a large saucepan melt the butter over medium heat. When it has foamed, add the shallots and cook them until translucent, about 3 to 4 minutes. Add the lettuce and the peas—reserving about ½ cup for the final garnish—salt and sugar. Cover the pan and cook gently for 10 minutes.

2. Transfer the peas to the bowl of a food processor fitted with a steel chopping blade and purée, or pass them through a food mill. This will have to be done in batches. Any liquid not used to purée the peas should be reserved in the pan. Once they are puréed, pass the peas through a sieve to eliminate the pea skins.

3. Add the stock and water to the puréed peas and continue to cook the soup over medium heat for 5 to 7 minutes.

DID YOU KNOW? Frozen tiny peas need no further cooking if they are to be used in salads. Once they are defrosted, they may be used directly or briefly rinsed under warm water for a slightly softer texture.

4. Add the ham and reserved peas. Taste for seasonings. Serve with croutons, if desired.

Winter Squash, Apple, and Walnut Soup

Serves 6

One of the joys of the supermarket is finding ingredients in ready-to-use, time-saving form. This is true of frozen butternut squash, which is already cleaned, cooked and puréed without losing its taste. Combine the purée with unsweetened applesauce, chopped walnuts, and cream into a magnificent bright-orange soup with a warm, delicate flavor.

Frozen vegetables are wonderful for soups or purées where the texture is less important. Make sure the boxes or bags are sealed tightly to avoid freezer burn and use them within 6 to 8 months.

2 12-ounce packages frozen puréed winter
    (butternut) squash, defrosted
2 tablespoons unsalted butter
1 cup unsweetened applesauce
1 cup light or heavy cream
¼ cup ground toasted walnuts
2 teaspoons dried chervil, crumbled
½ teaspoon ground mace
Salt and white pepper to taste
½ cup toasted walnut pieces for garnish

1. Combine all the ingredients except the walnuts to be used for garnish in a large saucepan and stir to blend well. Cook the soup over medium heat until warmed through, about 6 to 8 minutes. Ladle the soup into bowls and add a few chopped walnut pieces in the center.

Easy Glazed Pearl Onions

Serves 4 to 6

Here is another easy and quick way to make use of your Frozen Foods aisles. These pearl onions are simple to glaze with beef stock and a little sugar. A splash of vinegar added at the end perks up the flavor. My son Justin always asks for them at Thanksgiving, when we mix them with peas.

Tiny pearl onions are often scarce in the supermarket. For that reason, and to save a *lot* of time, I find that the large 16-ounce bags of these round gems are a great savings—especially at holidays when I'm called upon to cook for 12 to 20. I find that if I remove only the excess ice from the onions they hold their shape better.

2 tablespoons unsalted butter
1 16-ounce package frozen pearl onions
3 tablespoons sugar
1½ cups beef stock
3–4 tablespoons red wine vinegar
Salt and freshly ground pepper to taste

1. Rinse the onions in a strainer, just to separate them and remove extra ice. Blot them on paper towels.

2. In a large, heavy skillet, heat the butter over high heat. When it has foamed, add the onions and sugar and continue cooking for 5 minutes, shaking often, until the onions are lightly colored. Add the beef stock, adjust the heat to medium high, and continue cooking until the liquid is almost completely evaporated, about 20 to 25 minutes. Stir in the vinegar, cook for 30 seconds, season with salt and pepper, and serve.

Creamed Spinach

Serves 8

I am always amazed at how much people love well-seasoned creamed spinach. It is wonderful served plain or as a filling for hollowed-out tomatoes or potato baskets.

This version takes advantage of frozen spinach— an excellent alternative to the fresh vegetable.

2 10-ounce packages frozen leaf or chopped
   spinach *or* 2½ pounds fresh, washed and stems
   removed
½ teaspoon salt
2 tablespoons unsalted butter
1 large onion, peeled and finely chopped
2 tablespoons unsalted butter
2 tablespoons unbleached all-purpose flour
1 cup milk
½ teaspoon paprika
⅛ teaspoon ground red pepper
Generous pinch of freshly ground nutmeg
Salt and freshly ground black pepper to taste

1. In a medium-size saucepan, cook the spinach according to the package directions, drain well, and set it aside. *Or* shake most of the water from the fresh spinach, place it and the salt in a large, deep saucepan, cover, and cook it until tender, about 5 to 7 minutes. Drain well in a strainer.

2. Melt 2 tablespoons of butter in the saucepan over medium-high heat. When it has foamed, add the onion and sauté it for 6 to 8 minutes, or until lightly colored. Combine the spinach with the onion.

3. Melt the remaining 2 tablespoons of butter in a small saucepan over medium-high heat. When it has foamed, add the flour and beat it with a wire whisk over medium-low heat for a few minutes to cook but not brown the flour. Pour the milk in all at once, and beat until the mixture is smooth and thick. Add the paprika, red pepper, nutmeg, salt, and pepper; scrape this white sauce (béchamel) into the spinach-onion mixture; and stir to blend.

Convenient Vegetarian Lasagna

Serves 8 to 12

This recipe is a testament to the value of convenient frozen vegetables. When time is short, or you can't make it to the supermarket, most of these ingredients will wait for you already cleaned and cut up in your freezer. They are easily folded into the basil-flavored ricotta filling. This colorful, aromatic lasagna will feed you and a goodly tribe of your friends remarkably well.

Boxes and bags of frozen vegetables adorned with an endless variety of sauces and in exotic combinations have multiplied over recent years. The pictures look so tempting, especially when otherwise the same old boring vegetables stare you in the face. Unfortunately, many of the packaged seasonings contain a generous dollop of chemicals, and the vegetables end up being a sorry imitation of the promised product. Stick to the flash-frozen individual vegetables.

DID YOU KNOW? Since frozen chopped onions are difficult to brown due to the moisture they contain, they are best used in stews and soups where a sweet, subtle, uncaramelized flavor is sought. To have them color, they must be blotted very dry on paper towels. At this point, it is usually faster to chop a fresh onion.

2 pounds whole-milk or low-fat ricotta
4 eggs
1 cup Parmesan cheese
⅓ cup chopped flat-leaf parsley *or* 2 tablespoons dried
2 tablespoons chopped fresh basil *or* 2 teaspoons dried
Freshly ground black pepper to taste
½ cup olive oil
1 12-ounce package frozen chopped onions, defrosted and squeezed very dry (see Note)
1 cup frozen sliced carrots, defrosted and squeezed dry
1 10-ounce package frozen cut red and green peppers, defrosted and squeezed dry
1 16-ounce package frozen chopped broccoli, defrosted and squeezed dry
1–1½ pounds QUICK HOMEMADE FETTUCINE (page 383) or store-bought fresh pasta left in broad strips, and cut into lengths to fit a lasagna pan *or* dried pasta, cooked according to package directions and drained
3 cups CHUNKY HOMEMADE TOMATO SAUCE (page 377) or prepared spaghetti sauce
2 cups shredded mozzarella cheese

1. In a large bowl combine the ricotta cheese with the eggs, Parmesan cheese, parsley, basil, and pepper, and stir to blend well.

2. In a large saucepan, heat the olive oil until fragrant, about 1 minute over high heat. Stir in the onions and sauté them for 5 to 6 minutes, stirring occasionally. They will become translucent but not brown. Add the carrot slices and cook for 2 minutes; then add the peppers and broccoli. Stir all the vegetables together, adjust the heat to medium, and let them cook until tender, another 5 to 6 minutes. Scrape the vegetables into the ricotta cheese and mix well.

3. Preheat your oven to 350°F.

4. Using a lasagna dish about 11 × 14 inches, ladle about 1 cup of the sauce into the bottom of the dish and spread it evenly with a spatula. Place 2 lengths of the fresh pasta lengthwise in the dish, or enough of the cooked dried pasta to cover the bottom of the dish. Spread about 4 cups of the filling over the pasta, using a spatula or rubber scraper to even it out. Sprinkle 1 cup mozzarella over the filling.

5. Place 2 more lengths of pasta over the filling and mozzarella. Ladle 1 more cup of sauce over the pasta, and then scrape the remaining filling into the lasagna dish and spread evenly. Cover with 2 to 3 more lengths of pasta, using a piece of the third length only if necessary to cover the filling. Ladle the last cup of sauce over the pasta and sprinkle on the remaining mozzarella cheese.

6. Cover the top of the pan with aluminum foil, place it in the preheated oven, and bake for 50 minutes until hot and bubbling. Remove the pan from the oven, let it stand for at least 10 minutes, carefully uncover, and cut the lasagna into 8 to 12 servings.

NOTE: The easiest way to drain whole packages of frozen vegetables is to let them defrost, then puncture 3 or 4 holes in one end, and gently squeeze the water out.

Very Berry Compote

Makes about 5 cups

Spoon this combination of berries, orange juice, and spices on your favorite breakfast fare. It's superb on WILD RICE, PECAN, BUTTERMILK WAFFLES (page 317), CRISPY CREAM OF WHEAT GRIDDLE CAKES (page 310), or HEAVENLY BLUES (page 315). Or try it over ice cream and chocolate brownies.

The beauty of this sauce is that frozen fruits can go directly from the freezer to the saucepan. Remember to buy individually quick-frozen fruits, rather than those in sugar syrups. The quality of the fruit is generally higher and you can use only the portion needed at one time and return the remainder to the freezer. Seal the bag tightly and replace it as quickly as possible.

1 12-ounce package frozen raspberries
1 12-ounce package frozen blueberries
1 20-ounce package frozen strawberries
½ cup dark or light raisins
1 10-ounce jar raspberry jelly
1 stick cinnamon
12 whole cloves
Grated zest of 1 orange
½ cup orange juice
2 tablespoons finely chopped candied ginger

1. Combine the berries, raisins, jelly, cinnamon, cloves, orange zest, orange juice, and ginger in a large, nonaluminum saucepan and bring to a boil over medium-high heat. Once the jelly has melted, lower the heat and let the mixture boil slowly for about 1 hour, stirring occasionally, until it is slightly thickened. Remove from the heat and let it stand for about 20 minutes. As the compote stands, it will become thicker. Serve it warm or cool. It will last several weeks in your refrigerator.

Easy Orange Sherbet

Makes 1 pint

This is a very quick and easy way to make orange sherbet, especially if you keep frozen orange juice on hand in the freezer. Use it with ORANGE SEGMENTS IN ORANGE SAUCE WITH ORANGE SHERBET (page 93), or as a filling for hollowed-out oranges.

Frozen orange juice now comes in several varieties in the market: low-acid, home-style with more pulp, and regular. Frozen, the cartons of citrus juices last up to 6 months in your freezer. Other fruit juices last for 10 to 12 months. Refrigerate once the juice has been reconstituted and use within 5 to 6 days.

¾ cup water
¾ cup sugar
½ cup *undiluted* orange juice concentrate
2 egg whites

1. Combine the water and sugar in a small saucepan and, over high heat, bring just to a boil. Remove the pan from the heat, pour the syrup into a jar, and let it cool. *Or*, let it cool in the saucepan.

2. When the sugar syrup is cooled, combine it with the orange juice, pour the mixture into a flat metal brownie pan, cover, and place it in the freezer until solid, 3 to 4 hours.

3. Cut the frozen juice into squares, and place it along with the egg whites in the bowl of a food processor fitted with a steel blade. Process until the mixture is frothy and pale orange in color. Cover again, and return it to the freezer for 2 hours.

Honeydew-Cantaloupe Semi-Freddo

Serves 6

This is a dessert to literally "whip up" for your friends. With a couple of bags of frozen melon balls, this Italian soft-style frozen dessert is made in minutes in a food processor. Once the fruit is puréed, it will keep for a couple of hours in the freezer before hardening. Serve 1 scoop of each flavor with some crisp cookies for a light dessert.

Like the name says, this dessert is only "semi-cold." The texture is softer than frozen sherbert or ice cream.

¾ cup sugar
¾ cup water
2 20-ounce bags frozen melon balls
2 tablespoons lemon juice
1 egg white
2 tablespoons lime juice
1 egg white

1 Combine the sugar and water in a small saucepan and bring it just to a boil to dissolve the sugar crystals. Pour the syrup into a glass jar and chill until cold. *Or,* let it cool in the saucepan.

2. Separate the melon balls into cantaloupe and honeydew. You should have about 3½ to 4 cups of each. Place the cantaloupe balls in a food processor fitted with a steel chopping blade with ½ cup of the sugar syrup and process briefly just until the melon is almost smooth, about 10 seconds. Add the lemon juice and 1 egg white and process just until light in color and smooth, about 10 seconds. Scrape the semifreddo into a freezer container, cover, and place in the freezer for up to 2 hours before serving. (If your freezer is not very cold, this dessert may stay soft longer.)

3. Repeat the process with the honeydew balls, using the lime juice and egg white.

NOTE: This simple dessert may be made with many fruits by cutting the fruit into bite-size pieces and freezing them first on a cookie sheet. Or use any of the other frozen fruits without sugar. Any one of these semi-freddi are wonderful eaten right away. When they become too solid, process again.

DID YOU KNOW? If you have several frozen egg whites that have been defrosted, measure out 2 tablespoons for the equivalent of 1 large egg white. One egg yolk measures 1 tablespoon.

An Ice Cream Mix-In Party

One of the latest crazes sweeping fancy ice cream parlors is the "mix-in" idea, a fun, creative way to make your own signature blend of frozen fantasy. The scheme is that basic ice cream flavors are combined with ingredients such as crushed cookies, candies, or nuts, then blended with spatulas and served somewhat soft in a bowl to each guest. It's sort of like a make-it-yourself sundae. The common ingredients for mixing in are found in your market, and this is a different idea for a very spontaneous, casual dessert.

Allow about a pint of ice cream for every 2 guests.

TOPPINGS

Chopped candy bars—Heath Bars, Butterfingers, Nestle's Crunch, Mounds
Chopped cookies—Oreo, chocolate chip
Toasted coconut, granola, raisins, butterscotch chips, chopped nuts, etc.

1. Place a generous serving of ice cream and the mix-ins on a clean large acrylic, formica, or marble surface. Stir the mix-ins in quickly until blended, then spoon the mixture into a bowl. Top with whipped cream, nonpareils, a cherry, and sauces, too.

The Ultimate Raspberry Chocolate Sauce

Makes 2½ cups

When it comes to chocolate sauces, I like mine dark, rich, and allied with the slightly acidic taste of raspberries for a fuller dimension in taste. This sinfully decadent sauce blends cocoa, sugar, cream, and butter with the puréed fruit for a thick topping to slather on ice cream, pound cake, or brownies. (Some of my friends say to forget the ice cream and serve a bowl of this sauce with a spoon!)

While frozen raspberries are marvelous puréed for this sauce, sherbet, and ice cream, you cannot expect them to look as beautiful as the fresh product. If you want to preserve as much of their shape as possible when using them for decoration, keep them separate and frozen until ready to serve. Without a lot of handling, there will be a number of presentable berries in the package.

1 12-ounce package individually quick-frozen raspberries, defrosted
¾ cup Dutch process cocoa
¾ cup heavy cream
4 tablespoons unsalted butter, softened
1½ cups sugar
⅓ cup light corn syrup

1. Purée the raspberries in a food processor fitted with a steel blade, then pass them through a fine strainer. Or pass them through a food mill. Set aside.

2. In a medium-size heavy saucepan, whisk together the cocoa and heavy cream. Add the butter, sugar, corn syrup, and raspberries and stir until well blended. Place the pan over medium heat and slowly bring the mixture to a boil, stirring often. Once it reaches a boil, let it continue to boil slowly for 8 minutes *without* stirring. Remove the pan from the heat and pour the sauce into a container. Let it cool for 15 minutes if serving it hot or cover and refrigerate until needed. It will last for at least 1 month. The sauce may be reheated slowly.

Praline Candy Ice Cream Cups

Serves 8

These festive dessert cups take advantage of the premium-quality ice cream sold in every supermarket. And who doesn't like ice cream? Here, it is served in a crunchy candy cup made from ground Amaretti —Italian almond macaroons, found with other imported cookies—and caramelized almonds. Serve it with THE ULTIMATE RASPBERRY CHOCOLATE SAUCE (page 417) or purchased hot fudge topping. I have used vanilla, coffee, and strawberry ice creams. But there are so many wonderful flavors now, the choice is up to you.

Buying "gourmet" ice creams is expensive. Pints may cost more than gallons of other, less-rich brands. Personal taste is important. If the ice cream is served nude—relying solely on the flavor and texture— without additional adornment, then serve the best. However, when it will be sauced, mixed with other ingredients (see AN ICE CREAM MIX-IN PARTY on page 417), or used as part of another confection, a good-quality, less-costly product will never be noticed. All ice creams are best when used within 2 to 4 months.

Unsalted butter to grease a piece of aluminum foil
½ cup sugar
2 tablespoons water
¾ cup (3 ounces) slivered almonds, toasted until rich brown
10 pair Amaretti cookies, crumbled
3 tablespoons unsalted butter, melted
1 quart premium-quality ice cream

1. Lightly butter a piece of aluminum foil.

2. In a small, heavy saucepan, combine the sugar and water and bring them to a boil over high heat. Let the mixture bubble slowly, continuously swirling the syrup but not stirring it, for about 6 minutes, or until it is a rich amber color. If some sugar crystals begin to burn, rinse down the side of the pan with a brush dipped in water. Immediately remove the pan from the heat, stir in the almonds, and scrape the mixture onto the aluminum foil, separating the pieces with a couple of forks. Set aside to cool.

3. Once the almonds have cooled, add them with the cookie crumbs to the bowl of a food processor fitted with a steel blade and process into very fine crumbs. Scrape them into a small bowl, add the butter, and toss to mix evenly.

4. Line a muffin tin with 8 foil or colored liners. Spoon in about 3 tablespoons of the crumb mixture into each cup, and push the crumbs against the bottom and sides. Place the candy cups in the freezer to harden for about ½ hour. The cups may be made several days in advance and left ready to fill or already filled and lightly covered with foil. Reserve any extra crumbs.

5. Scoop a large ball of ice cream into each cup, and sprinkle on extra crumbs. If the ice cream has softened, return the cups to the freezer until firm. Serve with or without sauce. The muffin liners may be pulled off leaving an attractive ridged pattern.

NOTE: As a variation, before adding the ice cream scoops, place 1 tablespoon of THE ULTIMATE RASPBERRY CHOCOLATE SAUCE (page 000) in the bottom of each cup and let it harden for about 40 minutes in the freezer.

DID YOU KNOW? Until recently, ice cream was considered a generic product and package labeling of ingredients was not required. With the advent of the new age of ice cream, this has changed, although some companies still do not comply with this. Take a look to see if the product is really pure dairy cream with natural sugar, honey, and other ingredients. Products with air whipped into them will deflate quickly with a little stirring.

Look for foil and colored muffin liners in the Kitchen Tools section. Another fun idea is to buy the mini-muffin tin and liners, line them with a generous tablespoon of crumbs, and use mini scoops of several flavors of ice cream. Each guest may have a couple of different cups.

Suggested Menus from the Supermarket

T hese Strategy Pages are meant to offer suggested menus for entertaining that may be used on different occasions. As with ingredient selection, the choice of these recipes is not etched in stone. You may wish to prepare some of the dishes and supplement them with purchased or personal favorites. In fact, the next chapter discusses how to make "supermarket take-out food" look and taste like your own.

There are, however, some general guidelines to consider for successful menu planning.

PREPARATION

For me, the most important factor is that a majority of the work be done ahead of time so that I may spend time with my guests.

Special order meats, produce, and other needs at least a week in advance, and *be sure* to recheck the order a few days before you need it. Markets have a way of forgetting or getting orders mixed up.

All table settings, platter selection, beverage storage, and appropriate garnishes (where possible), should be decided upon ahead of time.

Some dishes may be partially prepared in advance and finished at the last minute. Others can be made, frozen, and then reheated.

Be realistic. Select only a few dishes that require the majority of preparation at the last minute. Be sure to consider the number of burners, broilers, and ovens you have as well as refrigeration space. Also think about how many hands are required for stirring, chopping, etc.

Where possible, clean up as you go during preparation and during the meal to avoid a last-minute pile up. Sometimes a conscientious high-school student will be grateful for a little extra money for washing dishes.

FOOD SELECTION

Consider seasonality. Lighter foods, chilled or at room temperature, work well in the summer. They may be prepared early, before the day becomes hot. A more substantial meal takes away the chill in the winter. Foods that are appropriate to the season will usually be fresher and a better buy, as well.

Make use of color. You have a giant paintbox of colors to choose from in the market. Think about the balance of hues and shades as you select dishes. You may want to select a color scheme appropriate to the setting or the time of year. But, remember that we see our food before we taste it.

Textures and shapes should be mixed. All-puréed or all-crunchy foods are less satisfying than a combination of smooth, soft, firm, and rough. If your plate has thin rectangular slices of meat on it, then sliced carrots and a purée of spinach afford contrasting optical and taste sensations.

Use creamy or rich foods sparingly. You can serve a greater variety of courses when moderation is used.

Let the menu be appropriate to the guest list. If the group is not familiar with game meat or unusual delicacies, choose foods that will make everyone comfortable and happy. Menus where children will be present, unless the kids are quite sophisticated, should include choices that they are sure to eat.

Don't forget to think about garnishes. They need not be complicated. Even a poached chicken breast will look more glamorous with a sprig of watercress and a cherry tomato next to it. Again, look in the next chapter for some new serving ideas.

Finally, have some familiar recipes in your repertoire that you can make with no hesitation. Each new dish requires concentration. When you are trying several at once, select some that can be made ahead of time.

A Colorful South-of-the-Border Brunch Buffet

Brunch is that strange meal we Americans have put together that is some distance from breakfast, but not quite lunch. This menu has some of both dishes to pick and choose from. Why not have a little fun with this one? If you can find a piñata, it would make a great centerpiece. Buy heavy-duty plastic plates, napkins, and crepe-paper streamers in several colors and make it a fiesta. Tie two different colors of paper napkins together with a flower or ribbon, and don't forget a pitcher of Bloody Marys, Margaritas, or Sangria, if you're up for it.

*Crispy Cream of Wheat Griddle Cakes
with Very Berry Compote (page 414)*

•

Orange, Jicama, Watercress, and Olive Salad (page 92)

•

Mexican Ranchers' Eggs (page 282)

•

Corny Cheesey Popovers (page 275)

•

Mexican Cole Slaw (page 28)

•

Margarita's Fruit Salad in a Honeydew Melon (page 88)

•

Mexican Chocolate Cake (page 346)

Tote Cuisine: A Pack-and-Go Picnic

Here's where supermarkets and you can shine. Take along decorative paperware, casually elegant fare, and your best spirits. If you only feel like making a couple of dishes, take-out departments are loaded with plenty of choices. But before stuffing the cartons into your hamper, glance at *Simple Ideas for Enhancing Purchased Foods* in the next chapter. And remember how attractive edible containers are. Serve the Mustard Custard in a hollowed-out red bell pepper, for example. Wrap foods tightly and leave them in the refrigerator until the last possible minute to prevent any spoilage. Markets do sell insulated chests, too.

Artichokes Stuffed with Russian Potato Salad (page 20)

•

Made-to-be-Leftover Meat Loaf with Cranberry, Pepper, and Onion Conserves
on French Bread (page 85)

•

Pita Pockets filled with Sprouts and Lean and Moist Turkey Breast
with Mustard Custard (page 367)

•

Colorful Corn Salad (page 407)

•

Molasses Spice Cookies (page 328)
Irish Oatmeal Hermits (page 327)

A Sunday Afternoon Tea

This is the opportunity for the whole family and all generations to get together. Of course you want to be there, too, to catch up on all the latest chatter. So have a good mix of sweet and savory finger foods— some hot, some cold—plenty of hot tea with lemon, sugar, and milk close by, and some hot cocoa or cider for the kids. There are lots of prepared foods—like smoked salmon from the Deli—to add to the tea table. Lay cotton lace over a printed table cloth for an old-fashioned feeling. Add small bunches of flowers and candles, too.

Cocoa Pecans (page 336)

•

Whole Wheat Cream Puff Shells with Tarragon Chicken Salad (page 120)

•

Smoked Salmon on Thinly Sliced Whole Grain Bread

•

Vermont Cheddar and Maple Crackers (page 271)

•

Warm Individual Apple Strudels (page 73)

•

Lemon Shortbread Cookies (page 325) and Other Crisp Cookies

•

Chocolate Carrot Brownies (page 334)

A Party with Just Hors d'Oeuvres

Everyone loves hors d'oeuvres. In fact, the great mistake we often make in entertaining is to feed our guests too much before we sit down. Here, there's no problem with that, because after this, the party's over! Remember some of these dishes are easily prepared in advance and/or frozen, like the Puffy Asparagus and Cheese Gougère and Joanna's Country Pâté. Everything else is fine made beforehand. For the mixture to be satisfying, you will need hot and cold foods with a variety of tastes and textures. Food that is too highly seasoned will overshadow all the other flavors. And, don't put everything out at once. Let the selection change during the course of the party.

Tapenade with Raw Vegetables (page 370)

•

Mini Shrimp Spring Rolls (page 223) with Gingery Peanut Dipping Sauce (page 368)

•

Curried Corn Nut and Sunflower Seed Nibble (page 335)

•

Puffy Asparagus and Cheese Gougère (page 272)

•

Joanna's Country Pâté (page 193) with Plum-Pear Ketchup (page 104)

•

Mediterranean Tomato Tart (page 405)

•

Squid Caponata (page 222)

•

Roasted Eggplant with Tahini on Endive Leaves (page 33)

•

Vermont Cheddar and Maple Crackers (page 271)

Express Register Dinner: 12 Items or Less

At the end of the day when time is short and all the supermarket registers have lines 7 to 8 deep, you need to be resourceful about how to prepare an attractive meal. Look over the Take-Out department for foods that you can "dress up." It helps to have a few staples like a can of chicken stock, some olive oil, seasonings, and rice on hand. And you can carefully layer 2 or 3 vegetables into one Salad Bar container, separating them at home.

Winter Squash, Apple, and Walnut Soup (page 410)

•

Devilish Crunchy Chicken (page 135)
Sautéed Broccoli, Cauliflower, and Carrots
Wild Pecan Rice

•

Honeydew-Cantaloupe Semi-Freddo (page 416)
with Cookies

NEEDED TO BUY

2 packages frozen puréed squash
1 jar applesauce
½ pint cream
4 ounces walnuts
1 chicken
2 lemons

1 large container from the Salad Bar of broccoli, cauliflower, and carrots mixed
1 box Wild Pecan Rice
2 20-ounce packages frozen melon balls
1 package cookies

WHAT YOU NEED TO HAVE ON HAND

mace and chervil *or* substitute nutmeg and parsley
butter

olive oil
salt and white or black pepper
egg whites

Dinner for Two

Cooking for two should be just as festive as for six or eight. It is especially fun when you can share the chores, then sit down together. If there is only one cook, this menu is designed to have the work done pretty much ahead of time. While you can select recipes that make two servings, another strategy is to cook for four and freeze or refrigerate the second half for another meal. Make a small amount of the Curried Corn Nuts and Sunflower Seeds or store the rest for another day. Divide the Grilled Chèvre on Endive with Red Pepper Sauce recipe in half. Make two strawberry tarts and reserve the remaining custard for another dessert, like pound cake with custard and fresh fruit. It's like a mini Queen Victoria's Christmas Trifle.

Curried Corn Nut and Sunflower Seed Nibble (page 335)

•

Baked Chèvre on Red Pepper Sauce and Endives (page 274)

•

Quick Paella with Monkfish (page 246)
Thick Sliced Italian or French Bread

•

Individual Strawberry Crème Brûlée Tarts (page 106)

A Casual Outdoor Dinner

This is meant as a casual outdoor dinner for you and a couple of friends. Cook the corn in the husk on the grill along with the marinated steak. Prepare everything else—the sherbet, cookies, tomato coulis, and seviche—ahead of time. The zucchini gratin may be served hot or warm. Minted ice tea or frosty beers would help to cool things down.

Avocado and Scallop Seviche with Endive Leaves (page 221)

•

Steak 'n' Stout (page 184)
Zucchini Gratin with Tomato Coulis (page 63)
Fresh Corn on the Cob

•

Nutmeg-Scented Cantaloupe Sherbet (page 81)
with Molasses Spice Cookies (page 328)

A Lighter Meal for Low-Calorie Entertaining

It takes creative thinking to come up with a meal that is satisfying, beautiful, and elegant without wrecking everyone's diet. Throughout this book, I have tried to include some recipes that meet these criteria. When slimming down recipes, remember that color, texture, and lots of taste are especially important so we don't feel as though we are suffering. The food *must* be beautiful. Once again, very little work is left to be done at the end in this menu. The game hens, mixed vegetables, and rice may be served hot or at room temperature, depending on the weather.

Spicy and Crunchy Low-Cal Tofu Dip and Raw Vegetable Basket (page 270)
Grilled Marinated Turkey Bites (page 138)

•

Individual Red Pepper Salmon Mousses (page 231)

•

Indian Game Hens Marinated in Yogurt and Spices (page 148)
Sautéed Snow Peas, Radishes, and Cherry Tomatoes (page 51)
Basmati Rice with Mint

•

Mosaic of Peaches and Berries in Wine (page 95)
Deceptively Decadent Cheesecake (page 296)

A Do-Ahead Cold Buffet for Summer

When the weather is warm, our desire to slave over a hot stove wanes. The secret to this menu is that everything, save placing the food on the table, can be done almost a day ahead of time. Last minutes are reserved for assembling already prepared ingredients. Your table should be ready beforehand, too. Festive mushroom baskets with "vegetable flowers" (page 444) set a casual but decorative table.

Squid Caponata (page 222)

•

Roasted Eggplant with Tahini on Endive Leaves (page 33)

•

Green Bean and New Potato Salad from Vernon (page 36)

•

A Platter of Cheeses with Dilled Potato Bread (page 321)

•

Chicken, Pecan, Avocado, and Wild Pecan Rice Salad (page 386)

•

Chilled Whole Cod Tonnato (page 250)

•

Curried Corn Nut and Sunflower Seed Nibble (page 335)

•

Baskets of Fresh Fruit

•

Blackberry Tart (page 78)

•

Chilled White Wine Soufflé with Apricot Sauce (page 288)

For Thanksgiving and the Next Day

When planning your Thanksgiving dinner, you can save a lot of work the morning after Thanksgiving if you cook a little extra the night before the holiday. In our house we still roast a bird large enough to have leftovers for sandwiches, soup, and Two-Day-After Turkey Hash. The Cranberry Holiday Braid is delicious warm from the oven or reheated the next morning.

Winter Squash, Apple, and Walnut Soup (page 410)

•

Roast Turkey with Gravy and Stuffing
Easy Glazed Pearl Onions with Peas (page 410)
Holiday Cranberry Carrots (page 31)
Baked Yams
(make 2 extra)

•

Spicy Pumpkin Mousse (page 340)
Molasses Spice Cookies (page 328)

THE NEXT DAY
Two-Day-After Turkey Hash with Apple Sauce (page 143)
Day-After Thanksgiving Sweet Rye and Yam Muffins (page 318)

•

Salad

•

Cranberry Holiday Braid (page 323)

A Classic French Dinner

This is a menu for when you want to feel that you are in an elegant French setting. How you present it will make the difference between two- and three-star dining. So take a few extra minutes with the garnishes. For a beautiful but unusual table setting, look on page 442 for the Large Purple Cabbage Flower, Chrysanthemum Onions, and Votive Candles. Only the racks of lamb need last-minute preparation. Why not serve the pâté in the kitchen? It's a good place for guests to break the ice while you take care of last-minute preparations. The raspberry tart and coffee might await you in the living room, so tired bodies have a chance to stretch and talk to other guests on the way to this meal's finale.

Pheasant Pâté (page 151)

•

French Pea Soup (page 409)

•

Rack of Lamb Persillade (page 190)
Creamed Spinach in Tomatoes (page 411)
Those Potatoes! (page 54)

•

Green Salad with Chèvre and Grapes

•

Raspberry Chocolate Tart (page 348)

A Glamorous Celebration

Sometimes we want to go "all out." This dinner is for one of those occasions, and the ingredients are luxurious: lobster, quail, port, and Stilton cheese. The menu is colorful and a balance of simple and complex flavors. Set an elegant table to go with this menu. Look at the suggestion on page 447 for adding flowers, perhaps tiny rose buds, to a potted plant. Make the cheese palmiers, sorbet, stuffing for the squabs, salad without the dressing, pears and cheese, and cookies ahead of time. It is important that you only offer the lightest hors d'oeuvres with this meal to insure your guests are not overstuffed. A bottle of champagne would be an appropriate beginning. Switch to a full-bodied red for the squabs.

Crisp Cheese Palmiers (page 403)

•

Lobster Timbales with Riesling Beurre Blanc (page 234)

•

Mandarin Cranberry Sorbet (page 339)

•

Roasted Squabs Stuffed with Turnips, Olives, and Figs (page 158)
Steamed Broccoli Florets, Sautéed Carrots, Cauliflower Purée (page 32)

•

Salad of Mixed Greens with Mustard Vinaigrette (page 363)

•

Poached Pears with Stilton Cream (page 99)
Pogachel and other Cookies (page 329)
or
The Ultimate Decadent Orange-Chocolate Dacquoise (page 351)
(if you want an all-out finale)

·10·

ENTERTAINING FROM THE SUPERMARKET

INTRODUCTION

Until recently, the idea of entertaining from the supermarket might have seemed like a strange one. Although it was a fine place for everyday shopping, elegant prepared foods and the accessories for a special occasion were missing. When you wanted someone else to take care of an entire event, you called a caterer. For many people, this is still the case. However, if you haven't looked around your market lately, you might be surprised at what you will find.

The biggest area of expansion in the entire supermarket business is in the realm of Take-Out, Prepared Foods, and Catering. This reflects the current need for convenience as a result of our changing lifestyles. In many homes, either both partners work, there is a single parent, or other interests draw one away from the home and kitchen. The time crunch has curtailed our running from one food boutique to the next. Yet, the desire to entertain remains constant.

Recognizing these trends, supermarkets have started to add trained personnel to meet the needs of their customers. Chances are a chef or even a sophisticated consulting company is directing these changes. In Deli cases, mundane commercially made salads share space with more contemporary combinations of ingredients prepared on the premises. Nearby, fresh soups, vegetables, entrées, and desserts may be displayed. Throughout the store, in the Meat, Poultry, Fish, and even Produce departments, there are fresh foods which are ready to eat or to be cooked at home.

While the prices may seem more expensive, these foods can save you a lot of time and effort for everyday or special meals. They are worth trying. You will find that some are wonderful; others are best forgotten. Across this country, the quality ranges from superior to mediocre. By investing the time to familiarize yourself with the services available, your results will be more predictable.

Entertaining can be a combination of store-bought and homemade foods. That is what this last chapter is all about. By "doctoring up" and "dressing up" already prepared foods, you make them special. Toss a pasta salad with a simple vinaigrette or a handful of fresh vegetables to perk up the taste and appearance. Or pack a chicken or rice salad in a ring mold and unmold it on a large platter with curly endive leaves for a border. Add cucumber "scales" to a piece of poached fish. Or, serve some tartar sauce in a hollowed-out red bell pepper. Supermarkets are full of garnishes, centerpieces, and serving containers that are imaginative and inexpensive.

To meet an even broader range of needs, some supermarkets rent or sell almost any service or piece of equipment for catering your party from musicians or bartenders to chafing dishes and glassware. Depending on state laws, this may also include wine and spirits to accompany your meals. It is worth exploring these supermarket services. They are working to make entertaining easier and more enjoyable for all of us, including the host/chef.

TAKING TAKE-OUT ONE STEP FURTHER

As supermarket Deli departments expand to include more prepared foods from salads to entrées to desserts, customers are discovering a whole new way of purchasing food for elegant or casual dining that entails less work and time. As good as some of these items taste, for store-bought food to look and taste homemade, simple garnishes, seasonings, or additional ingredients may be helpful.

Before You Buy

Before deciding to buy ready-made items or have the market cater your entire party, a little detective work of your own will give you a better idea of the final results.

1. Give a good look at the foods that are on display in the Take-Out department. Do the selections look fresh? As salads sit, acidic vinegar or lemon juice leaches out the color of vegetables. Cream- or mayonnaise-based salads develop an unattractive skin if not turned or stored correctly. The edges of sliced meats will brown and curl as they dry out. Ask when foods were prepared. Does the store make its own? Are there preservatives? Does it move quickly (a good indication of quality)? And, how long and under what conditions have they been stored?

2. How is each preparation displayed? Bowls and platters should be neat and clean. If there is not a separate serving utensil for each preparation, then utensils should be washed after each use. Food should not be left out of refrigeration for a long time, as it deteriorates quickly. What does the market do with the food that is left over each day?

3. Watch that the clerk who serves you has not been snacking and then handling your food. Gloves and a hat or some protection against falling hair should be worn.

4. *Always* ask to taste at least a few (if not all) of the items you are considering buying to get an idea if the foods are well seasoned and made without preservatives. Unfortunately, many great-looking salads are made with bottled or packaged dressings and have a chemical taste. Chickens are routinely brushed with bottled barbecue sauce or packaged seasonings. Find out what is in the food.

5. Discuss quantities with the clerk. He or she should be able to tell you how much you will need for light or heavy eaters. Be sure to indicate if this choice will be served alone or with other items. (See the introduction to this chapter about catering managers and party planners.)

6. Freshly packaged prepared foods sold in the Deli department should have the date of preparation stamped on the serving container along with reheating and storage directions. Trays should be sealed and neatly organized. Most foods are best used within a day or two unless otherwise indicated.

7. Whenever possible, order larger quantities in

advance to save time and to insure that the particular selection is in good supply.

8. Pick up perishable prepared foods toward the end of your shopping, especially if you will be in the market for a long time. Refrigerate them as soon after purchase as possible.

SIMPLE IDEAS FOR ENHANCING PURCHASED FOOD

These suggestions are meant as a guide only. There is a never-ending number of ways to dress up food. Once you look over these ideas using familiar Deli and Take-out fare, I'm sure you will have several of your own.

1. Pasta is incredibly porous and in salads it often absorbs most of the flavor and vinaigrette before you are ready to eat it. Ask what variety of oil, vinegar, and herb was used and then add a little more of them just before serving. Or, make some MUSTARD VINAIGRETTE (page 363).

2. Vegetable salads dressed with an acid-based sauce lose their color and texture when prepared in advance. Why not blanch a few broccoli or cauliflower florets from the Salad Bar or some frozen tiny peas, and toss them in for vibrancy of color, taste, and texture. Toasted nuts are another crunchy addition.

3. Potato salad will taste brighter with some fresh parsley, or a little sour cream and freshly chopped dill. You can also add a shredded hard-cooked egg and chopped small pickles. Serve the salad in a hollowed-out green pepper. This works for macaroni salad, too.

4. Marinated cucumber-and-onion salad will taste special if you drain it, add some plain yogurt, chopped fresh dill and/or mint, and serve it in hollowed-out tomatoes as a side dish. Add leftover chicken or shrimp and serve with pita bread.

5. Purchased cole slaw tastes better with some caraway seeds, finely shredded carrots and a chopped green apple stirred in. Serve it with Jarlsberg cheese and brown bread.

6. Mayonnaise-based chicken and turkey salads will be refreshed with a few drops of lemon juice and some finely chopped celery or onion. Cut off one end of a pita bread and open the pocket. Add some shredded lettuce, alfalfa sprouts, sunflower seeds, and sliced tomato along with a scoop of one of these salads for a delicious lunch or light supper.

7. Or, make a chicken salad curried by adding curry powder, lemon juice, sliced radishes, sliced almonds, and raisins. Serve in a small melon half cut with a zigzag pattern.

8. Prepared tuna salad will taste livelier with a little red wine vinegar, dried chervil, and freshly diced celery. Scoop it into a split avocado. Garnish with a lemon twist and a parsley sprig.

9. Toast flour tortillas with thinly sliced Muenster or Jack cheese on top in a 400°F oven until the cheese is hot and bubbling. Top with some sour cream, a thinly sliced pickled jalapeño pepper (from a jar), some salsa, or a little mole sauce. Top with a second tortilla, and bake for a few minutes longer. Cut into wedges and serve.

10. For nachos, buy taco chips, cover them with shredded cheddar cheese, add a thin slice of jalapeño pepper on top of each, and bake until hot.

11. Make individual pita-bread pizzas. For the cheese base for two 7-inch pitas: Combine 1 cup ricotta cheese, 1 egg, 1½ tablespoons chopped basil *or* 1½ teaspoons dried, ½ cup Parmesan cheese, 1 teaspoon olive oil. Spread the cheese over the pitas and top with a thin layer of spaghetti sauce and thin slices of pepperoni; or thinly sliced zucchini, yellow squash, and red pepper lightly brushed with oil, etc. Bake for 15 minutes in a preheated 425°F oven.

12. Prepared soups often benefit from fresh herbs, a splash of vinegar, a little cream, and/or freshly ground black pepper.

13. Buy a prepared croissant, split it, place some thin slices of ham and Swiss cheese on top, and grill it until bubbling and hot. A touch of Dijon mustard will help, too. Or, fill the croissant with tuna or chicken salad.

14. Make a "Muffaletta"—a New Orleans-style hero sandwich. Buy a large round Italian or French bread. Slice off the top and hollow out the center. Start by spreading the inside with about ¾ cup of any salad (olive, onion, etc.) in a vinaigrette. Add ½ pound of ham, ½ pound thinly sliced salami, ⅓ pound thinly sliced provolone, lettuce, and tomato slices. Replace the top of the bread, wrap tightly in plastic wrap, and refrigerate for a couple of hours. Then unwrap and cut into wedges.

15. Decorate poached fillets or a whole salmon with cucumber slices (see page 252) or thinly sliced lemons and dill.

16. Whole filets of beef or roasted chickens may be reheated and presented on a platter with mashed potatoes, carrots, or CAULIFLOWER AND POTATO PURÉE (page 32) piped around the edge. Run it under the broiler for a little color. Serve with a sprig of watercress and a couple of cherry tomatoes, too.

17. Fresh mint, Grand Marnier, lemon juice, and shredded coconut all enhance fruit salads. Add prepared fruit salad to hollowed-out grapefruit halves or melons, including the fresh fruit with the purchased fruit. Or serve a large spoonful over a mound of purchased rice pudding.

18. Fruit preserves mixed with softened butter are a perfect topping to serve with purchased muffins.

19. Custard baked in disposable individual aluminum cups can be unmolded and served with THE ULTIMATE RASPBERRY CHOCOLATE SAUCE (page 417) or purchased fudge sauce. Add some chocolate shavings on top of a dollop of whipped cream.

20. Decorate dessert mousses with whipped cream piped around the edge in a decorative design, or carefully spoon them into purchased (or made) dessert cups—chocolate or pastry—and top with fresh fruit or whipped cream.

21. Serve baked apples with a mound of French vanilla ice cream with crumbled candied nuts on top.

DECORATIVE SERVING CONTAINERS TO MAKE

1. Buy a large round French bread, cut off the top, about ¼ the way down, and hollow it out (be sure to save the bread for bread crumbs or croutons). Toast it briefly, line the bottom with foil, and use it to serve VEAL AND SAUSAGE MEATBALLS (page 201) or even MY DYNAMITE ALL-TIME FAVORITE CHILI (page 177). If your market has a whole black bread, it is stunning to hold colorful little sandwiches. Line the platter with some rich-looking leaves, like beet greens.

2. Choose a large purple or green cabbage. If it does not sit steady, cut off a narrow slice from the root end. Cut off the top about ¼ the way down, and hollow out a space in the cabbage large enough to accommodate a pint or half-pint plastic container from the market. Use it for dips or sauces. Fill extra plastic containers and keep them refrigerated until needed. Then simply replace the empty with the filled one.

3. Lemons, limes, or oranges when hollowed out become festive cups to hold sorbets (see LIME SORBET, page 91), relishes, and dipping sauces. Cut them in half with a zigzag pattern and leave a narrow strip to become a handle, if it won't be in the way.

4. Cucumbers may be scored around the outside, hollowed out into little cups about 2½ inches in height and filled with a fish mousse, mashed potatoes, or condiments.

5. Split zucchini in half lengthwise. Hollow them out leaving a ½-inch border, then chop and sauté the zucchini meat and combine it with rice, chopped parsley, seasonings, and grated Swiss cheese. Refill the shells, bake and serve as a vegetable side dish.

6. Pumpkins make handsome tureens in which to serve PUMPKIN BLACK BEAN SOUP (page 373) or MY DYNAMITE ALL-TIME FAVORITE CHILI (page 177). Hollowed-out melons also make tureens for MINTED WATERMELON SOUP (page 108) and MARGARITA'S FRUIT SALAD (page 88).

7. Use tablequeen squash as individual soup or stew bowls, or use spaghetti squash for CHILI (page 178).

8. Large red, yellow, green, or purple peppers make a beautiful medley of containers for dipping sauces or condiments. Use two or three colors at once. See MOROCCAN LAMB IN PEPPERS (page 186). Cut off a tiny slice from the bottom if the peppers do not stand steady.

9. Stuffed potato skins have been used for everything from taco fixings to chicken salad.

10. The hollowed-out skins of avocados can be filled with guacamole.

11. Corn and flour tortillas make great individual serving baskets, as in MEXICAN RANCHERS' EGGS (page 282) or MEXICAN SHRIMP BASKETS (page 242).

12. And tomatoes will hold tossed or MARINATED THREE ONION SALAD (page 46) or CREAMED SPINACH (page 411).

A Few Supermarket Centerpiece Ideas

INTRODUCTION

Years ago, my wonderful friend Karen Berk, a talented food stylist and cooking teacher, shared a number of her secrets for carving vegetables into fanciful centerpieces. I was so taken with her inspiration that I almost never purchase ready-made table decorations.

Original and easy centerpieces that are fun to make are available at your supermarket. They usually cost less than a formal arrangement from the florist. Each of the following ideas is only a jumping-off point. Look around; you'll discover a world of possibilities as you do your shopping.

Large Purple Cabbage Flower, Chrysanthemum Onions, and Votive Candles

The large green leaves for this display should come from your garden. Even pine boughs will do. Use this arrangement on a round or oval table.

1 medium to large purple cabbage
3 large white, yellow, or red onions, regularly shaped
6 6-inch bamboo skewers
Large flat leaves, such as aurelia or small branches of rhododendron
2–3 low votive candles in colors of your choice

1. FOR THE CABBAGE Cut off a narrow slice at the base of the cabbage so that it stands straight and steady. Discard any blemished outer leaves. With a large, sharp chef's knife, make a cut from the top of the cabbage *almost* to the base. Don't cut the cabbage through.

2. Make a second cut perpendicular to the first. Continue making 2 more cuts, dividing the cabbage into 8 sections. Depending on how large the cabbage is, divide each of the sections into 2 or 3 smaller sections, using a small paring knife (see illustration). Place the cabbage in a large bowl or sink filled with ice water for at least 18 to 24 hours, until the leaves twist and curl back and the cabbage resembles a large flower. Add ice occasionally. This may also be done in a garbage bag. Once the leaves have curled, the cabbage may be drained and stored in a plastic bag in the refrigerator for up to 1 week.

Cabbage

3. FOR THE ONIONS Slice the thinnest layer possible off the root ends so that each onion sits straight. Remove only the papery outside of the onions. About ¼ the way from the root, run 1 skewer through the onion and out the other side. Run the second skewer

onion

perpendicular to this (see illustration). The skewers will prevent your cutting through the onions.

4. Make 4 cuts, as for the cabbage. Make several smaller cuts with a small paring knife to divide the segments into strips about ½ inch wide near the skewers. Fill a large bowl with hot water and several tablespoons of salt. Add the onions and let them soak for at least 1 to 3 hours, until they open into a chrysanthemum. Or add 2 cups of warm water to a large Ziploc bag with a few drops of yellow or red dye (found near baking staples). Add the onions and let them color for at least 1 to 3 hours. Most of the smell should disappear by this point. Onions should be fairly soft to look like flowers. Drain on paper towels. As they sit, the "petals" will curl in slightly, making them look more real.

5. ASSEMBLE THE DISPLAY Place the cabbage in the center of your table, or on a small plate to protect the finish. Slip the stem end of the leaves or branches under the cabbage, using as many as needed to encircle it. Place the "chrysanthemums" around the cabbage with the votive candles near each one. If you get candles with a scent, this will mask any onion smell. Light the candles before having guests come in to sit down.

NOTE: Anytime you use fresh leaves that will come in contact with food, you should make sure that they are not poisonous. Since food is not touching this display, you are safe. However, check with any poison information center; many universities have them.

Mushroom Basket with Beet Tulips and Mini-Vegetable Flowers

Ask the Produce manager if he will give you the light wood basket used for shipping mushrooms. They measure 14 × 5 × 7 inches and can be saved and used many times not only for centerpieces, but also to hold cutlery for casual buffets. If you are inclined, they can be spray-painted or even stenciled. This is a nice arrangement for a rectangular or buffet table. Most of the supplies for this can be reused.

1 mushroom basket
2–3 potatoes (any kind)
7–8 bunches curly parsley
3–5 beets, about 2½ to 3 inches in diameter
3–5 12-inch bamboo skewers
3–5 drinking straws
1–2 large bunches of scallions with long greens
Straight dressmaker pins
1 package enoki mushrooms (optional)
2–3 miniature squashes (optional)
2–3 5-inch bamboo skewers

1. Place the potatoes on the bottom of the mushroom basket. Add the parsley bunches, packing them in fairly tightly.

2. **MAKE THE TULIPS** Trim and peel the beets with a vegetable scraper. Pare the plain end into a slight point. Reserve the greens for another arrangement, if desired (see page 446). Cup the beet in the palm of your hand. With a small paring knife, carefully make an incision the length of the beet almost to the bottom, cutting in at a 45-degree angle, and cutting about ½ to ¾ inch deep (see illustration). Make a second incision about ⅛ inch to the right and cut until this incision joins the first, removing a small wedge of beet. Make the next incision about ¾ inch to the right and repeat the smaller cut next to it. Continue in the same manner around the beet, removing about 7 wedges in all. The wedges should all come together at the top of the beet.

3. Once all the wedges have been removed, reinsert your knife in back of each "petal," and gently work the knife down in back of the petal in front of it, to loosen each petal from the core of the beet. Place the beet in cold water while carving the others. (Beet juice does stain, so wear an apron to protect your clothes.)

4. ASSEMBLE THE BASKET Insert a 12-inch skewer into each tulip. Cut the green portions from the scallion. (Reserve the white part for cooking.) Slide a straw on each skewer, and then the scallion. Stick the tulip well into the potato base. To make leaves, slit a 6-inch length of scallion. Trim 1 end into a point, and curl it back. Attach it with a straight pin near where the tulip goes through the parsley. Repeat with the other tulips.

5. Break the enoki mushrooms into clusters, and slip them into the parsley. Attach the miniature squash to the smaller skewers, and position them in the parsley, as well. Once the arrangement is assembled, mist the parsley often to keep it looking perky before placing it on the table. The beets and squash may be brushed with a little vegetable oil to give them a nice luster. If preparing this several hours ahead, drape plastic bags over the arrangement to prevent drying out.

AS AN AUTUMN VARIATION: Use fresh yellow and orange marigolds instead of the carved flowers. Attach them with narrow skewers, make a dramatic bow with some purchased orange, yellow, and brown plaid ribbon, and stick it on with pins or glue. Even brilliant-colored autumn leaves lend a seasonal touch when used around the basket.

ANOTHER AUTUMN IDEA: Buy a butternut squash about 10 inches in length. Cut off the smaller end,

and hollow out the squash with a long, sharp knife, leaving about a ½-inch border. Work until you come to the seeds in the bulbous section. Scrape this clean. The top of the "vase" may be left plain or scalloped. Fill it with beet "tulips," onion "chrysanthemums," beet greens and/or real flowers.

AN EASTER CENTERPIECE

This arrangement uses the same mushroom basket and parsley as above. Make pastel or brightly colored Easter eggs; putting designs on them is even prettier. Use several eggs (see illustration). This may be done with hard-cooked or hollowed eggs. Even candied jelly beans may be added. Add streamers of curled paper ribbon. Make "place cards" by marking each guest's name on an egg with a crayon before it is dyed. Rest the eggs on a little stand made by fastening a narrow strip of colored paper together into a ring.

Or use a spectacular glass or silver bowl piled high with colored Easter eggs. Line the bowl with pretty green leaves. Leave 1 or 2 eggs on the table in a nest of gaily colored ribbons.

NOTE: To hollow eggs, make a tiny hole in the smaller end of the egg with a sharp needle. Make a slightly larger hole at the other end, and push the needle in several times to break the yolk. Place your lips over the smaller hole and blow the egg into a bowl. Soak hollowed eggs in warm water, then drain and dry them.

ROSES, TULIPS, OR DAISIES "GROWING" IN A POTTED PLANT

I have often surprised guests with this centerpiece of potted baby ivy or fern with little roses or other plants growing from them. It is so easy and quick, and you can use many different containers, from a spackleware or copper colander to a beautiful Chinese porcelain bowl. The results are stunning each time.

1 purchased (or owned) plant in a plastic pot of a size to fit inside a decorative container. You can transplant the plant for your party and repot it later, as well.
1 decorative container
1 bunch tulips, roses, or mixed flowers
12 plastic floral vials (see Note)

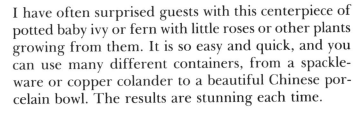

1. Place the plant in the decorative container. The vines or leaves should cover the plastic pot. Snip the flower stems to about 5 to 7 inches in length depending on how high your plant is. Slip each flower into a little vial filled with water, and push it into the soil. If the flowers are very tiny, 2 or 3 may be put into each vial. For tulips, I save the leaves and add one along with each flower.

NOTE: Plastic floral vials cost about $.05 to $.10 each in a Floral department or florist shop. They may be reused forever.

A HOLIDAY CENTERPIECE

Using the same potted plant as above, choose a festive holiday container, add juniper cuttings and miniature glass or wooden ornaments attached with pipecleaners wrapped around bamboo skewers stuck into the plant. Some fresh cranberries or a bow will add a festive touch of color.

And, don't overlook

The wonderful greens available to line baskets, platters, and form the base for salads:

- purple savoy cabbage
- kale
- red and green chard
- single leaves of radicchio

The beauty of real vegetables or fruits as a "still life" centerpiece directly on the table, in a rustic basket or handsome bowl:

- ripe tomatoes—plum or cherry
- eggplants—purple, Japanese, and white
- artichokes
- red chard
- cauliflower
- red apples
- ripe pears—Bartlett, Anjou or seckel
- walnuts in the shell
- purple grapes in clusters

Found objects

- antique or decorative cookie tins
- apple and other reusable baskets
- dried flowers
- small decorative jars for individual arrangements and name cards

GLOSSARY

al dente (to the tooth) usually referring to pasta or vegetables that are cooked until just tender yet retaining some "bite."

bain marie a method of cooking foods over or in another vessel that contains water.

bard to cover lean meat, poultry, or fish with a thin layer of fat to keep it moist during cooking.

baste to moisten the surface of foods with a liquid or fat while cooking.

beurre manié usually equal parts of softened unsalted butter and flour kneaded together and used as a last-minute thickener of sauces, soups, and stews.

blanch to partially cook foods in boiling water to set the color, remove an outside skin (such as with nuts), or to soften the texture of vegetables. In many cases, vegetables are immediately plunged into cold water to stop the cooking and retain the color.

boil to cook food in rapidly bubbling liquid.

braise a moist-heat method of cooking foods in a covered pan, usually used with larger, tougher cuts of meat.

broil to cook foods under a direct heat source. (Grilling is the same but the heat source is below the food.)

broth/stock the liquid derived from slowly simmering bones, herbs, and aromatic root vegetables in large quantities of water. The foundation for many dishes.

chop to cut into coarse, irregular pieces.

clarify to remove impurities in stocks or milk solids in butter. Clarified butter can be heated to a much higher temperature without burning.

deglaze to stir a liquid into a hot pan that has been used for sautéing or roasting foods, thereby incorporating and dissolving the browned cooking solids that remain in the pan. A good source for pan sauces and juices.

dice to cut foods into small, uniform cubes.

emulsion the binding of two normally insoluble ingredients into a suspension. Oil with vinegar or butter and egg yolks in Hollandaise sauce, are examples.

gratiné to run food under a broiler to add additional color.

julienne to cut foods into thin, matchstick-like strips.

lard to insert small strips of fat into lean meats to make them more tender and flavorful.

mince to chop finely.

mirepoix a classic combination of aromatic vegetables: carrots, celery, and onions or leeks, frequently used as the foundation for stocks and stews.

mise en place all ingredients for a specific recipe gathered together. (Getting your "mess in place"!)

poach to submerge foods in a gently simmering liquid.

purée to turn a solid food into a semi-liquid state.

reduce to boil a liquid to reduce the volume and concentrate flavors.

refresh to plunge hot food into cold water to arrest the cooking and set the color or to reconstitute, as with dried herbs.

roast a dry-heat method of cooking, usually in an uncovered, shallow pan.

roux equal parts by weight of flour and fat cooked together to create a thickening agent. It may be cooked to various stages from white to lightly colored to dark brown, depending on its final use.

sauté to cook foods quickly in a small amount of fat over high heat.

simmer the stage just below boil when bubbles just begin to break the surface.

steam to cook foods over rapidly boiling water in a covered pan.

sweat to soften vegetables in a minimum amount of fat in a covered pan over low heat.

INDEX

451

vinegar, 364
balsamic, 209
rabbit in red wine and
balsamic, sauce, 207–209

waffles, wild rice, pecan,
buttermilk, 317–318
walnut(s):
crescents, chocolate-dipped
butter, 331–332
date and nut meringue kisses,
336–337
pastry crust, 311–313
winter squash and apple soup,
410
watercress:
orange, jicama and olive salad,
92–93
sauce, cool and tangy, 63
stuffed chicken breast Italiana,
126–128
watermelon soup, minted,
108–109

Wehani rice pudding, 392–393
whole stuffed sea bass (or red
snapper) en croute with
confetti beurre blanc, 259–
261
whole wheat cream puff shells
(pâte à choux), 313–314
wild rice, pecan, buttermilk
waffles, 317–318
wine:
chilled white, soufflé with
apricot sauce, 288–289
Late Harvest Johannisberg
Riesling beurre blanc, 281
lobster timbales with Riesling
beurre blanc, 234–236
mosaic of peaches and berries
in, 95–97
pears poached in port with
Stilton cream, 99–100
pork cutlets for fall, 195–197
red, and balsamic vinegar
sauce, rabbit in, 207–209

red, Basque chicken in, with
olives and peppers,
130–131

yam(s):
and rye muffins, sweet, day-
after-Thanksgiving,
318–319
Southern salad, 406–407
yogurt, 269, 277
buying, 268
cucumber raita, 277
Indian game hens marinated in
spices and, 148–149
orange-honey sauce for fruit,
277–278
sauce, 47

zabaglione sauce, broiled pineapple slices with, 102–103
zucchini, 63
blossoms, fried, 45
gratin with tomato coulis, 63–
64